Moura Quayle
November 2019

Strategic Leadership
Across Cultures

Strategic Leadership Across Cultures

The GLOBE Study of CEO Leadership Behavior and Effectiveness in 24 Countries

Robert J. House
University of Pennsylvania

Peter W. Dorfman
New Mexico State University

Mansour Javidan
Thunderbird School of Global Management

Paul J. Hanges
University of Maryland

Mary F. Sully de Luque
Thunderbird School of Global Management

Los Angeles | London | New Delhi
Singapore | Washington DC

Los Angeles | London | New Delhi
Singapore | Washington DC

FOR INFORMATION:

SAGE Publications, Inc.
2455 Teller Road
Thousand Oaks, California 91320
E-mail: order@sagepub.com

SAGE Publications Ltd.
1 Oliver's Yard
55 City Road
London EC1Y 1SP
United Kingdom

SAGE Publications India Pvt. Ltd.
B 1/I 1 Mohan Cooperative Industrial Area
Mathura Road, New Delhi 110 044
India

SAGE Publications Asia-Pacific Pte. Ltd.
3 Church Street
#10-04 Samsung Hub
Singapore 049483

Acquisitions Editor: Patricia Quinlin
Production Editor: Laura Barrett
Copy Editor: Megan Markanich
Typesetter: C&M Digitals (P) Ltd.
Proofreader: Eleni Georgiou
Indexer: Rick Hurd
Cover Designer: Candice Harman
Marketing Manager: Liz Thornton
Permissions Editor: Jennifer Barron

Copyright © 2014 by SAGE Publications, Inc.

Library of Congress Cataloging-in-Publication Data

House, Robert J.
Strategic leadership across cultures : the globe study of CEO leadership behavior and effectiveness in 24 countries / Robert J. House, University of Pennsylvania, Peter W. Dorfman, New Mexico State University, Mansour Javidan, Thunderbird University, Paul J. Hanges, University of Maryland, Mary F. Sully de Luque, Thunderbird School of Global Management.

pages cm
Includes bibliographical references and index.

ISBN 978-1-4129-9594-8 (hardcover)

1. Leadership—Cross-cultural studies. 2. Chief executive officers—Cross-cultural studies. 3. Strategic planning—Cross-cultural studies. 4. Organizational behavior—Cross-cultural studies.
I. Global Leadership and Organizational Behavior Effectiveness Research Program. II. Title.

HD57.7.H68 2014
658.4'092—dc23   2013020373

13 14 15 16 10 9 8 7 6 5 4 3 2 1

Contents _____

Foreword _____

B eing asked to write a foreword to the GLOBE project's third book gives me the rare opportunity to fully appreciate how "ancient" I am in the field of cross-cultural comparative management and how my longitudinal view of the subject may benefit this endeavor. My "review" of cross-cultural organizational psychology and management is not a technical one. For me, this is an emotional journey—seeing, feeling, and influencing the progression of the field since its embryonic stage in the late 1960s. Working alongside, sometimes collaboratively and at other times argumentatively, with pioneering contributors such as Bernie Bass, Harry Triandis, and Geert Hofstede I am in awe as I witness how researchers and practitioners conjoined their studies into a major and highly pertinent discipline.

Many readers will probably find it surprising that Comparative and International Management courses in MBA programs in the United States were only endorsed by AACSB around 1985. Indeed, there was only one textbook available at the time—I know because it so happened that I wrote it (Ronen, 1986).

As pointed out by the authors of this volume, the field was characterized by scarcity of data at its early stages, experiencing a dramatic change only in the past two decades or so. Large multinational studies are expensive, cumbersome, and characterized by a myriad of both technical and conceptual problems (e.g., language barrier, back translation, the cultural outlook of investigators vs. respondents, variance among subjects, organizations, ownership, and so on). It is a small miracle that such a project can be completed in a timely manner, as planned, and with comprehensibly intelligent results. In itself, this merits a big round of applause for the GLOBE researchers—both leaders and other team members. While potentially intimidating, the GLOBE success should serve as inspiration to new (or old) scholars in the field.

The historical unfolding of the field thus reflects the true magnitude of the contribution of the GLOBE project to comparative and cross-cultural management. The scarcity of available comparative field documentation was acutely felt. For years, we had but one source of data. Indeed, many significant multicountry comparative publications (e.g., Hofstede, 1976, 1980; Ronen & Kraut, 1977; Sirota & Greenwood, 1971) have all relied on the international survey data that was collected within a single multi-national corporation (MNC).

The 1980s were a period of growing cultural awareness. Cross-cultural managerial training tended to be hands on, in expatriate contexts. Fueled by the increasing share of foreign operations (and revenues) of U.S. and European MNCs, cross-cultural training manuals, courses, and seminars proliferated the management field. Not only was data scarce but so was theoretical reasoning. I recall the symposium, organized by Peter Dorfman and myself at the annual meeting of the Academy of Management in 1991, in which we assembled recognized leaders in the field to speculate to what extent prevailing theories would hold in different cultural settings. So little did we know, even then, about leadership in different cultures. And where such evidence had accumulated, it was often limited to the comparison of just a few single countries.

Advances in communication sciences and new statistical techniques encouraged cooperation among researchers, increased the volume of relevant grants, and enabled a growing body of multicountry comparative studies. Anecdotal evidence as well as scientific publications reporting cross-cultural employee and manager attitudes and behaviors have (and often still do) attributed observed differences to the mere fact that the compared samples came from different societies, countries, or cultures. The findings were inter-esting and challenging, and at times even useful in terms of practical adapta-tion to the "foreign" cultures. However, more comprehensive causal models were still lacking. Not surprisingly, the real transformation in scientific rigor occurred when rather than associating the cross-cultural national dif-ferences in work attitude and behavior to the mere *origin* of the sample— that is, the country or geographic zone—scientifically anchored *causes* were required as explanatory variables.

One of Hofstede's main achievements and thus influence was indeed his pioneering contribution to this challenge. He showed that data retrieved from employees and managers in a large number of countries (subsidiaries) could be analyzed to provide insights into cultural values that could predict leaders' and employees' attitudes and behaviors. This legacy and subsequent consolidation of the field during the 1980s in both the United States and Europe as well as the wealth of periodicals reporting cross-cultural studies in psychology, organizational behavior, and management created fertile grounds for creative visionaries. When Bob House and his colleagues Peter Dorfman, Mansour Javidan, and Paul Hanges started to develop and design this monumental research project more than two decades ago, I was over-whelmed by the breadth of their vision, their innovative theoretical concep-tualization, and the scientific rigor they embraced in their planned research.

It was later that the extent of their leadership became fully apparent, as they led the project and coordinated the work of the country co-investigators (CCIs). The monumental effort and result of the collaboration of over 250 CCIs from all populated continents has been an unprecedented research project. I was fortunate enough to see the project unfold from a short distance, as I was asked to be a discussant at some of the teams' symposia at annual meetings of the Academy of Management. I shared from afar the team's progress and excitement—sometimes mixed with envy, sometimes with frustration but always with sheer admiration.

The 20-year-long Global Leadership and Organizational Behavior Effectiveness (GLOBE) Research Program set the goal of empirically determining the role of culture in leadership behavior and effectiveness. It contributed to building evidence-based managerial and leadership theories and practices. The team's focus in the 1990s was to develop a method by which to define and measure national cultural practices (i.e., "as is") and values (i.e., "should be") as described by employees in a variety of organizational employment and simultaneously to identify which leadership attributes are consistent with and are likely to succeed in these cultures. And indeed, the results demonstrated that societal culture values predicted leadership expectations as endorsed in these societies. This was an extension of the hypothesis developed by House, Wright, and Aditya (1997), known as the cultural congruence hypothesis.

To date, the scientific harvest has been immense and its impact on leadership scholarly publications enormous. With two award-winning massive published volumes behind them, delineating leadership in culture-based organizational context among 62 societies (House, Hanges, Javidan, Dorfman, & Gupta 2004) and portraying an in-depth profile of 27 European societies (Chhokar, Brodbeck, & House 2007), and more recently, the special issue of the *Journal of World Business* (2012) that was devoted entirely to global issues in leadership that emerged from the project (in addition to numerous other articles), the GLOBE project has been a rich source for cross-cultural data mining.

The present volume follows the tradition of the previous stages and offers a document that is based on sound theoretical models and that provides practical insights to executives and researchers alike. It endeavors to analyze managerial attributes, styles, behavior, and outcomes of senior executives and CEOs in terms of their strategic leadership paradigms and behavior effectiveness across cultures. The goal was to assess whether such leadership behaviors are directly influenced by cultural dimensions or whether culture indirectly influences leadership through leadership expectations. Relating culture values and practices to leadership attributes is an achievement that contributes to the lean body of such information to date. Of 112 leadership attributes that were isolated cross-culturally in GLOBE 2004, the researchers found 22 leadership attributes to be universally desirable, 8 leadership attributes were found to be universally undesirable, and 35 leadership attributes are culturally contingent (desirable in some, undesirable in others). Mapping out these attributes into behavioral items in the current volume, I am certain the current volume opens a new vista in cross-cultural leadership research.

In this latest phase of the GLOBE Project, researchers tested relationships between observed leadership behaviors of CEOs, societal leadership expectations (i.e., culturally endorsed implicit leadership theory [CLT] attributes), as well as between leadership and organization effectiveness. While rigorous empirical research on CEOs is in its infancy, the focus has so far been on outcomes rather than drivers of CEO behavior. Surveying over 5,000 senior executives who directly report to over 1,000 CEOs in 1,015 organizations in 24 countries, the current volume finds that cultural values do not directly predict leadership behavior. Instead, they drive the cultural expectations that in turn drive leader behaviors. In other words, the researchers found that leaders are perceived to be effective if their behaviors are congruent with societal expectations. While the achievement is outstanding, this finding leaves room for future research: How can CEOs change the status quo if they are successful only when they enact behaviors that are consistent with cultural expectations? We rely on CEOs, top management teams (TMTs), and upper echelon executives to change and reshape organizational realities, yet in effect, the current volume shows that they are influenced by their own societal culture and its value-based expectations concerning adequate leadership etiquette.

Treading where others have not (or hardly) gone before, I must agree with the authors of this volume that before this phase of the GLOBE project, there simply wasn't enough data to determine if CEO Charismatic leadership is universally effective or varies in importance and impact across cultures. Nor did we know if the same set of leadership behaviors can capture the essence of Charismatic leadership. Their results point to the importance of leaders who are visionary, performance oriented, inspirational, and decisive and who personify high levels of integrity. While Charismatic leadership may be an obviously desired behavior, the researchers were surprised that Team-Oriented and Humane-Oriented leadership were also deemed important. And yet, one wonders if this is indeed such a surprising finding considering the globalizing, computerizing virtual world in which networks and the human interrelatedness are increasingly endorsed. In fact, the authors report that among earlier GLOBE (2004) findings, the Humane-Oriented leadership expectations (i.e., CLTs) were rated as being only slightly important for outstanding leadership. However, the current empirical results found that Humane-Oriented leadership behavior has a huge impact on TMT Dedication and is the *most* predictive of all leadership behaviors for TMT Commitment. These findings are important not only by themselves but also in pointing to an emergent lacuna in which organizational leadership and behavior could be tied to the growing body of business-related networks.

Just as leadership is a new word in the dictionary, although the linguistic concept has been around for at least 5,000 years, one may also say that cross-cultural variation in the field of organizational behavior and industrial psychology is a relatively young arena—just about 50 years old, struggling in a long tradition of scientific research. Dealing with slow-to-change cultural variation, we can only hope that we will be able to "unpack the black box of culture" as it impacts leadership and leadership effectiveness across cultures. With cultural clustering related to organizational behavior, values, and attitudes remaining nearly unchanged throughout four decades of study (Ronen & Shenkar, 2010), it seems that the chances are in our favor.

The current volume has set out to understand and empirically measure the nature and drivers of CEO leadership behavior, the drivers of CEO leadership effectiveness, the relationship between CEO leadership behavior and effectiveness, and the impact of the new fit index between CEO leadership behavior with CLTs as well as assess the leadership distinctions between the high-performing CEOs (i.e., superior), and underperforming CEOs (i.e., inferior). These are big promises—all of which are competently and skillfully achieved from design to analysis, to synthesis, to integration, and conclusion. Notwithstanding, the cultural experience is still very much driven by the Western–American worldview (the Europeans were rightfully skeptical of models developed in North America), and much is clearly desired to further develop leadership concepts from other cultural perspectives in order for us to truly appreciate the notion of leadership in all its cultural colors.

Walking the walk, the leading researchers of the GLOBE project should be recognized for their own cultural colors and commended for their openness, positive collaboration, and information transparency that are manifested in this volume. Based on personal experience and encounter with a myriad of opposing attitudes in the field, I feel confident to assume that these traits greatly contributed to the overall success of the project and the ability to extract such wealth of in-depth valuable cross-cultural information over the span of two decades or more.

Writing the foreword of a massive volume that reports yet another stage of the GLOBE monumental multinational research project, and probably the ultimate pinnacle with respect to implications of cross-cultural comparison of CEOs, is to me personally not only a meaningful professional experience but also an encompassing process. It began almost half a century ago when very few of our colleagues were interested in or were touched by the excitement of international research and theoretical applications. As research in the field continues to evolve, I can only hope for additional active participation and involvement on my part. In the meanwhile, I am sufficiently content to be an official, albeit honorary, part of the GLOBE team.

Simi (Simcha) Ronen

Dedication

A massive project like GLOBE that spans over two decades needs the support of many individuals to succeed. The latest phase of GLOBE, like its previous phases, was possible only with the generous support and hard work of large numbers of individuals. We owe a debt of gratitude to our many colleagues all over the world who collected data in their countries. They are the GLOBE country co-investigators (CCIs) who worked very hard to collect data from over 1,000 CEOs in over 1,000 corporations and over 5,000 senior executives in 24 countries. We are also thankful to those CEOs and senior executives who agreed to participate in this unique research project. In addition, four individuals deserve special mention for their contribution to this book. Gary Yukl's careful review of the manuscript as it was being crafted illuminated areas that could be clarified, provided new insights for our findings and offered important suggestions for future research. The GLOBE project was helped immeasurably by Juliet Aiken who worked tirelessly for many years conducting complex statistical analyses. Renee Brown helped with many aspects of manuscript preparation and editing. Finally, Megan Markanich, our SAGE copy editor, provided sage editing and advice under very tight deadlines. We sincerely thank all of these people for their dedication and expertise in contributing to this latest GLOBE project.

We especially thank our spouses—Sharon Dorfman, Soheila Yazdanbakhsh, Carol Hanges, and Edgard Luque—and dedicate this book to them. They have been supportive, understanding, patient, and loving beyond anything we could ask for. During the past 10 years, we spent a huge number of days and weeks meeting away from home and being totally consumed with our work on this book. All along, our spouses patiently and lovingly encouraged us. This book would not have been possible without them at our sides. Also, we'd like to especially thank, and dedicate this book to, Tessa House, who cared so dearly and lovingly for our friend and colleague Bob House during his last years of ill health. We have the utmost admiration for Tessa as a spouse and a human being. She is an inspiration to us all.

Acknowledgments_____

Our Fantastic Journey With Robert J. House
_____ and Our Farewell to a Dear Colleague

We write this book with much joy and also sadness. Bob House is not with us any longer, so we felt a need to write this brief note to bring closure to an always wonderful and sometimes challenging long-running set of professional relationships and friendships.

This book closes a very important chapter in the 20-year GLOBE research program and brings to an end Bob House's impressive publication record and the countless hours, days, weeks, and months of individual and collective work by us and many of our GLOBE colleagues.

It was in 1991 that Bob House contacted Mansour, Peter, and Paul individually to discuss his ideas about a new research program. Very simply put, he was curious about whether or not leadership means the same thing in different countries and whether country culture impacts people's notion of leadership. Our conversations were intriguing and energizing. Having a research conversation with Bob was an exciting experience. We started to get more and more serious about the idea. Bob started to draft the proposals for research funding. Each one of us started to do a variety of things. Our first milestone was the first gathering of the GLOBE team of researchers, sponsored by Mansour Javidan, at University of Calgary in Canada in 1994. Three of us, Peter, Mansour, and Paul plus several other colleagues worked very closely with Bob to collect and manage the data from over 60 countries. Our research has produced many award-winning publications. Bob's intellectual and scholarly contributions were always invigorating and intriguing. We miss our regular weeklong meetings with Bob at Wharton.

Upon completion of the data collection for Phase 2 of GLOBE, in the late 1990s, Bob, Paul, Mansour, and Peter had to divide the work of writing the first book, which we all refer to as the "blue book," published by SAGE in 2004. Due to health issues and also the massive amount of work, Bob played more of an oversight role. Paul Hanges conducted all the statistical analyses throughout the project. He also wrote the relevant chapters of the blue book regarding research design and statistical analyses. Mansour Javidan managed the relationships with CCIs in many countries and worked closely with the authors of the various chapters on dimensions of country cultures. He also wrote several of the chapters in the blue book. Peter Dorfman wrote the main chapters related to culture and leadership and worked with other authors (including Paul Hanges) of the remaining chapters on leadership. While Bob was not directly involved in writing the chapters, he was always ready to help. We spent hundreds of hours on the phone with Bob, and he always had a funny joke to tell before we started with the serious topics. Our work culminated in a weeklong meeting in Toronto to go over all the chapters and put the finishing touches.

In the late 1990s and early 2000, Bob, Mansour, Paul, and Peter started to discuss the next steps for GLOBE. As always, Bob did not lack ideas. He started talking about a *CEO study* where we would test some of the findings of the blue book. The blue book showed us what managers in different societies expect from their leaders. The next logical question for us was the following: Do effective leaders act according to the expectations in their societies? Bob was becoming increasingly interested in this question. Three of us (Mansour, Paul and Peter) were quite busy with the writing of the blue book, so we were not as focused on this interesting question as Bob was. But any chance we had, we would always enjoy a conversation with Bob about this question and how to test it. As part of our division of labor, Bob focused increasingly on drafting the proposal for the next phase of the GLOBE project, the CEO study, as its principal investigator (PI). Peter, Paul, and Mansour agreed to be co-principal investigators with the understanding that the first priority for the three of us was to finish the blue book.

Bob developed the framework and submitted a proposal for funding that was successful and officially started Phase 3 of GLOBE. Mary Sully de Luque was a postdoctoral fellow working with Bob and agreed to manage the data collection process for this research. She spent countless hours working with tens of CCIs in over 20 countries and managed the GLOBE database throughout the CEO project.

As co-principal investigators, we were focused on the blue book. Once the blue book was successfully launched, we joined Bob and Mary to complete this third phase. Due to serious health issues, Bob was unable to join our discussions of the next steps. Mary handed the collected database to Paul and Peter, and they worked closely to design new research methodologies for the required analyses. Paul focused on the statistical work needed to produce the expected results. Peter agreed to be the project manager for the design and writing of this book. Over the past 2 years, we have spent many 4-day meetings at University of Maryland and Thunderbird School of Global Management. We have worked closely as a group and as individuals to write this book. We have spent countless hours reviewing the statistical results and their implications and on the design of the chapters of the book. Each chapter is written primarily by one individual and reviewed numerous times by at least one coauthor.

As always, we have had much joy in these discussions, but we missed Bob. His intellectual rigor and wit were sorely missed. We wish he could be with us.

Mansour Javidan

Peter Dorfman

Paul Hanges

Mary Sully de Luque

About the Authors _____

Robert J. House received his PhD in management from The Ohio State University. He went on to hold faculty appointments at The Ohio State University, University of Michigan, City University of New York, and the University of Toronto. In 1988, he was appointed the Joseph Frank Bernstein Professor Endowed Chair of Organization Studies at the Wharton School of the University of Pennsylvania.

A prolific writer, he authored more than 130 journal articles, several of which have been reprinted in numerous anthologies. Among the multiple awards conferred, House received the award for Distinguished Scholarly Contribution to Management, the Eminent Leadership Scholar award, and the ILA Lifetime Achievement award, as well as many awards for outstanding publications. He also authored two papers, which are Scientific Citations Classics.

House was the principal investigator (PI) and founder of the GLOBE Research Program. Further, he founded a nonprofit foundation to sustain the GLOBE Project beyond his tenure, including a board of directors and a constitution. House was a fellow of the Academy of Management, American Psychological Association, and Society for Industrial/Organizational Psychology (SIOP). House's major research interests were varied but focused on relationships among power, personality, and leadership in contributing to organizational performance. The last two decades of his life focused on the implications of cross-cultural variation for effective leadership. Professor House passed away November 1, 2011.

Peter W. Dorfman is professor emeritus of management at New Mexico State University. He recently held the Bank of America Professorship in the Department of Management. He is currently chairman of the board of directors and president of GLOBE Foundation. His master's degree and PhD are from the University of Maryland. His articles on leadership, cross-cultural management, and employee discrimination have appeared in *Leadership Quarterly, Academy of Management Journal, Academy of Management Review, Academy of Management Perspectives, Organizational Dynamics, Journal of Management, Journal of World Business, Advances in*

International Comparative Management, Journal of International Business Studies, Journal of Applied Psychology, and *Advances in Global Leadership.* Dr. Dorfman's current research involves investigating the impact of cultural influences on managerial behavior and leadership styles. He has been a co-principal investigator of the two decades-long GLOBE Research Project. As part of GLOBE, he has been a member of the GLOBE coordinating team, an executive board member, and an editor of the Society for Industrial and Organizational Psychology (SIOP) award-winning book *Culture, Leadership, and Organizations: The GLOBE Study of 62 Societies.*

Mansour Javidan Multiple award-winning educator and author Dr. Mansour Javidan received his MBA and PhD from the Carlson School at the University of Minnesota. He recently stepped down as dean of Research and is currently the Garvin Distinguished Professor and director of Najafi Global Mindset Institute (www.globalmindset.com) at the Thunderbird School of Global Management in Arizona.

Mansour is past president and chairman of the board of the GLOBE Research Foundation. He is a coeditor of the first GLOBE book, which won the SIOP award for The M. Scott Myers Award for Applied Research in The Workplace.

Dr. Javidan is designated an expert adviser by the World Bank and a senior research fellow by the U.S. Army. He has published in *Harvard Business Review, Journal of International Business Studies, Organization Science, Strategic Management Journal, Academy of Management Perspectives, Leadership Quarterly, Management International Review, Organizational Dynamics, Journal of Applied Behavioral Sciences,* and *Journal of World Business.*

He is past editor of global leadership for the *Journal of World Business.* He is a fellow of the Pan Pacific Business Association and was named in Lexington's 2001/2002 Millennium Edition of the North American Who's Who Registry and Empire's 2003 Who's Who Registry.

Paul Hanges is professor, industrial/organizational psychology, of the Department of Psychology at the University of Maryland. He is also an affiliate of the University of Maryland's R. H. Smith School of Business and the Zicklin School of Business (Baruch College). He is on the board of directors of OBA Bank. Paul's research centers on three themes: (1) human resource practices, team/organizational diversity, and organizational climate; (2) leadership, team-processes, and cross-cultural issues; and (3) dynamical systems theory. He has written over 80 articles and book chapters. His publications have appeared in such journals as *Advances in Global Leadership, American Psychologist, Psychological Bulletin, Journal of International Business Studies,* and *Leadership Quarterly.* His research has won the M. Scott Myers Award for Applied Research from SIOP twice: in 2004 for being an editor of the first GLOBE book and in 2011 for his work on human resource selection processes. Paul is a fellow of the American Psychological

Association, Association for Psychological Sciences, and the Society for Industrial/Organizational Psychology (SIOP), and he was a founding member of the GLOBE Foundation and has been a principal investigator (PI) of this project since its inception.

Mary Sully de Luque is an associate professor of management at the Thunderbird School of Global Management. She is currently a member of the board of directors of GLOBE Foundation and has been extensively involved in GLOBE Phase 3 research since 2000. She was a senior research associate for the first GLOBE book.

Dr. Sully de Luque's research interests include the influences of culture on leadership effectiveness, stakeholder decision making, feedback processes in the work environment, and human resource management (HRM). She is academic co-director of Project Artemis, a program that helps women entrepreneurs develop and grow businesses in emerging markets and has served as faculty member for the Goldman Sachs 10,000 Women Project.

She has presented her research at international conferences and has published in such journals as *Administrative Science Quarterly, Academy of Management Review, Journal of International Business Studies,* and *Academy of Management Perspective,* as well as many book chapters. Along with the GLOBE book editors, she won the 2005 M. Scott Myers Award for Applied Research in the Workplace from the Society for Industrial and Organizational Psychology (SIOP). In 2008, she won the Western Academy of Management Ascendant Scholar award for outstanding early career research.

List of Country Co-Investigators[1]

Adetoun, Bolanle Akande, Economic Community of West African States Executive Secretariat (Nigeria)

Alas, Ruth, Estonia Business School (Estonia)

Antino, Mirko, Universidad Complutense de Madrid (Spain)

Barrasa, Angel, University of Zaragoza (Spain)

Bhal, Kanika T., Indian Institute of Technology, Delhi (India)

Bobina, Mariya, University of Iowa (Russia)

Bodur, Muzaffer, Boğaziçi University (Turkey)

Bostjancic, Eva, University of Ljubljana (Slovenia)

Bourantas, Dimitris, Athens University of Economics and Business (Greece)

Catana, Alexandru, Technical University of Cluj-Napoca (Romania)

Catana, Doina, Technical University of Cluj-Napoca (Romania)

Chen, Yi-Jung, National Kaoshiung University of Applied Science (Taiwan)

Debbarma, Sukhendu, Tripura University (India)

de Hoogh, Annebel H. B., University of Amsterdam (Netherlands)

den Hartog, Deanne N., University of Amsterdam (Netherlands)

DeVries, Reinout, Vrije University (South Pacific: Fiji, Solomon Islands, Tonga, Vanuatu)

[1]The country co-investigators (CCIs) collected the data relevant to their countries. The countries they represented are in parentheses following their names and their institutional affiliations.

Dorfman, Peter, New Mexico State University (Mexico)

Duarte, Roberto Gonzalez, Federal University of Minas Gerais (Brazil)

Dzuvichu, Rosemary R., Nagaland University (India)

Evcimen, Idil, Istanbul Technical University (Turkey)

Fenn, Mathai, The Talk Shop, Bangalore (India)

Fischman, David, Fischman and Associates (Peru)

Fu, Ping Ping, Chinese University of Hong Kong (China)

Garagozov, Rauf, Center for Strategic Studies under the President of the Republic of Azerbaijan (Azerbaijan)

Gil Rodríguez, Francisco, Universidad Complutense de Madrid (Spain)

Grachev, Mikhail, Western Illinois University (Russia)

Gupta, Vipin, California State University—San Bernadino (India)

Howell, Jon, New Mexico State University (Mexico)

Jone, Kuen-Yung, Kaohsiung Medical University (Taiwan)

Kabasakal, Hayat, Boğaziçi University (Turkey)

Khan, Mohamed Basheer Ahmed, Pondicherry University (India)

Kharbihih, Hasina, Impulse NGO Network, Shillong (India)

Konrad, Edvard, University of Ljubljana (Slovenia)

Koopman, P. L., Vrije University (Netherlands)

Lang, Rainhart, Chemnitz University of Technology (Germany)

Lin, Cheng-Chen, National Pingtung University of Science & Technology (Taiwan)

Liu, Jun, Renmin University (China)

Martinez, Boris, Universidad Francisco Marroquín (Guatemala)

Mathew, Mary, Indian Institute of Science, Bangalore (India)

Munley, Almarie E., Regent University (Guatemala)

Ortiz, José Agustín, Universidad Peruana de Ciencias Aplicadas—UPC (Peru)

Palin, Gary, Elon University (United States)

Papalexandris, Nancy, Athens University of Economics & Business (Greece)

Paquin, Anthony R., Western Kentucky University (South Pacific: Fiji, Solomon Islands, Tonga, Vanuatu)

Pathak, R. D., University of the South Pacific (South Pacific: Fiji, Solomon Islands, Tonga, Vanuatu)

Peng, T. K., I-Shou University (Taiwan)

Prieto, Leonel, Texas A&M International University (Mexico)

Quigley, Narda, Villanova University (United States)

Rajasekar, James, Sultan Qaboos University (India)

Reddy, Lokanandha Irala, KKC Group of Institutions, Puttur (India)

Reddy, S. Pratap, Dhruva College (India)

Rodríguez Muñoz, Alfredo (Spain)

Rohmetra, Neelu, Jammu University (India)

Saran, Pankaj, EMPI Business School (India)

Sharma, Dinesh, Indian Institute of Technology Bombay (India)

Shrivastava, Mrinalini, United Nations, Guinea Bissau (India)

Srinivas, E.S., Indian School of Business, Hyderabad (India)

Steyrer, Johannes, Vienna University of Economics & Business (Austria)

Sully de Luque, Mary F., Thunderbird, School of Global Management (United States)

Tanure, Betania, Pontificia Universidade Católica—PUC-MG (Brazil)

Thierry, Henk, Tilburg University (Netherlands)

Thomas, Fr. Vattathara M., Don Bosco Institute, Guwahati (India)

Tuulik, Krista, Estonian Entrepreneurship University of Applied Sciences (Estonia)

van den Berg, Peter T., Tilburg University (Netherlands)

Waldman, David, Arizona State University (United States)

Washburn, Nathan, Thunderbird, School of Global Management (United States)

Wilderom, Celeste P. M., University of Twente (Netherlands)

Wollan, Melody L., Eastern Illinois University (United States)

1 Societal Culture and Leadership

GLOBE History, Theory, and Summary of Previous Findings

The 21st century should be, if it is not already, the century of international management research.

—Tsui, Nifadkar, and Ou (2007)

Culture is the greatest of all moderators.

—Harry Triandis (1993)

To succeed in this complex business environment, leaders will need to adopt a set of characteristics and traits that enables them to move fluidly across different cultures.

—James Turley, chief executive officer (CEO)
of Ernst & Young (2010)

The importance of executive leaders to the success of their organizations is widely acknowledged (cf. Finkelstein, Hambrick, & Cannella, 2009; Zaccaro & Klimoski, 2001). The Global Leadership and Organizational Behavior Effectiveness (GLOBE) research project presented in this book has the principal goal of determining how societal leadership expectations influenc executive leadership behavior and effectiveness. The current project is a continuation of the previous GLOBE research started in the early 1990s whereby investigators have been studying the interrelationships among societal culture, societal effectiveness, and societal leadership expectations. However, in contrast to earlier GLOBE research (House, Hanges, Javidan, Dorfman, & Gupta, 2004), the focus of this book is on executive leadership behavior and its effectiveness. Specifically, our study focuses on the behavior and performance of chief executive officers (CEOs) and their top management teams (TMTs).

Although there are compelling reasons for understanding the influence of societal culture on leadership and organizational processes, only during the past two decades has there been an increased interest in studying leadership in multiple cultures (including non-Western cultures). Contemporary reviews of leadership theories by cross-cultural researchers generally espouse the perspective that leadership theories developed and tested in one culture may not apply to other cultures (Aycan, 2008; Dickson, Castaño, Magomaeva, & Den Hartog, 2012). While this perspective about the importance of cultural contingencies has recently gained acceptance, many prominent leadership theories were either developed before this zeitgeist or tacitly assumed that leadership processes and theories generally transcend cultures (Dorfman, 2004). Yet convincing evidence exists that there are inherent limitations in transferring theories across cultures; what works in one culture may not be valid in other cultures. As Triandis (1993) suggested in the quote given at the beginning of the chapter, because societal culture has proven to be an important moderator in social science research, leadership researchers should be able to "fine-tune" theories by investigating cultural variations as moderators or parameters of those theories.

In addition, by focusing on potential cross-cultural effects, researchers are more likely to uncover new relationships by including a much broader range of variables often not considered in contemporary theories, such as the importance of religion, language, ethnic background, history, or political systems (Chemers, 1993). Essentially, cross-cultural research may identify limiting conditions and specific cultural differences that are relevant for understanding leadership processes and outcomes (Yukl, 2013). In short, GLOBE investigators believe that cross-cultural researchers should thoughtfully view current leadership theories within a contingency framework whereby cultural variables are incorporated as antecedents and/or moderators. With this contingency perspective, we may begin to answer a fundamental question as to the extent to which leadership theories generated and tested in one culture generalize to different cultures (Yukl, 2013). The present project attacks this question from the GLOBE theoretical basis presented by House and colleagues (2004) and subsequently revised from the results of previous GLOBE efforts.

Practical reasons also exist for understanding the role of societal cultures' influence on leadership and organizational processes. The knowledge gained from cross-cultural research will assist organizations in the selection and development of leaders with the necessary multicultural skills to become effective in multicultural environments (see the Turley (2010) quote at the beginning of the chapter). This knowledge can directly improve firm performance and profitability as CEOs strive to increase their firm's presence and sales in foreign markets. As William Green (former chairman and CEO of Accenture) (2009) stated, it is important to focus on growing market share and expanding business in key geographic markets with a special emphasis on Brazil, Russia, India, China, South Korea, and Mexico. In one recent survey of more than 500 senior executives at 100 corporations, the Economist Intelligence Unit (EIU) (Bolchover, 2012) reported that 75% of the respondents' corporations were planning to compete in foreign markets. Another survey of 520 senior business executives reported that 50% of these executives expect their corporations to receive more revenue from foreign markets than from their domestic markets (Turley, 2010). Pursuing global markets, global supply chain partners, and global talent pools are high priorities for contemporary corporations, and cross-cultural leadership skills are critical to success. As Howard and Wellins (2008) noted, "Mobilizing teams and working across cultures" are the top two vital leadership competencies for developing globally successful leaders. The importance of developing globally minded executives has also not been lost on emerging market multinationals (EMMs) who increasingly view global business savvy to be a key to their success (Foster, 2008). In short, increased global exposure of corporations has raised managerial interest in understanding national cultures and their influence on executives and corporations.

Robert House founded the GLOBE research program in 1991 to enhance the scholarly literature on this important topic. GLOBE is a multiphase, multimethod, multisample project in which investigators spanning the world are examining, among other things, the interrelationships between societal culture and organizational leadership. Over 200 social scientists and management scholars from nearly 69 cultures representing all major regions of the world are engaged in this programmatic series of cross-cultural leadership studies. We studied 62 countries in the first two GLOBE phases and 24 countries in the latest phase of GLOBE. Of the latter 24 countries, 17 were in common with the first two phases (in total, 69 countries were represented in the combined research). We studied over 900 domestic corporations in the 62 countries in Phases 1 and 2 and over 1,000 corporations in Phase 3.

In this chapter of the book, we describe the rationale, theory, and findings from the GLOBE project up to this latest (i.e., Phase 3) study. We summarize our perspectives on culture and leadership—what we now know, what we still don't know, and what we may soon know. The chapter ends with a discussion of why we chose to proceed with the CEO study reported in this book. Chapter 2 reviews the current state of literature regarding the intriguing relationship between culture and leadership. Chapter 3 describes our rationale, hypotheses, research design, and analytical strategy. Insights gained from our 20-year effort, along with the extant literature, have enabled us to modify our original theoretical model (House et al., 2004) to the one presented in Figure 1.1. We intend to provide evidence throughout this book that leadership matters, executive leadership matters greatly, and societal cultures influence the leadership behaviors that are expected and effective.

GLOBE: A Primer

Since its inception in the early 1990s, the GLOBE project has grown into an enormous research effort involving more than 200 researchers from multiple academic disciplines located throughout the world. GLOBE investigators set out to explore the fascinating and complex effects of culture on leadership and organizational effectiveness. Among our goals, we strove to make the project applicable to many facets of cross-cultural interaction beyond simply conducting an in-depth study of societal culture and organizational behavior. To this end, GLOBE 2004 stated the following:

> At the present time there is a greater need for effective international and cross-cultural communication, collaboration, and cooperation, not only for the effective practice of management but also for the betterment of the human condition. Ample evidence shows that cultures of the world are getting more and more interconnected and that the business world is becoming increasingly global. As economic borders come down, cultural barriers will most likely go up and present new challenges and opportunities in business. When cultures come into contact, they may converge on some aspects, but their idiosyncrasies will likely amplify. The information resulting from the GLOBE research program can be used as a guide when individuals from different cultures interact with each other. (House et al., 2004, p. 1)

Some scholars believe that worldwide distribution of movies, TV programs, restaurant chains, travel, MBA programs, and educational exchange opportunities (Child & Tayeb, 1983; Werther, 1996; Yavas, 1995) will result in cultural uniformity. However, cultural differences have been the proverbial "elephants in the room," and businesses ignore them at their peril currently and in the future. Cultural misunderstandings have led to numerous failures in cross-cultural mergers, acquisitions, and market penetration (Stahl & Javidan, 2009). Furthermore, in a recent survey of CEOs, executives identified mobilizing teams and working across cultures as the *top* two critical leadership competencies in their corporations (Howard & Wellins, 2008). In another survey of 1,000 internationally oriented Chinese companies (*China Daily*, 2012) these executives indicated the major challenge in establishing overseas business was cultural differences. Further, complexity theory suggests that even with free-flowing information, pockets of cultural heterogeneity will persist, emerge, and flourish (Marion & Uhl-bien, 2001). As Nisbett (2003) has shown, thousands of years of history are behind the unique development of cultures around the world, and it is simplistic to expect massive convergence of thinking in a few years.

GLOBE Theoretical Model

The GLOBE theoretical model (House et al., 2004) was proposed as a fully integrative theory linking culture, leadership, and organizational effectiveness. The theory not only relates national culture to aspects of leadership and organizational processes but also asserts that culture has a sustained influence on societal human welfare and the economic success of that culture. Our theory, which continues to guide the GLOBE research program, is an integration of implicit leadership theory (ILT) (Lord & Maher, 1991), value–belief theory of culture (Hofstede, 1980; Triandis, 1995), implicit motivation theory (McClelland, 1985), and structural contingency theory of organizational form and effectiveness (Donaldson, 1993; Hickson, Hinings, McMillan, & Schwitter, 1974). We readily acknowledge that the original GLOBE theory has benefited from further research conducted by GLOBE scholars (Chhokar, Brodbeck, & House, 2007) and many other cross-cultural researchers (cf. Leung, Bhagat, Buchan, Erez, & Gibson, 2005). Modifications of the original GLOBE model have been made due to research results acquired over two decades of the GLOBE project and from additional knowledge gained by researchers worldwide.

The central proposition in GLOBE's research is that the attributes and characteristics that differentiate societal cultures from each other may also suggest organizational practices and leader attributes/behaviors that will be frequently enacted and effective in that culture. We believe that the validity of the GLOBE theory can be inferred from tests of specific relationships theorized in the GLOBE model rather than with attempts to develop an omnibus test. The version of the GLOBE model presented in this book (see Figure 1.1) is a modification of the one originally presented by House, Wright, and Aditya (1997) and subsequently changed in GLOBE 2004 (House et al., 2004). Constructs and relationships shown by solid lines refer to relationships among constructs tested in the previous phases of GLOBE. We showed that societal cultural values and practices predict societal phenomena and leadership expectations (i.e., culturally endorsed implicit leadership theories, or CLTs). Relationships shown by dashed lines and boxes with dark blue backgrounds are those to be tested in the present study. We intend to examine the relationship among cultural values, cultural leadership expectations (i.e., CLTs), and leadership behavior and effectiveness. Relationships shown by dotted lines will be examined in the future.

Figure 1.1   Modified GLOBE Theoretical Model 2013

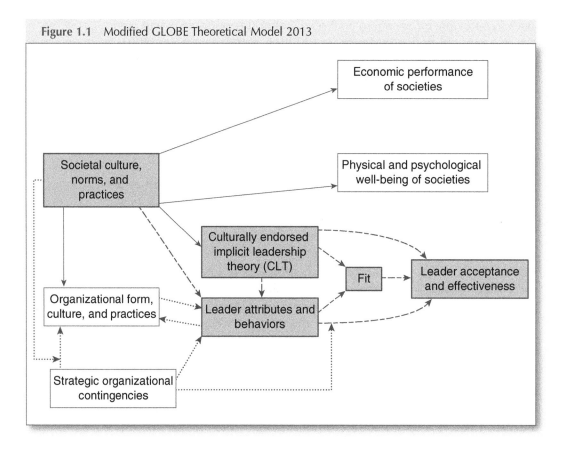

Focus of GLOBE 2004 and GLOBE 2007

GLOBE researchers' initial focus in the 1990s was twofold: First, they developed a method to define and measure national cultural practices and values. Second, they strove to identify which leadership attributes are consistent with—and likely to succeed in—these cultures. It should be noted that in the 1990s GLOBE researchers also had goals of determining *how* cultural values and practices influence societal and organizational effectiveness. An important feature in GLOBE research was to identify cultural *practices* that define cultures as they now exist (i.e., as is); in contrast, cultural *values* are defined as what societies desire in the future (i.e., should be). GLOBE researchers found that cultural practices (but not values) are associated with a large variety of societal phenomena such as economic performance and societal health. In contrast, cultural values (and not practices) are associated with desirable leadership qualities. As an example, we found that Power Distance (values) is a positive predictor of the predictor of perception of effectiveness for Self-Protective leadership behaviors and a negative predictor perception of effectiveness for Charismatic/Value-Based leadership and Participative leadership behaviors. The complete findings for these analyses were published in *Culture, Leadership, and Organizations: The GLOBE Study of 62 Societies* (House et al., 2004).

For convenience and brevity throughout this book, the two GLOBE book publications are referred to as GLOBE 2004 (House et al., 2004) and GLOBE 2007 (Chhokar et al., 2007). In addition, when describing the project we use terms such as *our project* or *we* to refer to GLOBE researchers as a single entity. The GLOBE 2007 book was structurally different from the GLOBE 2004 book. The former was structured around nine cultural dimensions whereas the latter provided in-depth country-specific analyses of cultural values, practices, and leadership expectations. The latter also included extensive findings from a variety of qualitative analyses along with the quantitative findings in GLOBE 2004.

In GLOBE 2007, we also described numerous instances where 10 regional clusters of countries (e.g., Latin American countries) were culturally unique from each other (and within each cluster) regarding differences in perceptions of effective leadership qualities. Consider the following examples that highlight cultural differences. Leaders in Hong Kong (Confucian Asian cluster) are substantially influenced by Confucian values for order, compliance, and acceptance of authority: a predisposition that results in a more autocratic leadership style. They are very opportunistic, seize every opportunity to become affluent, and generally exhibit a paternalistic and benevolent autocratic style (Chow, 2007). The French (Latin European Cluster) place a high value on human equality with an accompanying anticapitalist tradition, but the French leader is expected to reconcile contradictions such as hierarchy and equality, order, and liberty (Castel, Deneire, Kurc, Lacasagne, & Leeds, 2007). Interestingly, French leaders in general are expected to be well educated and "cultivated" (i.e., classically educated). Insights such as these, which combine both quantitative and qualitative data, are found in GLOBE 2007's 25 culture-specific chapters.

Figure 1.2 presents the countries grouped into the culture clusters as presented in GLOBE 2004. This figure also includes all countries in the current CEO study.

We believe that GLOBE 2004 and GLOBE 2007 advanced cross-cultural research in several ways. As previously mentioned, in GLOBE 2004 we measured 62 societal cultures along nine cultural dimensions for both cultural practices and cultural values. This distinction between practices and values has been acknowledged as an important addition to cross-cultural research (Triandis, 2004; preface to GLOBE 2004). In addition, GLOBE's cultural measures continue to be used in international business research (Parboteeah, Hoegl, & Cullen, 2008), but debate remains as to the precise meaning of each construct (Graen, 2006; Hofstede, 2006; Javidan, House, Dorfman, Hanges, & Sully de Luque, 2006; Peterson, 2004). We also empirically validated our measures to establish each scale's reliability and construct validity. Perhaps most importantly, we assessed the degree of aggregation among societal and organizational members so that we had

Figure 1.2   All Countries in GLOBE 2004 and Current GLOBE CEO Study

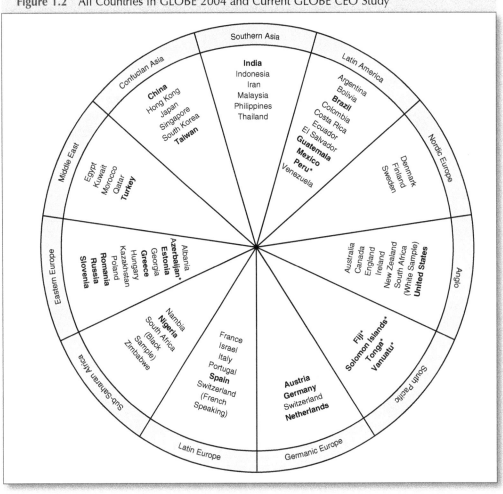

Note: Twenty-four countries in the current GLOBE CEO study are bold. Countries not in the GLOBE 2004 study are indicated by an asterisk.

confidence that our samples accurately reflected the reported societal and organizational cultures. Unfortunately, the validity of aggregation has often been ignored in previous cross-cultural research (cf. Hofstede, 1980). We determined which economic and human conditions are associated with these cultural dimensions. In addition, we assessed the confluence between national cultures and the human condition (with extensive supporting data) as well as relationships among national and organizational cultures and desired leadership qualities. Practical implications for leadership development resulting from GLOBE research have been advanced and adopted by university MBA programs worldwide. For example, the paper by Javidan, Dorfman, Sully de Luque, and House (2006) provides MBA students with a sound basis for conceptualizing worldwide leadership differences.

Specific GLOBE Research Questions for GLOBE 2004 and GLOBE 2007

Specific objectives and research questions pertaining to the entire GLOBE research program are listed next. Selected findings from the research project are presented in Table 1.1 Essentially, the glue that holds the objectives together can be summarized as our effort to develop reliable survey instruments that enable us to independently measure cultural practices and values; determine which principles of leadership and organizational processes transcend cultures; and link together cultural, leadership, and organizational elements. Our specific objectives were to accomplish the following:

1. Develop reliable survey instruments to independently measure cultural practices and values (using a sound theoretical base and exacting psychometric standards).

2. Ascertain how attributes of societal cultures affect the economic, physical, and psychological welfare of members of the societies studied (e.g., determine the relationship between societal cultural variables and international competitiveness of societies).

3. Identify and group the 62 societal cultures into a limited set of regional clusters and validate the culture groupings.

4. Determine which leader behaviors, attributes, and organizational practices are universally expected to be effective across all cultures.

5. Use ILT to create leadership profiles that are endorsed differently across cultures (i.e., determine which leader behaviors, attributes, and organizational practices are accepted and effective in only some cultures).

6. Group 112 leadership attributes into more parsimonious leadership dimensions (*primary* dimensions) and demonstrate how they can be grouped into secondary (*global*) leadership dimensions.

7. Establish which attributes of societal and organizational cultures are expected to influence the acceptance and effectiveness of specific leader behaviors in a culture.

8. Determine how attributes of a societal culture affect the values and practices of organizations within that culture.

9. Investigate whether distinct industry contexts (e.g., finance as compared to food industry) influence societal and organizational culture dimensions or culturally endorsed leadership attributes.

Table 1.1   Summary of Objectives and Findings from GLOBE 2004 and GLOBE 2007

	Objectives	Findings	Examples
1.	Develop reliable survey instruments to identify and measure societal and organizational cultural practices *and* values.	Nine cultural dimensions were identified that differentiate attributes of societal and organizational cultures for 62 societies.	The United States, China, and Hong Kong were among the highest scoring societies for Performance Orientation practices.
2.	Determine the relationship between selected cultural dimensions and economic and psychological well-being of societies.	Many significant relationships exist between selected cultural dimension practices and economic health and positive human conditions.	Societal Performance Orientation, Future Orientation, and Uncertainty Avoidance are positively related to most measures of economic health. Societal health is negatively related to Power Distance and In-Group Collectivism.
3.	Group 62 societal clusters into regional clusters.	The 62 societal clusters were grouped into 10 regional clusters.	The Nordic Europe culture cluster consisted of Denmark, Sweden, and Finland.
4.	Determine which leadership attributes are universally endorsed or refuted.	Twenty-two leadership attributes were universally endorsed; 8 attributes were universally refuted.	*Trustworthy, just,* and *honest* were universally endorsed; *egocentric* and *dictatorial* were universally rejected.
5.	Determine which leadership attributes are culturally contingent. Use implicit leadership theory (ILT) to create leadership profiles that are differently endorsed across cultures.	Thirty-five qualities were culturally contingent. Leadership profiles were created for each of 10 culture clusters.	*Cautious, cunning,* and *compassionate* were culturally contingent attributes. The Latin America societal cluster scored highest on the Team-Oriented global leadership dimension.
6.	Group 112 leadership attributes into more parsimonious leadership dimensions.	Twenty-one primary leadership dimensions were formed out of the 112 leadership attributes; these were consolidated into global leadership dimensions.	The Charismatic/Value-Based global leadership dimension is comprised of six primary dimensions (e.g., one is charisma-inspirational).

	Objectives	Findings	Examples
7.	Determine relationships between culture dimensions and leadership dimensions.	The nine cultural dimension values are differentially related (at the societal and organizational) level to the six global leadership factors.	Performance Orientation and Gender Egalitarianism cultural values are strongly and positively related to desirability of Participative leadership.
8.	Determine how attributes of societal cultures influence organizational cultures.	Organizational practices and values mirror the societies in which they are comprised.	Organizations with high Performance Orientation are found within societies with high Performance Orientation.
9.	Determine if distinct industry contexts (e.g., food) influence societal and organizational culture dimensions as well as leadership culturally endorsed implicit leadership theories, or CLTs.	Industry has a limited direct influence on GLOBE findings, but evidence suggests a more subtle industry X society interaction.	Societal culture moderated relationships between organizational culture and leadership preferences for food and telecommunications but not in the financial services industry.
10.	Provide a more in-depth understanding of cultures and leadership processes within specific nations by integrating qualitative and quantitative data.	Qualitative data were obtained from 25 countries and reported in GLOBE 2007. Numerous culture-specific aspects of leadership emerged.	New Zealand leadership styles demand straight-talking, non-self-promoting, and strong rejection of bureaucratic leaders. Chinas' leadership remains welded to Confucian ideology but aggressively learns from the West.

The following two sections summarize GLOBE's perspectives of culture, leadership, and the intriguing interaction between them.

GLOBE Perspectives on Culture

Unfortunately, there is no universally agreed-upon definition among social scientists for the term *culture*. However, consistencies are found among definitions; when used by social scientists, the term *culture* typically refers to a set of parameters of collectives that differentiate each collective in a meaningful way, with a focus on the "sharedness" of cultural indicators among members of the collective. For Project GLOBE, culture is defined as follows:

Shared motives, values, beliefs, identities, and interpretations or meanings of significant events that result from common experiences of members of collectives that are transmitted across generations.

GLOBE researchers conceptualized and measured nine cultural dimensions after reviewing the available literature, paying particular attention to Geert Hofstede (1980); Trompenaars and colleagues (1996); and Inglehart, Basanez, and Moreno (1998). The nine GLOBE cultural dimensions are (1) Performance Orientation, (2) Assertiveness, (3) Future Orientation, (4) Humane Orientation, (5) Institutional Collectivism, (6) In-Group Collectivism, (7) Gender Egalitarianism, (8) Power Distance, and (9) Uncertainty Avoidance. We should note that the emphasis on culture in GLOBE 2004 was understandable for several reasons. First, given the earlier groundbreaking work in this area by Hofstede (1980), it was only natural for researchers to compare GLOBE findings to his seminal research findings. This is particularly true with respect to the ranking of societal cultures (i.e., nations) along various cultural dimensions (e.g., individualism/collectivism), which mirrors Hofstede's (1980) earlier research at IBM. Second, in the process of designing and conducting the first two phases of the GLOBE project, we broadened the scope to include an understanding of how cultures affect both economic performance and the human condition. Third, GLOBE cultural dimensions can be applied to both societies and organizations. For each, careful attention was given to levels of analysis issues. Listed here are brief definitions of the nine cultural dimensions. Culture construct definitions, example questionnaire items, and national exemplars of the extremes are presented in Table 1.2.

Performance Orientation: The degree to which a collective encourages and rewards (and should encourage and reward) group members for performance improvement and excellence.

Assertiveness: The degree to which individuals are (and should be) assertive, confrontational, and aggressive in their relationship with others.

Future Orientation: The extent to which individuals engage (and should engage) in future-oriented behaviors such as planning, investing in the future, and delaying gratification.

Humane Orientation: The degree to which a collective encourages and rewards (and should encourage and reward) individuals for being fair, altruistic, generous, caring, and kind to others.

Institutional Collectivism: The degree to which organizational and societal institutional practices encourage and reward (and should encourage and reward) collective distribution of resources and collective action.

In-Group Collectivism: The degree to which individuals express (and should express) pride, loyalty, and cohesiveness in their organizations or families.

Gender Egalitarianism: The degree to which a collective minimizes (and should minimize) gender inequality.

Power Distance: The degree to which members of a collective expect (and should expect) power to be distributed equally.

Uncertainty Avoidance: The extent to which a society, organization, or group relies (and should rely) on social norms, rules, and procedures to alleviate unpredictability of future events. The greater the desire to avoid uncertainty, the more people seek orderliness, consistency, structure, formal procedures, and laws to cover situations in their daily lives.

Table 1.2   Culture Construct Definitions, Sample Questionnaire Items, and Country Score Examples

Performance Orientation: *The degree to which a collective encourages and rewards group members for performance improvement and excellence.*				
Specific Questionnaire Item	**Cultural Characteristics and Country Examples**	**Country Dimension Scores (*Practices*)**		
		Low	**Med.**	**High**
Students are encouraged (should be encouraged) to strive for continuously improved performance.	In countries that score high on this cultural practice, such as the United States and Singapore, businesses are likely to emphasize training and development. In countries that score low, such as Russia and Greece, family and background count for more.	Greece (3.20) Russia (3.39) Italy (3.58)	Spain (4.01) Japan (4.22) India (4.25)	China (4.45) United States (4.49) Singapore (4.90)

Assertiveness: *The degree to which individuals are assertive, confrontational, and aggressive in their relationships with others.*				
Specific Questionnaire Item	**Cultural Characteristics and Country Examples**	**Country Dimension Scores (*practices*)**		
		Low	**Med.**	**High**
People are (should be) generally dominant in their relationships with each other.	People in highly assertive countries, such as the United States and Austria, tend to have can-do attitudes and enjoy competition in business. Those in less assertive countries, such as Sweden and New Zealand, prefer harmony in relationships and emphasize loyalty and solidarity.	Sweden (3.38) New Zealand (3.42)	China (3.76) Italy (4.07) Ecuador (4.09)	Spain (4.42) United States (4.55) Austria (4.62)

Future Orientation: *The extent to which individuals engage in future-oriented behaviors such as delaying gratification, planning, and investing in the future.*

(Continued)

(Continued)

Specific Questionnaire Item	Cultural Characteristics and Country Examples	Country Dimension Scores (*Practices*)		
		Low	Med.	High
More people live (should live) for the present rather than for the future (scored inversely).	Organizations in countries with high Future Orientation practices, such as Singapore and Switzerland, tend to have longer-term horizons and more systematic planning processes, but they tend to be aversive to risk taking and opportunistic decision making. In contrast, corporations in the least Future Oriented countries, such as Russia and Argentina, tend to be less systematic and more opportunistic in their actions.	Russia (2.88) Argentina (3.08) Italy (3.25)	China (3.75) Indonesia (3.86) United States (4.15)	Austria (4.46) Switzerland (4.73) Singapore (5.07)

Humane Orientation: *The degree to which a collective encourages and rewards individuals for being fair, altruistic, generous, caring, and kind to others.*

Specific Questionnaire Item	Cultural Characteristics and Country Examples	Country Dimension Scores (*Practices*)		
		Low	Med.	High
People are generally (should be generally) very tolerant of mistakes.	People in high Humane Orientation societies are urged to provide social support to each other. The need for belonging and affiliation motivates people. Countries such as Egypt and Malaysia rank very high on this cultural practice; countries such as France and Germany rank low.	Germany (3.18) France (3.40) Singapore (3.49)	Australia (4.28) New Zealand (4.32) Canada (4.49)	Egypt (4.73) Malaysia (4.87) Philippines (5.12)

Institutional Collectivism: *The degree to which organizational and societal institutional practices encourage and reward collective distribution of resources and collective action.*

Specific Questionnaire Item	Cultural Characteristics and Country Examples	Country Dimension Scores (*Practices*)		
		Low	Med.	High
Leaders encourage (should encourage) group loyalty even	Organizations in collectivistic countries, such as Singapore and	Greece (3.25)	United States (4.20)	China (4.77)

Specific Questionnaire Item	Cultural Characteristics and Country Examples	Country Dimension Scores (*Practices*)		
		Low	Med.	High
if individual goals suffer.	Sweden, tend to emphasize group performance and rewards whereas those in the more individualistic countries, such as Greece and Brazil, tend to emphasize individual achievement and rewards.	Argentina (3.66) Brazil (3.83)	Egypt (4.50)	Singapore (4.90) Sweden (5.22)

In-Group Collectivism: *The degree to which individuals express pride, loyalty, and cohesiveness in their organizations or families.*

Specific Questionnaire Item	Cultural Characteristics and Country Examples	Country Dimension Scores (*Practices*)		
		Low	Med.	High
Employees feel (should feel) great loyalty toward this organization.	Societies such as Egypt and Russia take pride in their families and also take pride in the organizations that employ them. In contrast, the United States scores relatively low for In-Group Collectivism but higher in the previously described Institutional Collectivism.	Denmark (3.53) New Zealand (3.67) United States (4.25)	Japan (4.63) Israel (4.70) Brazil (5.18)	Russia (5.63) Egypt (5.64) China (5.80)

Gender Egalitarianism: The degree to which a collective minimizes gender inequality.

Specific Questionnaire Item	Cultural Characteristics and Country Examples	Country Dimension Scores (*Practices*)		
		Low	Med.	High
Boys are encouraged (should be encouraged) more than girls to attain a higher education (scored inversely).	Not surprisingly, European countries generally had the highest scores for gender egalitarian practices. Egypt and South Korea were among the most male-dominated societies in GLOBE. Organizations operating in gender egalitarian societies tend to encourage tolerance for diversity of ideas and individuals.	S. Korea (2.50) Egypt (2.81)	Germany (3.10) New Zealand (3.22) United States (3.34)	Canada (3.70) Sweden (3.84) Denmark (3.93)

Power Distance: *The degree to which members of a collective expect power to be distributed equally.*

(Continued)

(Continued)

Specific Questionnaire Item	Cultural Characteristics and Country Examples	Country Dimension Scores (*Practices*)		
		Low	Med.	High
Followers are (should be) expected to obey their leaders without question.	A high Power Distance score reflects unequal power distribution in a society. Countries that scored high on this cultural practice are more stratified economically, socially, and politically; those in positions of authority expect—and receive—obedience. Firms in high Power Distance countries such as Thailand, Brazil, and France tend to have hierarchical decision making processes with limited one-way participation and communication.	Denmark (3.89) Netherlands (4.11)	Canada (4.82) United States (4.88) China (5.04)	France (5.28) Brazil (5.33) Thailand (5.63)

Uncertainty Avoidance: *The extent to which a society, organization, or group relies on social norms, rules, and procedures to alleviate unpredictability of future events.*

Specific Questionnaire Item	Cultural Characteristics and Country Examples	Country Dimension Scores (*Practices*)		
		Low	Med.	High
Most people lead (should lead) highly structured lives with few unexpected events.	Organizations in high Uncertainty Avoidance countries, such as Singapore and Switzerland, tend to establish elaborate processes and procedures and prefer formal detailed strategies. In contrast, firms in low Uncertainty Avoidance countries, such as Russia and Greece, tend to prefer simple processes and broadly stated strategies. They are also opportunistic and enjoy risk taking.	Russia (2.88) Hungary (3.12) Greece (3.39)	United States (4.15) Mexico (4.18) England (4.65)	Germany (5.22) Singapore (5.31) Switzerland (5.37)

GLOBE Perspectives on Leadership

Similar to the "culture" definition problem, it is widely acknowledged that there is no universal consensus on the definition of *leadership* (Bass, 2008; Yukl, 2010). However, most definitions embody the concepts of influence and the accomplishment of objectives—that is, how leaders influence others to accomplish group or organizational objectives. Interestingly, from the very start of the GLOBE project, researchers noticed that the definition and construct of leadership itself clearly varies across cultures. For instance, the status and influence of leaders vary considerably as a result of cultural forces in the countries or regions in which the leaders function. Some cultures—such as American, Arabian, Asian, English, Eastern European, French, German, Latin American, and Russian—tend to romanticize the concept of leadership and consider it to be important in both political and organizational arenas. In these cultures, leaders are commemorated with statues or memorialized in the names of major avenues, boulevards, or buildings. In contrast, many people of German-speaking Switzerland, the Netherlands, and Scandinavia seemed to be more skeptical about the concept of leadership and leaders for fear that they will accumulate and abuse power. In these countries, it is difficult to find public commemoration of leaders.

One goal of the initial GLOBE conference (held in 1994 at the University of Calgary in Canada) was to create a working definition of leadership. We immediately found ourselves debating the role of leaders, their importance, and the attributes important for outstanding leadership. Anecdotal evidence that emerged during this discussion supported our initial beliefs about the countrywide variance of leadership concepts. After lengthy debates, GLOBE researchers reached a consensus for a working definition of leadership that reflected the group's diverse viewpoints. The following definition emerged:

> Leadership is the ability of an individual to influence, motivate, and enable others to contribute toward the effectiveness and success of the organizations of which they are members.

During the 1994 conference, we also spent considerable time discussing the best way to initiate the project's implementation—asking important administrative questions as to who will coordinate the project and how to recruit country co-investigators (CCIs), as well as creating an anticipated timeline for implementation and completion of the project. Decisions were made that focused our efforts and led to the development of the sequencing of the project. For the leadership portion, we wanted to focus on leadership attributes that were believed to be critical for outstanding leadership. Later in the project's development we used this information to assess actual leadership behavior—the focus of the present book.

Culturally Endorsed Implicit Leadership Theory—The Twenty-One Primary Culturally Endorsed Implicit Leadership Theory Leadership Dimensions and Six Global Culturally Endorsed Implicit Leadership Theory Leadership Dimensions

GLOBE's theoretical framework is built on the foundation of implicit leadership theory (ILT) (Lord & Maher, 1991) to develop our CLT (House et al., 2004). While ILTs are analyzed at the individual level of analysis, CLTs are aggregated at the societal level. Numerous examples demonstrate how societal cultures can shape the ILT of their members (Javidan, Dorfman, Howell, & Hanges, 2010). In countries with relatively high Power Distance values (e.g., Russia and Iran), children typically learn that the father is the ultimate authority in the family, and they show strong respect and deference to him. In such cultures, the CLT reflects elements of power and autocratic leadership. As adults, employees in organizations in such cultures are more accepting of high Power Distance values and autocratic leadership styles in organizations. While not the entire story, Vladimir Putin's rise to power and continuing presence as president and/or prime minister of Russia reflect the desirability of strong powerful leaders in this high Power Distance society.

For the initial phases of GLOBE, we designed an instrument called the Leader Attributes and Behavior Questionnaire. We decided not to use previously developed leadership instruments and scales (e.g., LMX and MLQ) because they were mostly developed in Western countries. Furthermore, because our objective was to compare cross-cultural differences in leaders and leadership, our strategy was to cast as wide a net as possible with respect to the attributes and behaviors to be assessed. We decided to go beyond leadership constructs currently in the research zeitgeist such as charismatic, transformational leadership, or dyadic leadership. As a result, the instrument contained leadership attributes reflecting a wide variety of skills, styles, behaviors, and personality traits. In short, our instrument was cross-culturally designed, included both leadership attributes and behaviors, and measured a wide range of theoretical constructs.

The first author, along with other GLOBE colleagues, developed a comprehensive list of leadership attributes and behaviors based on available research literature and personal reflections from many scholars in numerous countries. We created a list of 382 leadership attributes eventually winnowed down by a series of statistical procedures to 112 leader attribute and behavior items. These leadership items embodied a wide variety of traits, behaviors, and abilities potentially relevant to leadership emergence and effectiveness. For each item in the survey, a brief definition or example of the item clarified the construct to minimize language difficulties, and elaborate translation and back-translation procedures were developed to minimize language misunderstandings. (The complete procedure can be found in Chapters 6 through 11 by House and colleagues [2004].) Leader attributes were rated 1 through 7 with 1 indicating "This behavior or characteristic greatly inhibits a person from being an outstanding leader" and 7 indicating "This behavior or characteristic contributes greatly to a person being an outstanding leader."

After generating the 112 attributes, the next step in making sense of these disparate items was to group them using various conceptual and statistical procedures. Statistical analyses used data from the survey of over 17,000 managers in 62 societies (House et al., 2004). This resulted in a formation of *two levels* of leadership dimensions. The first level consists of 21 *primary* leadership dimensions (e.g., visionary leadership). To further understand the underlying construction of CLTs, a second-order factor analysis of these 21 primary dimensions produced the second level leadership dimensions that we refer to as 6 *global* leadership dimensions. In other words, the initial 112 attributes were used as the basis for the 21 primary leadership dimensions, which in turn are collapsed into the 6 global leadership dimensions (see Table 1.3). The conceptual linkage of the 21 primary dimensions to these 6 global dimensions is discussed in Chapter 2. Major GLOBE terms found throughout the book are defined in Appendix A. The global leadership dimensions are briefly defined as follows:

Charismatic/Value-Based leadership: Broadly defined to reflect the ability to inspire, motivate, and expect high performance outcomes from others based on firmly held core values.

Team-Oriented leadership: Emphasizes effective team building and implementation of a common purpose or goal among team members.

Participative leadership: Reflects the degree to which managers involve others in making and implementing decisions.

Humane-Oriented leadership: Reflects supportive and considerate leadership but also includes compassion and generosity.

Autonomous leadership: A newly defined global leadership dimension referring to independent and individualistic leadership attributes.

Self-Protective leadership: From a Western perspective, this newly defined global leadership dimension focuses on ensuring the safety and security of the individual and group through status enhancement and face-saving.

We believe the assessment of a wide variety of skills and behaviors in the GLOBE research instruments is a strength of our research. Many of the 21 primary leadership dimensions closely match those found in the research literature (e.g., visionary leadership). However, only some of the 6 "global" leadership dimensions, which were previously presented, match similar leadership dimensions found in previous cross-cultural research (e.g., Charismatic/Value-Based leadership). This discrepancy is likely due to several factors.

Table 1.3 Global and Primary Culturally Endorsed Implicit Leadership Theory Dimensions and Attributes Comprising Each Dimension

Leadership Dimensions		Leadership Attributes
Global Leadership Dimensions	**Primary Leadership Dimensions**	**Leadership Attributes**
I. *Charismatic/Value-Based leadership* (4.5–6.5)*	Charismatic 1: Visionary	Foresight Prepared Anticipatory Plans ahead
	Charismatic 2: Inspirational	Enthusiastic Positive Morale booster Motive arouser
	Charismatic 3: Self-Sacrificial	Risk taker Self-sacrificial Convincing
	Integrity	Honest Sincere Just Trustworthy
	Decisive	Willful Decisive Logical Intuitive
	Performance oriented	Improvement-oriented Excellence-oriented Performance-oriented
II. *Team-Oriented leadership* (4.7–6.2)	Team 1: Collaborative team orientation	Group-oriented Collaborative Loyal Consultative
	Team 2: Team integrator	Communicative Team builder Informed Integrator

Leadership Dimensions		Leadership Attributes
Global Leadership Dimensions	Primary Leadership Dimensions	
	Diplomatic	Diplomatic Worldly Win-win problem solver Effective bargainer
	Malevolent (reverse scored)	Hostile Dishonest Vindictive Irritable
	Administratively competent	Orderly Administratively skilled Organized Good administrator
III. *Participative leadership* (4.5–6.1)	Nonparticipative (reverse scored)	Autocratic Dictatorial Bossy Elitist
	Autocratic (reverse scored)	Individually oriented Nondelegator Micromanager Nonegalitarian
IV. *Humane-Oriented leadership* (3.8–5.6)	Modesty	Modest Self-effacing Patient
	Humane orientation	Generous Compassionate
V. *Autonomous leadership* (2.3–4.7)	Autonomous	Individualistic Independent Autonomous Unique
VI. *Self-Protective leadership* (2.5–4.6)	Self-Centered	Self-Centered Nonparticipative Loner Asocial

(Continued)

(Continued)

Leadership Dimensions		
Global Leadership Dimensions	**Primary Leadership Dimensions**	**Leadership Attributes**
	Status conscious	Status conscious Class conscious
	Internally competitive (formerly labeled *conflict inducer*)	Secretive Normative Intragroup competitor
	Face-Saver	Indirect Avoids negatives Evasive
	Bureaucratic (formerly labeled *procedural*)	Habitual Procedural Ritualistic Formal

Note: *The italicized dimensions are global CLT leadership dimensions. They consist of several primary CLT leadership dimensions. The only exception is dimension V (Autonomous), which consists of a single dimension of four questionnaire items. It is considered both a primary dimension and global dimension.

The parentheses represent the range of country scores for the 62 societal cultures on a 7-point scale ranging from 1 (*greatly inhibits*) to 7 (*contributes greatly*) to outstanding leadership found in GLOBE 2004.

First, most of the previous leadership theory and research was created almost solely in western countries. For example, the GLOBE Self-Protective leadership dimension contains five primary dimensions including face-saving and self-centered—aspects of leadership not previously identified in the Western literature. Second, our research suggests that many of the prior leadership constructs and models developed specifically to account for exceptional performance (e.g., transformational leadership) insufficiently captures the variety of leadership behaviors critical for outstanding leadership. Third, the GLOBE scales were derived to explain cultural leadership differences between societies whereas the extant leadership literature was developed to explain individual leadership differences within a single society.

Nevertheless, the reader might notice that three of the six global CLT leadership dimensions (Charismatic/Value-Based, Team Oriented, and Participative) are closely related to prior leadership constructs found in the leadership literature. The Humane-Oriented leadership dimension is also fairly closely related to supportive leadership, another well studied leadership construct. However, we found two leadership dimensions that have not been typically associated with "Western" oriented leadership: Autonomous leadership, which emulates an independent and individualistic aspect of leadership, and Self-Protective, which may hold more negative connotations from a Western perspective since it has not been previously considered in the leadership literature. Eastern leadership perspectives such as face-saving and status consciousness are characteristics of this dimension that may be more important when viewed from a non-Western perspective.

Universally Desirable Leadership Attributes and Dimensions

As noted by Yukl (2010), one of the most important research questions addressed in GLOBE is the extent to which there are uniform beliefs across cultures about effective leadership attributes. Our results indicated that of the 112 leadership attributes in the survey, 22 were identified as universally desirable. The worldwide grand mean score exceeded 6.0 on a 7-point scale and, 95% of the societal average scores for these attributes was greater than 5.0 on a 7-point scale. For example, the attributes of "trustworthy, just, and honest" met the criteria to be considered universally desirable (see Table 1.4).

Because these individual attributes were subsequently grouped into 21 primary leadership dimensions, GLOBE researchers were able to determine the extent to which the 21 dimensions are also universally desirable. The criteria for determining if a dimension is universally desirable were the same criteria used for the attributes previously identified. The mean ratings on these scales were above 6.0 and 95% of the societal average scores for these scales were greater than 5.0 on a 7-point scale. Therefore, GLOBE researchers determined that 4 of our 21 primary leadership *dimensions* met the criteria for universal desirability: (1) performance orientation, (2) visionary, (3) integrity, and (4) inspirational. What this means is that leaders in all GLOBE countries studied are expected to develop a vision, inspire others, and create a successful performance-oriented team within their organizations while behaving with honesty and integrity—easier said than done.

Universally Undesirable Leadership Attributes and Dimensions

The following criteria were used for determining whether attribute was a universally undesirable attribute. The worldwide grand mean score for the attribute had to be less than 3.0 on a 7-point scale, and 95% of the societal average scores for the attribute were less than 3.0 on a 7-point scale. Eight leadership attributes were identified as universally undesirable (e.g., attributes including irritable, egocentric, ruthless, dictatorial). Going up a level of analysis from the individual attribute level to our primary leadership dimension level, not unexpectedly we found that the "malevolent" primary dimension met our criteria for a universally undesirable leadership dimension (i.e., 95% of the countries rated it lower than a 3.0 and its grand mean score was less than 3.0).

Table 1.4 Societal Ratings for Universally Desirable, Undesirable, and Culturally Contingent Leadership Attributes

Universally Positive

Leadership Attribute	Ratings	
	Mean	SD
Trustworthy	6.36	0.39
Dynamic	6.28	0.34
Decisive	6.21	0.33
Intelligent	6.18	0.38
Dependable	6.17	0.36
Plans ahead	6.17	0.37
Excellence oriented	6.16	0.42
Team builder	6.15	0.39
Encouraging	6.14	0.29
Confidence builder	6.14	0.34
Informed	6.13	0.41
Honest	6.11	0.45
Effective bargainer	6.10	0.39
Motive arouser	6.07	0.51
Win–win problem solver	6.06	0.36
Positive	6.04	0.45
Foresight	6.02	0.33

Universally Negative

Leadership Attribute	Ratings	
	Mean	SD
Nonexplicit	2.30	0.35
Dictatorial	2.12	0.45
Loner	2.07	0.40
Ruthless	2.06	0.42
Asocial	2.05	0.49
Egocentric	2.02	0.39
Irritable	1.98	0.34
Noncooperative	1.69	0.35

Culturally Contingent

Leadership Attribute	Ratings				
	Mean	SD	Minimum	Maximum	Range
Ambitious	5.85	0.61	2.69	6.73	4.04
Logical	5.84	0.44	3.89	6.58	2.69
Sincere	5.83	0.59	3.99	6.55	2.56
Enthusiastic	5.74	0.53	3.72	6.44	2.72
Intuitive	5.72	0.51	3.72	6.47	2.75
Orderly	5.58	0.42	3.81	6.34	2.53
Willful	5.47	0.84	2.98	6.48	3.51
Worldly	5.18	0.70	2.48	6.54	4.05
Self-sacrificial	5.06	0.60	3.07	5.96	2.88
Sensitive	4.83	0.87	1.95	6.35	4.39
Intragroup competitor	4.70	0.68	3.00	6.49	3.49
Compassionate	4.63	0.64	2.69	5.56	2.88
Procedural	4.62	0.72	3.03	6.10	3.06
Unique	4.61	0.49	3.47	6.06	2.59
Status conscious	4.51	0.73	1.92	5.89	3.97
Formal	4.37	0.63	2.22	5.47	3.25
Risk taker	4.13	0.74	2.14	5.96	3.82

Universally Positive			Universally Negative			Culturally Contingent					
Leadership Attribute	Ratings		Leadership Attribute	Ratings		Leadership Attribute	Ratings				
	Mean	SD		Mean	SD		Mean	SD	Minimum	Maximum	Range
Just	6.02	0.37				Class conscious	4.11	0.76	2.53	6.09	3.55
Communicative	6.02	0.48				Intragroup conflict avoider	4.00	1.04	1.84	5.74	3.90
Motivational	6.00	0.39				Independent	3.94	0.68	1.67	5.28	3.61
Coordinator	6.00	0.40				Self-effacing	3.94	0.86	1.82	5.23	3.41
Administrative skilled	6.00	0.50				Autonomous	3.79	0.77	1.63	5.14	3.51
						Cautious	3.73	0.77	2.03	5.81	3.77
						Evasive	3.33	0.82	1.52	5.67	4.14
						Domineering	3.20	0.76	1.60	5.14	3.54
						Habitual	3.17	0.66	1.86	5.38	3.51
						Individualistic	3.14	0.78	1.67	5.99	4.32
						Indirect	3.01	0.56	2.16	4.86	2.70
						Subdued	3.00	1.17	1.27	6.18	4.90
						Micromanager	2.86	0.80	1.38	5.00	3.62
						Elitist	2.74	0.77	1.61	5.00	3.39
						Ruler	2.67	0.64	1.66	5.24	3.58
						Cunning	2.47	0.95	1.26	6.38	5.11
						Provocateur	2.44	0.85	1.38	6.00	4.62

Note: Numbers represent mean values for the 64 societal cultures on a 7-point scale ranging from 1 (*greatly inhibits*) to 7 (*contributes greatly*) to outstanding leadership. These data represent the original data of the 62 countries published previously (House et al., 2004) plus an additional two countries added to the data set (Estonia and Romania).

SD = standard deviation.

Scores above 4 indicate this CLT leadership dimension contributes to outstanding leadership.

Scores below 4 indicate this CLT leadership dimension inhibits outstanding leadership.

Culturally Contingent Leadership Attributes and Dimensions

From a cross-cultural perspective, however, the most interesting attributes and dimensions are those that are *culturally contingent*—desirable in some cultures, of neutral importance in some, and undesirable in others. We might expect that cultures differ on the effectiveness of specific leadership qualities given that cultural attitudes differ in their conceptions and favorability of the leadership construct itself. From the original 112 attributes, GLOBE found that 35 attributes should be considered as culturally contingent. These attributes yielded country-level scores above and below the scale midpoint of 4 (scale range of 1 to 7). A look at these attributes proved informative. By definition they are desirable in some cultures and undesirable in others, such as the attribute "ambitious" (with a societal score ranging from 2.85 to 6.73). "Elitist" is another example, with a societal score range of 1.61 to 5.00. From a humanistic perspective, one might predict that being compassionate and sensitive might be universally endorsed; however, they were not. From a Western perspective, one might also expect that being cunning and domineering would be universally refuted, but they were also culturally contingent. Many of these attributes fell into the self-centered and autonomous primary leadership dimensions. For instance, although the attribute "individualistic" had a grand culture mean of 3.11 (slightly inhibits outstanding leadership), individual national culture scores ranged from a low of 1.67 (somewhat inhibits) to a high of 5.10 (slightly contributes). Similarly, the attribute status conscious ranged in value from a low of 1.92 (somewhat inhibits) to a high of 5.77 (moderately contributes).

Going up a level of analysis from the 112 individual attributes to our 21 primary leadership dimensions, we found 7 primary leadership dimensions to be culturally contingent (Javidan et al., 2010). They are as follows:

1. *Self-Sacrificial* (country scores range from 3.92 to 6.07): This dimension indicates an ability to convince followers to invest their efforts in activities that do not have a high probability of success, to forgo their self-interest, and make personal sacrifices for the goal or vision.

2. *Status conscious* (country scores range from 2.34 to 5.81): This dimension reflects a consciousness of one's own and others' social position, holding an elitist belief that some individuals deserve more privileges than others.

3. *Internally competitive* (formerly labeled conflict inducer; country scores range from 2.92 to 5.04): This dimension reflects the tendency to encourage competition within a group and may include concealing information in a secretive manner.

4. *Face-Saver* (country scores range from 2.01 to 4.75): This leadership dimension reflects the tendency to ensure followers are not embarrassed

or shamed, maintains good relationships by refraining from making negative comments, and instead uses metaphors and examples.

5. *Bureaucratic* (formerly labeled procedural; country scores range from 2.79 to 4.95): This dimension emphasizes following established norms, rules, policies and procedures and habitually follows regular routines.

6. *Humane orientation* (country scores range from 3.31 to 5.59): This dimension emphasizes empathy for others by giving time, money, resources, and assistance when needed; shows concern for followers' personal and group welfare.

7. *Autonomous* (country scores range from 2.23 to 4.67): This dimension describes tendencies to act independently without relying on others; it may also include self-governing behavior and a preference to work and act separately from others.

Which GLOBE Cultural Dimensions Influence Leadership Expectations?

We employed hierarchical linear modeling (HLM) (Hofmann, 1997; Hofmann, Griffin, & Gavin, 2000) to test for relationships among GLOBE's cultural dimensions and the six global CLT dimensions. In GLOBE 2004, we presented findings that linked specific cultural dimensions (e.g., Performance Orientation values) to specific leadership dimensions (e.g., Team-Oriented leadership). This linkage indicated the relationships between cultures scoring high or low on each cultural dimension and the desirability of specific leadership dimensions thought to contribute to outstanding leadership. That is, for *each* of the six *global leadership dimensions*, we found significant relationships predicting their desirability based on GLOBE cultural dimension *values* (see Table 1.5). As an example, note that Participative leadership is highly desirable in societies that also value Performance Orientation, Gender Egalitarianism, and Humane Orientation cultural dimensions; however, Participative leadership is not highly desired in societies with high values for Power Distance, Uncertainty Avoidance, and Assertiveness. Thus, the Germanic European and Anglo cultures were strong supporters of Participative leadership, whereas the Confucian Asian and Eastern European cultures were less supportive.

To further understand the relationships between culture and leadership, we employed HLM to test for congruence among GLOBE's nine cultural dimensions and the seven culturally contingent primary leadership dimensions. Relationships among cultural dimension values and the culturally contingent leadership primary dimensions are presented in Table 1.6. As one example of our findings, we can see the effect Power Distance values have on several leadership dimensions. High Power Distance values are positively

Table 1.5   Societal Culture Dimensions as Predictors of Culturally Endorsed Implicit Leadership Theory (CLT) Leadership Dimensions

Societal Culture Dimensions (values)	Culturally Endorsed Implicit Leadership Theory Leadership Dimensions					
	Charismatic/ Value-Based Leadership	Participative Leadership	Self-Protective Leadership	Humane-Oriented Leadership	Team-Oriented Leadership	Autonomous Leadership
Performance Orientation	++	++	–	+	+	++
Humane Orientation	+	++		++	+	– –
Uncertainty Avoidance		– –	++	++	++	
In-Group Collectivism	++		–		++	
Power Distance	– –	– –	++			
Gender Egalitarianism	++	++	– –			
Future Orientation	+			+	+	
Assertiveness		–		++		
Institutional Collectivism						– –

Note: + indicates a positive relationship between the culture dimension and CLT; ++ indicates strong positive relationship between the culture dimension and CLT; – indicates a negative relationship between the culture dimension and CLT; – – indicates a strong negative relationship between the culture dimension and CLT.

associated with high desirability of status conscious, bureaucratic, and internally competitive leadership. Conversely, we can examine each leadership dimension and see which culture dimensions are influential. For instance, bureaucratic leadership was viewed as contributing to outstanding leadership in societal cultures that highly valued Uncertainty Avoidance, Power Distance, and Institutional Collectivism. Javidan and colleagues (2010) have provided a full description of all culturally contingent findings.

In summary, GLOBE researchers verified through carefully developed measures and analyses that although some leadership qualities are positively desired or negatively undesired across the world (vision and malevolence, respectively), others are not (compassionate). We also believe that culturally contingent leadership qualities will be most problematic for leaders acting in multinational contexts.

Table 1.6 Relationships Among GLOBE's Cultural Dimensions and Culturally Contingent Leadership Dimensions

	Uncertainty Avoidance	Power Distance	Institutional Collectivism	Humane Orientation	Performance Orientation	In-Group Collectivism	Assertiveness	Gender Egalitarianism
Status Conscious	++	++					– –	–
Bureaucratic	++	++	++					
Autonomous			– –		–	– –		
Face-Saver				+	– –		–	
Humane Orientation				++			–	
Self-Sacrificial			++		++	++		
Internally Competitive		++				–	+	– –

Note: + indicates positive hypothesized relationship; ++ indicates positive hypothesis and results that support hypothesis; – indicates negative hypothesized relationship; – – indicates negative hypothesis and results that support hypothesis.

Country Clusters and Ideal Leadership Qualities _____

The regional clustering of the GLOBE cultural dimensions was based on a conceptual and empirical process with significant involvement of the country co-investigators (CCIs) (Gupta & Hanges, 2004). The initial 10 societal grouping of GLOBE participant countries was increased to 11 with the addition of countries in the South Pacific. The current societal groupings of the GLOBE participant countries are the following: Anglo, Eastern Europe, Latin America, Latin Europe, Confucian Asia, Nordic Europe, Sub-Saharan Africa, Southern Asia, Germanic Europe, South Pacific, and Middle East. GLOBE expected that these cultural clusters would be helpful for understanding the CLT prototypes (i.e., individuals' belief systems about what contributes to or impedes outstanding leadership) that exist in the societies comprising our 10 culture clusters. In practical terms, clusters offer a valuable framework for handling the intricacies of multicultural ventures. That is, the knowledge that managers gain from cluster information may enable them to appreciate the application of particular management practices, policies, and human resources across cultural boundaries. Each cluster has its own expectations with regard to desired leadership qualities. Table 1.7 provides a summary of leadership expectations in all country clusters (with the exception of the South Pacific cluster that was new to the current CEO project).

In concert with the culture-specific view of leadership, GLOBE 2004 reported that clusters of associated countries (such as those found in Latin American or Germanic European groupings) differed with respect to their perceived importance of specific leadership attributes necessary for outstanding leadership. For instance, Latin American managers viewed team orientation as being much more important than the German managers did whereas the German managers viewed participation as more important than did the Latin American managers. Large cross-cultural differences concerning the importance of attributes such as "cunning, compassionate, or cautious" attest to the variety of beliefs regarding effective leadership (Javidan, Dorfman, et al., 2006). However, in contrast to these "culture-specific" beliefs, GLOBE also found considerable universality in positively viewed attributes such as "being trustworthy, just, and honest," or negatively viewed attributes such as "loner, ruthless, and egocentric." We concur with Bass (2008) when he noted that "images of the ideal leader, *prototypes*, tend to vary from one country and culture to another, at the same time, some prototypical traits generalize across countries" (p. 1021).

Differences of opinion about effective leadership also exist among countries within a culture cluster (e.g., Anglo or Latin American cluster). For instance, in New Zealand (Anglo cluster) there is a strong tendency to reject the "tall poppy" and enforce the "tall poppy syndrome" where New Zealanders are likely to cut down to size those who consider themselves high achievers. Lack of deference to anyone in a leadership position is a

Table 1.7 Ranking of Societal Clusters Using Absolute Culturally Endorsed Implicit Leadership Theory (CLT) Scores

Charismatic/Value-Based Leadership	Team-Oriented Leadership	Participative Leadership	Humane-Oriented Leadership	Autonomous Leadership	Self-Protective Leadership
higher	*higher*	*higher*	*higher*	*higher*	*higher*
Anglo L. America Southern Asia Germanic E. Nordic E.	L. America	Germanic E. Nordic E. Anglo	Southern Asia Sub-Saharan A. Anglo	E. Europe[1] Germanic E. Confucian A. Southern Asia Nordic E.	Southern Asia Middle East Confucian A. E. Europe
Sub-Saharan A. L. Europe E. Europe Confucian A.	E. Europe Southern Asia Nordic E. Anglo L. Europe Sub-Saharan A. Germanic E. Confucian A.	L. America L. Europe Sub-Saharan A.	Confucian A. L. America Middle East E. Europe Germanic E.	Anglo Middle East L. Europe Sub-Saharan A. L. America	L. America Sub-Saharan A. L. Europe
Middle East	Middle East	E. Europe Southern Asia Confucian A. Middle East	L. Europe Nordic E.		Anglo Germanic E. Nordic E.
lower	*lower*	*lower*	*lower*	*lower*	*lower*
Charismatic/Value-Based Leadership	Team-Oriented Leadership	Participative Leadership	Humane-Oriented Leadership	Autonomous Leadership	Self-Protective Leadership

Note: The placement of each societal cluster indicates the relative rank of this cluster compared with other clusters with regard to the size of the absolute scores on this dimension. For example, the Anglo cluster is the highest in rank for Charismatic/Value-Based leadership, indicating that this leader dimension had the highest score (absolute measure) compared with other clusters. Using the Tukey HSD (or honestly significant difference) analysis, clusters in the top band are significantly different from those in the bottom band. The clusters in the middle band are placed between these extremes for heuristic purposes. Societal clusters within each block are not significantly different from each other.

L. America = Latin America; Germanic E = Germanic Europe; Nordic E. = Nordic Europe; Sub-Saharan A. = Sub-Saharan Africa; L. Europe = Latin Europe; Eastern E. = Eastern Europe; Confucian A. = Confucian Asia;

[1]Societal clusters in this column are ranked in order; however, there are no significant differences among them.

norm in responding to New Zealand leaders (Kennedy, 2007). Indeed, a strong egalitarian position and high levels of participation are expected of leaders. In contrast, in the United States (also in the Anglo cluster), Americans romanticize leaders and treat them as cultural heroes. They are considered special individuals who are often ascribed superhuman attributes and who carry the hopes and fears of others (Hoppe & Bhagat, 2007) despite overwhelming evidence that attributions to leadership influence are often overblown (Meindl, Ehrlich, & Dukerich, 1985; Pfeffer, 1977).

GLOBE Leadership and Culture: Summary of Specific Findings From GLOBE 2004 and GLOBE 2007 and Why We Initiated GLOBE 2013

To summarize, the GLOBE research program was designed to develop and test elements of a unified leadership theory that integrates what we already know about leadership effectiveness within a cross-cultural framework (House et al., 2004). Our meta-goal was to integrate these streams of research to predict both organizational and societal leadership effectiveness. The GLOBE project, as reported in GLOBE 2004 and GLOBE 2007, made significant progress in accomplishing many of our initial objectives. We found that it was possible to develop psychometrically sound instruments to measure cultural practices and values. In testing our theory, we also found significant relationships among many cultural dimensions and economic success and societal human welfare. In addition, countries with similar cultural norms and values were identified and their GLOBE groupings validated.

We were also able to determine which cultural forces primarily drive expectations that individuals have for their prototypical leaders and the behaviors expected to be enacted by their leaders. Further, we found that expected leadership styles vary in accordance with culturally specific values and expectations. For instance, using multilevel statistical analysis (hierarchical linear modeling, or HLM), we found that Participative leadership is highly desired in societies that value Performance Orientation, Gender Egalitarianism, and Humane Orientation but is less desired in societies with high cultural values for Power Distance, Uncertainty Avoidance, and Assertiveness. Thus, the Germanic European and Anglo cultures were strong supporters of Participative leadership whereas the Confucian Asian and Eastern European cultures were less supportive of this leadership style (see Table 1.5). However, while it may be somewhat of a cliché, for each question answered in GLOBE 2004 and GLOBE 2007 we identified several others that became the focus and rationale for this, the third phase of the GLOBE project.

In the new GLOBE Phase 3 CEO study reported in this book, we sought to answer additional questions that have significant theoretical and practical applications to leadership success and organizational behavior. Our efforts were partly guided by the belief that while executives are likely to have the greatest influence on organizational success, surprisingly the study of executive effectiveness across cultures is remarkably scant. As Wang, Waldman, and Zhang (2012) noted, most research on strategic leadership has been conducted in Western countries, especially in the United States. It simply isn't clear if, how, or when executive leadership might be sensitive to cultural influences. While several excellent scholarly books and articles on executive leadership provide useful insights, there is no unified theory specifically addressing cultural influences. To add to the considerable complexity of leadership research, the globalization process marches unabated, but as Kwok Leung and colleagues (2005) pointed out, studies of cross-cultural leadership lag embarrassingly behind the more practical concerns and interests of multinational firms.

Our decision to proceed with the GLOBE Phase 3 CEO study was partially due to the scarcity of theoretically based knowledge regarding how culture affects leadership, as well as practical concerns related to CEOs leading a multinational workforce. The following research question guided our project: What is the *process* or mechanisms by which national cultures influence *executive* leadership behaviors? We know from a substantial variety of cross-cultural leadership studies that culture partly shapes leadership processes, but we know much less about the precise mechanisms by which it does so. We intend to test our belief that leadership expectations within a culture explain the "how and why" of leader behavior in that culture. If leadership expectations (exemplified by a country's CLTs) are important, then shouldn't CEO success be predicated on the match between culturally desirable leadership qualities and actual executive leadership? The obvious answer to this question is *yes*—to be effective, leaders should "walk the talk" expected of them. Unfortunately, the importance of this match between follower expectations and leader behavior remains speculative; in fact, some leaders have succeeded by behaving counter to societal norms and pursuing a countercultural style. A case in point is the brilliant Steve Jobs, cofounder of Apple, whose domineering, aggressive, and intense personality (Deutschman, 2000), ran counter to the U.S. penchant for a more participative leadership style.

Another question relates to the actual effectiveness of specific leadership behaviors. Fortunately, based on decades of leadership research (e.g., Bass, 2008; Yukl, 2010), we can predict that certain leadership styles will be more strongly related to organizational success than others; however, research is much less clear as to which leadership styles are most sensitive to cultural influences. We will also investigate the prevailing "common wisdom" among academics that there are universally effective leadership behaviors such as those found within a Charismatic/Value-Based leadership style. Not to give too much away at this point, but as we were conducting this CEO study we came up with many additional fascinating questions and issues that were not part of the original study objectives. For instance, is it possible to delineate and empirically characterize the truly superior from inferior CEOs, and do the characteristics or qualities of these "quality" CEOs remain invariant across cultures? Here is another question that surfaced as we progressed with the study: Is the prevailing adage found in both popular and academic research true—that visionary leadership, not effective management, separates truly effective CEOs from those who are less effective? The answer might surprise you as to which leadership dimensions are most important from the 21 leadership behaviors measured in the current project.

The following chapter reviews and examines the cross-cultural leadership literature to help us define what critical questions remain unanswered regarding effective leadership across cultures. This review also resolves methodological issues in the research design related to the numerous challenges presented when conducting a cross-cultural study (e.g., common source variance). The literature review leads to Chapter 3 where research questions for the present project are presented as formal research objectives. It is here that we discuss what we know and don't know regarding the tangled web of culture and leadership. Because the extant literature on *executive* leadership across cultures is scant, we need to rely on the GLOBE integrated theory, cross-cultural leadership studies of mid-level managers, and studies of executive leadership conducted within a specific culture (e.g., Wang, Tsui & Xin, 2011). Chapter 2 presents a literature review of current knowledge about leadership considered from a cross-cultural perspective. Chapter 3 further describes the theoretical rationale for our GLOBE Phase 3 CEO study and presents research objectives addressed by our current research.

2 Selective Review of the Literature on Culture, Leadership, and Upper Echelon Theory

Be tender as a dove and shrewd as a snake.

—Taiwan CEO

I believe that leaders should keep a certain distance from the followers. I do not put on airs, but because of the way I manage, people are all afraid of me.

—Chinese CEO

My strengths are in having a vision where we are going, looking at things strategically, willing to take risks, pushing the envelope.

—U.S. CEO

To be effective, you must be able to pound the table; otherwise, no one will listen to you. If you are being familiar with your employees they are more careless and irresponsible.

—Azerbaijan CEO

Our decisions are made in collaborative formats, where all of us discuss the issues . . . this helps us function as a unified corporation, and we know each other so well that we can think on the same issues and how to resolve them.

—Guatemalan CEO

The research presented in this book is focused on chief executive officers (CEOs) in over 1,000 corporations in 24 countries. We studied over 1,000 CEOs and more than 5,000 members of top management teams (TMTs) to understand the relationship between national culture, societal expectations of leaders, CEO leadership behavior, and such outcome measures like TMT Dedication and Firm Competitive Performance.

Our work is informed by two distinct and—so far—unrelated streams of work: (1) the literature on the relationship between national culture and leadership styles and behaviors generally referred to as the cross-cultural leadership literature and (2) the literature on the attributes, styles, behaviors, and outcomes of senior executives, TMTs, and CEOs—typically called the upper echelon theory, executive leadership theory, or strategic leadership theory. In this chapter, we offer a select review of these two diverse literatures.

Cultural Influences on Leadership Processes _____

In this chapter, we review the current cross-culture leadership literature regarding the influence of culture on leadership. It is not an exhaustive review but one that highlights research that continues to drive our thinking about leadership in different cultural contexts. We start with a short introduction about leadership, emphasizing the often-overlooked fact that cultures differ considerably in how they view leaders and the importance of leadership. We review compelling theoretical and practical reasons for understanding why culture matters. We also present a general review of cultural influences on leadership by discussing three contrasting narratives as to potential universal and/or culture specific leadership processes. Because the present CEO study is concerned with observed leadership behavior, our review presents knowledge about the relationship between leadership expectations, actual leader behavior, and leadership effectiveness. We chose to organize the empirical cross-culture leadership literature in terms of the GLOBE six global leadership dimensions discussed in the first chapter (i.e., Charismatic/Value-Based, Team-Oriented, Participative, Humane-Oriented, Autonomous, and Self-Protective leadership). The last section of this chapter presents information regarding executive leadership because it is the goal of the present project to merge two separate streams of research—influence of culture on leadership and executive leadership.

The quotes at the beginning of the chapter attest to the variety of views held by CEOs in different nations as to effective management strategies. Their personal views clearly differ, but to what extent are they due to culture or other noncultural factors inherent in all people (e.g., personality) or to specific organizational and industry imperatives (e.g., manufacturing versus service industries)? Along the way, we review what we believe are compelling reasons to delve into this particularly difficult and vexing area of cross-cultural research. As noted by Smith and Hitt (2005), cross-cultural research is not for the faint of heart. It is difficult, time consuming, and often frustrating, but the potential rewards are both theoretically and practically important. And, on a positive note, it is often fun, surprising, and knowledge enhancing.

GLOBE's Definition of Leadership

While the subject of leadership has generated thousands of academic papers, articles, and books, there is no *single consensually agreed upon* definition of leadership. Perhaps this is because the word *leadership* is a relatively new addition to the English language; it appeared approximately 200 years ago in writings about political influence in the British Parliament (Bass, 2008). However, we know from Egyptian hieroglyphics that symbols for *leader* have existed as early as 5,000 years ago. Simply put, leaders have existed in all cultures throughout history. Yet researchers typically define leadership in terms of their particular perspectives and interest. Stogdill (1974), perhaps humorously, suggested that "there are almost as many definitions of leadership as there are persons who have attempted to define the concept" (p. 259). Some researchers emphasize the motivating, visionary, and dynamic change aspects of leadership (e.g., Bennis & Nanus, 1985; Katz & Kahn, 1978; Richards & Engle, 1986; Schein, 1985); others emphasize the nature of directing and influencing individuals to accomplish group goals (e.g., Hemphill & Coons, 1957; Rauch & Behling, 1984).

Most current definitions of leadership include the core concept of creating a compelling *vision* and *influencing* followers for the purpose of achieving important outcomes. A catchy colloquial definition of leadership that captures this essence would be that leadership is the capacity to convert the leader's vision into reality (Bennis & Nanus, 1985). A more precise definition describing the actual process is the following: "Leadership is the process of influencing others to understand and agree about what needs to be done and how it can be done effectively, and the process of facilitating individual and collective efforts to accomplish the shared objectives" (Yukl, 2013, p. 7). In the initial GLOBE research meeting in 1994 at University of Calgary in Canada, we attempted to adequately define leadership even though there were differing viewpoints representing the combined wisdom of researchers from 40 countries. We agreed that a definition should contain elements of influence, motivation, and achieving organizational success. Thus, GLOBE's final definition is as follows: "Leadership is the ability of an individual to influence, motivate, and enable others to contribute toward the effectiveness and success of the organizations of which they are members."

An Appreciation of Cultural Influences on Leadership

The quotes presented in the beginning of this chapter should alert us to striking cultural differences in the most basic concepts of leadership. For instance, one should not be surprised that Americans mentally situate leaders (in spatial orientation) at the front of a group as it is almost a given in the United States that leaders lead from the front, not the rear. Consider that during the primary debates prior to the 2012 U.S. presidential election, Republican candidates went out of their way to deride President Obama's leadership by suggesting that he is most comfortable *leading from behind*. For Westerners, as suggested by Naisbitt (1982), leading means "finding a parade and getting in front of it" (p. 162). Yet this may not be the norm in all societies. For example, Singaporeans are more likely to represent leaders *behind* the group—all the better to watch over the group and protect it from threats, disruption, and failure (Menon, Sim, Ho-Ying Fu, Chiu, & Hong, 2010). Similarly, the admonition by Chinese general Lao Tzu "to lead the people, walk behind them" (Grothe, 2004, pp. 5–6) is contrary to Western perspectives about the spatial orientation of leaders in front of their followers.

Schyns, Kiefer, Kerschreiter, and Tymon (2011) were able to demonstrate, in a visual form, very basic cultural differences in implicit leadership theories (ILTs). They used an exercise whereby participants from different cultures "drew their leader" by asking them to make a drawing of their leader and include the leader's characteristics and what they did or did not do. While the drawings often contained words indicating charismatic qualities across all cultures, Americans typically focused on the leader's skills, characteristics, and behaviors while East Asian and Latin participants placed their leader in a wider social context by describing an effective leader as "in the same boat with the followers" where [personal characteristics] are just one aspect of the leadership process" (Schyns et al., 2011, p. 403). In a follow-up discussion, one North American participant indicated incredulously the following: "You cannot be serious. How can it be the role of effective leaders to look after the families of employees?" Obviously paternalistic leadership was far from this American's concept of an effective leader in contrast to Asian concepts of effective leadership.

Evidence from several sources suggests that some connotations associated with being a leader are distinctly, if not uniquely, American (Peterson & Hunt, 1997b) due to strong individualistic cultural predispositions (Hofstede, 2001; House, Hanges, Javidan, Dorfman, & Gupta, 2004). In one influential leadership article, Meindl, Ehrlich, and Dukerich (1985) went so far as to assert that Americans (over) "romanticize" leaders and view leadership qualities as the "sine quo non" for heading up (Graumann & Moscovici, 1986) various organizations irrespective of the specific context (e.g., for-profit, and nonprofits, military and volunteer organization alike). In contrast, Europeans historically seem less enthusiastic about leadership than are Americans. As one example, Graumann and Moscovici (1986) wrote, "When we Europeans say leader, we think, as if by conditioned reflex, of Hitler . . . no one would forget the havoc the leadership principle wreaked in Germany's history and in ours" (pp. 241–242).

To cite additional examples of cultural leadership variations, we could mention a number of nations that specifically downplay the importance of leadership due to understandable cultural values. In Holland, for instance, consensus and egalitarian values are highly esteemed (Hofstede, 1993), and anecdotal evidence suggests that the Dutch believe the concept of leadership is overvalued. Swedish managers also question the desirability of managing as they perceive it isolates them from their coworkers (Hoppe, 2004). New Zealanders' strong emphasis on egalitarianism encourages leaders to engage in participative leadership but with humility so the leader doesn't fall into the category of the "tall poppy syndrome" (i.e., the need to cut high achievers down to size; Kennedy, 2007). In contrast, some nations portray leaders in terms of great strength. For Latin Americans, the term *El Patrón* (leader) connotes a directive or authoritarian style with a leader's propensity to delegate work, seldom use teams, and act assertively (Romero, 2004). The transitional society in Russia today makes it difficult to present a single leadership prototype, but to survive, the leader has to demonstrate strength, be action oriented, energetic, and courageous in such an unstable environment (Grachev, Rogovsky, & Rakitski, 2007).

As one last example of major cultural contrasts, consider how American and Japanese CEOs handle success and failure. In Japan, CEOs likely credit subordinates for organizational accomplishments while de-emphasizing their own role as contributors to organizational success (Bass & Yokochi, 1991). Most interestingly, while American leaders willingly accept credit for positive outcomes, concordant with the notion of leadership control and responsibility (Salancik & Meindl, 1984), logically they should in turn accept blame for failure. While some resign before being tossed out by the board of directors, clearly, many don't. An example of the former was American Airlines CEO Gerard Arpey who resigned without taking severance pay when the airlines filed for bankruptcy in 2011 (Jilani, 2011). In contrast, the notorious case of corporate abuse and accounting fraud perpetrated by Enron CEOs Jeffrey Skilling and Kenneth Lay, and CFO Andrew Fastow attest to individual malfeasance and reluctance to accept blame. Tony Hayward, the CEO of BP, was reluctant to resign and accept responsibility even after presiding over one of the world's worst environmental catastrophes with the oil spill in the Gulf of Mexico. In contrast, Masataka Shimizu, CEO of the Japanese utility TEPCO, accepted company responsibility for the nuclear accident that occurred after the earthquake and tsunami in 2011 (Tabuchi, 2011). These examples and others led Dickson, Castaño, Magomaeva, and Den Hartog (2012) to suggest the following:

> Leaders in individualistic societies may be seen as the cause for an organization's success, but are less likely to be held accountable for an organization's failures, while in collectivistic societies, top leaders are less often seen as the sole source of the organization's success, but are more frequently held accountable for the organization's failures. (p. 488)

Empirical Evidence for the Statistical "Effect Size" Regarding Cultural Variation in Leadership

While the research literature and anecdotal evidence consistently points to the conclusion that culture clearly influences leadership processes, we need to ask questions related to the "effect size" of influence. It seems reasonable to ask when, how, and *to what extent* cultures differ regarding their concepts of leaders and leadership, and to what extent are these differences empirically related to leadership effectiveness?

There are several distinct literature streams that address cultural influence on leadership processes. The first stream includes studies investigating culture as an antecedent or moderator of leadership effectiveness. Many recent reviews of cross-culture leadership are organized along these lines (cf. Aycan, 2008). While most of these studies demonstrate statistically significant effects as to cultural influences on leadership, information regarding the *magnitude* of the effect of culture is difficult to determine. Unfortunately, few studies present the actual variance accounted for by culture (i.e., effect size). For instance, most only report a finding that culture somehow influences the findings such as a differing rank order of factors respondents found important to leadership quality. The second literature stream contains information about leaders and leadership specific to individual countries such as leadership in Russia in contrast to the United States, Mexico, or other countries (cf. Chhokar, Brodbeck, & House, 2007). This second stream also includes studies that specifically address *emic* leadership constructs such as "guanxi" in China (Earley, 1997) or paternalistic leadership found in Latin America and Asia (Dorfman & Howell, 1988). It makes little sense to examine the extent to which emic constructs vary across *all* cultures as they might only be meaningfully understood and embedded in specific cultures.

The third literature stream, which is much smaller in volume, includes research studies that empirically calculate the effect sizes of leadership phenomena across nations or cultures. As noted by Brodbeck and Eisenbeiss (in press), to empirically quantify the magnitude of cross-cultural effects on leadership, one needs large national or cultural samples or meta-analytical designs. The GLOBE 2004 project calculated effect sizes (i.e., coefficient of determination) for country-level differences on each of their six major global leadership dimensions.

The largest effect sizes in the GLOBE study were found for Self-Protective leadership (36%) and the smallest for Autonomous (14%), meaning that countries vary greatly in their beliefs that Self-Protective leadership qualities enhance or inhibit outstanding leadership. Conversely, countries do not vary greatly in their desirability of Autonomous leadership qualities; most countries scored from neutral to negative regarding the desirability of this leadership dimension. Charismatic/Value-Based and Participative leadership dimensions were scored between the two extremes (20% and 21% for effect sizes, respectively) as did Team-Oriented and Humane-Oriented (15% and 18% for effect sizes, respectively). Two other points are worthy of note regarding these GLOBE findings. First, when countries are grouped into culture clusters, the variance accounted for decreases since the clusters mask country differences. Second, differences among individuals within each country are also masked by combining respondents' data into an aggregated country score.

Meta-analyses can also answer questions regarding the empirical impact of cultures on leadership. In one such meta-analytical study sampling of 20,073 participants in 18 countries, Leong and Fischer (2011) studied cultural differences in transformational leadership behavior. Their study examined *actual* transformational leadership behavior in contrast to the GLOBE studies to date that examined the desirability of this leadership behavior. Leong and Fischer (2011) found significant variability among countries on the means for transformational leadership. In fact, 50% of the variance in mean scores for transformational leadership was among societies. Furthermore, they found societal culture had an important effect whereby managers in more egalitarian societies were seen as engaging in more transformational leadership and managers in higher power distance countries were seen as engaging in less transformational leadership. They concluded that due to significant countrywide variability, transformational leadership is, therefore, not universal as previously suggested by Bass (1997) and Den Hartog and colleagues (1999). An alternate conclusion is that transformational leadership is universal but is of the kind previously described by Bass (1997) as variform functional universal—effective everywhere but in differing magnitudes. Interestingly, Leong and Fischer's (2011) findings also support early GLOBE (House et al., 2004) predictions regarding the cultural influences of power distance and egalitarianism values on Charismatic/Value-Based leadership. High power distance values are associated with less desirability of Charismatic/Value-Based leadership while high gender egalitarian values are associated with increased desirability of Charismatic/Value-Based leadership. Current GLOBE research examines the extent to which executives engage in Charismatic/Value-Based leadership behavior, whether this behavior (and others) is related to cultural expectations, and the extent to which this behavior is effective.

Managerial Implications for Understanding Cultural Influences on Leadership

Managers in the United States have long been concerned with managing employees from diverse cultural backgrounds. According to current human resource management (HRM) thinking, effective diversity management can lead to an organization's strategic advantage (Landy & Conte, 2010). For multinational organizations, practical knowledge is certainly critical in managing people with diverse values, beliefs, and expectations. Perhaps obviously, the globalization of labor markets and migration of labor is increasingly characteristic of contemporary international and multinational organizations; however, domestic organizations in most industrialized countries are also confronted with multinational workforces due to expanding international workforce migration. For example, 12% of Germany's workforce is of non-German ethnic origin with significant numbers from many countries in Asia, Africa, Europe, and the (former) USSR (Biffl, 2012). As another example, while the majority of businesses in Singapore are founded and staffed with ethnic Chinese, an increasing number of their employees are Indian, Malaysian, and Filipino. What may not be obvious, however, is that circumstances of modern life often *force* collaboration among people of different national origins irrespective of their wish for close interaction or not. For example, operations of nongovernmental organizations (NGOs) and multinational military alliances include work relationships among cultures that have not had the best prior interactions.

Multinational companies formed from international joint ventures (IJVs) and other strategic alliances are often confronted with a workforce representing vastly different national cultures. These IJVs provide unique opportunities to understand the process by which culture influences leadership effectiveness. Consider that in the past 30 years, the number of multinational organizations and NGOs have proliferated with an increasingly diverse intercultural mix of foreign ownership, management, and employees (Bass, 2008). Case studies of IJVs demonstrate the importance of intercultural compatibility where IJV failure can be partially attributed to cultural conflicts at executive leadership levels. For instance, the disastrous joint venture between Daimler Benz and Chrysler failed partially because of numerous cultural incompatibilities including corporate and national culture differences (Waller, 2001).

This increased interdependency among nations has occurred through economic integration with well-known examples such as the European Union (EU), regional and global trading entities (e.g., NAFTA [North American Free Trade Agreement] and ASEAN [Association of Southeast Asian Nations]), and the omnipresence of the World Trade Organization (WTO). Perhaps less well known are the numerous preferential and free trade blocs with hundreds of interlocking country members and *billions* of citizens within their purview (*CIA World Factbook,* n.d.; World Trade Organization's Regional Trade Agreement Database, 2012). For example, the preferential and free trade area of "AANZFTA-ASEAN+3" refers to a trading bloc of the 10 ASEAN member states (Brunei Darussalam, Cambodia, Lao PDR, Indonesia, Malaysia, Myanmar, the Philippines, Singapore, Thailand and Viet Nam, plus China, Japan, and South Korea) along with Australia and New Zealand. These countries have a combined population of more than 2 billion people! While leadership disasters attributed to cultural conflicts make the news more so than success stories, effective global leadership is not only possible but normal given leaders with the requisite education, experience and personal qualities (cf. Hollenbeck & McCall, 2003). Unfortunately, the demand for experienced global leaders exceeds the supply and a severe shortage of experienced global leaders is often cited as a major limitation of organizations wishing to expand globally into new markets (Beechler & Javidan, 2007).

International understanding and experience is becoming a must for globally minded CEOs (McCall & Hollenbeck, 2002). Résumé requirements have changed drastically in the past 10 years with 70% of current Standard & Poor's (S&P) Fortune 100 company CEOs having had senior management responsibilities overseas (Wolgemuth, 2010).

Magnusson and Boggs (2006) reported that international experience is an important asset associated with ascension to the CEO position of large corporations. Further, they found that CEO international experience is greater in firms that are highly international in terms of sales and assets. While the following example may be atypical, consider how the CEO of Siemens AG appeared well suited for leading a huge multinational organization. Siemens AG, a German engineering conglomerate, has 15 divisions and 420,000 employees located in 190 countries. It has products in a wide variety of sectors including lighting, energy, finance, and health care among others. It should be obvious that Siemens executives need to work compatibly with employees from numerous national cultures—a job seemingly well suited for (CEO) Peter Loscher (as of February 21, 2013). His cross-cultural experiences included an education in Austria, the United States, and Hong Kong, as well as holding management positions in Spain, the United States, Germany, the United Kingdom, and Japan.

Major leadership challenges also exist in governmental and other nonprofit organizations that operate in a multicultural world. The seemingly endless list of international nonprofit organizations attests to interdependencies among cultures. It is estimated that more than 50,000 NGOs such as the famine relief organization Oxfam (2013) and humanitarian-aid Médecins Sans Frontières (Doctors Without Borders, 2013) have an international focus (Union of International Associations, 2012). While their humanitarian goals are laudable, many international organizations such as the United Nations and the International Red Cross are plagued by long-festering disputes among countries; leaders of these organizations must contend not only with international problems but also with their own organization's inter- and intracultural problems (Bass, 2008). As a concrete example, the United Nations Children's Fund (UNICEF) operates in 190 countries within the UN framework. However, while an overriding goal is to provide a better future for children, there are intraorganizational squabbles over the degree to which local issues and priorities should govern their activities (in contrast to a "one size fits all" solution for all nations).

Military alliances are also prime examples of a mélange of cultures that by necessity must work effectively together. Obviously there is a huge potential for cultural conflict. Consider that during the Afghanistan and Iraq wars, combined North Atlantic Treaty Organization (NATO) military forces measured in the hundreds of thousands (2003 to the present). At one time, forces in Afghanistan included more than 130,000 troops from 48 contributing countries under the command structure of lead nations comprising very different cultures (including the United States, Italy, Turkey, Germany, and the United Kingdom (International Security Assistance Force, 2013). As of 2010, the U.S. military had contingents in 150 countries, exercising both peace-keeping and warring functions (U.S. Department of Defense, 2010). Added to this mix of oftentimes strained relationships among nations, NATO forces have the conundrum of simultaneously fighting terrorism as well as winning the "hearts and minds" of local citizens. Conflicting goals and cultural differences among contributing nations present daunting leadership challenges for any international military command structure (e.g., NATO).

The successful transformation of a national or newly conceived multinational organization to a global network of seamless, interconnected, and integrated operations is no easy task. From a leadership perspective, it requires the ability to work with individuals from both inside and outside the corporation, who represent diverse technical and cultural backgrounds, to help achieve the organization's goals (Beechler & Javidan, 2007). Perhaps, surprisingly, while it is almost an axiom that successful leaders choose leadership styles that reflect an understanding of their national culture and social institutions (cf. Cullen, 1998), the empirical evidence proving it is sparse. Current GLOBE research challenges our understanding of what really makes an effective global leader. We think you may be surprised by several key findings.

Theoretical Reasons for Understanding Cultural Influences on Leadership

From a scientific and theoretical perspective, compelling reasons exist for considering the influence of culture on leadership processes. Early cross-cultural leadership research often had the purpose of validating leadership theories developed solely in Western countries (cf. Dorfman, 2004). The results of these studies were decidedly mixed and often criticized as not being sensitive to cultural differences. While in general, cross-cultural researchers react negatively to the notion of universal laws, the often-found effectiveness of transformational and Charismatic/Value-Based leadership comes close to being considered universally effective (Bass, 1997).

Cross-cultural researchers respond to claims of universality that it is the unique *behaviors* required to enact general leadership styles such as transformational leadership that likely reflect the diversity among cultures (Smith & Peterson, 1988). However, GLOBE researchers typically believe that there has been a false dichotomy between these "universalist and culturally unique" perspectives. Our findings generally support a nuanced view of cultural influence, where we found some leadership attributes to be universally desired but also demarcating cultural variation with regard to cultural contingencies (Javidan, Dorfman, Howell, & Hanges, 2010). Examples of the former include visionary leadership whereas cultural contingencies were found for a number of other leadership behaviors such as bureaucratic and self-sacrificial leadership.

We know there are inherent limitations in transferring theories across cultures, which are well noted in the literature (Chemers, 1997; Poortinga & Malpass, 1986; Ronen, 1986; Ronen & Shenkar, 1985)—what works in one culture may not necessarily work in another culture). A more subtle view may be that through cross-cultural research we might determine which aspects of a leadership theory are culturally universal and which aspects are culturally unique. As Triandis (1993) suggested, leadership researchers will be able to "fine-tune" theories by investigating cultural variations as parameters of the theory. Chemers (1983) also suggested that this research helps us uncover new relationships by forcing the researcher to consider a broader range of noncultural variables. Continuing this thought, Yukl (2008) noted that "examination of cross-cultural differences may cause researchers to pay more attention to possible effects of situational variables not usually included in current theories of leadership (e.g., religion, language, history, laws, political systems, ethnic structures)" (p. 437). In fact, Beechler and Javidan (2007) developed the logical argument that cross-cultural leadership research is a subset of global leadership research since the latter forces a researcher to carefully consider national institutions in addition to cultural differences (e.g., the role of political imperatives in the conduct of Korean businesses).

Cultural variations may therefore highlight relationships among theoretical constructs, specify important theoretical boundary conditions, or even cause us to rethink the very basic nature of leadership itself. As one example, theories promoting participatory leadership may be valid for relatively sophisticated employees in developed countries but less valid for employees in less developed countries where egalitarian values may not be highly valued. Nevertheless, this somewhat patronizing view may not reflect reality in countries whose culture seems to be rapidly changing (e.g., China) or in cultures whose citizens are becoming more independent and worldly due to communication advances such as e-mail, Facebook, and Twitter. What we do know is that our theories must be able to help us understand the nature of leadership influence on people of different cultures and, hence, their different interpretations of organizational reality.

Answering Basic Research Questions About Cultural Influences on Leadership

Yukl (2006) challenged researchers to answer the following four questions regarding cultural influences on leadership:

1. What are the differences in the conceptualization of leadership behavior and leadership prototypes?

2. What are the differences in the beliefs about effective leadership behavior?

3. What are the differences in the actual patterns of leadership behaviors and styles?

4. What are the differences in the relationship of leadership behaviors to outcomes such as subordinate motivation, satisfaction, and performance?

Considerable progress has been achieved in answering questions 1 and 2. The extent to which ideal leader prototypes vary across cultures has been addressed early on by Gerstner and Day (1994) and more completely by GLOBE (Chhokar et al., 2007; House et al., 2004). Cultures certainly influence how societies view their leaders and their beliefs about effective leadership processes. While some leadership functions by necessity are identical across cultures (e.g., creating a compelling vision for the direction of the company), it has become an article of faith that leadership styles and behaviors will vary across cultures to accomplish these functions. But how much do the actual patterns of leadership and the effectiveness of these patterns vary across cultures (questions 3 and 4)? Do cross-cultural researchers oversell the notion of cross-cultural differences instead of universals? Further, what evidence supports the assertion that the magnitude of cultural influences on leadership varies by the *specific* leader behavior under consideration (e.g., visionary versus participatory leadership)? The present GLOBE project provides evidence to answer questions 3 and 4.

Coming of Age: The Proliferation of Cross-Cultural Leadership Studies

The field of cross-cultural, international, and global leadership has come of age. Prior to the mid-1980s, relatively few leadership studies were concerned with the impact of cultural influences on leadership. Many early studies suffered from limitations of scope, were methodologically suspect, focused mainly on the generalizability of U.S.- and Western-oriented leadership theories, and, in general, lacked a coherent cultural framework to interpret findings (Dorfman, 1996; Peterson & Hunt, 1997a). Fortunately, the situation has changed dramatically in the past 20 years. Dickson, Den Hartog, and Mitchelson (2003) went so far as to assert that there has been an explosion in the amount of cross-cultural leadership research. Strong evidence for increased interest can be found in numerous research outlets. For instance, the *Annual Review of Psychology* periodically features chapters on leadership and cross-cultural organizational behavior (Avolio, Walumbwa, & Weber, 2009; Gelfand, Erez, & Aycan, 2007). Relatively recent reviews of international leadership research by Dickson and colleagues (2003); Dorfman (2004); and Dorfman & House (2004) further indicate progress in this field. The most recent *Bass Handbook of Leadership* (Bass & Bass, 2008) contains a monumental 68-page chapter on globalization and cross-national effects on leadership. Current reviews by Aycan (2008) and Brodbeck and Eisenbeiss (in press) further attest to ongoing interest. Finally, we should note that special issues of the *Journal of World Business and Organizational Dynamics* (in 2012) are devoted entirely to global issues in leadership and contain several chapters specifically on reviews of cross-cultural leadership (Dickson et al., 2012; Wang, Waldman, & Zhang, 2012).

Unfortunately, while there clearly is increased interest in the cross-culture leadership field, Brodbeck and Eisenbeiss (in press) noted several continuing problems. First, there are very few large-scale multination studies that examine culture and leadership *concurrently*. They noted the following:

> To our knowledge, only two large scale multi-nation studies address culture and leadership concordantly, thereby also sampling managerial populations from various organizations. One project began with Smith and Peterson's (1988) early work about leadership, organizations, and culture, along the lines of which an event management evaluation model was developed and refined (e.g., Smith, Wang, & Leung, 1997). Their approach culminates in a 47 nation study about event management styles of nearly 7,000 managers (Smith, Peterson, & Schwartz, 2002). The other project is GLOBE (Global Leadership and Organizational Behavior Effectiveness), a multi-nation ($N = 62$), multi-industry ($N = 3$), multi-organization ($N > 900$), multi-level (country, industry, organization, $N = 17,000$ middle level managers), multi-method (quantitative-comparative and qualitative-interpretative), and multi-investigator study about societal culture, organizational culture, leadership, and performance, with more than 170 management and social scientists participating from the countries studies.

The second problem with cross-cultural leadership research relates to the first where Brodbeck and Eisenbeiss (in press) noted that the moderating effects of culture on leadership have been investigated mainly in small to mid-scale studies. These studies have been adequately reviewed by Bass (2008) and Tsui, Nifadkar, and Ou (2007). Specific findings are noted in the following sections when they bear on the current GLOBE project, but the fact remains that it becomes very difficult, if not impossible, to generalize findings beyond the specific cultures involved in small to midsize projects. To help place the results of the present study in context, the following literature review is organized around GLOBE's six global leadership behaviors identified in previous sections.

Three Competing Theoretical Propositions Regarding Cultural Influence on Leadership

One of our goals in the present project is to discover the extent to which *specific* leader behaviors are effective across countries and/or in specific national cultures, and why. These questions are subsumed under a meta-issue often labeled as a contrast between the perspectives of "universal versus culture specific" or "culture common versus culture unique." The perspectives can be stated as propositions that differ in the extent to which effective leadership is characterized by the congruence, or lack of congruence, between endemic cultural forces and specific styles, behaviors, and images associated with leaders. We propose that there are three propositions that speak to this issue (universality, cultural congruence, and cultural difference). Each enjoys some empirical support, but none have been explicitly tested with executives worldwide. Nevertheless, their contrasts have significant theoretical and practical significance as discussed in more detail below.

Fortunately, researchers now have an increasing wealth of knowledge and a set of tools that enable us to describe and measure cultures and cross-cultural variation. The well-known cultural studies of Hofstede (1980, 2001) and Smith and colleagues (2002) are exemplars of the continuation of the cultural anthropological tradition with strong implications for organizational behavior. The series of studies by Smith and Peterson (cf. 1995) and GLOBE (Chhokar et al., 2007; House et al., 2004) are research programs that focus on the measurements of both culture and measurement of leadership. The key question is to know when cultural universals and differences exist so we can better understand and predict effective leader behaviors and increase personal and organizational success. This is true whether we are concerned with leadership acceptance and effectiveness of expatriates or host country nationals figuring out why "foreigners" act the way they do.

Universality of Leader Behaviors

This proposition asserts that there are some leader behaviors that are universally, or near universally, accepted and effective. Organizational researchers in the "universal" camp note pan-cultural similarities in management processes worldwide. After all, managerial leaders face common problems across the globe—how to organize, motivate, and influence others to accomplish organizational goals. The "culturally common" camp is represented by the current zeitgeist in the strong belief that Charismatic/Value-Based and transformational leadership are just about universally valued and effective; empirical research now supports this notion (House et al., 2004; Leong & Fischer, 2011). The current form of the culturally common camp is embodied in what might be called the *near universality of leadership proposition;* it simply means that some leadership behaviors will be universally accepted, enacted and effective. Of course, the actual behavioral enactment and leadership effectiveness may differ somewhat across societies thus hedging the "universality" notion to reflect a position of "near universality" (in contrast to complete universality).

Despite wide-ranging differences in cultural norms across countries studied, there is some support for the proposition of universality for some (but probably not most) leadership behaviors. Bass, Burger, Doktor, & Barrett (1979) found that managers from 12 culturally diverse countries indicated a desire to get work done while using less authority. Similarly, Smith and Peterson (1995) found that managers in 30 countries reported satisfaction with events for which they were delegated substantial discretion. Transformational leadership has been found to be more acceptable and effective than transactional leadership in most empirical studies across multiple cultures including Canada (Howell & Avolio, 1993; Howell & Frost, 1989), India (Pereira, 1987), Japan (Bass, 1997), the Netherlands (Koene, Pennings, & Schreuder, 1991), and Singapore (Koh, Terborg, & Steers, 1991), as well as the United States (Bass & Avolio, 1993).

Several specific hypotheses relating culture to leadership processes will be tested throughout this book. One such hypothesis, given the previous discussion of universality, might take the position that because Charismatic/ Value-Based leadership has been universally endorsed as contributing to outstanding leadership (House et al., 2004), it will prove to be an effective leadership behavior. Even if this global leadership behavior proves to be universally effective, GLOBE researchers are interested in the extent to which all six subdimensions of their global Charismatic/Value-Based leadership dimension are equally effective across cultures. If Charismatic/ Value-Based leadership proves to be effective in all cultures, then a fascinating question arises concerning which *type* of universality it exemplifies. That is, Bass (1997) used concepts from Lonner (1980) to identify several different kinds of universality. *Simple* universality, for example, exists with the emergence of leaders in all societies throughout history. A *variform* universal exists when a universal phenomenon exists but is clearly influenced by culture. Mahatma Gandhi and Winston Churchill exemplify this type of universality in that both were charismatic leaders, but each inspired followers in quite a different manner. As another example of a variform universal, Brodbeck, Chhokar, and House (2007) identified four distinct "species" of Participative leadership found across a subset of countries where all highly desired Participative leadership (discussed further later in the chapter). A third type of universal is labeled a *functional universal*—a relationship between variables that is universal. However, culture can affect the size of relationships as in the case where there is significant variance across cultures in the *degree* of leadership effectiveness of even universally desirable leadership behaviors. Bass (1997) referred to this variability as a *variform functional universal*. The present project will empirically determine if any of the leadership attributes universally endorsed in GLOBE 2004 similarly result in universal leadership effectiveness, and if so, what type of universality they constitute.

Cultural Congruence (Effective Leadership requires a cultural match)

Cross-cultural researchers generally can be found in the "cultural congruence" camp where managerial processes and leadership styles are expected to be differentially effective depending on congruency with the societies' culture. This cultural congruency hypothesis has become an axiom or article of faith among cultural theorists (Dorfman, 2004). This proposition asserts that cultural forces affect the kind of leader behavior that is usually accepted, enacted, and effective within a collective. Accordingly, behavior that is consistent with collective values will be more acceptable and effective than behavior that represents conflicting values.

The following examples illustrate the cultural congruence proposition. Nations in Hofstede's research that have high power distance and collectivism scores experience a tendency to accept leader behaviors that are consistent with high scores on these dimensions. For instance, the heavy emphasis placed by Asian managers on paternalism (Dorfman & Howell, 1988; Farmer & Richman, 1965) and group maintenance activities (Bass et al., 1979; Bolon & Crain, 1985; Ivancevich, Shweiger, & Ragan, 1986) is consistent with countries that are culturally highly collective. Hofstede's Uncertainty Avoidance scores are associated with behaviors exhibiting less risky entry into foreign markets and more full disclosure of accounting information. McClelland (1961) found that achievement motivation reflected in grammar school books was predictive of entrepreneurial behavior 25 years later. In individualistic societies, people prefer individual rather than group-based compensation practices and exhibit greater willingness to take risks (Erez, 1997). These empirical findings support the congruence proposition.

One almost irrefutable cultural-congruence rejoinder to the "near universality camp" is that there are leadership constructs that are truly emic and found only in very specific cultures. For instance, the Chinese concept of guanxi (often simplistically described as personal relationships) and the Japanese emphasis of *wa* (harmony) are not found in Western conceptualizations of leadership. Nor is paternalistic leadership (which is typically found in the collectivist and high power distance cultures of Asia and Latin America) a desired leadership style in the West (Aycan, 2006, 2008).

A corollary of the cultural congruence proposition is that violation of cultural norms by leaders or managers will result in dissatisfaction, conflict, and resistance on the part of followers or subordinates and, at times, lower the performance of leaders and their work units and subordinates. Anecdotal examples from the literature on expatriate adjustment illustrate lowered productivity and satisfaction if collective norms and expatriate values conflict (Lindsay & Dempsey, 1985; Weiss & Bloom, 1990). However, while the cultural congruence hypothesis is taken as an article of faith among culture theorists, available empirical evidence is sparse (House, Wright, & Aditya, 1997). We believe that a rigorous test of this proposition is important for both practical and theoretical reasons.

Cultural Difference (Effective Leadership May Require Deviance From Existing Culture)

House, Wright, et al. (1997) developed a cultural difference position that can be juxtaposed to the cultural congruence proposition found in the present research. According to this proposition, increased task performance of followers, organizations, and institutions in societies will be induced by the introduction of selected values, techniques, and behavior patterns that are *different* from those commonly valued in the society (note that in our specific meaning of the construct, it does not mean that there simply are differences among cultures but that sometimes leaders must go against the grain of their culture). The rationale for this hypothesis is that by being different in respect to some culturally accepted behaviors, leaders introduce more changes of the kind required for innovation and performance improvement. The present project does not explicitly test this hypothesis but remains an intriguing notion for future research.

To summarize, the central issues presented in the above sections can be described in terms of three competing narratives. In the first narrative, because there are universally desirable leadership qualities (e.g., visionary leadership), leaders should strive to maximize these behaviors irrespective of cultural expectations. In contrast, the second narrative suggests that effective leaders *must* act in accordance with cultural expectations, hence the importance of knowing one's culture and what leadership styles should be effective in that culture (e.g., high levels of Participative leadership in the individualistic United States). By definition, leadership behaviors that deviate from expectations are expected to be counterproductive. To make the contrasting theoretical positions even more complex, House and colleagues (1997) discussed the possibility of a third narrative, that of a *cultural difference proposition* (in contrast to the *cultural congruency proposition*) whereby it might be advantageous for a leader to differ from cultural expectations—thereby violating cultural norms. History is replete with examples of business leaders who are famous for going against the zeitgeist.

We know of no prior research that empirically and competitively tests all three narrative positions. To foreshadow present GLOBE findings, we will lend support not only to those who firmly believe in cultural uniqueness but also to those who believe that there are commonalities among cultures when it comes to effective leadership. In general, however, our research does not support "the one best way of leading" to be maximally effective across diverse cultures. The devil, however, is truly in the details.

Linking Cognitive Psychology to Cross-Cultural Leadership

The social information processing literature (Croker, Fiske, & Taylor, 1984) provides an important conceptual framework to help explain the mechanisms by which cultural values impact leadership. Models developed from this literature illustrate how cultures shape the basic ways people collect, store, organize, and process information about each other. In fact, Avolio, Walumbwa, and Weber (2009) noted that "for more than 25 years, a great deal of the work on cognitive psychology and leadership focused on how implicit theories and prototypes affected the perceptions of leaders and followers" (p. 427).

As presented in Chapter 1, the central proposition of the GLOBE research project and associated integrated theory has been that the attributes and characteristics that differentiate a societal culture are predictive of leader attributes and behaviors that are most frequently enacted and most effective in that culture. We built on the foundation of implicit leadership theory (ILT) (Lord & Maher, 1990) and culturally endorsed implicit leadership theory (CLT) (House et al., 2004; Javidan et al., 2010) to present a theoretical framework linking national culture, organizational culture, and leadership.

The following propositions formally express the major assertions of ILT.

1. Leadership qualities are attributed to individuals, and those individuals are accepted as leaders on the basis of the degree of congruence between the leader behaviors they enact and the ILT held by the attributers.

2. ILTs constrain, moderate, and guide the exercise of leadership; the acceptance of leaders; the perception of leaders as influential, acceptable, and effective; and the degree to which leaders are granted status and privileges.

The basic conceptualization of ILT is that people have general ideas about leaders and leadership that include the personal qualities and behaviors necessary to be an effective leader. These general ideas can be further described in terms of implicit beliefs, convictions, and assumptions concerning attributes and behaviors that distinguish leaders from followers, effective leaders from ineffective leaders, and moral leaders from evil leaders. From these abstract notions, individuals develop a mental representation (i.e., prototype) typical of leaders in various contexts (e.g., what constitutes excellent leadership in voluntary organizations versus leadership in military contexts). Clearly, this cognitively oriented perspective about leadership assumes that leadership is partly in the eye of the beholder. Further, while these mental representations about leadership may be held both consciously and unconsciously by followers, the encoding and retrieval of leader-relevant information depends partly on these mental representations (Shondrick, Dinh, & Lord, 2010). The mental process is thought to involve the match between the ideal leadership (i.e., the leadership prototype) and the characteristics and behaviors of the leader in this comparison.

In support of this assertion, Epitropaki and Martin (2005) found the closer the match between an employee's endorsement of specific ILTs to their manager's ILT profile, the better the quality of interactions with the leader. In short, one's image of an *ideal* leader is a fundamental aspect of ILT theory and is critical to perceptions of leadership effectiveness (van Quaguebeke, van Knippenberg, & Brodbeck, 2011). Recently, conceptualizations regarding ILT have progressed to include more dynamic models that suggest how ILTs change with new information provided about a leader. This "connectionist approach" recognizes that the elements in various categories may shift in importance and in how they are grouped together over time and across situations (Hanges, Dorfman, Shteynberg, & Bates, 2006). Recent developments in ILT by Lord and colleagues continue to elucidate the precise kinds of mental representations characteristic of ILTs (Shondrick et al., 2010).

Cultural Differences in Implicit Leadership Theories

Shaw (1990) suggested three effects that culture can have on leadership schemas. He hypothesized that culture affects (1) the attributes believed to be typical of leaders (i.e., schema content), (2) the cognitive complexity and differentiation among the schema content (i.e., schema structure), and (3) the level of automaticity involved in processing a leadership encounter. Some evidence exists to confirm Shaw's hypotheses about the influence of culture on leadership schemas. O'Connell, Lord, and O'Connell (1990) found that national culture plays a role in influencing the content of leader attributes and behaviors perceived as desirable and effective by individuals in that culture. Other studies, such as those by Gerstner and Day (1994), found that the prototypicality of specific leader attributes varied across cultures for university students from eight nations. As expected, attributes that were seen as most characteristic of business leaders varied across cultures—no single trait was rated in the top five as being most prototypical across all eight nations.

More recent studies provide additional evidence that leadership perceptions are influenced by culture. Chong and Thomas (1997), for instance, suggested that leadership prototypes of two ethnic groups in New Zealand influenced the amounts of leadership behaviors experienced. Mehra and

Krishnan (2005) found that the Indian cultural orientation of Svadharma (following one's own duty) is related to conceptions of successful leadership. Casimir and Waldman (2007) reported significant differences among white-collar employees from China and Australia regarding traits important for effective leadership. Australians rated traits that attenuate power differences among leaders and followers (e.g., friendly) higher than did Chinese. Importantly, they also found differences depending on the requirements of the leadership role in addition to cultural influences. Using student samples from Turkey and the United States, Ensari and Murphy (2003) investigated the extent to which Charismatic leadership perceptions were based more on individual prototypical leadership characteristics or company performance outcomes. While the co-occurrence of high company performance and a charismatic prototype in the vignette led to the highest attributions of charisma for both samples, they found significant differences between the individualistic U.S. and collectivistic Turkish samples. The charismatic prototype was more salient for the U.S. sample and company performance outcomes were more important for the collectivistic Turkish sample. These studies, while important, were limited in size, scope, and sample selection such that their theoretical significance and generalizability are limited.

GLOBE Contributions to Implicit Leadership Theory and Culturally Endorsed Implicit Leadership Theory

A major part of the GLOBE research program was designed to capture the ILTs of societies and empirically determine the degree of commonality and differences within and among nations. GLOBE's 2004 extension of ILT to the cultural level of analysis (labeled culturally endorsed leadership theory, or CLT) found support for Shaw's hypothesized relationship between culture and leadership schema content (Dorfman, Hanges, & Brodbeck, 2004). GLOBE researchers found a high and significant within-society agreement with respect to questions concerning the effectiveness of leader attributes and behavior. Furthermore, many cultural dimension values were associated with specific leadership prototypes. For instance, high Performance Orientation values were positively associated with Participative leadership as a component of respondents' CLT profile of outstanding leaders (Javidan, 2004). GLOBE researchers also determined that culturally similar societies could be clustered together (Gupta & Hanges, 2004) and meaningful differences exist in the content of the CLT profiles of different clusters (Dorfman et al., 2004). For example, the Anglo (or English-speaking) cluster of countries particularly value Charismatic/Value-Based leadership whereas the Latin American cluster most highly valued Team-Oriented leadership.

Two studies published by GLOBE researchers (as part of Project GLOBE) further attest to the existence and importance of CLTs. Den Hartog and colleagues (1999) presented evidence that attributes of

Charismatic/Value-Based leadership are universally endorsed as contributing to outstanding leadership. This study also provides evidence that leadership prototypes vary by hierarchical levels within an organization; ILTs held for top managers and CEOs differ from those held for effective supervisors. In the second study, using a different subset of GLOBE data for European cultures, Brodbeck and colleagues (2000) presented convincing evidence that clusters of European cultures sharing similar cultural values also share similar leadership concepts. This study will be described in more detail later in the chapter.

GLOBE's Universal and Cultural-Specific Leadership Dimensions and Their Relationships to the GLOBE Cultural Dimensions

To recapitulate GLOBE 2004 findings, we answered major questions addressing the extent to which specific leader characteristics and actions are universally endorsed as contributing to effective leadership. GLOBE 2004 identified a number of primary leader attributes (i.e., skills, characteristics, or behaviors) that are universally viewed as contributors to leadership effectiveness and somewhat fewer that are universally viewed as impediments to leader effectiveness. Perhaps most interestingly, many leader attributes or behaviors were found to be culturally contingent—that is, considered to be contributors in some cultures and impediments in others (e.g., independent, cunning, subdued) (see Chapter 21, GLOBE [House et al., 2004]; Javidan et al., 2010). However, the actual leadership enactment of these culturally common and culturally specific attributes remains a matter to be studied; therefore, it is a major issue examined in this book. Nonetheless, glimpses of how leaders enact the attributes can be found in the culture specific chapters of GLOBE 2007.

A Targeted Review of Cross-Cultural Leadership Based on GLOBE's Six Global Leadership Behaviors

A primary goal of the present GLOBE project is to empirically determine the actual enactment and effectiveness of the six global leadership behaviors identified as important in the prior GLOBE phases (reported in GLOBE 2004 and GLOBE 2007). As stated earlier, research presented in this book focuses on executive level leadership behaviors at two levels and their effectiveness within and across multiple cultures. Because we focus our research on GLOBE's 6 global leadership behaviors (and 21 primary leadership behaviors that combine to make the 6 global leadership behaviors), our literature review is organized around the following 6 global leadership dimensions: Charismatic/Value-Based, Team-Oriented, Participative, Humane-Oriented, Autonomous, and Self-Protective. These are the 6 second-level dimensions whereas the 21 primary dimensions are at the first level of analysis and subsequently collapsed into the 6 global, or secondary dimensions.

The reader might notice that of the six global CLT leadership dimensions, two are closely related to prior leadership constructs found in the extant leadership literature (Charismatic/Value-Based and Participative leadership). Nevertheless, we should note that the following review of cross-cultural leadership was oftentimes difficult because of the differing conceptions and measurement of similarly labeled constructs such as Charismatic/Value-Based and/or Transformational leadership. GLOBE has developed two other leadership dimensions, Humane-Oriented and Team-Oriented, that have some commonality with leadership constructs in the literature. The GLOBE Humane-Oriented construct has a commonality with supportive leadership— a well-studied leadership construct. The leadership of teams is an important domain of leadership, but the GLOBE Team-Oriented leadership behavior is distinctly different from the typical team literature in that it focuses on specific behaviors important for team success.

Finally, there are two additional GLOBE leadership behaviors that are very different from those found in Western-oriented leadership research. The first is Autonomous leadership, which represents independent and individualistic aspects of leadership. The second is Self-Protective leadership, which may hold more negative connotations from a Western perspective since it has not been previously considered in the leadership literature. Eastern leadership perspectives such as face-saving and status consciousness are characteristics of this global leadership dimension that may be more important when viewed from a Chinese and East-Asian perspective (Earley, 1997).

We start with a review of the most widely studied leadership behaviors, those of charismatic and transformational (C/T) leadership. Please note that by necessity, throughout our review, we take a certain amount of liberty in placing research studies into our already formed leadership categories. For instance, we will review the cross-cultural literature for C/T leadership in the GLOBE leadership behavior category titled next as "Charismatic/Value-Based Leadership."

Charismatic/Value-Based Leadership

This GLOBE construct is broadly defined to reflect the ability to inspire, motivate, and expect high performance outcomes from others based on firmly held core values. *Charisma,* a Greek word meaning "divinely inspired gift," embodies the leadership influence resulting from personal identification with extraordinary leaders. Such leaders may be found in politics (e.g., Ronald Reagan, Bill Clinton, Mahatma Gandhi, John F. Kennedy), religion (e.g., Christ, Mohammed, Moses), and business (e.g., Bill Gates, Steve Jobs, Mary Kay Ash who founded Mary Kay Cosmetics). The major charismatic theories include those by House (1977); Conger and Kanungo (1987); and Shamir, House, and Arthur (1993). They are considered "neo-charismatic" because they depart somewhat from the original conception of charisma by Weber (1947). The importance of the charismatic theories lies in their focus on the emotional attachment followers have to leaders because of the leader's appealing vision, confidence, optimism, and self-sacrifice (Jacobsen & House, 2011).

GLOBE's conceptualization and measurement of Charismatic/Value-Based leadership includes visionary, inspirational, and self-sacrifice attributes along with less noted but still important attributes of integrity, decisiveness, and performance orientation. (The development, measurement, and validation of GLOBE's six global leadership constructs can be found in Hanges and Dickson [2004, pp. 136–137]). The new formal GLOBE definition of Charismatic/Value-Based leadership used throughout the book is the following:

Charismatic leaders inspire their followers with a desirable and realistic vision that is decided based on appropriate analysis and high performance expectations. They are viewed as sincere, decisive and credible because of their integrity and willingness to sacrifice their own self-interest.

This leadership behavior dimension was developed from GLOBE 2004 data where a second-order maximum likelihood exploratory factor analysis of GLOBE 2004 CLT data revealed a six-factor solution. Charismatic/Value-Based leadership was identified as a major leadership dimension. It was comprised of six primary leadership factors. In examining the definitions of each primary factor presented here, one can see that in addition to the statistical analysis they are conceptually linked together in the following manner: First and foremost, the visionary and inspirational leadership are critical aspects of Charismatic/Value-Based leadership. They are brought together where a performance-oriented leader accomplishes goals by being seen by subordinates as having integrity, being decisive, and at times, being self-sacrificial for the good of the group or organization. These six primary leadership dimensions are defined as follows:

1. *Visionary:* This dimension describes a leader who clearly articulates his/her vision of the future, and makes plans and acts based on future goals.

2. *Inspirational:* This dimension describes leaders who inspire others, increase morale of subordinates, and are energetic and confident.

3. *Self-Sacrificial:* This dimension indicates an ability to convince followers to invest their efforts in activities that do not have a high probability of success, to forgo their self-interest, and make personal sacrifices for the goal or vision.

4. *Integrity:* This dimension indicates a leader who is honest and trust-worthy, keeps his/her word, and speaks and acts truthfully.

5. *Decisive:* This dimension indicates leaders who make decisions firmly, quickly, and logically and are insightful.

6. *Performance oriented:* This dimension describes leaders who set high goals, seek continuous improvement, and are excellence oriented for themselves and subordinates.

To summarize, according to GLOBE 2004, Charismatic/Value-Based leadership includes the conventional attributes of vision, inspiration, and self-sacrifice. However, it goes beyond these attributes and includes three other important dimensions: integrity, decisiveness, and performance orientation. For ease of discussion for the remainder of the book, the Charismatic/Value-Based leadership factor will often be referred to as Charismatic leadership without "Value-Based." We always, however, want to differentiate GLOBE's construct from that of the popular press's use of the term to indicate a person with a "charming and larger than life, over the top" personality. We will provide more about this distinction later in the book.

The following literature review also includes transformational leadership theories and research studies because they, like charismatic theories, focus on how leaders appeal to followers' values and emotions and both theoretical perspectives are often considered in tandem. Transformational leadership theories were developed from basic conceptualizations of James McGregor Burns (1978), whose popular book on political leadership greatly influenced the field of organizational leadership. The major transformational theory of leadership was developed by Bass (1985, 1990, 1997), but other theorists such as Bennis and Nanus (1985) and Kouzes and Posner (1987) have contributed to the understanding of how leaders are able to transform organizations. According to Bass (cf. 1997), leaders motivate followers in two distinctly different but important ways. Transformational leaders inspire followers to transcend their own interests for superordinate goals. They do this through a number of means—idealized influence or charisma, inspirational motivation, intellectual stimulation, and individualized consideration (Bass & Avolio, 1993). In contrast, transactional leadership motivates followers by providing task guidance, correcting performance flaws, and rewarding successful efforts—essentially using an exchange or transaction process with followers. Followers are motivated by self-interest and achieve an implicit bargain with the leader: "You work for me, do what I tell you, and I'll reward you when you perform well." The most often used survey instruments for studies investigating transformational leadership (e.g., see the Multifactor Leadership Questionnaire [MLQ], next) include subdimensions for each factor, but these subdimensions are often very highly intercorrelated, and composite scores are frequently used in research representing the transformational factor.

Because many of the leadership behaviors are similar to both C/T theories, some writers use the terms *transformational* and *charismatic* interchangeably. Yet, as noted by Yukl (2013), there are important distinctions to keep in mind. The essence of charismatic theories lies in the perception that the leader is extraordinary whereby followers rely on the leader for guidance and inspiration. For transformational theories, extraordinary performance can result from inspiring and developing followers without a total personal identification and attachment to the leader. Nonetheless, we offer five reasons for reviewing studies that fall under the C/T rubric. First, the most important elements of each (inspirational and visionary leadership) are common in both theories. As Bass (1985) noted, charisma is a necessary component of transformational leadership and, in fact, is the "idealized influence" factor in his survey research instrument (i.e., MLQ). Second, C/T leaders inspire followers with their enthusiasm and encouragement when pursuing high standards. Third, C/T theories provide explanations for the exceptional influence leaders can have on followers. Fourth, in most research studies, leaders who score high on transformational leadership also score high on charisma. And fifth, because transformational leadership is often considered a broader construct than charismatic leadership, one can study both by using the transformational Multifactor Leadership Questionnaire (MLQ), which was developed by Bass and Avolio (1997), or the transformational leadership scale, which was developed by Podsakoff, MacKenzie, Moorman, and Fetter (1990). Each of these includes charismatic components.

Evidence Regarding Charismatic and Transformational Leadership

Empirical evidence supports many of the key propositions in charismatic and transformational (C/T) theories (Yukl, 2013). In a meta-analytic test of transformational and transactional theories, Judge and Piccolo (2004) found that increased motivation, satisfaction, and effectiveness of leaders were related to transformational leadership. Clearly, these theories resonate with leadership researchers, but what evidence is there that these constructs are universally important or, conversely, are subject to cultural nuances? Because of the timeliness of these theories, which coincided with the increased interest in cross-cultural leadership, we have quite a few empirical studies that speak to the issue of universality for these neo-charismatic theories. First of all, we can infer from the gestalt of all cross-cultural research studies that the importance of C/T leadership seems to be universally acknowledged. In a review of cross-cultural studies of transformational leadership, Bass (1997) was unequivocal in his enthusiasm for the overriding influence of transformational leadership over transactional leadership. We first examine evidence regarding the general endorsement of C/T leadership and then review studies empirically determining its effectiveness.

Endorsement of Charismatic and Transformational Leadership

Several studies using GLOBE's data set attest to most aspects of C/T leadership as being universally endorsed (e.g., Den Hartog et al., 1999). Recall that as previously described, the GLOBE Charismatic leadership dimension includes the following six primary leadership dimensions: (1) visionary, (2) inspirational, (3) self-sacrificial, (4) integrity, (5) decisive, and (6) performance-oriented. Evidence points to the universal endorsement of all but the self-sacrificial element. The universal endorsement for charismatic qualities, however, does not mean that they are enacted in exactly the same manner across cultures or that there aren't meaningful differences in its endorsement across cultures. As House and colleagues (2004) demonstrated, this leadership dimension was most strongly endorsed in cultures with Performance Orientation and Gender Egalitarianism values and those that rejected Power Distance values.

One of the first studies using a subset of GLOBE leadership data was conducted by Brodbeck and colleagues (2000) who investigated the cultural variation of leadership prototypes across 22 European countries. They presented evidence that clusters of European cultures sharing similar cultural values also share similar leadership concepts. A country dendrogram indicated that two major country clusters emerged—a North/West European region and a South/West European region (the French constituted a separate cluster). Two findings are noteworthy. First, the leadership prototypicality dimensions among countries were highly correlated with cultural dimensions of a non-GLOBE study of contemporary Europe (Smith, Dugan, et al. 1996), and these relationships are fairly stable over time. Second, they suggest that knowledge about differences in leadership prototypes across European countries can help expatriate managers anticipate potential problems in cross-cultural interaction. For instance, leadership attributes such as autonomy are more strongly associated with outstanding leadership in Germanic countries (e.g., Austria) than in Latin European countries (e.g., Portugal).

Using GLOBE data, Brodbeck, Frese, and Javidan (2002) developed a semantic network of West German leadership concepts and found that the most positive leadership prototype contained attributes of integrity, inspiration, and performance orientation. This "most positive prototype," however, also contained attributes of team orientation and administrative competence. On the basis of these combined attributes, they concluded that a German version of transformational leadership contains elements of charisma along with team integrative behaviors and hence labeled it as transformational/charismatic. Holmberg and Akerblom (2006) concluded that while C/T leadership is also endorsed in Sweden, it is not an important *and* distinguishing feature of Swedish leadership as was Team-Oriented and Participative leadership. That is, Sweden positions itself in the middle of all

62 GLOBE countries in its rating of the desirability of C/T leadership (desirable but not any more so than other GLOBE countries), but high in ratings for Team-Oriented and Participative leadership in comparison to the other GLOBE countries.

A sampling of additional studies supports the perceived importance of C/T leadership in various world cultures. In a qualitative cross-cultural study involving interviews of Australian and Chinese business executives, Deng and Gibson (2009) found that transformational competencies are believed to contribute to effective leadership. Similarly, Boehnke, Bontis, DiStefano, and DiStefano (2003) found that in descriptions of company examples of outstanding organizational performance, transformational leadership represented the clear majority of executive descriptions. Furthermore, only a few variations in emphasis existed among six different regions of the world leading researchers to conclude that transformational leadership behaviors are indeed universally desirable. Also, as reported earlier, Ensari and Murphy (2003) found that both Turkish and U.S. (student) samples perceived leaders to be charismatic when descriptions including prototypical charismatic leadership characteristics were combined with high company performance outcomes. Finally, in another study using GLOBE data, Paris, Howell, Dorfman, and Hanges (2009) found that while Charismatic leadership was the most highly endorsed CLT leadership dimension, females endorsed it more so than did males.

Behavioral Research Investigating Universality of Charismatic and Transformational Leadership

The universal preference for many charismatic and transformational (C/T) qualities and leadership actions, however, does not mean that leadership enactment is identical across cultures or that there aren't meaningful differences in endorsement and effectiveness across cultures. Tsui and colleagues (2007) reviewed several cross-cultural studies investigating the importance and effectiveness of C/T behaviors. One study cited was that by Dorfman and colleagues (1997), who examined the impact of charismatic leadership across five cultures. Charismatic leadership was one of six behaviors derived from popular contingency theories and showed universally positive impacts for the five cultures. Interestingly, while charismatic leadership had positive effects on employee outcomes such as satisfaction with supervision for all countries, it had no direct impact on job performance.

Using a field study of employees from the emerging economies of China, India, and Kenya, Walumbwa and Lawler (2003) investigated the moderating impact of collectivism on the relationship between transformational leadership and work related outcomes. They concluded that transformational leadership had positive impacts on all levels of collectivism. Interestingly, in another study set in India, Palrecha, Spangler, and

Yammarino (2012) found that while transformational leadership did, in fact, predict employee performance, it was not as successful as two other theories in predicting employee performance. The two other theories were the Nurturant-Task (NT) theory by Sinha (1980, 1995) and an organization specific theory (labeled RDO—a pseudonym for a specific organization). In addition, only the transformational factor of individualized support led to higher job performance. This study was unique in several respects as the researchers employed qualitative and quantitative approaches, used job performance as the dependent variable in contrast to the usual employee attitude variables, and employed a competitive test between competing models.

Javidan and Carl (2005) examined the profiles of Canadian and Taiwanese upper level managers to determine similarities and differences of perceived leadership styles. While they showed similarities on several leadership styles within the C/T genre, such as visionary and self-sacrifice, differences emerged regarding specific attributes. For instance, the item "conveys a clear sense of direction to subordinates" was common to both profiles; however, other items were different as well as the item factor loadings. In another study which used a meta-analytical strategy, Leong and Fischer (2011) found that transformational leadership behaviors covaried with several cultural values aligned with Schwartz and Hofstede models. Managers in egalitarian contexts were seen as engaging in more transformational behaviors as were managers in mastery-oriented contexts. This finding regarding gender egalitarian values is in concert with GLOBE 2004 findings whereby egalitarian cultural values were strongly related to the desirability of charismatic leadership.

In a study of the effects of executives' stakeholder and economic values, Waldman and colleagues (2006) found that an emphasis on stakeholder values was related to visionary leadership. Specifically, in this 17-country GLOBE study, executives who believed in stakeholder values relating to the well-being, safety, and working conditions of workers and welfare of the local community were more likely to exhibit visionary leadership than those who didn't perceive these values as important. In turn, visionary leadership indirectly, through extra employee effort, was related to firm performance.

Results from a two-culture study of transformational leadership by Jung, Yammarino, and Lee (2009) also support the universality of transformational leadership. This methodologically sophisticated and complex study examined leadership effectiveness with multiple moderators and mediators in U.S. and Korean samples. Same-source bias was eliminated in tests of moderating factors. Among several important findings, they concluded that transformational leadership operated at the individual level of analysis and was very effective across both cultures. Furthermore, they concluded that because the effect of transformational leadership on work outcomes is so powerful in collectivistic cultures, it would be effective regardless of followers' attitudes (e.g., trust) toward their leaders. In another methodologically sophisticated study, Kirkman, Chen, Farh, Chen, and Lowe (2009) similarly found positive effects for transformational leadership. In addition, they determined that individual-level power distance orientation moderated the relationship between transformational leadership and procedural justice perceptions; more positive relationships occurred when the power distance orientation was lower, rather than higher.

Using data from 12 European countries, Elenkov and Manev (2005) found that the sociocultural environment (e.g., Power Distance) influenced both transformational and (what they refer to as) developmental/transactional leadership. Results are complex but generally point to the importance of transformational and developmental/transactional leadership. They speculated that none of the leadership factors would be universally endorsed in different societal cultures. The same authors, based on data from 27 EU countries, found that the level of senior expatriates' visionary-transformational leadership impacted the rate of a firm's innovation adoption (Elenkov & Manev, 2009). Cultural intelligence had a positive moderating effect (i.e., increased effect) on the leadership-outcome relationship for organizational innovation but not product market innovation.

In one of the few non-Western studies of *executive* leadership, Wang, Tsui, and Xin (2011) found that charismatic behaviors of articulating a vision and being creative and risk-taking was related to firm performance for Chinese executives. These factors also had significant bivariate correlations with employee attitudes such as organizational commitment. Through structural equation modeling, however, they interpret their results in a non-traditional manner as supporting the importance of charismatic leadership dimensions as being part of "task-focused CEO leadership behaviors." These task-focused behaviors directly influenced firm performance whereas relationship focused behaviors (e.g., showing benevolence) indirectly impacted firm performance through positive employee attitudes.

Spreitzer, Perttula, and Xin (2005) not only found that transformational leadership generally predicted leadership effectiveness in leaders from Asia and North America but also found that the effectiveness of most factors depended on the cultural dimension of traditionality. These researchers had the immediate superior of the focal leader rate the focal leader's effectiveness. Also, in an intriguing departure from most cross-cultural leadership studies, the immediate superiors also assessed their own cultural values. Despite the positive influence of transformational leadership on subordinate outcomes, there was an interesting interaction effect. For all cultural samples, they found that leaders who "scored high on setting a vision were also viewed as *less* effective by superiors who were more traditional than by superiors who are less traditional" (Spreitzer et al., 2005, p. 221). Interestingly, country of affiliation did not have the same important moderating influence as did the individualized cultural value of traditionality.

To conclude the literature review so far, relatively few empirical cross-cultural studies do not support the almost universal appeal of C/T leadership and its effectiveness. As one example not supporting the effectiveness of C/T leadership, Pillai, Scandura, and Williams (1999) found that transformational leadership did not result in higher levels of satisfaction in Colombia, the Middle East, or India. They concluded that being less involved with followers and being more directive are more appropriate for these regions. Cultural nuances of transformational leadership may also be apparent across cultures as Shahin and Wright (2004) found that the specific elements of transformational leadership in Egypt and other Middle Eastern countries varied from other parts of the world. Specifically, they delineated a leadership factor called "enthusiastic leadership" which contained Bass and Avolio's (1997) elements of inspirational motivation and intellectual stimulation.

Another complicating factor in investigating the effects of transformational leadership is that the constructs themselves are multifaceted and definitions vary considerably among originators of the theories (cf. Bass, 1985; House & Shamir, 1993). Even within a particular theory (e.g., Bass & Avolio, 1997), the conceptualization and operational measurement of the construct has changed over time. Although this may be laudable in terms of the ultimate scientific goal of understanding leadership processes, it creates numerous problems for the cross-cultural researcher. For instance, compared to the original factor structure presented by Bass (1985), how should researchers interpret more recent findings of different factor structures by Echavarria and Davis (1994) in the Dominican Republic; Den Hartog, Van Muijen, and Koopman (1994) in the Netherlands; and Koh (1990) in Singapore?

In summary, the totality of findings indicates that charismatic and transformational (C/T) leadership are routinely endorsed, and leaders who enact these qualities tend to be more successful than those who don't. However, while overwhelming research evidence supports the universality of transformational leadership, there are some counter findings previously cited. Nonetheless, we remain cognizant that the specific *behaviors* that constitute these leadership dimensions may vary from culture to culture. To date, however, we simply have insufficient evidence to indicate how, when, or why specific C/T behaviors vary across cultures, or whether the effectiveness will fall into the universal or near universal category.

When starting this phase of the GLOBE project, we anticipated that C/T leadership would most likely constitute a variform functional universal (i.e., universally important, but vary somewhat as to its effectiveness depending on culture). Another observation from this literature review is that the level of sophistication of behavioral studies varies greatly as does the quality of the journals publishing the research. We hope to reverse that trend in the current GLOBE research. While we are much further along in understanding the influence of C/T leadership across cultures, numerous questions remain unanswered, among them the following:

1. Does the level of CEO C/T *enactment* vary by countries and cultures?

2. Does the impact of C/T leadership take the form of a variform functional universal whereby the level of influence may vary across countries, but is always a positive influence?

3. To the extent that C/T leadership *impact* varies across cultures, which elements of C/T leadership are most important? Unfortunately, because the subscales of transformational leadership are often highly correlated, cross-cultural researchers tend to collapse the scales into a single factor that precludes answering this question.

4. Does C/T leadership behavior *impact* both attitudinal and performance outcomes?

5. Will the level of *enactment* of C/T leadership mirror that found in leadership prototype studies—that is, high enactment found in cultures that most strongly endorse this leadership dimension?

6. How does the *variability* of enactment (across cultures, across CEOs) of C/T leadership compare to the enactment of other leadership behaviors?

Team-Oriented Leadership

Teams and teamwork are ubiquitous structural entities and mechanisms for carrying out work in modern organizations, yet there are many kinds of teams with differing goals and team composition. While groups and teams share many characteristics, teams typically are interacting groups characterized by reciprocal influence, significant interdependency, a strong sense of identification, and common goals and are, after all, engaged in teamwork (Katzenbach & Smith, 1993). Bass (2008) related the following humorous story:

> I commented to an Egyptologist at the Temple of Luxor how remarkable it was to see four fellahin with only ropes skillfully maneuvering a ten-ton stone block. "Oh," he replied, "they have been doing that kind of teamwork for the past five thousand years!" (p. 756)

The study of groups, teams, and leadership of teams has a long past, and many competent reviews are available through textbooks (cf. Yukl, 2013) and numerous journal publication outlets (Aguinis & Kraiger, 2009; Bass, 2008; Burke et al., 2006). Our interest, however, is in the leadership of teams and the differential influence of Team-Oriented leadership across cultures. As explained next, the GLOBE Team-Oriented leadership dimension is defined in terms of effective team building and implementation of a common purpose or goal among team members.

The GLOBE Team-Oriented leadership behavior is defined as follows:

> Team-oriented leaders are loyal to their teams and care for the welfare of their team members. They use their administrative and interpersonal skills to manage the team's internal dynamics and to create a cohesive working group.

A second-order maximum likelihood exploratory factor analysis of GLOBE 2004 CLT data revealed a major leadership dimension that was labeled Team-Oriented leadership (Hanges & Dickson, 2004, pp. 136–137). Team-Oriented leadership dimension includes the following primary leadership dimensions: (1) collaborative team orientation, (2) team integrator, (3) diplomatic, (4) malevolent (reverse scored), and (5) administratively competent. They are defined as follows:

1. Collaborative team orientation: This dimension indicates a leader who is concerned with the welfare of the group and is collaborative and loyal.

2. Team integrator: This dimension indicates a leader who gets members to work together and integrates people into a cohesive working unit to achieve group goals.

3. Diplomatic: This dimension describes leaders who are diplomatic and skilled at interpersonal relations.

4. Malevolent: This dimension reflects leaders who are dishonest, vindictive, and deceitful and act negatively toward others (reverse scored in our analysis).

5. Administratively competent: This dimension reflects leaders who are administratively skilled and well organized. They can effectively coordinate and control activities of the team members.

Despite the variety of constructs in the Team-Oriented dimension, they are conceptually linked through a common thread of understanding how a leader manages team dynamics and promotes teamwork. While collaborative team orientation and team integrator are important for promoting and developing teams, the remaining three dimensions are also important. Effective leaders are skilled at interpersonal relations (i.e., diplomatic) and are generally viewed as benevolent (e.g., not malevolent). Perhaps surprisingly, we found that team-oriented leaders are also "administratively competent" (House et al., 2004). This finding is consistent with Mintzberg (2006) who, while agreeing with other researchers that strategic management roles such as developing a vision and inspiring followers are critical, asserts that being a competent manager is also critical to effective leadership—good management and leadership cannot be separated.

To summarize, the leadership of teams should be studied from multiple perspectives because of the variety of teams prevalent in modern organizations. There are cross-functional teams, self-managed teams, top-level executive teams, and virtual teams to name a few besides the generic "work teams" prevalent in almost all organizations (Zaccaro, Rittman, & Marks, 2001). The variety of leadership roles managing a team is also as varied as there are types of teams. Leadership of teams is a complicated and multifaceted endeavor since team leadership functions may include planning, organizing, networking, representing, and engaging in team development. Some leadership behaviors necessary to carry out these leadership roles are the same as for C/T and Participative leadership (the latter discussed in the following section). For instance, leaders might help create a vision and purposeful direction for the team, which is characteristic of C/T leadership. They may lead teams in a more or less participative manner. In addition, leaders need to develop teamwork and resolve conflicts among team members (Yukl, 2013). In fact, we do know a good deal about creating effective teams (cf. Hackman, 2002). What we don't know very much about, however, is team leadership from a cross-cultural perspective. And what makes a review of cross-cultural leadership of teams particularly difficult is that relevant articles may be concealed within other topics such as transformational and participative leadership, as well as under specific leadership functions (e.g., planning).

Because the current GLOBE research project concerns specific leadership behaviors directly related to team building, coaching, integrating members, and managing the team in a competent manner, we limit our literature review to these types of leadership behaviors. The following cross-cultural studies relate to this GLOBE dimension.

Endorsement of Team-Oriented Leadership

According to country-level ratings, the GLOBE 2004 Team-Oriented dimension was perceived to be at least somewhat important in enhancing effective leadership. Its moderately positive ratings and country variability, however, begs the question as to its universality. When examining the results, the Southern Asia, Confucian Asia, Eastern Europe, and Latin America clusters report Team-Oriented leadership to be particularly critical for effective leadership. This comports with the generally believed contributions of collectivist values for these parts of the world. In fact, statistical HLM tests revealed that GLOBE cultural dimensions of In-Group Collectivism and Uncertainty Avoidance are the most important in predicting this CLT leadership dimension. Organizations that value the expression of pride, loyalty, and interdependence will include the Team-Oriented CLT as part of the prototypical CLT leadership dimensions for effective leadership. In addition, the more the society reports valuing the reduction of uncertainty, the more they report endorsing Team-Oriented leadership. Members of societies who have collectivist (in-group) values and who want to reduce uncertainty are likely to have leadership prototypes that emphasize Team-Oriented leadership attributes.

Behavioral Research Investigating Team-Oriented Leadership

In their cross-cultural study, Boehnke and colleagues (2003) found that team building was a major factor represented in many executive descriptions of outstanding company performance (as was transformational leadership mentioned previously). However, in contrast to the almost universal emphasis of transformational factors among all samples, team building stood out in the American and Southern European regions but much less so in the Far Eastern region. This finding presents an obvious paradox with respect to the highly individualistic American executives and collectivistic East. The authors speculated that it may be because of the emphasis on teamwork in the Far East that these executives failed to see (or mention) teamwork although it is an ingrained aspect of their work life. Perhaps akin to American individualism as a defining cultural factor, Americans are inveterate joiners of organizations and teams. Irrespective of the rationale for the Boehnke and colleagues' (2003) findings, they lead one to question the relative effectiveness of leadership that is directly oriented to team building cross-culturally.

Another aspect of the previously mentioned Shahin and Wright (2004) study of Egyptian leadership reveals the importance of a "social integration" leadership dimension. The items comprising this factor are clearly related to GLOBE's Team-Oriented dimension (e.g., "I encourage members of my group to discuss work-related problems together" [Shahin & Wright, 2004, p. 506]). The presence of this factor reinforces the strong Egyptian emphasis on maintaining harmony and social integration in the workplace. In contrast, GLOBE 2004 results indicate that team orientation was not particularly important in the Germanic cluster and was very low in the Middle East cluster of countries. Using the GLOBE database, Paris and colleagues (2009) examined gender differences in the endorsement of leadership prototypes. One conclusive finding was that, in general, female managers endorsed Team-Oriented leadership more so than did male managers. They also found that the differences between male and female managers varied across nations; for example, gender differences in rating the Team-Oriented prototype were much smaller in the United States than in Hong Kong or Guatemala.

Investigating team cohesiveness across cultures, Wendt, Euwema, and Van Emmerik (2009) found that the cultural dimension of individualism/collectivism (I/C) moderated the impact of both directive and supportive leadership on team effectiveness. Their study used data from a large consulting group database (Hay Group) with employees from 615 organizations, approximately 30,000 managers, and more than 130,000 team members representing 80 countries. Supportive leadership had positive effects on cohesiveness while directive leadership had negative effects; these effects were stronger in individualistic societies. Interestingly, the levels of both directive and supportive leadership were lower in individualistic countries compared to collectivistic countries. Unexpectedly, despite the moderating effect of I/C, it did *not* directly relate to team cohesiveness.

Several observations may be useful to understand the literature review of Team-Oriented leadership. First, while an abundance of studies point to the considerable impact of leadership influencing team effectiveness (e.g., Bass, 2008), they typically employ leadership measures not specifically designed to directly test the importance of team-oriented leader behaviors but instead use commonly found measures in the leadership literature. For example, the Wendt and colleagues' (2009) study employs measures of supportive and directive leadership in their study of team cohesiveness. As another example, the study of transformational leadership in Korea by Jung, Butler, and Baik (1998) found that this leadership style was highly correlated with group cohesiveness.

In summary, perhaps it is obvious by now, but the present GLOBE study differs from almost all previous studies in that GLOBE researchers developed new measures of Team-Oriented leadership instead of employing leadership measures found in the literature that are more tangential to team effectiveness (e.g. supportive leadership). Second, because the GLOBE Team-Oriented CLT dimension was multifaceted, we developed separate measures for each facet (similar to the differing facets of transformational leadership by Bass and Avolio (1997). These facets are (1) collaborative team orientation, (2) team integrator, (3) diplomatic, (4) malevolent (reverse scored), and (5) administratively competent. Third, like the Wendt and colleagues' (2009) study, the current GLOBE study also investigates the direct and indirect effect of culture on team cohesiveness.

Participative Leadership

Because a central aspect of management involves decision making (Mintzberg, 1973), it is not surprising that individuals affected by management decisions often desire to have an input in the decision making process. Supervisors often struggle with the extent to which subordinates should participate and become involved in organizational decisions. The decision-making process or procedure is often described in terms of a continua, where extremes are characterized from decisions made by supervisors without asking for input by others (i.e., autocratic and/or directive leadership) to subordinates being given complete authority and responsibility (i.e., delegation). Participation falls somewhere in between and may take the form of consultation and/or joint decisions to arrive at a conclusive decision.

The GLOBE Participative global leadership dimension reflects the degree to which managers involve others in making and implementing decisions. GLOBE's Participative leadership dimension is defined as the following:

> Participative leaders believe that employees can contribute to decision making and should be engaged in the process of decision making and implementation. They also believe that debate, discussion, and disagreement are a natural part of good decision making and should not be suppressed.

A second-order maximum likelihood exploratory factor analysis of GLOBE 2004 CLT data revealed a third major leadership dimension, which we labeled Participative leadership (Hanges & Dickson, 2004, pp. 136–137). Two primary leadership factors, participative and autocratic (reverse scored), statistically formed this second-order leadership factor. The following is the description of each primary factor:

1. *Participative:* This dimension reflects leaders who share critical information with subordinates and give them a high degree of discretion to perform work.

2. *Autocratic:* This dimension indicates leaders who are dictatorial, do not tolerate disagreement, and expect unquestioning obedience of those who report to them (reverse scored for the global Participative leadership dimension).

To summarize, according to GLOBE 2004, Participative leadership reflects the view that employees can contribute to decision making and should be engaged in the process of decision making and implementation. It also reflects the view that debate, discussion, and disagreement are a natural part of good decision making and should not be suppressed.

Similar to the enormous amount of research on C/T leadership, the effects of Participative leadership have been the object of hundreds, if not thousands of studies since the pioneering research by Lewin, Lippitt, and White (1939). Comprehensive reviews and meta-analyses are found in Bass (2008); Leana, Locke, and Schweiger (1990); and Sagie & Koslowsky (2000).

Complicating the study of participative leadership behavior is the fact that its nature, concepts, and definitions vary tremendously in the literature. Distinctions between concepts of participation, delegation, joint decision making, and directive/autocratic decision making are possible; however, as Bass (2008) noted, most leaders exhibit all these modes but in differing frequencies and amounts depending on the situation. Unlike the relatively consistent positive endorsement and effects of C/T leadership, results for participative leadership are more mixed. Yukl (2013) noted, "The results from research on the effects of participative leadership are not sufficiently strong and consistent enough to draw any firm conclusions . . . [it] sometimes results in higher satisfaction, effort, and performance, and at other times it does not" (p. 111). Another distinction between C/T and participative leadership in the literature is that there are relatively few contemporary cross-cultural studies examining how this behavior is enacted and its effectiveness across cultures. Before addressing more recent cross-cultural studies examining participative leadership, it is useful to review a few of the earlier research findings.

Endorsement of Participative Leadership

The classic cross-cultural study by Haire, Ghiselli, and Porter (1966) demonstrates cultural nuances regarding the importance and likely enactment of participative leadership. One goal of this seminal study was to determine if managerial attitudes are essentially the same across nations or if they differ from country to country. Questionnaire responses were obtained from more than 3,600 managers in 14 nations. Eight leadership items covered issues relating to an average subordinate's capacity for leadership and initiative, a leader's attitude toward sharing information and participation, and attitudes toward authority and control. One striking finding was that while managers from all countries espoused democratic management styles and favored participative leadership, managers from most countries held a low opinion of whether subordinates had the capacity for leadership and initiative. More so than managers in other countries, American managers believed that individuals have the necessary requisites for democratic leadership—the potential to exhibit initiative and share leadership responsibilities.

GLOBE 2004 found that overall, while Participative leadership was generally viewed favorably by respondents from all cultures, their endorsement of it as a contributor to effective leadership also varied considerably among cultures. Further, the Participative leadership dimension was not endorsed (i.e., rated as highly) as the Charismatic and Team-Oriented leadership dimensions. The highest endorsement of participative attributes was in the Anglo, Germanic, and Nordic cultures, followed by Latin Europe, Latin America, and Sub-Saharan Africa. The lowest endorsement came from Southern Asia, Eastern Europe, Confucian Asia, and Middle East. In addition to the variability across cultures, there also was considerable variability within cultures for this dimension. The popularity of participative leadership in the Western and European leadership literature seems to confirm preconceived notions about these cultures (Bass, 1990). That is, members of societies who report high performance-oriented and gender egalitarian values and also have a high tolerance for uncertainty will likely value Participative leadership. Also using the GLOBE database, Paris and colleagues (2009) examined gender differences in the endorsement of leadership prototypes. In general, female managers endorsed Participative leadership more so than did male managers. Furthermore, the cultural dimension of Gender Egalitarianism moderated the size of gender differences; Gender Egalitarianism increased females' desire for Participative leadership.

To sum up, the belief in individual capability is but one reason for the many varieties of participative decision making across cultures. Reinforcing the notion of variability in participative approaches, Sagie and Aycan (2003) proposed seven alternative models in their cross-cultural analysis of participative decision making that coexist with differing levels of cultural Power Distance and collectivism. Particularly striking was the observation that in individualistic and low Power Distance countries, employees' suggestions must be operated on in order for them to believe that supervisors were participative—not so for high Power Distance and collectivistic societies. From GLOBE 2004 findings, we might speculate that in high Power Distance societies, lower level employees are thought to have less skills and capabilities; hence, they typically do not expect that their input would be given much credence. This observation was affirmed when one of the present authors participated in a GLOBE focus group in Mexico. The discussion revealed that leaders were thought to be participative simply by asking subordinates for their opinions, even if the supervisor ignored their input or made a decision that was contrary to their ideas (Dorfman & Howell, 1997). As one participant opined, "My supervisor is very participative. He asks me my opinion and tells me what to do." In another study that concurs with the importance of congruence between culture and participation, Newman and Nollen (1996) examined performance of work units in a single large U.S.-based corporation with work units across Europe and Asia. Units located in high Power Distance locations were most successful when participation was low; conversely, units located in low Power Distance locations were most successful when participation was high.

The Smith and Peterson (1988) event management model also speaks to the issue of participative leadership. Their model has proven useful to address the way many typical events in organizational life are interpreted from a cross-cultural perspective. For instance, managers often need to select new employees and they might rely on various sources of guidance to make a decision. In a 47-country study, Smith and colleagues (2002) asked managers how much they relied upon eight sources of meaning (e.g., formal organization rules, national norms, specialists) for common managerial activities such as selecting a new employee or handling poor subordinate performance. They found that managers' reliance on subordinate information through a participative process was higher in cultures characterized by individualism, low power distance, and egalitarian values. Interestingly, they suggest that the reliance on hierarchical sources is most prevalent in African nations in contrast to the usually cited Asian nations. The event management leadership process has also been the focus of several studies in China (Smith, Peterson, & Wang, 1996). Western managers from the United States and Britain relied more upon their own experience and training; however, in China, rules and procedures were more salient. In another study (Smith et al., 1997), mid-level Chinese managers in Chinese joint ventures reported a much stronger reliance on widespread beliefs within their own country as a source of guidance than had been found in other nations in earlier studies.

In an effort to develop a more culturally nuanced view of participative leadership, Brodbeck and Eisenbeiss (in press) identified four "species" of Participative leadership for a subset of countries, all of which share very high scores on the GLOBE 2004 Participative leadership dimension. They suggested the following:

Each describes how the high endorsement of participative leadership manifests itself and is rooted in the respective cultures' societal cultural practices and values: (a) as an opposition to non-participative, auto-cratic, or directive leadership; (b) as a principle to organize interactions at work between 'labor and capital' (or management) in a participative way; (c) as a set of personal competencies apparent in leadership conduct; and (d) as a set of communication behaviors like listening and inviting suggestions from others. (Brodbeck & Eisenbeiss, in press)

As these authors suggested, while all these cultures highly endorsed Participative leadership in the GLOBE 2004 study, they are quite different from each other and only a more emic approach can unearth these subtleties. Chhokar and colleagues (2007) provided additional country-specific information regarding the endorsement of Participative leadership.

Behavioral Research Investigating Participative Leadership

The extent to which subordinates should become involved in organizational decisions continues to be a fruitful area for leadership researchers. Perhaps one of the best-known and valid models of participative leadership was developed by Vroom and Yetton (1973) and subsequently modified by Vroom and Jago (1988). This model of participation is labeled the normative decision model that specifies the type of decision procedures most likely to be effective in alternative situations. For Vroom and Yetton (1973), the type of participative approach should be evaluated in terms of the subordinate's contribution to effective performance, not because of the romance of participative approaches that seem to be particularly desirable in Western leadership literature. The model helps supervisors decide on the most appropriate level of subordinate participation using decision rules based on the importance of making a high quality decision as well as likely subordinate acceptance of the decision. The model identifies situations where the most appropriate decision process for the supervisor might be more autocratic, consultative, or completely participative (the latter when there is an attempt to reach a consensus and a group decision is likely acceptable).

The quality of decisions and decision acceptance by subordinates are focal aspects of the model. While the model has changed through the years, one of its stable and central aspects is its suggested diagnostic procedure to help leaders determine the optimal amount of subordinate involvement in decisions. This theory has proved to be one of the most valid contingency theories of leadership (Yukl, 2013). We also have some evidence showing how this theory fares in non-Western cultures. For instance, Bottger, Hallein, and Yetton (1985) investigated the behavioral intent to engage in participative leadership among 150 managers from Australia, Africa, Papua New Guinea, and the Pacific Islands. They used standard Vroom–Yetton (1973) methodology where managers (mentally) chose a level of participation for problem solving among prespecified problem sets. Results indicated that participation was highest for all managers in situations of low structure and low power compared to situations of high structure and high power.

That is, when managers feel relatively powerless and problems are not structured, managers from all nations favor a participative style.

Another validation effort of the Vroom–Jago (1988) normative decision model was conducted by Bohnisch, Ragan, Reber, and Jago (1988) for Austrian managers. Similar to findings in America, the responses for the "problem sets" were significantly related to behavior in actual situations, although there was a less than perfect correspondence between the leaders' behavioral intentions and actual responses. U.S. managers more frequently chose autocratic decision-making styles whereas Austrian managers more frequently chose group consultation. Consistent with these results, the "mean level of participation" score revealed that Austrian managers were significantly more participative than U.S. managers. Perhaps the most interesting finding that showed when conflict among subordinates is likely, U.S. managers become more autocratic while Austrian managers become more participative. Using similar methods, Reber, Jago, and Bohnisch (1993) determined that German, Austrian, and Swiss managers were the most participative, Polish and Czech managers the most autocratic, and U.S. and French managers between the extremes. Two other findings were particularly interesting. First, unlike managers of other nations, Polish managers were more likely to be participative for trivial matters, in contrast to important issues. Second, Austrian managers became more participative when resolving conflicts among subordinates in contrast to more autocratic behaviors by French, Finnish, U.S., Polish, and Czech managers. Finally, predictions about participation based on a culture's Power Distance scores were generally supportive in that participation scores were higher for lower Power Distance cultures.

In addition to the stream of research initiated by Vroom and Yetton (1973), studies by Heller and Wilpert (1981) and Heller, Drenth, Koopman, and Rus (1988) bear examining for their relevance to Participative leadership. Both studies were complex, time consuming, large-scale cross-national research efforts that had the purpose of understanding how various macro (e.g., country) and micro (e.g., specific task) factors influence leader decision making and participative processes in organizations.

Heller and Wilpert (1981) obtained survey data and feedback from group discussions with 1,600 managers sampled from 129 organizations across eight nations (Israel, Spain, the United Kingdom, Germany, the Netherlands, the United States, France, and Sweden). Managerial decision making was conceived as varying along a continuum (decision without explanation, decision with explanation, prior consultation, joint decision, delegation), and a "decision centralization score" was computed for each manager indicating the manager's degree of centralized (authoritarian) versus participative decision making. Some of the findings relevant to participative leadership include (1) small but consistent covariance between subordinates' perceptions of supervisory participation and subordinates' own job satisfaction, (2) significant differences among managers' self-descriptions of their decision-making styles across nations (e.g., Israeli managers described their decision making as more centralized than did Swedish managers), (3) managers' decision-making style was much more influenced by micro-level variables close to the decision maker (e.g., type of decision to be made) than by macro-level variables such as the manager's country, and (4) an absence of country/culture clusters as might have been expected from prior theorizing (e.g., a Nordic vs. Latin-European cluster).

The study by Heller and colleagues (1988) provides further evidence regarding decision-making processes across nations. This study, like the Heller and Wilpert (1981) study, also employed multiple research methods using multinational samples (the United Kingdom, the Netherlands, and Yugoslavia). As previously found, decision making varied greatly with the type of decision required, and the researchers were able to detect influences due to "organizational culture" that lead to more or less centralization. Yet evidence for country differences was not clear and, as previously found by Heller and Wilpert (1981), no cultural patterns emerged as might be predicted by a cultural typology such as Hofstede's (1980).

In a comparison of Turkish and American first-line supervisors, Kennis (1977) found that American supervisors were perceived to be more participative and considerate than Turkish supervisors but equal in structuring behaviors. However, whereas participation, consideration, and structure were related to satisfaction with supervision for Americans, only the consideration score was related to satisfaction with supervision for the Turkish sample.

The cross-cultural field study by Dorfman and colleagues (1997) provides further evidence of the variable effects of participative leadership. While the findings showed complete universality for three leader behaviors (including supportive behaviors, contingent reward, and charismatic), the effects of participative leadership were culturally contingent. Specifically, the researchers were struck by the fact that the United States was unique in that it was the only culture where participative leadership had a significant positive effect on the job performance of subordinates. The high individualism of the United States (Dorfman et al., 1997) combined with the highly participative U.S. management climate likely contribute toward the culturally unique results regarding participative leadership behaviors in the U.S. sample.

What can researchers conclude regarding the effectiveness of participative leadership in cross-cultural contexts? Unfortunately, findings are more complex when viewing the importance of participative leadership in cross-cultural situations than when viewing findings from Western cultures. We think it is safe to conclude that both the enactment and effectiveness of participative leadership follows the cultural congruency perspective discussed earlier in the chapter. For cultures that are more individualistic, low on power distance and can tolerate a significant amount of uncertainty, participative leadership will be accepted, enacted, and effective.

Humane-Oriented Leadership

A fourth major leadership dimension labeled Humane-Oriented leadership was revealed in a second-order maximum likelihood exploratory factor analysis of GLOBE 2004 CLT data. This dimension includes two primary leadership dimensions labeled (1) modesty and (2) humane orientation. GLOBE's definition of Humane-Oriented leadership is as follows: "Humane-oriented leaders are unpretentious, show humility, and are reticent to boast. They are empathetic and likely to help and support team members in a humane manner by offering resources and other forms of assistance." The two globe primary dimensions of Humane-Oriented leadership are as follows:

1. Modesty: This dimension reflects leaders who do not boast, are modest, and present themselves in a humble and unassuming manner.

2. Humane orientation: This dimension emphasizes empathy for others by giving time, money, resources, and assistance when needed. It reflects concern for followers' personal and group welfare.

Besides including studies directly related to Humane-Oriented leadership, this review also contains studies concerning the supportive, considerate relationship and employee-centered behaviors because of their conceptual overlap with GLOBE's Humane-Oriented leadership dimension. Due to lack of research on the modesty dimension, the following review mostly concerns the humane orientation dimension. We realize that while prior research on considerate and supportive leadership does not overlap 100% with GLOBE's Humane-Oriented leadership dimension, it has some of the same components—particularly related to employee support and empathy. With that caveat in mind, the following review should provide a reasonable indication of what we might find regarding the enactment and effectiveness of Humane-Oriented leadership behavior.

Endorsement of Humane-Oriented Leadership

In general, GLOBE societal cultures and "culture clusters" (House et al., 2004) report Humane-Oriented leadership as being slightly important but not critical in contributing to outstanding leadership. The average Humane-Oriented CLT score for this dimension was 4.88, with a country range of 3.80 to 5.60 (on a 7-point scale). GLOBE country cluster rankings indicate that four clusters may be singled out as particularly endorsing this characteristic in enhancing effective leadership: Southern Asia, Anglo, Sub-Saharan Africa, and Confucian Asia. In contrast, the Nordic European, Latin European, and Germanic clusters rated Humane-Oriented leadership as not particularly effective. As expected, GLOBE's Humane Orientation cultural values strongly predicted desirability of Humane-Oriented leadership (House et al., 2004). The Humane Orientation *cultural dimension* of societies indicates high overall concern for the well-being of their members. This, in turn, contributes to the endorsement of Humane-Oriented leadership. As Yukl (2013) pointed out, "Humane oriented values encourage supportive leadership behaviors such as being considerate of a subordinate's needs and feelings, showing sympathy when a subordinate is upset, . . . and acting friendly and accepting" (p. 368).

Our findings in GLOBE 2004 showed large country-level differences in the endorsement of Humane-Oriented leadership (i.e., CLTs). Brodbeck and colleagues (2002) revealed an interesting picture regarding the importance of Humane-Oriented leadership in Germany. They indicated that while it contributed to a positive leadership prototype in Germany, which they labeled the "humble collaborator," it was toward the midpoint of the scale (going from negative to positive leadership attributes). They attributed this finding to the extremely low scores for Germany on the Humane Orientation cultural dimension.

Potential gender differences in the endorsement of a Humane-Oriented leadership style have been the subject of several GLOBE based studies. Results from the Paris and colleagues (2009) study were surprising because, contrary to much of the extant literature (cf. Eagly, Johannesen-Schmidt, & van Engen, 2003), females did not differ from males in their endorsement of the global CLT of Humane-Oriented leadership. Male and female managers alike rated this dimension equally as a weak contributor to outstanding leadership across 27 countries. This finding is inconsistent with the conventional wisdom that female managers are more considerate, supportive, and kind than male managers (Tung, 2004). However, in another study based on the same GLOBE database across 27 countries (Aiken, Dorfman, Howell, & Hanges, 2012), the authors examined gender differences in desirability of the two primary leadership dimensions of humane orientation and modesty. They found that females rated the primary dimension of humane orientation as more important than did males. There were no differences on the desirability of the modesty dimension. In other words, men and women do not differ on their views of the global CLT of Humane-Oriented leadership consisting of the two primary dimensions of humane orientation and modesty. They do, however, differ on the more specific primary dimension of humane orientation.

Behavioral Research Investigating Humane-Oriented Leadership

To understand the potential impact of Humane-Oriented leadership, we have to rely on past research that is complementary to the GLOBE Humane-Oriented leadership construct. Fortunately, considerable cross-cultural research has investigated the effectiveness of considerate and supportive leadership originally developed in The Ohio State University (e.g., Fleishman, 1953; Fleishman, Harris, & Burtt, 1955) and the University of Michigan research programs (Bowers & Seashore, 1966; Likert, 1961, 1967). Recent cross-cultural studies continue to support previous findings (Dorfman, 2004) that worldwide, considerate, and supportive leadership behaviors will increase subordinates' satisfaction with both their job and their supervisor (Agarwal, DeCarlo, & Vyas, 1999; Bass, 2008; Euwema, Wendt, & Van Emmerik, 2007; Lok & Crawford, 2004; Wendt et al., 2009). The evidence regarding a "people oriented" leadership *for individual job and firm performance* is not nearly so clear. For instance, Dorfman, Howell and colleagues (1997) found that supportive leadership had a direct impact on job performance in Mexico, an indirect impact on job performance through reducing role ambiguity in south Korea, and no impact on job performance for the United States samples.

The near universality of positive effects for leader supportiveness with respect to employee attitudes should not be surprising since supportive leaders show concern for followers and are considerate and available to listen to followers' problems. An empirical study of top-level Chinese managers found that showing benevolence (i.e., showing love and care for subordinates) was related to both employee attitudes and firm performance (the latter through employee attitudes such as organizational commitment) (Wang et al., 2011). Contrary findings regarding supportive leadership are infrequent but do occur (Bennett, 1977; Scandura, Von Glinow, & Lowe, 1999). For instance, Kennis (1977) found that American supervisors were perceived to be more considerate and participative than Turkish supervisors but equal in structuring behaviors. However, whereas consideration, participation, and structure were related to satisfaction with supervision for Americans, only the consideration score was related to satisfaction with supervision for the Turkish sample. Evidence also exists that cultures differ in the perceived importance of managerial consideration/supportive behaviors (Bass et al., 1979) and often differ in the factor structure of leadership scales measuring consideration (Anderson, 1983; Ayman & Chemers, 1983).

Truthfully, because the GLOBE Humane-Oriented leadership dimension is only tangentially related to the leadership consideration and support literature, we have relatively little to go on in predicting this leadership behavior. The GLOBE 2004 CLT ratings of this dimension would lead us to predict that it will have a positive but relatively little effect on leadership effectiveness.

Autonomous Leadership

This newly defined global leadership dimension was also developed in GLOBE 2004 research and refers to leadership that is independent and individualistic. The endorsement of this dimension in GLOBE was measured by a single primary leadership dimension labeled "autonomous," which contains the following attributes: individualistic, independent, autonomous, and unique. This dimension describes tendencies to act independently without relying on others; is self-governing and includes a preference to work and act separately from others. GLOBE's definition of Autonomous leadership is as follows:

> Autonomous leaders have extreme confidence in their own abilities and lack respect for others' abilities and ideas. They view themselves as unique and superior to others and as a result, prefer to work independently and without much collaboration with colleagues or direct reports.

The corresponding autonomous CEO behaviors in the present study include acting independently, self-governing and not relying on others, and being individualistic by behaving in a manner different from peers. Perhaps colloquially, the leadership style that comes to mind might be that of the John Wayne movie character if he were to head up a major corporation. Or the extreme case of the CEO of (the now defunct) Tiger Oil whose leadership independence is best exemplified in his memos whereby among other things, he stated the following:

> In case anyone does not know who owns Tiger Oil company, it is me, Edward Mike Davis . . . Do not let anyone think that they are the owner but me. There is one thing that differentiates me from my employees, I am a known son-of –a bitch, do not speak to me when you see me, if I want to speak to you, I will do so.

In short, according to GLOBE 2004, autonomous leaders have extreme confidence in their own abilities and lack respect for others' abilities and ideas. They view themselves as unique and superior to others and as a result, prefer to work independently and without much collaboration with colleagues or direct reports.

Endorsement of Autonomous Leadership

In the GLOBE 2004 project, Autonomous leadership attributes were generally viewed within each country cluster as being neutral to negative with respect to contributing to or impeding effective leadership. The average score for this dimension was 3.79, with a country range of 2.30 to 4.70 (on a 7-point scale). The country rating scores portray the Sub-Saharan Africa, Middle East, Latin Europe, and Latin America clusters as rejecting this factor whereas the Eastern Europe and Germanic Europe clusters saw it in a more positive light. In the Brodbeck and colleagues (2000) study of cultural variation of leadership prototypes across 22 European countries, they reported that autonomy was a primary factor differentiating

European countries from Anglo, Nordic, Latin, and Near European countries. In a more targeted study of German managerial leadership, Brodbeck and colleagues (2000) clarified how an individualistic leadership prototype can be viewed positively in Germany. Autonomous German leaders may be seen as unique, independent, and individualistic and who generally stay apart from the crowd. This prototype is represented by Alfred Herrhausen, former president of Deutsche Bank, who was described as an individualist, an outsider, often reserved and distanced with a high need for recognition.

In a study linking national culture, organizational culture, and leadership attributes, two GLOBE cultural values were related to the endorsement of Autonomous leadership (Javidan et al., 2010). As predicted, collectivism values (specifically, Institutional Collectivism) were negatively related to the Autonomous leadership dimension. In addition, Performance Orientation values were positively related to Autonomous leadership. In sum, members of societies and organizations with high performance-oriented and individualistic values will have a positive view of autonomous leaders.

We know of no empirical behavioral research investigating the effectiveness of Autonomous leadership behaviors.

Self-Protective Leadership

A second-order maximum likelihood exploratory factor analysis of GLOBE 2004 CLT data revealed this sixth major leadership dimension labeled Self-Protective leadership (Hanges & Dickson, 2004, pp. 136–137). GLOBE's definition of Self-Protective leadership is as follows:

> Self-protective leaders have a deep desire to succeed among a group of colleagues and direct reports who may act as competitors for the leaders' position and success. To protect themselves, they defer to positions of power, hide information which might advantage potential competitors, follow rules and policies to avoid risk, and interact carefully with others to ensure they leave a positive impression.

This leadership dimension includes five primary leadership dimensions labeled (1) self-centered, (2) status conscious, (3) internally competitive (formerly labeled *conflict inducer*), (4) face-saver, and (5) bureaucratic (formerly labeled *procedural*). (The label changes for GLOBE's conflict inducer and procedural primary leadership dimensions were made to clarify the constructs and make the labels more consistent with the attribute items). The primary Self-Protective leadership dimensions are defined as follows:

1. Self-Centered: This dimension reflects a leader who is self-absorbed, is a loner, is aloof, and stands off from others.

2. Status conscious: This dimension reflects a consciousness of one's own and others' social position, holding an elitist belief that some individuals deserve more privileges than others. A status conscious leader adjusts his or her style of leadership and communication according to the status of the individual(s) he or she is dealing with.

3. Internally competitive (formerly labeled *conflict inducer*): This dimension reflects the tendency to view colleagues as competitors and to conceal information due to a lack of willingness to work jointly with others.

4. Face-Saver: This leadership dimension reflects the tendency to ensure followers are not embarrassed or shamed. A face-saving leader maintains good relationships by refraining from making negative comments and instead uses metaphors and analogies.

5. Bureaucratic (formerly labeled *procedural*): This dimension emphasizes leaders who habitually follow established norms, rules, policies, procedures, and routines.

To summarize, according to GLOBE 2004, self-protective leaders have a deep desire to be viewed as successful among a group of colleagues and direct reports who may act as competitors for the leaders' position and success. They take a number of steps to protect their position and career. To begin with, they are highly deferential to positions of power. Secondly, they hide information that in any way might advantage others who could be competitors. Third, they tend to follow rules and policies to avoid risk and finally they are careful in how they interact with others to make sure they leave a positive impression. This style of leadership is reminiscent of a Machiavellian approach to leadership (Machiavelli, 1532/1961).

Endorsement of Self-Protective Leadership

Almost all respondents in the 10 GLOBE clusters viewed the Self-Protective CLT dimension as an impediment to effective leadership—some strikingly so as reflected by the low absolute and relative scores for the Anglo, Germanic Europe, and Nordic Europe clusters; yet the Confucian Asia and Southern Asia clusters viewed Self-Protective leadership in an almost-neutral manner (with some attributes of this factor being viewed positively, such as face-saving). The construct of saving face within Asian societies is well established, and we might speculate that face-saving leadership will be more easily accepted and effective in Asian cultures in contrast to Western cultures (Earley, 1993). Richard Brislin (personal communication, 2000), when referring to GLOBE data, suggested that the concept for Asian cultures actually reflects "group-protective" and "self-protective" elements and, therefore, would be viewed more positively in the Confucian Asia and Southern Asia clusters.

All five of the primary leadership dimensions comprising the global Self-Protective leadership dimension were statistically grouped together by a second-order factor analysis in GLOBE 2004. Of the five primary dimensions, only the notion of bureaucratic leadership is found as a distinct leadership construct in the literature. Of course, the concepts of status and face-saving, and being self-centered are found in various literatures, but none has appeared specifically as leadership dimension as they are in GLOBE. The GLOBE primary dimension of being internally competitive is a fact of organization life but has not appeared in the leadership literature perhaps because of its negative connotation.

Regarding bureaucratic leadership, Weber (1947) expressed the positive aspects of legal authority found in bureaucracies (i.e., obedience to the office and rules rather than the person) in contrast to the other two types of legitimate authority of charismatic and patrimonial authority. Contemporary leadership literature has typically portrayed bureaucracies and bureaucratic leadership in a negative fashion (Bensman & Rosenberg, 1960). However, contrary assertions have made a positive case for bureaucracies. Goodsell (1983), for instance, citing evidence from Kohn's (1971) study of individuals who worked in bureaucratic firms, found that individuals in bureaucratic organizations were actually more self-directed, more receptive to change, and showed greater flexibility than those working in nonbureaucratic firms and agencies. In this book, we will examine the relationship between bureaucratic leadership and effectiveness across cultures.

The concept of status has a long history within the leadership literature (cf. Barnard, 1951). Higher status individuals, due to their position or expertise within an organization, are more likely to emerge as leaders and engage in influence activities. Numerous empirical studies have affirmed the almost obvious finding that high-status managers have greater influence over subordinates than lower status managers (Bass, 2008). Nevertheless, being aware of one's status and acting accordingly may or may not be well received by subordinates. In GLOBE (House et al., 2004), the desirability of being aware of one's status and class consciousness were highly variable across cultures. For example, ratings for status consciousness varied from a societal low of 1.92 to a high of 5.77 on a 7-point scale, likely indicating huge cultural variability in the desirability of this leadership attribute. In the present GLOBE project, the effectiveness of status consciousness leadership will be examined.

Behavioral Research Investigating Self-Protective Leadership

We know of no behavioral research investigating most of GLOBE's Self-Protective leadership behaviors. As previously discussed, we can speculate about its actual level or enactment and the effectiveness of each, but empirical research is lacking. However, because of the generally negative ratings of self-centered leadership and internally competitive leadership in GLOBE (House et al., 2004), we expect that they will also be viewed negatively. The effectiveness of status conscious, bureaucratic, and face-saving leadership behaviors may be more nuanced and depend on the specific cultures studied. Overall, however, we expect that Self-Protective leadership attributes and behaviors would be part of an effective leadership prototype of members of societies valuing high power distance and reduced uncertainty. In this book, we will examine the relationship between Self-Protective leadership behaviors and effectiveness across cultures.

_____ Strategic Leadership and Upper Echelon Theory

In the previous sections of this chapter, we have reviewed the literature on cross-cultural leadership, but as noted, there is limited work on executive leadership from a cross-cultural perspective. Our research presented in this book has the overriding goal of bridging these two separate streams of literature— (1) cross-cultural leadership primarily studied at the middle management level and (2) strategic leadership primarily studied in Western contexts.

Perhaps surprisingly to nonacademic audiences, there is an ongoing scholarly debate as to the *actual* importance of executive leadership in contrast to the widely held public perception that executives are *the fundamental* key to organizational success or failure. There is a school of thought that argues for limited executive impact. The rationale is based in several streams of thought. Attribution theory suggests that leaders are given excessive credit for success of an organization. Meindl and colleagues (1985), in the now seminal article titled "The Romance of Leadership," made the point that the attributions of successful leadership increase as a causal explanation in cases of extreme organizational or team performance even when leaders lack actual control in the fate of organizations in their charge. Similarly, as noted by Yukl (2010), "more attributions are made for someone who occupies a high-level position with substantial prestige and power, especially in cultures where leaders are viewed as heroic figures" (p. 133). These views of limited leadership influence are supported by several literature streams that present a deterministic view of environmental constraints that severely limit the flexibility of executives. For instance, population ecology asserts that the growth of enterprises from birth, growth, to death is constrained by available resources such that individual leadership influence is minimal (Hannan & Freeman, 1977). Institutional theory likewise views the leader's influence as limited due to the necessity of conforming to external expectations and limitations, thus mimicking the choices of other successful organizations (Finkelstein, Hambrick, & Cannella, 2009).

On the other hand, there are several arguments that executives are critical to organizational success. CEOs hold the highest formal leadership position within an organization and, because of their position legitimacy, exert the most powerful leadership role. Executives run the firm, setting organizational priorities, developing organizational structures, and determining the importance of multiple and conflicting goals and objectives. While their actions are subject to board approval in publicly held firms they often have input as to who sits on the board and exhibit great influence over board actions. Through multiple layers of management, they can motivate or demotivate subordinates through an almost infinite number of rewards and punishments for success or failure. Prominent executives such as Herb Kelleher at Southwest Airlines, Jack Welch at GE, and Louis Gestner at IBM channeled these organizations to great success. Conversely, the actions by incompetent, unethical, and/or rogue executives such as Jeffrey Skilling and Kenneth Lay at Enron, and Richard Fuld at Lehman Brothers, devastated their organizations.

The logic that was just described has led several researchers to argue that senior executives have a substantive impact on the performance of their firm (see Bass, 1990; Cannella & Monroe, 1997; Hunt, 1991, for detailed reviews). Yukl's (2008) flexible leadership theory (FLT), for instance, integrates the diverse fields of leadership, strategic management, HRM, and organizational change. The crux of the FLT is that senior leaders improve organizational performance by influencing decisions about management programs and systems, decisions about the competitive strategy for the organization, and the use of specific leadership behaviors in interactions with subordinates. According to FLT, the actions and decisions of senior leaders directly influence performance determinants such as the organization's adaptation to the external environment, which in turn relates to overall organizational effectiveness (e.g., ability to survive).

The more recent stream of work is focused on how and in what way CEOs and senior executives impact the performance of their firms. A highly influential theory of executive influence is the upper echelon theory (Hambrick & Mason, 1984). Rooted in Child's (1972) notion of strategic choice, this school of thought argues that organizations are reflections of top managers' cognitions and values. This approach has more recently grown into a more comprehensive model called strategic leadership (Finkelstein & Hambrick, 1996), which attributes organizational outcomes to decisions and choices made by senior executives (Cannella & Monroe, 1997). The basic argument in strategic leadership is that the way senior executives view their opportunities and challenges—and how they process and interpret the information they receive—is impacted and restricted by their values, personalities, and cognitions (Cannella & Monroe, 1997).

Two points are important to note about the strategic leadership literature: First, while the theory contends the impact of the personality and values of senior executives, most of the empirical work has tended to use the more easily accessible demographic variables as surrogates for the more difficult to measure psychological variables. The surge of interest in demographic variables led researchers to raise concerns about their use. Priem, Lyon, and Dess (1999) raised fundamental questions about the meaning and construct validity of demographic variables. Similarly, Boal and Hooijberg (2001) questioned nomological validity of strategic leadership theory and called for a "moratorium on the use of demographic variables as surrogates for psychological constructs" (p. 523).

Secondly, the strategic leadership literature has tended to focus on TMTs without a distinction between the CEO as the leader and other senior executives. Rather, CEOs and other senior executives are clustered into a group that Hambrick and Mason (1984) called upper echelon and Cyert and March (1963/1992) called dominant coalition (Peterson, Smith, Martorana, & Owens, 2003). Several authors have raised concerns about lack of attention to CEOs as separate from the TMT. Hambrick (1994) pointed out the following:

> Perhaps out of a zeal to move away from undue focus on the single top executive, researchers of top groups have been noticeably silent on the distinct role and impact of the group leader. As Jackson (1992) points out, there has been a tendency in top management team research to simply include the CEO as a member of the group, averaging in his or her characteristics in establishing overall group characteristics. Yet, everyday observation and a wealth of related literature indicates that the top group leader has a disproportionate, sometimes nearly dominating influence on the group's various characteristics and output. (p. 180)

Zaccaro and colleagues (2001) also raised a similar concern that "although there is a large and growing literature on TMTs, few studies have focused specifically on the relationship between the executive leader and his or her team, and specifically how executive leaders manage or lead their teams" (p. 193).

In response to the two concerns that were just stated, researchers have recently started to focus on CEOs and how they can impact the firm's performance (Colbert, Kristof-Brown, Bradley, & Barrick, 2008; Ling, Simsek, Lubatkin, & Veiga, 2008b; Waldman, Ramirez, House, & Puranam, 2001; Waldman, Javidan, & Varella, 2004). Peterson and colleagues (2003) showed that the five factors of CEO personality (conscientiousness, emotional stability, agreeableness, extraversion, and openness) affect TMT dynamics, and TMT dynamics in turn are related to firm performance. For example, extroverted CEOs were viewed as dominating their TMTs, and CEOs who were open-minded were associated with TMTs that demonstrated intellectual flexibility.

Eisenhardt and Bourgeois (1988) examined the impact of CEO leadership style and found that a less dominating style by the CEOs resulted in greater sharing of information, a consensus style of decision making, a more collaborative TMT, and a greater focus on group rather than individual goals. Flood and his colleagues (2000) also tested the relationship between CEO leadership style and TMT effectiveness and found that laissez-faire and authoritarian styles impacted team dynamics negatively and reduced TMT effectiveness.

Perhaps the most studied aspect of CEO leadership in the recent literature is the link between CEO charismatic and transformational (C/T) leadership style and TMT effectiveness and firm performance. Waldman and Yammarino (1999) postulated that charismatic CEOs will foster top management cohesion and will cascade their style in lower levels through role modeling. They will also produce higher firm results by creating consensus across the organization about higher performance expectations. Agle, Nagaragan, Sonnenfeld, and Srinivasan (2006) posited that C/T CEOs can influence firm results due to (1) their ability to overcome inertial forces that prevent organizations from adapting to their environments, (2) their ability to inspire employees and other stakeholders, and (3) their ability to create cohesion in the organization.

Despite the theoretical and intuitive appeal of the above insights, empirical evidence on the relationship between CEO charisma and firm performance is mixed (Agle et al., 2006). Waldman and colleagues (2001) found no direct relationship between CEO charisma and firm performance but found that charismatic CEOs were associated with firm performance under conditions of environmental uncertainty. Tosi, Misangyi, Fanelli, Waldman, and Yammarino (2004) also found no direct relationship between CEO charisma and firm performance. Similarly, Agle and colleagues (2006) showed that CEO charisma was unrelated to firm performance. In contrast, Waldman and colleagues (2004) showed that CEO charisma was related to firm performance but no moderating effect for environmental uncertainty. Ling and colleagues (2008a) also found that C/T CEOs had a significant direct effect on both objective and subjective measures of firm performance in small privately held firms. Ling and colleagues (2008b) also showed that transformational leaders were associated with more cohesive TMTs, more decentralization of responsibilities, higher risk-taking propensities, and higher levels of corporate entrepreneurship. Finally, in the most recent study available, Wang and colleagues (2011) showed that Chinese CEOs can achieve higher levels of firm performance by both focusing on task performance activities (through charismatic leadership) and by inducing positive attitudes of employees through their relationship oriented behaviors.

To summarize, rigorous empirical research on CEOs seems to be in its infancy. Only a few studies have focused on how CEOs can influence firm outcomes and have found rather conflicting results. The extant literature seems to be almost all based in North America and with North American executives. The only exception is the study by Wang and colleagues (2011), who studied Chinese CEOs. There is no comparative study of CEOs across countries and cultures. Furthermore, the existing literature examines how and what aspects of CEO's behaviors and styles can result in positive or negative outcomes. But there is little study of *why* CEOs behave the way they do. There is limited existing literature on what explains CEO behavior. The focus has so far been on the consequences of CEO behavior and not on drivers of CEO behavior. But if we can understand why CEOs behave the way they do, we will be better able to help modify their behavior and improve their performance.

As will be explained in the next chapter, our research is designed to help fill the previously stated two gaps. We will present a large-scale study of over 1,000 CEOs across 24 countries, and we will examine not just the consequences of their behaviors and styles but also the cultural drivers of their behavior.

3

Rationale, Theoretical Framework, Hypotheses, Research Design, and Snapshots of Findings

The rationale for conducting this new GLOBE project on executive level leadership follows from previous findings of GLOBE 2004 and GLOBE 2007 (Chhokar, Brodbeck, & House, 2007; House, Hanges, Javidan, Dorfman, & Gupta, 2004) as well as recent world events. Indeed, the importance of global leadership was highlighted by the central focus of the 2013 economic forum of world leaders in Davos, Switzerland (*The Economist*, 2013). This GLOBE project adds to the global leadership discussion by empirically assessing effective CEO leadership in 24 different countries.

Previously, in GLOBE 2004, we demonstrated that each country has a culturally endorsed implicit leadership theory (CLT), which represents that country's expectations from the leaders in that society. In other words, it is a profile of societal leadership expectations. We showed that each CLT consists of 21 primary dimensions that were further consolidated into 6 global dimensions. We further showed that societal cultural values predicted the CLTs or the leadership expectations desired in different societies. These leadership expectations were described as attributes and characteristics that are culturally endorsed (hence the construct of culturally endorsed implicit leadership theories, or CLTs). For instance, Performance Orientation cultural values positively predicted the degree to which Charismatic and Team-Oriented leadership attributes (two of the six global leadership dimensions of CLT) were expected and desired in leaders.

We also found that some leadership attributes are universally desired, others universally refuted, and still others culturally contingent. From a cross-cultural viewpoint, the most interesting findings relate to the aspects of leadership that are culturally contingent—that is, effective characteristics in some cultures and less effective, or even ineffective, in others.

We want to note that in this current project, our focus on cultural influences on CEO leadership behavior and effectiveness is in contrast to much of the prevailing strategic literature examining the influence of personality, individual demographics, and other organizational variables on executive behavior (Cannella & Monroe, 1997). It doesn't mean that these variables are not important, only that these variables are not the focus in this book. One issue yet unanswered by earlier GLOBE research concerns whether or not leadership behaviors are directly influenced by culture (i.e., cultural dimension such as Power Distance) or if culture indirectly influences leadership behaviors through leadership expectations (i.e., CLTs). The prevailing view from the literature seems to indicate a direct relationship—cultures impact leadership behaviors. In contrast, we predict that culture has an indirect effect whereby leaders in various cultures *enact* the behaviors that are culturally expected (CLTs). It stands to reason that behaviors that are widely believed to be appropriate and effective, and therefore most acceptable should normally be enacted except under extenuating circumstances. This *culture congruence hypothesis* was developed by House, Wright, and Aditya (1997), suggesting that leaders should generally not deviate substantially from what is expected in the culture. This argument is consistent with the discussion of tight and loose cultures/norms (Gelfand et al., 2011). Figure 3.1 presents the GLOBE model. Hypotheses tested in the present project are indicated by dashes.

Figure 3.1   Modified GLOBE Theoretical Model 2013

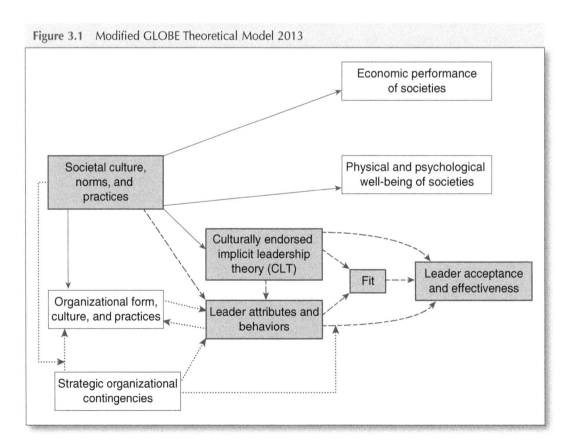

If the first research question concerns enactment of CEO leadership, a second question concerns the effectiveness of specific leadership behaviors such as Charismatic leadership. In forthcoming analyses, we will determine the relative effectiveness of our 6 global and 21 primary leadership behaviors. We will also determine if these relationships are universal (pan-cultural/culture common) or culturally contingent. From the past literature discussed in Chapter 2, the term *variform functional universal* may apply in contexts whereby charismatic behaviors, for example, may be universally desirable but differentially effective across societies. We expect that a number of additional leadership behaviors in this project will have positive effects as well (e.g., Team-Oriented leadership). Since GLOBE also found universally *undesirable* leadership attributes and negatively rated primary leadership behaviors, we might expect leadership enactment of them to correspondingly be ineffective (e.g., malevolent leadership). Still others may vary considerably in effectiveness across cultures (Participative and Self-Protective leadership). The six global leadership dimensions include the following:

- *Charismatic leadership:* Charismatic leaders inspire their followers with a desirable and realistic vision that is decided based on appropriate analysis and high performance expectations. They are viewed as sincere, decisive, and credible because of their integrity and willingness to sacrifice their own self-interest.
- *Team-Oriented leadership:* Team-oriented leaders are loyal to their teams and care for the welfare of their team members. They use their administrative and interpersonal skills to manage the team's internal dynamics and to create a cohesive working group.
- *Participative leadership:* Participative leaders believe that employees can contribute to decision making and should be engaged in the process of decision making and implementation. They also believe that debate, discussion, and disagreement are a natural part of good decision making and should not be suppressed.
- *Humane-Oriented leadership:* Humane-oriented leaders are unpretentious, show humility, and are reticent to boast. They are empathetic and likely to help and support team members in a humane manner by offering resources and other forms of assistance.
- *Autonomous leadership:* Autonomous leaders have extreme confidence in their own abilities and lack respect for others' abilities and ideas. They view themselves as unique and superior to others, and as a result, they prefer to work independently and without much collaboration with colleagues or direct reports.
- *Self-Protective leadership:* Self-protective leaders have a deep desire to succeed among a group of colleagues and direct reports who may act as competitors for the leaders' position and success. To protect themselves, they defer to positions of power, hide information that might advantage potential competitors, follow rules and policies to avoid risk, and interact carefully with others to ensure they leave a positive impression.

A third research question follows from the two previously given where we predict that CEO leadership effectiveness depends on the extent to which behaviors match cultural expectations. Testing this "congruency hypothesis" is another important aspect of the current project. As a formal proposition, we expect that the more a CEO leader's behavior is congruent with the country's leadership expectations (i.e., CLTs), the more we expect that leadership attempts by such individuals will be effective. It follows that such a leader will be perceived as legitimate, resulting in more highly motivated and committed subordinates. In this and the following chapter, we want to assess the behavioral consequences of the "fit" between the ideal leadership qualities and the enacted behaviors by the leader.

Because of a general interest in CEO effectiveness within and across countries, we intend to empirically examine the leadership profiles of the best and worst CEOs in our sample; we designate these as superior and inferior CEOs, respectively. We will provide evidence that the profiles of each differ in terms of leadership behaviors leading to top management team (TMT) outcomes and Firm Competitive Performance. For example, we will provide evidence that superior Austrian CEOs tend to show high levels of integrity while inferior Austrian CEOs show *very* low levels of integrity. Evidence is presented regarding the importance of the 6 global and 21 primary leadership behaviors in distinguishing the superior CEOs from the inferior CEOs.

In summary, the purpose of our new GLOBE project can be summarized by asking and answering the following research questions: (1) To what extent do societal cultural values and/or culturally endorsed implicit leadership expectations (CLTs) drive CEO behavior?; (2) Which specific CEO leadership behaviors influence TMT Dedication and Firm Competitive Performance?; (3) Does the congruency or fit between CEO leadership behavior and culturally endorsed leadership expectations (CLTs) make a difference as to TMT Dedication and Firm Competitive Performance?; (4) If both the level of CEO behavior and fit of behaviors to expectations are important, to what extent do both jointly contribute to TMT Dedication and Firm Competitive Performance?; (5) Are there leadership profile differences between superior CEOs and inferior CEOs?

Theoretical Framework Underlying the Present Project: The Importance of Implicit Leadership Theory Driving Executive Behaviors

Convincing evidence exists that individuals distinguish leaders from followers, effective leaders from ineffective leaders, and moral leaders from evil leaders on the basis of personal beliefs, convictions, and assumptions about leadership (House et al., 1997). As previously noted, GLOBE researchers are interested in the extent to which leaders at the highest organizational levels actually enact the behaviors that are culturally endorsed. It stands to reason that behaviors that are widely believed to be appropriate and effective—and therefore most acceptable—should normally be enacted except under extenuating circumstances. We intend to test this proposition. Unfortunately, the extant research literature is almost devoid of cross-cultural *executive* leadership studies (a welcome exception is the study of Chinese CEO leadership by Wang, Tsui, & Xin, 2011). And we know next to nothing about the actual empirical relationship between leadership expectations of societies (i.e., CLTs) found worldwide and executive behavior in these societies.

The process by which implicit leadership theories (ILTs) drive behavior may be both conscious and unconscious (Lord & Brown, 2004). Conscious awareness of one's ILT may occur when leaders engage in active thinking about their own leadership style. This may occur in situations that prompt introspection (e.g., seminars, performance evaluations, meetings, retreats) or when events and outcomes occur that are surprising, unexpected, and disappointing. Only when these events are truly novel does the typical person move into a more introspective mode regarding their ILT. More likely, this process of enacting a coherent mental representation of effective leadership is more unconscious as in the situations where managerial leaders establish selection criteria for hiring and promotions, serve as role models by setting personal examples, and socialize organizational members in a manner that reflects the broader culture in which they function.

Further, dominant cultural norms should reinforce leader behavior patterns and organizational practices that are expected and viewed as legitimate within a culture. In a sense, culture may simply limit the repertoire of acceptable strategies of action rather than being the *conscious* end value toward which action is directed (Swidler, 1986). That is, while people naturally know "how to act" in certain situations, they do not necessarily have to be able to espouse the "values" consistent with the action nor cognitively realize that a particular behavior is directed toward a specific value. Although both the "cultural dimensions/values" and "behavioral repertoire/ routines" explanations are valid causal mechanisms by which organizational behaviors become culturally contingent, the former are more established in the leadership literature.

The Importance of Congruency Between Executive Behaviors and the Culturally Endorsed Implicit Leadership Theories for Executive Effectiveness

Implicit leadership theory (ILT) posits that leaders are evaluated by the congruence between an individual's implicit beliefs about the characteristics of effective leaders and the leader's actual qualities, actions, and effectiveness (Lord & Maher, 1991; Offermann, Kennedy, & Wirtz, 1994).

That is, ILTs held by individuals influence the way they view the importance of leadership, the values they attribute to leadership, and the values they place on selected leader behaviors and attributes. For instance, perceptions of U.S. leadership effectiveness for President Barack Obama and prior president Ronald Reagan are influenced by both their actual proven effectiveness as well as the congruence between the perceiver's values, beliefs, and assumptions of leadership and his/her perceptions of Barack Obama's and Ronald Reagan's behavior. Both factors, one's ILT as well as a leader's actual proven effectiveness, influence the perceptions of leadership qualities. This being the case, both presidents are considered charismatic leaders but with vastly differing values and beliefs for the role of government. Conservatives and liberals alike admire Obama's eloquence, but each group sees his leadership behavior and effectiveness through their own perceptual lens; for example, whether Obama is deliberate or dithering seems to depend on one's political views. President Ronald Reagan was an exceptional role model to conservatives, but liberals considered him out of touch with the reality of most U.S. citizens with his "morning in America campaign."

Why Focus on Strategic Leadership?

A resurgence of interest in higher level leadership since the early organizational theories by Barnard (1938) and others reflects the growing importance of strategic leadership by executives and their top management teams (TMTs) (Finkelstein, Hambrick, & Cannella, 2009; Yukl, 2008; Zaccaro, 2001). While at one time there may have been a controversy as to the actual impact leaders have on organizations (Meindl, Ehrlich, & Dukerich, 1985), numerous case studies and sophisticated empirical research designs attest to how effective and ineffective leadership substantially influences organization success and prosperity (Hambrick, 2007; Klein, Dansereau, & Hall, 1994). The "strategic imperative" is clear as globalization creates unique and unprecedented opportunities for corporations but with a price of increased complexity, uncertainty, and high potential for failure. Beechler and Javidan (2007) noted the following:

> Corporations need a new and different breed of global leaders who can take decisions and actions that facilitate the development of the complex network of internal and external connections with individuals, teams, and organizations from many different political, social, and cultural systems.

While the role of national culture in shaping the values of executives has been heavily examined (Finkelstein et al., 2009), what has clearly been missing is empirical evidence showing how these values are enacted by executives and the effectiveness of these behaviors in multicultural environments.

Thus, the shift in focus from the study of leadership of mid-level managers to upper level leaders is rational because it reflects an increased interest in understanding how executives can transform their companies to cope with globalization, increasing international competition, and more rapid technological and social change (Boal & Hooijberg, 2001; Cannella & Monroe, 1997; Carpenter, Geletkanycz, & Sanders, 2004; Yukl, 2008, 2010). With few exceptions, however, few studies of executive level effectiveness are found in the cross-cultural literature. As previously mentioned, the study of Chinese executives by Wang and colleagues (2011) is an exception; note that this study involves executives from a single culture. The present GLOBE project will test the effectiveness of a wide variety of leadership behaviors across countries including the charismatic behaviors studied by Wang and colleagues (2011).

Research Objectives

1. *Understanding and empirically measuring the nature and drivers of CEO leadership behavior.*

A major objective of the present study is to determine whether cultural values and/or CLTs in a society predict the observed behavior of CEOs in that society. The cultural values and CLTs were measured in GLOBE 2004. We examine here the extent to which the cultural values and CLTs predict the observed behaviors of CEOs. The extant literature on cross-cultural leadership posits a direct effect of cultural values on behavior (Hofstede, 1993; Smith, Peterson, & Thomas, 2008), arguing that leaders internalize the cultural norms and values that are manifested in their behavior. Our rationale is somewhat different as we argue that CLTs are essentially espoused leadership theories of cultures, and it is these CLTs that influence behavior, not cultural values themselves. CLTs specify the behaviors that are widely believed to be appropriate and effective; they are how societies expect their leaders to behave. For example, CEOs who work in societies that expect their leaders to be participative tend to act in a participative manner. Leaders grow up learning and internalizing these expectations and will tend to enact them in leadership positions. CEOs epitomize the highest level of leadership and leadership success. To reach the CEO position, we expect leaders to master the art of acting according to expectations.

Our research empirically tests the hypothesis that cultural values predict CEO behavior. Furthermore, we test an alternative hypothesis that CLTs predict CEO leadership behavior. Our expectation is that cultural values indirectly predict behavior through the manifestation of culturally endorsed leadership expectations (i.e., CLTs).

2. *Understanding and measuring the drivers of CEO leadership effectiveness: the relationship between CEO leadership behavior and effectiveness.*

Our second objective is to determine the extent to which observed and reported CEO leadership behavior predicts CEO effectiveness. There is substantial research literature that theoretically and empirically demonstrates the relationship between specific leadership behaviors and various outcomes (Yukl, 2013). In our research, we measure CEO effectiveness in two ways: (2a) the effect of CEO leadership on his/her direct reports (members of TMT) and (2b) the effect of CEO leadership on the performance of the firm.

We test the hypothesis that CEO leadership behaviors predict TMT Dedication and Firm Competitive Performance. Specifically, we expect the following across countries:

a. CEO Charismatic leadership behavior will be positively related to TMT Dedication and Firm Competitive Performance.

b. CEO Team-Oriented leadership behavior will be positively related to TMT Dedication and Firm Competitive Performance.

c. CEO Participative leadership behavior will be positively related to TMT Dedication and Firm Competitive Performance.

d. CEO Humane-Oriented leadership behavior will be positively related to TMT Dedication and Firm Competitive Performance.

e. CEO Autonomous leadership behavior will be negatively related to TMT Dedication and Firm Competitive Performance.

f. CEO Self-Protective leadership behaviors will be negatively related to TMT Dedication and Firm Competitive Performance.

3. *Assessing the leadership distinctions between the high-performing CEOs (i.e., superior), and underperforming CEOs (i.e., inferior).*
The hypotheses in our model are tested using various statistical analyses including random coefficient modeling (RCM), which is frequently referred to in the organizational literature as hierarchical linear modeling, or HLM. Staying with the literature, we will label results when we use this technique as HLM. While critical and helpful, these statistical analyses can only tell part of the story. They only connect patterns or trends among the averages of variables of interest. Deviations from these averages are ignored or treated as error. Additional analyses contrasting the extremely effective and ineffective CEOs enhance our understanding of the "error term." Such analyses provide detailed information regarding each leadership dimension as well as country-specific profiles of outstanding leadership. For example, our statistical analyses as demonstrated in Chapter 8 provide evidence that, across countries, Charismatic leadership predicts effectiveness. Furthermore, as demonstrated in Chapter 7, Austrian CEOs generally enact low levels of Charismatic leadership. However, in Chapter 8 we will provide evidence that superior Austrian CEOs tend to show very high levels of

Charismatic leadership while inferior Austrian CEOs show very low levels of Charismatic leadership. Thus, the combined pieces of information help us answer theoretically meaningful and managerially relevant questions. Therefore, we test the following hypotheses: (3a) superior CEOs differ from inferior CEOs in their leadership behavior, and (3b) the nature and extent of the difference will vary across countries.

4. *Understanding and measuring the drivers of CEO leadership effectiveness: the impact of the fit between CEO leadership behavior with CLTs.*

It is our hypothesis that the fit between a CEO's behavior and his/her society's leadership expectations (CLTs) will predict the CEO's effectiveness. The closer the fit or congruence between CEO behavior and the society's CLT, the more committed and coherent the CEO's TMT and the more successful the CEO's company. We expect that the more congruent individual CEO leader behaviors are with the societies' leadership expectations (CLTs), (4a) the more dedicated and committed his subordinates/followers and (4b) the more successful the firm.

5. *Determining the differential and combined effect of "fit" and "behavior" in predicting CEO effectiveness.*

What is the differential and cumulative effect of both fit and behavior in predicting CEO effectiveness? As presented in objective 2, the extant literature on leadership provides ample evidence on the relationship between leadership behavior and leadership effectiveness (Yukl, 2013). As explained in objective 3, a key hypothesis driving the current research is that the fit between CEO leadership behavior and the society's leadership expectations predicts CEO effectiveness. It is thus logical to examine the differential and combined effect of these two sources: leadership behavior and the fit between leadership behavior and leadership expectations (CLTs). This is an important question because in previous GLOBE research (Dorfman, Hanges, & Brodbeck, 2004; Javidan, Dorfman, Howell, & Hanges, 2010), we identified leadership attributes that were universally desirable and some that were culturally contingent. We therefore expect—and empirically test—that for the universally desirable leadership dimensions, CEO effectiveness is predicted by the level of behavior rather than the fit between behavior and leadership expectations (i.e., CLTs). In contrast, for the culturally contingent CLTs, we expect the fit to predict CEO effectiveness.

Project Research Design

The full and complete research design is presented in the following chapter, but a summary is in order because of the project's complexity. For the project, we employed both quantitative and qualitative design elements. The primary aspect of the design employed survey research with more than 1,000 CEOs and their 5,000 direct reports (TMT members). Each CEO was required to have between six and nine TMT members reporting to him/her. The research design also specified using three independent sets of these TMT members with two to three TMT members in each set. The rationale for independent TMTs is as follows. The questionnaires completed by two of the TMT sets rated their CEO's leadership behaviors and personal reactions (e.g., Commitment). We want to note, however, that two sets of TMT members rated the CEO along the same leadership constructs *but with different items*. The third TMT set answered items related to demographics and financial performance of the firm along with their personal reactions. Figure 4.2 in the following chapter graphically shows the design of the current project. Table 3.1 presents a summary of the design (purpose, method, design, and results) for the previous GLOBE project (2004) and similar information for the design of the present project.

Table 3.1   GLOBE Phases 1, 2, and 3

GLOBE Phases 1 and 2			
Purpose	**Method**	**Design Strategy**	**Major Results**
• Design and implement multiphase and multimethod program to examine the relationship among national culture, leadership effectiveness, and societal phenomena • Identify leadership attributes critical for outstanding leadership • Develop Societal culture questionnaire • Develop Leadership questionnaire	• Involve a total of over 160 researchers from 62 national societies in the research project • Conduct individual and focus group interviews with mid-level managers in domestic organizations • Check items for relevance and understandability • Survey over 17,000 managers representing 951 organizations in 62 cultures	• Employ rigorous psychometric assessment procedures for scale items • Translate and back-translate survey instruments in each country • Conduct pilot tests in several countries • Control for common source error in research design • Use rigorous statistical procedures to ensure scales can be aggregated and reliable • Assess cultures and organizations on practices (i.e., as is) and values (should be)	• Validation of culture and leadership scales • Ranking of 62 societal cultures on nine culture dimensions • Grouping of 62 cultures into 10 culture clusters • Creation of 21 primary leadership and 6 global leadership scales • Determining relationships between culture dimensions and leadership dimensions • Determination of universally desirable and culturally specific leadership qualities (i.e., culturally endorsed

GLOBE Phases 1 and 2			
Purpose	**Method**	**Design Strategy**	**Major Results**
		• Use hierarchical linear modeling (HLM) to test hypotheses (culture to leadership) at organizational and societal level	implicit leadership theories, or CLTs)

GLOBE Phase 3			
Purpose	**Method**	**Design Strategy**	**Major Results**
• Determine the manner in which national culture influences executive leadership processes • Examine the relationship between leadership expectations (CLTs) and CEO behavior • Examine the relationship between CEO leadership behavior and effectiveness • Determine which CEO leadership behaviors are most effective	• Involvement of more than 40 researchers in 24 countries • 18 of the 24 countries previously completed Phase 1 and 2 in addition to Phase 3 • Interviews and surveys were conducted for 40 CEOs within each country • A total of more than 1,000 CEOs and 5,000 of their direct reports were respondents in the project • Previously defined leadership qualities from Phases 1 and 2 (i.e., CLTs) were converted into behavioral leadership items and combined into scales for Phase 3	• Between six and nine direct reports of each CEO assessed the CEO's leadership behaviors, their personal reactions, and firm performance • Common method and response variance eliminated through research design • Internally oriented top management team (TMT) outcomes included commitment, effort, and team solidarity • Externally oriented firm outcomes included competitive sales performance, and competitive domination of the industry	• Leaders tend to behave in a manner expected within their country • Cultural values do *not* have a direct effect on CEO behavior; rather, the effect is indirect through CLTs (i.e., leadership expectations) • For some leadership behaviors, both the fit of CEO behaviors (to expectations) and degree of leadership behavior predict effectiveness • Superior and inferior CEOs exhibit differing patterns of behavior within their country

Illustrative Examples of Findings From the Present GLOBE Project: A Snapshot of CEO Influence

Throughout the book, we will demonstrate that CEO leadership is important and that both commonalities and differences in CEO leadership behavior and effectiveness exist among the 24 countries studied. In addition, we concluded from earlier GLOBE research (2004, 2007) that leadership processes reflect the organizational and societal cultures in which they are imbedded. From our perspective, here are a few significant findings that are discussed in more detail later in the book.

Leadership Matters

As expected, we were not surprised to find that CEO behaviors have major influences on various outcomes related to TMT members' Dedication and Firm Competitive Performance. Charismatic leadership significantly predicted the Commitment, extra Effort, and Team Solidarity from TMT members across all cultures. In prior GLOBE research, we found that this leadership dimension was universally thought to lead to outstanding leadership. The following are quotes taken from CEO interviews regarding Charismatic leadership: "My strengths are in having a vision where we are going, looking at things strategically, willing to take risks, pushing the envelope" (U.S. CEO). "We have a vision for the future, we try to stay independent, minimizing our risk" (German CEO).

We found that the Team-Oriented global leadership factor, like the Charismatic factor, was very important in the new GLOBE study. Examples of the global Team-Oriented leadership factor are as follows: "I have formed a very good team and we started working, fast, aggressive, and showed very good results" (Russian CEO). "Our decisions are made in collaborative formats; this helps us function as a unified corporation" (Guatemalan CEO).

Perhaps surprisingly, earlier GLOBE research found that the rating of Humane-Oriented leadership indicated it was only slightly important to achieving outstanding leadership. The rating also varied across cultures (Javidan et al., 2010). Nonetheless, this leadership dimension was strikingly important in leadership effectiveness in the present research. The following are some statements taken from CEOs regarding Humane-Oriented leadership: "It is important that people should feel that they belong to an organization that cares about their personal growth" (South Pacific CEO). "We need to be clear about the human nature of our employees . . . we aspire to be a highly productive and humane company" (Mexican CEO).

Further, we found but did not predict that the importance of Humane-Oriented leadership would sometimes outperform the importance of another major leadership style—that of Participative leadership. The following are quotes taken from CEOs regarding Participative leadership: "I decided to adopt a more participative management approach, so I let myself make more informed decisions based on many views" (Greek CEO). "We have evolved into having a multilayer approach of both benevolent autocracy and participative management—we are moving to complete empowerment" (Indian CEO).

The Self-Protective global leadership factor was generally negatively perceived in GLOBE 2004 and GLOBE 2007, but the importance of primary leadership dimensions that comprise this factor often varied across nations (e.g., status conscious). The following are quotes taken from CEOs regarding Self-Protective leadership: "It is very hard to have a business in Azerbaijan if you have not developed good relations with different state officials and authorities who will protect you" (this quote refers to the favors granted to certain executives and often involves protection from excessive taxes and bribes, Azerbaijan CEO). "I am a very ambitious person and had too many fists in my face, and obstacles, I did not let myself be defeated" (Romanian CEO).

Examples of the sixth leadership factor, Autonomous, are as follows: "I would say, 98% of the time I did it alone . . . no one could teach me anything, since I knew the internal situation best, and have been there a long time" (German CEO). "I believe that leaders should keep a certain distance from the followers, I do not put on airs, but because the way I manage, people are all afraid of me" (Chinese CEO).

National Culture Is a Driver of Leadership Behaviors Through Cultural Expectations; Congruency With the National Culture Is Critical

In this latest GLOBE project, we demonstrate that national culture is a specific driver of leadership processes—leaders tend to enact the kind of leadership that is expected in a culture. However, the process of cultural influence is decidedly mediated through societal expectations (CLTs) of attributes and behaviors thought to constitute outstanding leadership. Prior GLOBE research (2004) led us to hypothesize that effective leadership depends on *"congruency* hypothesis of leadership" whereby CEO leadership effectiveness is predicated on the extent to which leaders *enact* the type of leadership actually *expected* (to be outstanding) within that society. Our current research in the present project presents empirical evidence to support this hypothesis. Before the concluding chapter of the book, we provide evidence about the most and least superior CEOs in our sample. We think you might be surprised by some of these results.

In summary, throughout the book, we provide evidence that leadership matters, executive leadership matters greatly, and that societal cultures influence the kind of leadership that is expected and effective. Our research contributes to existing literature in several ways. To begin, there is no study of CEOs and senior executives (i.e., TMT members) across cultures and countries. Our research is the first study of its kind to examine a large number (several thousand) of CEOs and senior executives in multiple countries. Second, we are the first to empirically examine directly the relationship between culture and leadership. Third, we use a multimethod and multisample approach including quantitative and qualitative research methods.

Fourth, most cross-cultural studies assess the impact of leadership in terms of internally oriented outcome measures (e.g., employee commitment and satisfaction) and do not assess externally oriented outcome measures such as Firm Competitive Performance. Our research examines the impact of senior executive leadership on Firm Competitive Performance along with the typical internally oriented measures across countries. Fifth, our measures of leadership behavior are derived from our 20-year-long programmatic research on cultural values and practices and leadership expectations across 62 cultures (the GLOBE 2004 and GLOBE 2007 studies). Managerial and theoretical implications are presented in the concluding chapters. We hope that you will find the project interesting, the results theoretically informative, and of practical importance for managers.

4 Research Methodology and Design

This chapter describes the research design used in GLOBE Phase 3. In Chapter 1, the history, theory, and some of the previous GLOBE findings were discussed. As mentioned, the first phase focused on the development and validation of a set of scales that were needed to test the constructs identified in the GLOBE conceptual model. In all, 21 primary leadership scales, nine dimensions of societal culture, and nine dimensions of organizational culture were assessed. Through two pilot studies, psychometric properties were evaluated for these scales. A complete description of the scale development and validation process is provided in the first major GLOBE book (Hanges & Dickson, 2004). The second phase of GLOBE empirically examined the conceptual model and many of its propositions (House & Javidan, 2004). Specifically, relationships were analyzed between societal and organizational culture on dimensions of culturally endorsed leadership, using the culture and leadership scales developed during Phase 1.

Phase 3, the current phase of the GLOBE project, tests the relationships between observed leadership behaviors of CEOs and societal culturally endorsed implicit leadership theory (CLT) attributes, as well as leadership and organization effectiveness. The purpose of this research is to learn about reported CEOs' behaviors and how they relate to societal expectations (CLTs), as well as the relationship between these behaviors and CEO and firm effectiveness in different societies.

In this chapter, we explain the methodology of this research in terms of sampling and assessment instruments. We describe the steps in identifying the countries in our research, samples of CEOs in each country, the development of constructs, and the scale development process.

Origins of GLOBE Phase 3

The planning of Phase 3 of the GLOBE project began as the data analyses for Phase 2 were being finished in 1998.[1] This new phase is focused on

---

[1]Two preliminary studies conducted during the mid-1990s in Egypt and Hong Kong provided insights into the development of GLOBE Phase 3.

reporting the actual behaviors that are enacted in the top echelon of leadership in organizations. The principal investigator (PI) of the Phase 3 project, Robert J. House, developed this initial idea from field research conducted with CEOs and their top management team (TMT) members in the Silicon Valley (see Delbecq, House, Sully de Luque, & Quigley, 2013, for a full history of the initial development of the current CEO project). With the primary goal of validating the actual effectiveness of leader behaviors that were identified as important in prior GLOBE phases, behavioral-based measures were developed to reflect the CLT attributes found in the 21 primary leadership dimensions. Once the development of these behavioral survey measures was finalized and the preliminary sample identified, GLOBE Phase 3 data-gathering commenced in early 2000. Researchers gathered a majority of these data from 2000 to 2004.[2] The processes for survey development and sample selection are further outlined in this chapter.

Funding for GLOBE Phase 3 was provided by a $350,000 grant from the National Science Foundation (NSF) through the Innovation and Organizational Change Program. The initial sample of scholars that gathered data for their respective countries could request funding to lessen their research expenses. In total, the NSF grant provided direct funding for research in 20 countries of this sample.[3] Moreover, many of the scholars were able to contribute funding for this study through a variety of grants from both local and national institutions. Additionally, several scholars financed their research through personal funds.

Specific Objectives of Phase 3

The primary goal of this research study centers on executive level leadership and its demonstrated effectiveness within and across multiple cultures. As explained in more depth in Chapter 3, the following is an overview of GLOBE Phase 3 objectives:

1. Understanding and empirically measuring the nature and drivers of CEO leadership behavior

2. Understanding and measuring the drivers of CEO leadership effectiveness: the relationship between CEO leadership behavior and effectiveness

3. Understanding and measuring the drivers of CEO leadership effectiveness: the impact of the fit between CEO leadership behavior with CLT

---

[2]The exception was for the data gathered in the U.S. sample, which were primarily gathered from 2004 to 2008.

[3]NSF grant SES-0080705 was awarded in 2000 to the GLOBE Research and Education Foundation, a nonprofit organization created by Robert House.

4. Determining the differential and combined effect of fit and behavior in predicting CEO effectiveness

5. Assessing the leadership distinctions between the high-performing CEOs (i.e., superior) and underperforming CEOs (i.e., inferior)

With these objectives as our guide, we commenced with developing our research methodology for GLOBE Phase 3. Throughout the next few chapters, we will articulate this process, beginning with identifying the samples of interest.

Participating Societies

All researchers involved in Phase 2 of the GLOBE project received a letter of invitation to participate in the current study. The invited sample of 62 societies was considered a convenience sample, because these researchers had been part of the previous research study to which we had access. Of this invited sample, a total of 16 countries completed the data-gathering process for Phase 3.

In addition, we invited scholars from several other countries who had not participated in the previous GLOBE sample. These contacts were made using the current GLOBE network of scholars based on their interest in cross-cultural leadership research and their willingness to provide infrastructure support. An effort was made to invite scholars from both developed and developing economies from every region of the world. A sample from the South Pacific Islands was gathered in an effort to glean information in seldom-studied regions and island cultures. Furthering the sample, several scholars independently contacted the first author requesting to take part in the study. Seven of these new societies completed the data-gathering process.

In total, 24 countries were included in the final data set. Table 4.1 shows the final list of countries that participated in GLOBE Phase 3, as well as the number of firms in each country from which data were gathered.

From this broad sample, a subset of societies overlapped between the GLOBE Phase 2 and Phase 3 samples, allowing comparison for 16 of the original societies. Additionally, two countries that were not a part of the original GLOBE studies, Estonia and Romania, gathered data for both Phase 2 and Phase 3. Thus, we were able to increase our total overlapping sample size to 18 societies across these phases of the project. The comparisons of CLTs with actual leader behavior were conducted using these 18 countries (see Table 4.1). Previously, in Chapter 1, we presented the countries in all GLOBE phases (please see Figure 1.2), with each of these countries placed within their respective regional cluster identified in GLOBE 2004. The countries in Phase 3 are bold in Figure 1.2. As you can see, almost all regions of the world are represented in this new CEO study

Table 4.1   Participating Countries and Number of Firms Per Country

Participating Countries in Phase 3	Number of Firms
Austria	40
Azerbaijan*	40
Brazil	37
China	97
Estonia	49
Fiji*	24
Germany	29
Greece	51
Guatemala	40
India	113
Mexico	42
Netherlands	53
Nigeria	47
Peru*	29
Romania	44
Russia	40
Slovenia	40
Solomon Islands*	20
Spain	35
Taiwan	40
Turkey	39
Tonga*	16
United States	44
Vanuatu*	6
Total number of firms in the study	1,015

Note: * = countries without the House, Hanges, Javidan, Dorfman, and Gupta (2004) culture and CLT data.

presented in this book. While a larger number of countries would be desirable, our current sample offers sufficient sampling of cultures to ensure meaningful tests of our cross-cultural hypotheses. That is, our sample includes countries from 9 out of 10 cultural clusters presented in GLOBE 2004 and therefore includes sufficient variability and diversity of cross-cultural phenomena of interest. Had this been a study of 24 countries representing only a small number of cultural clusters then it would face the limitation of range restriction and would be a biased test of cross-cultural hypotheses. In other words, in an ideal world we would like to obtain data from a large number of countries in all cultural regions. Practically, however, as suggested by Gupta and Hanges (2004, p. 179), it is critical to have as many cultural regions represented as possible.

We received formal correspondence from the country scholars that agreed to participate, indicating that their institutions would be providing infrastructure support for the duration of the GLOBE Phase 3 project. Representing their respective societies, these scholars, or country co-investigators (CCIs) as they are called, were from a variety of disciplines including management, business, economics, psychology, and even other disciplines such as linguistics, English, and political science. Table 4.2 shows information about our CCIs participating and representing the 24 countries in the study.

Table 4.2   Country Co-Investigator Names and Affiliations

Country	Title	Name	Affiliation
Austria			
	Professor	Johannes Steyrer	Vienna University of Economics and Business
Azerbaijan			
	Professor and Senior Research Fellow	Rauf Garagozov	Center for Strategic Studies under the president of the Republic of Azerbaijan
Brazil			
	Professor	Betania Tanure	Pontifícia Universidade Católica (PUC-MG)
	Professor	Roberto Gonzalez Duarte	Federal University of Minas Gerais
China			
	Associate Professor	Ping Ping Fu	Chinese University of Hong Kong
	Professor	Jun Liu	Renmin University
Estonia			
	Professor	Ruth Alas	Estonia Business School
	Professor	Krista Tuulik	Estonian Entrepreneurship University of Applied Sciences
Germany			
	Professor	Rainhart Lang	Chemnitz University of Technology
Greece			
	Professor	Nancy Papalexandris	Athens University of Economics and Business

(Continued)

(Continued)

Country	Title	Name	Affiliation
	Professor	Dimitri Bourantas	Athens University of Economics and Business
Guatemala			
	Assistant Professor	Almarie E. Munley	Regent University
	Research Associate	Boris Martinez	Universidad Francisco Marroquín
India			
	Associate Professor	Sukhendu Debbarma	Tripura University
	Assistant Professor	Rosemary R. Dzuvichu	Nagaland University
	Associate Professor	James Rajasekar	Sultan Qaboos University
	Rector President	Fr. Vattathara M. Thomas	Don Bosco Institute, Guwahati
	Professor	Vipin Gupta	California State University, San Bernadino
	Professor	Kanika T. Bhal	Indian Institute of Technology Delhi
	CEO	Mathai Fenn	The Talk Shop, Bangalore
	Director	Lokanandha Reddy Irala	KKC Group of Institutions, Puttur
	Chairman	S. Pratap Reddy	Dhruva College of Management
	Dean of Management Sciences	Mohamed Basheer Ahmed Khan	Pondicherry University
	President	Hasina Kharbhih	Impulse NGO Network, Shillong
	Associate Professor	Mary Mathew	Indian Institute of Science, Bangalore
	Professor and Director, Business School	Neelu Rohmetra	University of Jammu
	Vice President	Pankaj Saran	EMPI Business School
	Assistant Professor	Dinesh Sharma	Indian Institute of Technology, Bombay
	Fellow	Mrinalini Shrivastava	United Nations, Guinea Bissau
	Visiting Fellow	E S Srinivas	Indian School of Business, Hyderabad

Country	Title	Name	Affiliation
Mexico			
	Associate Professor	Leonel Prieto	Texas A&M International University
	Professor Emeritus	Peter Dorfman	New Mexico State University
	Professor Emeritus	Jon Howell	New Mexico State University
Netherlands			
	Assistant Professor	Annebel H. B. de Hoogh	University of Amsterdam
	Professor	Deanne N. Den Hartog	University of Amsterdam
	Professor Emeritus	P. L. Koopman	Vrije University
	Professor Emeritus	Henk Thierry	Tilburg University
	Assistant Professor	Peter T. van den Berg	Tilburg University
	Professor	Celeste P.M. Wilderom	University of Twente
Nigeria			
	Head, Gender Division	Bolanle Adetoun	Economic Community of West African States Executive Secretariat, Nigeria
Peru			
	President	David Fischman	Fischman and Associates
	Director of Educational Quality	José Agustín Ortiz	Universidad Peruana de Ciencias Aplicadas (UPC)
Romania			
	Professor	Alexandru Catana	Technical University of Cluj-Napoca
	Professor	Doina Catana	Technical University of Cluj-Napoca
Russia			
	Professor	Mikhail Grachev	Western Illinois University
	Assistant Professor	Mariya Bobina	The University of Iowa
Slovenia			
	Professor	Edvard Konrad	University of Ljubljana
	Assistant Professor	Eva Bostjancic	University of Ljubljana

(Continued)

(Continued)

Country	Title	Name	Affiliation
South Pacific: Fiji, Solomon Islands, Tonga, Vanuatu			
	Associate Professor	Anthony R. Paquin	Western Kentucky University
	Associate Professor	Reinout de Vries	Vrije University
	Professor	R. D. Pathak	University of the South Pacific
Spain			
	Professor	Francisco Gil Rodríguez	Universidad Complutense de Madrid
	Professor	Angel Barrasa	University of Zaragoza
	Assistant Professor	Alfredo Rodríguez Muñoz	Universidad Complutense de Madrid
	Assistant Professor	Mirko Antino	Universidad Complutense de Madrid
Taiwan			
	Professor	T.K. Peng	I-Shou University
	Associate Professor	Yi-Jung Chen	National Kaohsiung University of Applied Science
	Associate Professor	Kuen-Yung Jone	Kaohsiung Medical University
	Professor	Cheng-Chen Lin	National Pingtung University of Science and Technology
Turkey			
	Professor	Hayat Kabasakal	Boğaziçi University
	Professor	Muzaffer Bodur	Boğaziçi University
	Assistant Professor	Idil Evcimen	Istanbul Technical University
United States			
	Associate Professor	Mary Sully de Luque	Thunderbird School of Global Management
	Associate Professor	Melody L. Wollan	Eastern Illinois University
	Professor	David Waldman	Arizona State University
	Associate Professor	Nathan Washburn	Thunderbird School of Global Management
	Senior Lecturer	Gary Palin	Elon University
	Associate Professor	Narda Quigley	Villanova University

These CCIs provided direct assistance in the gathering of data in their respective countries. Most of the CCIs were native to the countries of interest. A notable exception to this was the South Pacific region, where a team of researchers coordinated the gathering of data across four island nations. One of the South Pacific region scholars helped gather data while serving in the Peace Corp after having received his PhD. Together, this team of three researchers was able to gather data from four countries and 61 firms in this seldom-researched region.

Participating Firms

Data were gathered from a total of 1,015 firms for the GLOBE Phase 3 study. Table 4.3 displays the overall firm demographics across the 24 participating countries. These descriptions provide an informed overview of the firms participating in this study.

Table 4.3 also shows that across countries, 54.3% of the firms were founder or family owned, with 30.4% investor owned. Overall, just 15.3% of firms reported either being owned by public/private partnership or owned by government. As most companies around the world are privately owned, this sample more closely reflects the type of firm ownership structure observed globally (Baer & Frese, 2003; van Dyck, Frese, Baer, & Sonnentag, 2005).

Table 4.4 provides a detailed percentage breakdown of firm ownership across our sample. In our sample, the country reporting the highest number of founder- or family-owned companies was Turkey with 88.9%, followed by Taiwan with 78.4%. Overall, eight countries reported that at least 60% of their firms were founder or family owned. Fiji reported 72.3% of their firms as investor owned, with Vanuatu (57.1%) and Azerbaijan (52.5%) as the only additional countries reporting more than half their firms as investor

Table 4.3   Overall Ownership of Firms

Ownership of Firms	Overall	
	N*	% n**
Founder/Family owned	485	54.3%
Investor owned	271	30.4%
Government owned	87	9.7%
Public/Private partnership	50	5.6%
Total	893	100.0%

Note: *N = number of organizations completing survey question. ** % n = percentage of organizations across countries.

Table 4.4 Firm Ownership Across Countries

	Overall		Austria		Azerbaijan		Brazil	
	N*		N	% c**	N	% c	N	% c
Founder/Family owned	485		20	51.3%	19	47.5%	16	51.6%
Investor owned	271		14	35.9%	21	52.5%	12	38.7%
Government owned	87		1	2.6%	0	0.0%	0	0.0%
Public/Private partnership	50		4	10.7%	0	0.0%	3	9.7%
Total	893		39	100.0%	40	100.0%	31	100.0%
	China		Estonia		Fiji		Germany	
	N	% c	N	% c	N	% c	N	% c
Founder/Family owned	48	55.2%	18	41.9%	3	27.3%	11	47.3%
Investor owned	2	2.3%	15	34.9%	8	72.3%	10	43.5%
Government owned	29	33.3%	7	16.9%	0	0.0%	2	8.7%
Public/Private partnership	8	9.2%	3	7.0%	0	0.0%	0	0.0%
Total	87	100.0%	43	100.0%	11	100.0%	23	100.0%
	Greece		Guatemala		India		Mexico	
	N	% c	N	% c	N	% c	N	% c
Founder/Family owned	24	50.0%	22	64.7%	44	44.0%	21	58.3%
Investor owned	16	33.3%	10	29.4%	22	22.0%	13	36.1%
Government owned	1	2.1%	0	0.0%	29	29.0%	2	5.6%
Public/Private partnership	7	14.6%	2	5.9%	5	5.0%	0	0.0%
Total	48	100.0%	34	100.0%	100	100.0%	36	100.0%
	Netherlands		Nigeria		Peru		Romania	
	N	% c	N	% c	N	% c	N	% c
Founder/Family owned	30	66.7%	27	62.8%	10	47.6%	18	40.9%
Investors owned	14	31.1%	13	30.2%	10	47.6%	20	45.5%
Government owned	1	2.2%	0	0.0%	0	0.0%	0	0.0%

	Netherlands		Nigeria		Peru		Romania	
	N	% c	N	% c	N	% c	N	% c
Public/Private partnership	0	0.0%	3	7.0%	1	4.8%	6	13.6%
Total	45	100.0%	43	100.0%	21	100.0%	44	100.0%

	Russia		Slovenia		Solomon Islands		Spain	
	N	% c	N	% c	N	% c	N	% c
Founder/Family owned	26	65.0%	15	39.5%	1	7.7%	22	62.9%
Investor owned	12	30.0%	16	42.1%	3	23.1%	13	37.1%
Government owned	0	0.0%	3	7.9%	9	69.2%	0	0.0%
Public/Private partnership	2	5.0%	4	10.5%	0	0.0%	0	0.0%
Total	40	100.0%	38	100.0%	13	100.0%	35	100.0%

	Taiwan		Tonga		Turkey		United States	
	N	% c	N	% c	N	% c	N	% c
Founder/ Family-owned	29	78.4%	1	50.0%	32	88.9%	26	65.0%
Investors-owned	7	18.9%	0	0.0%	3	8.3%	13	32.5%
Government-owned	0	0.0%	1	50.0%	1	2.8%	0	0.0%
Public/private partnership	1	2.7%	0	0.0%	0	0.0%	1	2.5%
Total	37	100.0%	2	100.0%	36	100.0%	40	100.0%

	Vanuatu							
	N	% c						
Founder/Family owned	2	28.6%						
Investor owned	4	57.1%						
Government owned	1	14.3%						
Public/Private partnership	0	0.0%						
Total	7	100.0%						

Note: *N = number of organizations completing survey question. ** % c = percentages of organization responses within country.

owned. Solomon Islands (69.2%) and Tonga (50.0%) showed the highest percentages of government-owned firms; however, these sample sizes are small. For countries with larger sample sizes, China and India indicated the largest percentage of firms owned by the government, with 33.3% and 29.0% reported, respectively.

Table 4.5 indicates the overall age of the firms participating in this study. The table shows that almost half of the firms in this sample have been in existence for at least 20 years or longer (45.6%). Younger firms, which are firms in operation for 10 years or fewer, comprised 31.4% of the companies sampled, with firms in existence for 10 to 19 years making up the balance of the sample (22.9%).

Table 4.6 shows the overall ages of the firms across countries that were included in this study. As displayed in the table, Russia reported that almost all the firms in their sample (90%) were less than 10 years old, as were both firms reported in Vanuatu. The countries indicating the next youngest firm samples are Azerbaijan (87.5%) and China (55.9%). By far, the largest number of countries had firms in their sample in existence for more than two decades. For 14 of the 24 countries included in the study, at least half of their firms had been in operation for at least 20 years. Brazil reported that 84.9% of their firms had been doing business for more than 20 years, with Fiji and the Netherlands reporting 81.8% and 79.1%, respectively. For firms that had been operating for up to two decades, Romania and the Solomon Islands both reported 45.4% of firms in this category, followed by Nigeria with 42.1%. Table 4.6 provides the diverse detail.

Next, Table 4.7 indicates whether the firms are managed either privately or professionally. To determine this, we asked if the founder, members of the founder's family, or two or more partners manage the firm, or alternately if the firm is managed by a hired CEO or hired executive committee. Mentioned previously, the overall column shows that out of the total number of firms, 61.7% utilize private management (i.e., managed by founder,

Table 4.5 Overall Age of Firms

Age of Firms	Overall	
	N*	% n**
Under 10 years	270	31.4%
10 to 19 years	197	22.9%
20 years and more	392	45.6%
Total	859	100.0%

Note: * N = number of organizations completing survey question. ** % n = percentage of organizations across countries.

Table 4.6   Age of Firms Across Countries

	Overall		Austria		Azerbaijan		Brazil		China	
	*N**		*N*	% c**	*N*	% c	*N*	% c	*N*	% c
Under 10 years	270		10	25.0%	35	87.5%	4	12.1%	47	55.9%
10 to 19 years	197		8	20.0%	4	10.0%	1	3.0%	18	21.4%
20 years or more	392		22	55.0%	1	2.50%	28	84.9%	19	22.6%
Total	859		40	100.0%	40	100.0%	33	100.0%	84	100.0%

	Estonia		Fiji		Germany		Greece		Guatemala	
	N	% c	*N*	% c	*N*	% c	*N*	% c	*N*	% c
Under 10 years	19	44.2%	2	18.2%	11	39.3%	9	18.7%	6	17.1%
10 to 19 years	15	34.9%	0	0.0%	9	32.14%	13	27.1%	4	11.4%
20 years or more	9	20.9%	9	81.8%	8	28.6%	26	54.2%	25	71.4%
Total	43	100.0%	11	100.0%	28	100.0%	48	100.0%	35	100.0%

	India		Mexico		Netherlands		Nigeria		Peru	
	N	% c	*N*	% c	*N*	% c	*N*	% c	*N*	% c
Under 10 years	15	20.5%	4	10.8%	2	4.6%	14	36.8%	9	37.5%
10 to 19 years	12	16.4%	6	16.2%	7	16.3%	16	42.1%	2	8.3%
20 years or more	46	63.0%	27	73.0%	34	79.1%	8	21.0%	13	54.2%
Total	73	100.0%	37	100.0%	43	100.0%	38	100.0%	24	100.0%

	Romania		Russia		Slovenia		Solomon Islands		Spain	
	N	% c	*N*	% c	*N*	% c	*N*	% c	*N*	% c
Under 10 years	8	18.2%	36	90.0%	12	31.6%	1	9.1%	4	11.8%
10 to 19 years	20	45.4%	4	10.0%	12	31.6%	5	45.4%	11	32.3%
20 years or more	16	36.4%	0	0.0%	14	36.8%	5	45.4%	19	55.9%
Total	44	100.0%	40	100.0%	38	100.0%	11	100.0%	34	100.0%

(Continued)

(Continued)

	Taiwan		Tonga		Turkey		United States		Vanuatu	
	N	% c	N	% c	N	% c	N	% c	N	% c
Under 10 years	10	27.8%	0	0.0%	3	9.1%	7	16.3%	2	100.0%
10 to 19 years	14	38.9%	0	0.0%	10	30.3%	6	13.9%	0	0.0%
20 years or more	12	33.3%	1	100.0%	20	60.6%	30	69.8%	0	0.0%
Total	36	100.0%	1	100.0%	33	100.0%	43	100.0%	2	100.0%

Note: *N = number of organizations completing survey question. ** % c = percentage of organization responses across countries.

the family of the founder, or two or more partners) and, further, 38.3% use professional management (i.e., hired CEO or hired executive committee). In all, 17 of the 24 countries reported that more than half of their firms employed private management. Perhaps this percentage is not surprising because the majorities of the firms in the study are privately owned and thus may tend to have the founder or founder's family at the management helm.

Table 4.8 reports the management of the firms across the 24 countries. This table shows that India has the largest number of privately managed firms (86.8%) followed by Taiwan (83.8%). Four countries (Turkey, Azerbaijan, Russia, and the United States) reported that at least 75% of their firms were privately managed. However, several countries sampled showed a higher employment of professional managers. Slovenia reported a higher employment of professional management (80.0%), followed by Estonia (72.3%). All combined, the countries of Fiji, Solomon Islands, Tonga, and Vanuatu reported greater use of professional managers with an overall South Pacific mean of 72%.

Table 4.7   Overall Management of Firms

Management of Firms	Overall	
	N*	% n**
Privately managed	492	61.7%
Professionally managed	305	38.3%
Total	797	100.0%

Note: *N = number of organizations completing survey question. ** % n = percentage of organizations across countries.

Table 4.8   Management of the Firm

	Overall		Austria		Azerbaijan		Brazil		China	
	N*		N	% C**	N	% c	N	% c	N	% c
Privately managed	492		21	52.5%	31	77.5%	16	53.3%	54	63.5%
Professionally managed	305		19	47.5%	9	22.5%	14	46.7%	31	36.5%
Total	797		40	100.0%	40	100.0%	30	100.0%	85	100.0%
	Estonia		Fiji		Germany		Greece		Guatemala	
	N	% c	N	% C	N	% c	N	% c	N	% c
Privately managed	10	27.0%	4	40.0%	12	50.0%	24	55.8%	18	64.3%
Professionally managed	27	73.0%	6	60.0%	12	50.0%	19	44.2%	10	35.7%
Total	37	100.0%	10	100.0%	24	100.0%	43	100.0%	28	100.0%
	India		Mexico		Netherlands		Nigeria		Peru	
	N	% c	N	% C	N	% c	N	% c	N	% c
Privately managed	79	86.8%	20	64.5%	22	61.1%	23	69.7%	10	55.6%
Professionally managed	12	13.2%	11	35.5%	14	38.9%	10	30.3%	8	44.4%
Total	91	100.0%	31	100.0%	36	100.0%	33	100.0%	18	100.0%
	Romania		Russia		Slovenia		Solomon Islands		Spain	
	N	% c	N	% C	N	% c	N	% c	N	% c
Privately managed	18	41.9%	30	75.0%	6	20.0%	2	18.2%	19	63.3%
Professionally managed	25	58.1%	10	25.0%	24	80.0%	9	81.8%	11	36.7%
Total	43	100.0%	40	100.0%	30	100.0%	11	100.0%	30	100.0%
	Taiwan		Tonga		Turkey		United States		Vanuatu	
	N	% c	N	% C	N	% c	N	% c	N	% c
Privately managed	31	83.8%	0	0.0%	22	78.6%	18	75.0%	2	28.6%
Professionally managed	6	16.2%	1	100.0%	6	21.4%	6	25.0%	5	71.4%
Total	37	100.0%	1	100.0%	28	100.0%	24	100.0%	7	100.0%

Note: *N = number of organizations completing survey question. ** % c = percentage of organization responses across countries.

In our sample of firms, Table 4.9 shows the overall major outputs of the organization, either products or services. We show an overall greater percentage of service output firms (42.6%) across the sample. However, we see an almost equal representation overall of product output firms (29.8%) with firms that have outputs, which are a combination of both products and services (27.6%). Although the overall sample of firms reflects a larger number of firms involved in services, there are diverse distributions of product and service firms throughout the countries.

Across the countries in our sample, Table 4.10 reports the overall output of the firms: products, services, or a combination of products and services. The distribution of products, services, or a combination of both shows variability across the overall sample of countries, with countries such as Turkey reporting firms producing more products (63.6%), other countries such as Peru with firms producing more services (60.0%), and still other countries such as Azerbaijan with a majority of firms producing both products and services (47.5%). The detailed table shows the country of Guatemala has a majority of firms that produce products (40.6%) and services (56.2%) but not both (3.1%). On the other hand, Russia reports that a majority of their firms are engaged in services (52.5%) and some firms with outputs of products and services (37.5%) but few firms with product outputs (10.0%).

Finally, Table 4.11 shows the overall percentage of total revenue generated by exports across firms in the sample. For those that reported revenues from exports, 81.6% of the firms engaged in domestically oriented activity, which is defined as having below 40.0% of revenue generated by exports. The table shows that 11.5% of the overall firms reported to be export dominated, which is defined as having 60.0% or more export-generated activity. Firms reporting balanced revenue generated by exports (between 40.0% and 60.0%) represented only 6.9% of this sample. For those firms reporting revenue by exports, clearly they generated most of their revenue domestically.

Table 4.9 Overall Firm Output: Products and Services

Firm Output: Products and Services	Overall	
	N*	% n**
Products	238	29.8%
Services	340	42.6%
Products and services	220	27.6%
Total	798	100.0%

Note: *N = number of organizations completing survey question. ** % n = percentage of organizations across countries.

Table 4.10   Organizational Output Across Countries: Products or Services

	Overall		Austria		Azerbaijan		Brazil		China	
	*N**		*N*	% c**	*N*	% c	*N*	% c	*N*	% c
Products	238		9	22.5%	6	15.0%	8	25.8%	29	34.9%
Services	340		18	45.0%	15	37.5%	12	38.7%	24	28.9%
Products and Services	220		13	32.5%	19	47.5%	11	35.5%	30	36.1%
Total	**798**		40	100.0%	40	100.0%	31	100.0%	83	100.0%
	Estonia		Fiji		Germany		Greece		Guatemala	
	N	% c	*N*	% c	*N*	% c	*N*	% c	*N*	% c
Products	5	16.7%	2	18.2%	11	42.3%	16	34.8%	13	40.6%
Services	14	46.7%	6	54.5%	7	26.9%	26	56.5%	18	56.2%
Products and Services	11	36.7%	3	27.3%	8	30.8%	4	8.7%	1	3.1%
Total	30	100.0%	11	100.0%	26	100.0%	46	100.0%	32	100.0%
	India		Mexico		Netherlands		Nigeria		Peru	
	N	% c	*N*	% c	*N*	% c	*N*	% c	*N*	% c
Products	19	31.7%	15	40.5%	11	27.5%	5	13.9%	5	25.0%
Services	28	46.7%	15	40.5%	21	52.5%	20	55.6%	12	60.0%
Products and Services	13	21.7%	7	18.9%	8	20.0%	11	30.6%	3	15.0%
Total	60	100.0%	37	100.0%	40	100.0%	36	100.0%	20	100.0%
	Romania		Russia		Slovenia		Solomon Islands		Spain	
	N	% c	*N*	% c	*N*	% c	*N*	% c	*N*	% c
Products	15	34.1%	4	10.0%	10	33.3%	1	11.1%	9	26.5%
Services	10	22.7%	21	52.5%	14	46.7%	6	66.7%	20	58.8%
Products and Services	19	43.2%	15	37.5%	6	20.0%	2	22.2%	5	14.7%
Total	44	100.0%	40	100.0%	30	100.0%	9	100.0%	34	100.0%

(Continued)

(Continued)

	Taiwan		Tonga		Turkey		United States		Vanuatu	
	N	% c	N	% c	N	% c	N	% c	N	% c
Products	16	42.1%	0	0.0%	21	63.6%	8	26.7%	0	0.0%
Services	8	21.0%	1	100.0%	4	12.1%	15	50.0%	5	71.4%
Products and Services	14	36.8%	0	0.0%	8	24.2%	7	23.3%	2	28.6%
Total	38	100.0%	1	100.0%	33	100.0%	30	100.0%	7	100.0%

Note: *N = number of organizations completing survey question. ** % c = percentage of organization responses within country.

Table 4.11 Firms' Total Revenue From Exports

	Overall	
Firms' Total Revenue from Exports	*N**	*% n***
Domestically oriented (below 40%)	475	81.6%
Balanced (40% to 60%)	40	6.9%
Export dominated (above 60%)	67	11.5%
Total	582	100.0%

Note: *N = number of organizations completing survey question. ** % n = percentage of organizations across countries.

Table 4.12 shows the percentage of total revenue generated by exports across firms in each of the 24 countries. The table shows several issues worth mentioning related to revenue generated by exports. First, we need to note that overall a number of firms in the sample did not report their data for this question. This may be a question that our TMT respondents believed too sensitive to report. Although it was stressed that all information would be strictly confidential, some respondents may not have been comfortable providing this information. Given that most of the firms in our sample were not publicly traded, this type of data may be considered competitive intelligence. That said, the majority of firms responding to this query indicated that they are domestically oriented firms. Thirteen of the 24 countries in this sample reporting revenue generated from exports (again, defined as having below 40% of revenue generated by exports) had at least 80% in predominantly domestically oriented activity. China and the Solomon Islands led the way with all of their sample firms generating revenues domestically. India (98.6%), Azerbaijan (97.5%), the United States (96.3%), and Brazil (96.0%) had firm samples that were mainly domestically focused. Further, Turkey was one of the few countries with their firms reported to be export dominated (again, defined as having 60.0% or more export generated activity) with 62.5%.

Table 4.12 Firms' Total Revenue From Exports

	Overall		Austria		Azerbaijan		Brazil		China	
	N*		*N*	% *c***	*N*	% *c*	*N*	% *c*	*N*	% *c*
Domestically oriented (< 40%)	475		15	48.4%	39	97.5%	24	96.0%	40	100.0%
Balanced (40% to 60%)	40		7	22.6%	1	2.5%	1	4.0%	0	0.0%
Export dominated (> 60%)	67		9	29.0%	0	0.0%	0	0.0%	0	0.0%
Total surveys completed	**582**		31	100.0%	40	100.0%	25	100.0%	40	100.0%
	Estonia		Fiji		Germany		Greece		Guatemala	
	N	% *c*	*N*	% *c*	*N*	% *c*	*N*	% *c*	*N*	% *c*
Domestically oriented (< 40%)	29	87.9%	11	100.0%	16	69.6%	29	93.5%	11	64.7%
Balanced (40% to 60%)	3	9.1%	0	0.0%	4	17.4%	1	3.2%	3	17.6%
Export dominated (> 60%)	1	3.0%	0	0.0%	3	13.0%	1	3.2%	3	17.6%
Total surveys completed	33	100.0%	11	100.0%	23	100.0%	31	100.0%	17	100.0%
	India		Mexico		Netherlands		Nigeria		Peru	
	N	% *c*	*N*	% *c*	*N*	% *c*	*N*	% *c*	*N*	% *c*
Domestically oriented (< 40%)	71	98.6%	29	76.3%	15	75.0%	9	81.8%	12	80.0%
Balanced (40% to 60%)	1	1.4%	4	10.5%	3	15.0%	2	18.2%	1	6.7%

(Continued)

(Continued)

	India		Mexico		Netherlands		Nigeria		Peru	
	N	% c	N	% c	N	% c	N	% c	N	% c
Export dominated (> 60%)	0	0.0%	5	13.2%	2	10.0%	0	0.0%	2	13.3%
Total surveys completed	72	100.0%	38	100.0%	20	100.0%	11	100.0%	15	100.0%

	Romania		Russia		Slovenia		Solomon Islands		Spain	
	N	% c	N	% c	N	% c	N	% c	N	% c
Domestically oriented (< 40%)	19	82.6%	5	62.5%	20	69.0%	11	100.0%	8	53.3%
Balanced (40% to 60%)	0	0.0%	0	0.0%	4	13.8%	0	0.0%	3	20.0%
Export dominated (> 60%)	4	17.4%	3	37.5%	5	17.2%	0	0.0%	4	26.7%
Total surveys completed	23	100.0%	8	100.0%	29	100.0%	11	100.0%	15	100.0%

	Taiwan		Tonga		Turkey		United States		Vanuatu	
	N	% c	N	% c	N	% c	N	% c	N	% c
Domestically oriented (< 40%)	17	77.3%	1	100.0%	11	34.4%	26	96.3%	7	100.0%
Balanced (40% to 60%)	1	4.5%	0	0.0%	1	3.1%	0	0.0%	0	0.0%
Export dominated (> 60%)	4	18.2%	0	0.0%	20	62.5%	1	3.7%	0	0.0%
Total surveys completed	22	100.0%	1	100.0%	32	100.0%	27	100.0%	7	100.0%

Note: *N = number of organizations completing survey question. ** % c = percentage of organization responses within country.

Table 4.13 shows that overall the participating firms represented a variety of industries. To categorize the industries in the sample, we used an industry standard classification, the North American Industry Classification System (NAICS). This classification system provided broad categories into which diverse industries can be grouped, such as manufacturing (i.e., electrical equipment, appliance and component manufacturing, and chemical manufacturing), retail trade (i.e., electronics and appliance stores; motor vehicle and parts dealers), finance and insurance (i.e., credit intermediation and related activities), and construction (i.e., industries in building, developing, and general contracting). Comprising 68.8% of the overall firm sample, the top five industry sectors are manufacturing (38.9%), retail trade (8.9%), finance and insurance (7.7%), information (7.4%), and wholesale trade (5.9%). Clearly, the manufacturing sector has the largest representation of industries in this study. The bottom five industry sectors that represent just 3.8% of our sample are (1) public administration (1.2%), (2) administrative, support, waste management, and remediation services (1.1%), (3) mining (1.0%), (4) utilities (0.4%), and (5) management of companies and enterprises (0.1%).

Table 4.13   Industry Sectors Overall

Industry Sector	N*	% n**
• Manufacturing	325	38.9%
• Retail trade	74	8.9%
• Finance and insurance	64	7.7%
• Information	62	7.4%
• Wholesale trade	49	5.9%
• Construction	39	4.7%
• Professional, scientific, and technical services	36	4.3%
• Accommodation and food services	32	3.8%
• Transportation and warehousing	32	3.8%
• Health care and social assistance	22	2.6%
• Arts, entertainment, and recreation	17	2.0%
• Real estate and rental and leasing	15	1.8%
• Educational services	14	1.7%
• Agriculture, forestry, fishing, and hunting	13	1.6%
• Other services (except public administration)	11	1.3%
• Public administration	10	1.2%
• Administrative, support, waste management, and remediation services	9	1.1%
• Mining	8	1.0%
• Utilities	3	0.4%
• Management of companies and enterprises	1	0.1%
Total	836	100.0%

Note: *N = number of organizations completing survey question. ** % n = percentage of organizations across countries.

In Table 4.14, we show the percentage of industries in each of the 20 sectors for each country reporting industry information. The table shows Turkey reporting that the vast majority of firms in their sample (89.7%) were in manufacturing, with few other sector industries represented in the sample. The countries of Germany (65.5%) and Taiwan (65.0%) reported the next highest percentage of manufacturing firms surveyed. The country having the fewest number of manufacturing firms sampled was Nigeria (10.6%). Among the countries showing greater diversity of industry sectors include Estonia, India, and the United States.

Table 4.14   Types of Industries Overall and By Country

Industry Sector	Total^ N*	Total^ % n**	Azerbaijan N	Azerbaijan % c***	Brazil N	Brazil % c	China N	China % c
—Accommodation and food services	32	3.8%			1	2.8%	6	6.4%
—Administrative, support, waste management, and remediation services	9	1.1%					1	1.1%
—Agriculture, forestry, fishing, and hunting	13	1.6%					1	1.1%
—Arts, entertainment, and recreation	17	2.0%					2	2.1%
—Construction	39	4.7%	2	5.0%	7	19.4%	5	5.3%
—Educational services	14	1.7%						
—Finance and insurance	64	7.7%	1	2.5%	3	8.3%		
—Health care and social assistance	22	2.6%			3	8.3%		
—Information	62	7.4%	9	22.5%	3	8.3%	1	1.1%
—Management of companies and enterprises	1	0.1%						
—Manufacturing	325	38.9%	11	27.5%	14	38.9%	46	48.9%
—Mining	8	1.0%					1	1.1%
—Other services (except public administration)	11	1.3%					3	3.2%
—Professional, scientific, and technical services	36	4.3%	2	5.0%	1	2.8%	4	4.3%
—Public administration	10	1.2%					1	1.1%
—Real estate and rental and leasing	15	1.8%					2	2.1%

Industry Sector	Total^		Azerbaijan		Brazil		China	
	N^*	$\% n^{**}$	N	$\% c^{***}$	N	$\% c$	N	$\% c$
—Retail trade	74	8.9%	8	20.0%	1	2.8%	10	10.6%
—Transportation and warehousing	32	3.8%	2	5.0%	2	5.6%		
—Utilities	3	0.4%						
—Wholesale trade	49	5.9%	5	12.5%	1	2.8%	11	11.7%
Total	836	100.0%	40	100.0%	36	100.0%	94	100.0%

Industry Sector	Estonia		Germany		Greece		Guatemala	
	N	$\% c$	N	$\% c$	N	$\% c$	N	$\% c$
—Accommodation and food services	3	7.0%			3	5.9%	2	5.1%
—Administrative, support, waste management, and remediation services	2	4.7%						
—Agriculture, forestry, fishing, and hunting								
—Arts, entertainment, and recreation	2	4.7%						
—Construction	1	2.3%	2	6.9%	1	2.0%	2	5.1%
—Educational services	1	2.3%	1	3.4%				
—Finance and insurance	3	7.0%	1	3.4%	11	21.6%	1	2.6%
—Health care and social assistance	1	2.3%	1	3.4%	1	2.0%		
—Information	1	2.3%	4	13.8%	7	13.7%		
—Management of companies and enterprises								
—Manufacturing	9	20.9%	19	65.5%	12	23.5%	18	46.2%
—Mining								
—Other services (except public administration)							1	2.6%
—Professional, scientific, and technical services					3	5.9%	2	5.1%
—Public administration	2	4.7%						
—Real estate and rental and leasing	1	2.3%			1	2.0%	1	2.6%
—Retail trade	5	11.6%	1	3.4%	8	15.7%	4	10.3%

(Continued)

(Continued)

Industry Sector	Estonia N	Estonia % c	Germany N	Germany % c	Greece N	Greece % c	Guatemala N	Guatemala % c
—Transportation and warehousing	6	14.0%			1	2.0%	2	5.1%
—Utilities							1	2.6%
—Wholesale trade	6	14.0%			3	5.9%	5	12.8%
Total	43	100.0%	29	100.0%	51	100.0%	39	100.0%

Industry Sector	India N	India % c	Mexico N	Mexico % c	Netherlands N	Netherlands % c	Nigeria N	Nigeria % c
—Accommodation and food services	3	4.5%	1	3.2%			8	17.0%
—Administrative, support, waste management, and remediation services					1	1.9%		
—Agriculture, forestry, fishing, and hunting	5	7.5%	1	3.2%			2	4.3%
—Arts, entertainment, and recreation	2	3.0%	1	3.2%	2	3.8%		
—Construction	1	1.5%			6	11.3%	1	2.1%
—Educational services	4	6.0%	1	3.2%			3	6.4%
—Finance and insurance	7	10.4%	1	3.2%			11	23.4%
—Health care and social assistance	3	4.5%			3	5.7%	3	6.4%
—Information	7	10.4%	1	3.2%	7	13.2%	4	8.5%
—Management of companies and enterprises	1	1.5%						
—Manufacturing	21	31.3%	18	58.1%	10	18.9%	5	10.6%
—Mining	1	1.5%						
—Other services (except public administration)					4	7.5%		
—Professional, scientific, and technical services	1	1.5%			4	7.5%	3	6.4%
—Public administration	4	6.0%			1	1.9%		
—Real estate and rental and leasing			1	3.2%	2	3.8%		
—Retail trade	4	6.0%	4	12.9%	5	9.4%	2	4.3%
—Transportation and warehousing	2	3.0%	2	6.5%	7	13.2%	5	10.6%

Industry Sector	India N	India % c	Mexico N	Mexico % c	Netherlands N	Netherlands % c	Nigeria N	Nigeria % c
—Utilities	1	1.5%						
—Wholesale trade					1	1.9%		
Total	67	100.0%	31	100.0%	53	100.0%	47	100.0%

Industry Sector	Peru N	Peru % c	Romania N	Romania % c	Russia N	Russia % c	Slovenia N	Slovenia % c
—Accommodation and food services					1	2.5%		
—Administrative, support, waste management, and remediation services							1	2.5%
—Agriculture, forestry, fishing, and hunting			1	2.3%				
—Arts, entertainment, and recreation							2	5.0%
—Construction	1	3.6%	6	13.6%	1	2.5%		
—Educational services					1	2.5%		
—Finance and insurance	5	17.9%	3	6.8%	5	12.5%	3	7.5%
—Health care and social assistance			1	2.3%	1	2.5%		
—Information	2	7.1%	2	4.5%	2	5.0%	4	10.0%
—Management of companies and enterprises								
—Manufacturing	6	21.4%	24	54.5%	16	40.0%	13	32.5%
—Mining	3	10.7%	3	6.8%				
—Other services (except public administration)	1	3.6%					1	2.5%
—Professional, scientific, and technical services	1	3.6%			3	7.5%	2	5.0%
—Public administration							1	2.5%
—Real estate and rental and leasing	1	3.6%			4	10.0%	1	2.5%
—Retail trade	8	28.6%	2	4.5%	3	7.5%	3	7.5%
—Transportation and warehousing			1	2.3%	1	2.5%		
—Utilities								

(Continued)

(Continued)

Industry Sector	Peru		Romania		Russia		Slovenia	
	N	% c	N	% c	N	% c	N	% c
—Wholesale trade			1	2.3%	2	5.0%	9	22.5%
Total	28	100.0%	44	100.0%	40	100.0%	40	100.0%

Industry Sector	Spain		Taiwan		Turkey		United States	
	N	% c	N	% c	N	% c	N	% c
—Accommodation and food services			1	2.5%			3	7.3%
—Administrative, support, waste management, and remediation services	1	2.9%					3	7.3%
—Agriculture, forestry, fishing, and hunting					3	7.7%		
—Arts, entertainment, and recreation	3	8.8%	2	5.0%			1	2.4%
—Construction			1	2.5%	1	2.6%	1	2.4%
—Educational services	2	5.9%	1	2.5%				
—Finance and insurance	3	8.8%	1	2.5%			5	12.2%
—Health care and social assistance	1	2.9%	2	5.0%			2	4.9%
—Information	4	11.8%	1	2.5%			3	7.3%
—Management of companies and enterprises								
—Manufacturing	13	38.2%	26	65.0%	35	89.7%	9	22.0%
—Mining								
—Other services (except public administration)							1	2.4%
—Professional, scientific, and technical services	6	17.6%	1	2.5%			3	7.3%
—Public administration			1	2.5%				
—Real estate and rental and leasing							1	2.4%
—Retail trade	1	2.9%	1	2.5%			4	9.8%
—Transportation and warehousing							1	2.4%
—Utilities							1	2.4%
—Wholesale trade			2	5.0%			3	7.3%
Total	34	100.0%	40	100.0%	39	100.0%	41	100.0%

Note: *N = number of organizations completing survey question. ** % n = percentage of organization responses across countries. *** % c = percentage of organization responses within country. ^ = industry sector information was not available for samples Austria, Fiji, Solomon Islands, Tonga, and Vanuatu.

Research Design

GLOBE Phase 3 CCIs were asked to obtain data from approximately 40 firms in their respective society. Using a stratified sampling strategy, we incorporated three different strata in our study (i.e., top management team [TMT] members, CEOs, and societies). Specifically, our Phase 3 sampling strategy required that data from each participating country meet the following criteria: (1) one group of respondents was CEOs, (2) half of the organizations were led by entrepreneurs and half were led by nonentrepreneur CEOs, and (3) at least six TMT members reporting directly to the firm's CEO needed to be surveyed from each firm.

Survey Procedures

A multiple survey and respondent approach was used to gather the data. First, the CCI contacted the respective firm CEO to set up an interview. The semistructured interviews conducted by the CCI averaged 60 to 90 minutes in length and covered a variety of topics related to the CEOs' leadership actions, strategic vision, organizational practices and their effectiveness, and firm competitive performance. At the conclusion of the interview, the CCI requested a list of names of members of the TMT or the immediate subordinates of the CEO (i.e., directly reporting subordinates and advisers). Generally, it was the CEO's administrative assistant who provided this list of names directly to the CCI. From this list of names, each CCI randomly assigned nine TMT members into three groups, each of which would receive three separate survey questionnaires.

Three separate forms of surveys were used in this study: Two surveys focused on leadership behavior, and one survey focused on both organization demographics and external firm performance. All three surveys had measures of internal TMT member performance. The two leadership-focused surveys were given to two separate groups of TMT members, with the various leadership behavior question items divided between the questionnaires. These leadership-focused surveys were developed based on the CLT dimensions found in the GLOBE Phases 1 and 2 research studies. The third survey, focused on organization processes and demographics as well as firm performance, was given to another group of TMT members. This third group of TMT members was selected because they had knowledge of, or access to, organizational performance information (i.e., finance and/or accounting) (see Figure 4.1).

Survey items were purposefully distributed across three distinct surveys for several reasons. First, we were concerned about the overall length of the surveys. Distributing the items across the three survey versions reduced the burden on our respondents. Second, the various TMT members had unique skill sets and information. Having three versions of the survey enabled us to include extra questions that were targeted to

Figure 4.1   Overview of Survey and Distribution Design in Phase 3

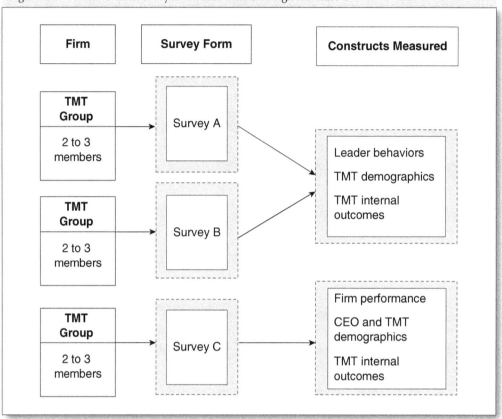

respondents (e.g., firm financial outcomes) based upon their specialized knowledge. Third, splitting the items across multiple survey versions allowed us to reduce same-source bias in our experimental design. It should be noted that we reduced same-source bias across measures as well as within measures (i.e., scale items were split between two different surveys for most leadership constructs). These methodological decisions were made by the first author of this volume and were informed by a series of pilot studies conducted earlier.[4]

More specifically, it was clear that a large number of items would be needed to measure the 21 CLT leadership behaviors as well as demographic and firm performance. Therefore, the decision was made that the leadership behavior items would be randomly split across two surveys (Survey A and Survey B). This design choice, as previously noted, reduced the influence of same-source bias in the measurement of CEO leadership

---

[4]These early studies were conducted in Egypt and Hong Kong, respectively. We would like to thank Irene Chow and her Hong Kong team as well as Aly Messallam and his Egypt team for their work that helped inform the current study.

behavior, which is often problematic in survey research (Podsakoff, MacKenzie, Jeong-Yeon, & Podsakoff, 2003). The third survey (Survey C) was designed to measure firm demographic variables as well as firm financial performance and other outcome measures. Thus, distributing our items among three versions of the survey accomplished our methodological goals. (We provide further detail regarding the development of these survey instruments and items in the next sections.) Figure 4.2 illustrates how these surveys were designed and distributed with respect to the focal content and assessment of key measures.[5]

CCIs were instructed to administer three survey forms to three separate groups of TMT members and to attain at least two of the three respondents for each survey. Thus, three randomly selected TMT members, who are subordinates of a respective CEO, were asked to complete the GLOBE Phase 3 Survey A, and three additional randomly selected TMT members were asked to complete GLOBE Phase 3 Survey B. These two survey questionnaire forms contained multiple survey items written to assess CEO behaviors related to each of the 21 primary CLT dimensions. Also included in these two surveys were items measuring internal performance outcomes, as well as TMT demographic information.

Figure 4.2   Model of Survey Design Process

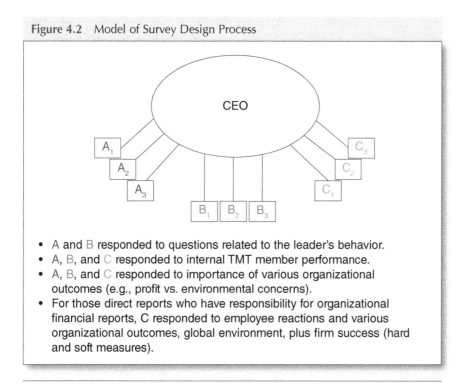

- A and B responded to questions related to the leader's behavior.
- A, B, and C responded to internal TMT member performance.
- A, B, and C responded to importance of various organizational outcomes (e.g., profit vs. environmental concerns).
- For those direct reports who have responsibility for organizational financial reports, C responded to employee reactions and various organizational outcomes, global environment, plus firm success (hard and soft measures).

[5]Earlier versions of this figure were presented in research by House, Dorfman, Sully de Luque, Hanges, & Javidan (2010), and Ashford, Sully de Luque, Wollan, Wellman, & DeStobbelier (2011).

Furthermore, a third survey questionnaire form was given to three additional TMT members to complete. This group of individuals tended to be somewhat different from the first groups of managers who were assigned the leadership surveys (Survey A and Survey B). This last group of TMT respondents was selected for their knowledge about the firm's strategy formulation process, environment, and economic performance. Within the GLOBE Phase 3 Survey C, items were included to assess organization processes and demographics, as well as external firm performance. Similar to the other two leadership-focused survey questionnaires, this third survey form included items assessing internal performance outcomes and TMT demographic information.

Once the TMT members' names were divided into the three groups receiving the different surveys, CCIs contacted the respondents to inform them that surveys would be arriving for them to complete. CCIs were asked to identify each questionnaire with a unique four-digit number before being sent to the TMT member, beginning with 0001 for the first organization, not using the same code twice. This four-digit code served as an identifier for each firm and to ensure confidentiality. Because all respondents were promised confidentially, no personal individual-level or firm-level identifying information was retained once the surveys were received (i.e., names of people or companies). Figure 4.3 depicts a mapping of the leadership dimension to the creation of a leadership behavior item.

TMT members are typically quite busy, so follow-up correspondence was required in many cases. Commonly, CCIs would need to follow up with TMT members via phone or e-mail if they had not received surveys back after 1 month. The time taken for completed surveys to be returned varied widely, ranging from several weeks to many months and sometimes over a year. CCIs would often be required to send a survey more than once. In cases where it seems that the TMT member would not be returning the survey, CCIs were urged to select a different name from the list of TMT members or contact the CEO to get another TMT name. As such, CCIs were encouraged to contact additional CEOs to repeat this process when necessary, to reach a proper sample size of 40 firms per country.

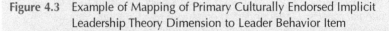

Figure 4.3   Example of Mapping of Primary Culturally Endorsed Implicit Leadership Theory Dimension to Leader Behavior Item

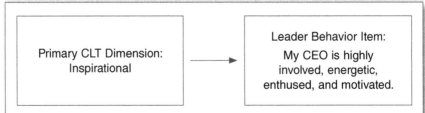

Primary CLT Dimension: Inspirational → Leader Behavior Item: My CEO is highly involved, energetic, enthused, and motivated.

Translation and Back-Translation Process

Potential misunderstandings and discrepancies about the meaning of items and constructs are among the most challenging problems for cross-cultural researchers. A translation and back-translation procedure was used to ensure that the conceptual intent was maintained in the translation of the questionnaires (Brislin, 1980). All surveys were first written in English and then translated by a bilingual speaker into the native language of the participating country. Following this, these surveys were back-translated into English by a separate bilingual scholar. All back-translated surveys were reviewed to check for accuracy of the item intent. When translation discrepancies were uncovered, CCIs were consulted and adjustments made to the translation in question, with follow-up discussion engaged if needed. Most discrepancies were resolved after the initial iteration. However, with more complex translation issues, the consultation between the CCI and GLOBE team researcher could entail several iterations before an accurate translation was attained.

All Phase 3 survey instruments were back-translated into the predominant nation language in countries where English was not the dominant language. Thus, the three survey instruments (Survey A, Survey B, and Survey C) were translated into 13 languages. Table 4.15 displays the language into which these surveys translated. For survey translations, those interested may contact the CCIs in the respective country to request translations.

Data Collection

Table 4.16 shows the guidelines of the data collection that were given to the CCIs as they prepared for the data collection process. Although we anticipated that the data collection process would take around a year to complete, the entire data collection process per country frequently took between 1 and 2 years to complete and sometimes longer.

Table 4.15 Survey Language Translations

Azerbaijani	Portuguese
Dutch	Romanian
English	Russian
Estonian	Slovenian
German	Spanish (4 versions)
Greek	Turkish
Mandarin	

Table 4.16   Guidelines of Data Collection Process for Country Co-Investigators

Step	Key Activities
1	• Back-translate the questionnaire, if required. • Return to PI to check translation. • CCIs may include additional items to supplement their own research (these are added to end of questionnaire).
2	• Develop list of potential CEOs to participate in the study.
3	• Contact CEOs to arrange appointments (this can take weeks or months if rescheduling is required).
4	• During interviews with CEOs, names of TMT members or immediate subordinates of CEOs (e.g., advisers, key personnel) are collected.
5	• Randomly select six TMT members or immediate subordinates of the CEO; assign three TMT members the GLOBE Phase 3 Survey A and the other three TMT members the GLOBE Phase 3 Survey B.
6	• Randomly select three TMT members or other executives knowledgeable about firm's strategic processes and economic performance. • Assign this group the GLOBE Phase 3 Survey C (these respondents need to be different from the other two groups of managers assigned the abovementioned surveys).
7	• Contact TMT members to notify them that they will be receiving surveys to complete; answer any questions TMT members may have about completion of surveys (e.g., they often want assurance that survey responses are confidential).
8	• Identify each questionnaire with a unique number before sending it out, and keep the name of company for each of these on file (i.e., identifier list).
9	• Prepare surveys to send to TMT members. • CCIs can deliver surveys to the firm—or more often, surveys will be mailed. • Arrange for proper postage—include self-addressed envelopes for TMT members to return completed surveys (make it as simple as possible for TMT members to participate).
10	• As completed surveys are returned, data is entered into file provided by PI. • Surveys are tracked to their corresponding firms using identifier codes.
11	• At least two TMT members' responses are required for each of the three surveys. • A follow-up phone call or e-mail is sent if completed surveys are not returned after 1 month from when they were sent to TMT members. • Sometimes it can take months to receive surveys, and surveys may need to be sent more than once to TMT members. • In cases where it is unlikely that a TMT is going to return completed surveys, a different name from the list of TMTs will be selected, or contact the CEO to obtain an additional TMT member name.
12	• Track firms and their TMT members diligently. • Since data will be collected from at least 40 firms, it is important to monitor firms closely and stay up to date. • Make note of firms that have not returned completed surveys

Step	Key Activities
13	• The entire data collection process can take approximately 1 year or more to complete. • Some firms may not return the minimum required number of completed surveys and are eliminated from the sample. • It may be necessary to contact additional CEOs and repeat this process in order to reach an adequate sample size of 40 firms per country.

Note: PI = principle investigator.

The GLOBE Sample of CEOs

The CEOs from over 1,000 firms participated in this study. Table 4.17 provides an overview of the length of time the CEOs had held their current position in the firm.

The majority of the CEOs had over 6 years in their leadership position (52.3%), with the next largest number of CEOs serving between 3 and 6 years (30.8%), and far fewer CEOs with tenure of less than 3 years (16.9%).

Table 4.18 shows the mean range of years that these CEOs have been leaders of their firms in each of the 24 countries. The largest number of CEOs had been in their leadership positions in their firms for more than 6 years, but there are some notable differences across countries. The table shows that within many of the Latin countries (e.g., Brazil, Guatemala, Mexico, and Spain) well over half of their firm leaders had been CEOs for more than 6 years. Spain reported the most number of CEOs with tenure more than 6 years (85.3%). Nonetheless, several countries had firms reporting lower mean tenure in their samples. The island nation of Vanuatu reported that a majority of their CEOs had less than 3 years' experience in firms (80.0%) and Russia reported the majority of their CEOs held

Table 4.17 CEO Tenure Overall

CEO Tenure	Overall	
	N*	% *n***
Under 3 years	152	16.9%
3 to 6 years	277	30.8%
Over 6 years	471	52.3%
Total	900	100.0%

Note: *N = number of organizations completing survey question. ** % *n* = percentage of organization responses across countries.

Table 4.18   CEO Tenure in Office Across Countries

	Overall		Austria		Azerbaijan		Brazil	
	N*	% n**	N	% c***	N	% c	N	% c
Less than 3 years	152	16.9%	5	12.5%	4	10.0%	1	3.2%
3 to 6 years	277	30.8%	13	32.5%	20	50.0%	10	32.3%
Over 6 years	471	52.3%	22	55.0%	16	40.0%	20	64.5%
Total	900	100.0%	40	100.0%	40	100.0%	31	100.0%
	China		Estonia		Fiji		Germany	
	N	% c	N	% c	N	% c	N	% c
Less than 3 years	14	16.3%	16	35.6%	3	37.5%	6	21.4%
3 to 6 years	28	32.6%	14	31.1%	2	25.0%	7	25.0%
Over 6 years	44	51.2%	15	33.3%	3	37.5%	15	53.6%
Total	86	100.0%	45	100.0%	8	100.0%	28	100.0%
	Greece		Guatemala		India		Mexico	
	N	% c	N	% c	N	% c	N	% c
Less than 3 years	1	3.6%	1	2.6%	25	22.5%	8	19.5%
3 to 6 years	9	32.1%	9	23.1%	65	58.6%	5	12.2%
Over 6 years	18	64.3%	29	74.4%	21	18.9%	28	68.3%
Total	28	100.0%	39	100.0%	111	100.0%	41	100.0%
	Netherlands		Nigeria		Peru		Romania	
	N	% c	N	% c	N	% c	N	% c
Less than 3 years	14	31.1%	11	26.2%	8	32.0%	5	11.4%
3 to 6 years	8	17.8%	8	19.0%	5	20.0%	4	9.1%
Over 6 years	23	51.1%	23	54.8%	12	48.0%	35	79.5%
Total	45	100.0%	42	100.0%	25	100.0%	44	100.0%

	Russia		Slovenia		Solomon Islands		Spain	
	N	% c	N	% c	N	% c	N	% c
Less than 3 years	5	12.5%	10	25.6%	2	15.4%	1	2.9%
3 to 6 years	25	62.5%	9	23.1%	7	53.8%	4	11.8%
Over 6 years	10	25.0%	20	51.3%	4	30.8%	29	85.3%
Total	40	100.0%	39	100.0%	13	100.0%	34	100.0%
	Taiwan		Turkey		United States		Vanuatu	
	N	% c	N	% c	N	% c	N	% c
Less than 3 years	1	2.6%	4	11.4%	3	7.0%	4	80.0%
3 to 6 years	10	26.3%	5	14.3%	9	20.9%	1	20.0%
Over 6 years	27	71.1%	26	74.3%	31	72.1%		0.0%
Total	38	100.0%	35	100.0%	43	100.0%	5	100.0%

Note: *N = number of organizations completing survey question. ** % n = percentage of organization responses across countries. *** % c = percentage of organization responses within country.

leadership positions between 3 and 6 years (62.5%). The country reporting the most evenly divided tenure among the CEOs within their firms was in Estonia.

Table 4.19 provides an overview of the age of the CEOs in the total sample. The table shows that CEOs between the ages of 41 and 50 encom-

Table 4.19   CEO Age Overall

	Overall	
CEO Age	N*	% n**
20 to 30 years	14	1.6%
31 to 40 years	174	20.2%
41 to 50 years	354	41.1%
51 to 60 years	257	29.8%
61 to 70 years	59	6.8%
71 to 80 years	4	0.5%
Total	862	100.0%

Note: *N = number of organizations completing survey question. ** % n = percentage of organization responses across countries.

passed 41.1% of the sample, with CEOs between the ages of 51 and 60 comprising the next largest group (29.8%). CEOs between 31 and 40 years old made up 20.2% of the overall sample.

Table 4.20 presents the country-specific data regarding CEOs range of age for our sample. While the majority of the countries had CEOs between 41 and 50 years, several countries had a broader range of ages. In the table, Brazil reported 73.5% of their sample of CEOs was over 50 years of age. The countries reporting the largest portion of their CEOs ages 50 years or younger were the countries of Estonia reporting 84.8% and China reporting 88.1% of their CEOs in this age range.

Table 4.20   CEO Age Across Countries

	Overall		Austria		Azerbaijan		Brazil	
	N*	% n**	N	% c***	N	% c	N	% c
20 to 30 years	14	1.6%						
31 to 40 years	174	20.2%	11	27.5%	6	15.0%	1	2.9%
41 to 50 years	354	41.1%	10	25.0%	30	75.0%	8	23.5%
51 to 60 years	257	29.8%	16	40.0%	4	10.0%	17	50.0%
61 to 70 years	59	6.8%	3	7.5%			7	20.6%
71 to 80 years	4	0.5%					1	2.9%
Total	862	100.0%	40	100.0%	40	100.0%	34	100.0%
	China		Estonia		Fiji		Germany	
	N	% c	N	% c	N	% c	N	% c
20 to 30 years	3	3.3%	4	8.7%				
31 to 40 years	40	43.5%	20	43.5%			4	13.8%
41 to 50 years	38	41.3%	15	32.6%	6	75.0%	10	34.5%
51 to 60 years	10	10.9%	4	8.7%	2	25.0%	11	37.9%
61 to 70 years	1	1.1%	2	4.3%			3	10.3%
71 to 80 years			1	2.2%			1	3.4%
Total	92	100.0%	46	100.0%	8	100.0%	29	100.0%
	Greece		Guatemala		India		Mexico	
	N	% c	N	% c	N	% c	N	% c
20 to 30 years			1	2.6%	1	2.5%	1	2.4%
31 to 40 years	8	16.7%	8	20.5%	6	15.0%	7	16.7%
41 to 50 years	18	37.5%	14	35.9%	19	47.5%	18	42.9%
51 to 60 years	17	35.4%	14	35.9%	14	35.0%	11	26.2%

	Greece		Guatemala		India		Mexico	
	N	*% c*	*N*	*% c*	*N*	*% c*	*N*	*% c*
61 to 70 years	5	10.4%	2	5.1%			5	11.9%
71 to 80 years								
Total	48	100.0%	39	100.0%	40	100.0%	42	100.0%
	Netherlands		Nigeria		Peru		Romania	
	N	*% c*	*N*	*% c*	*N*	*% c*	*N*	*% c*
20 to 30 years	3	6.8%						
31 to 40 years	7	15.9%	4	8.9%	4	16.0%	5	11.4%
41 to 50 years	18	40.9%	22	48.9%	9	36.0%	21	47.7%
51 to 60 years	11	25.0%	16	35.6%	9	36.0%	16	36.4%
61 to 70 years	5	11.4%	3	6.7%	3	12.0%	2	4.5%
71 to 80 years								
Total	44	100.0%	45	100.0%	25	100.0%	44	100.0%
	Russia		Slovenia		Solomon Islands		Spain	
	N	*% c*	*N*	*% c*	*N*	*% c*	*N*	*% c*
20 to 30 years	1	2.5%						
31 to 40 years	8	20.0%	14	35.9%	1	9.1%	9	25.7%
41 to 50 years	21	52.5%	14	35.9%	7	63.6%	8	22.9%
51 to 60 years	8	20.0%	7	17.9%	3	27.3%	15	42.9%
61 to 70 years	2	5.0%	4	10.3%			3	8.6%
71 to 80 years								
Total	40	100.0%	39	100.0%	11	100.0%	35	100.0%
	Taiwan		Turkey		United States		Vanuatu	
	N	*% c*	*N*	*% c*	*N*	*% c*	*N*	*% c*
20 to 30 years								
31 to 40 years	2	5.6%	7	18.9%	2	4.7%		
41 to 50 years	15	41.7%	15	40.5%	13	30.2%	5	100.0%
51 to 60 years	16	44.4%	12	32.4%	24	55.8%		
61 to 70 years	3	8.3%	3	8.1%	3	7.0%		
71 to 80 years					1	2.3%		
Total	36	100.0%	37	100.0%	43	100.0%	5	100.0%

Note: **N* = number of organizations completing survey question. ** *% n* = percentage of organization responses across countries. *** *% c* = percentage of organization responses within country.

Table 4.21 provides an overview of the gender distribution of the CEOs in the total sample. The table shows that female CEOs made up 7.6% of the total group, with male CEOs comprising the majority of the sample (92.4%).

Table 4.22 presents the country-specific data regarding the gender distribution of CEOs in our sample. While the majority of the countries had mostly male CEOs in their sample, several countries had a notable number of females in CEO positions as well. In the table, five countries had no female

Table 4.21 CEO Gender Overall

	Overall^	
CEO Gender	N*	% n**
Female	71	7.6%
Male	862	92.4%
Total	933	100.0%

Note: *N = number of CEOs. ** % n = percentage of CEOs across countries. ^ gender information was not available for the Fiji and Netherlands samples.

Table 4.22 CEO Gender Across Countries

	Overall		Austria		Azerbaijan		Brazil		China	
	N*	% n**	N	% c ***	N	% c	N	% c	N	% c
Female	71	7.6%	0	0.0%	0	0.0%	5	13.5%	6	6.2%
Male	862	92.4%	40	100.0%	40	100.0%	32	86.5%	91	93.8%
Total	933	100.0%	40	100.0%	40	100.0%	37	100.0%	97	100.0%
	Estonia		Germany		Greece		Guatemala		India	
	N	% c	N	% c	N	% c	N	% c	N	% c
Female	1	2.1%	3	10.3%	7	13.7%	5	12.5%	0	0.0%
Male	48	97.9%	26	89.7%	44	86.3%	35	87.5%	113	100.0%
Total	49	100.0%	29	100.0%	51	100.0%	40	100.0%	113	100.0%
	Mexico		Nigeria		Peru		Romania		Russia	
	N	% c	N	% c	N	% c	N	% c	N	% c
Female	0	0.0%	0	0.0%	4	13.8%	2	4.5%	8	20.0%
Male	42	100.0%	47	100.0%	25	86.2%	42	95.5%	32	80.0%
Total	42	100.0%	47	100.0%	29	100.0%	44	100.0%	40	100.0%

	Slovenia		Solomon Islands		Spain		Taiwan		Tonga	
	N	% c	N	% c	N	% c	N	% c	N	% c
Female	7	17.5%	2	10.0%	7	20.0%	8	20.0%	1	9.1%
Male	33	82.5%	18	90.0%	28	80.0%	32	80.0%	10	90.9%
Total	40	100.0%	20	100.0%	35	100.0%	40	100.0%	11	100.0%
	Turkey		United States		Vanuatu					
	N	% c	N	% c	N	% c				
Female	1	2.6%	2	4.5%	2	33.3%				
Male	38	97.4%	42	95.5%	4	66.7%				
Total	39	100.0%	44	100.0%	6	100.0%				

Note: *N = number of CEOs. ** % n = percentage of CEOs across countries. *** % c = percentages of CEOs within country. ^ complete gender information was not available for samples Fiji and Netherlands.

CEOs in their sample: Austria, Azerbaijan, India, Mexico, and Nigeria. On the other hand, three countries reported that female CEOs comprised 20% of their sample: Russia, Spain, and Taiwan.[5]

The most recent data reporting gender distribution of CEOs in Fortune 500 companies show that women currently hold 4.2% of CEO positions in both Fortune 500 and Fortune 1000 firms (Catalyst, 2013). Notably, although the U.S. sample is comprised of a diverse group of firms, this percentage of female CEOs closely mirrors the percentage of female CEOs reported in Fortune 500 companies, 4.5% and 4.2%, respectively.

_____ The GLOBE Sample of Top Management Teams

Responses from TMT members are the primary source of information of this study. The TMT members are in an optimal position to report on the leader behaviors of their CEOs, thus their expert perspective is the focus of our research. Following each of the CEO interviews, the CCIs obtained names of the immediate subordinates and members of the TMT (advisers, other key personnel) who report to the CEOs.

Overall, data were gathered from more than 6,000 TMT members across the firms for this study. The total number of respondents by country ranged from 29 TMT members (Vanuatu, South Pacific) to more than 600 TMT

---

[5]The exception was the island of Vanuatu, which reported 33.3% of female CEOs participated out of the total sample size of 6 CEOs.

members (China and India). Table 4.23 provides a detailed breakdown of the total TMT members per country.

Table 4.24 shows the overall age of the TMT members across the 24 countries participating in this study. The table shows that 65.4% of the total sample of TMTs ranged between 31 and 50 years of age, with an average age of 38.4 years. The next largest group of TMTs was reported

Table 4.23 Number of Top Management Team Respondents Per Country

Country	Mean Number TMT Respondents*
Austria	243
Azerbaijan	239
Brazil	217
China	646
Estonia	298
Fiji	68
Germany	164
Greece	282
Guatemala	241
India	685
Mexico	297
Netherlands	272
Nigeria	301
Peru	183
Romania	263
Russia	355
Slovenia	270
Solomon Islands	92
Spain	207
Taiwan	213
Tonga	51
Turkey	217
United States	337
Vanuatu	29
Total TMT respondents	6,170

Note: *Calculated by averaging TMT responses to age and gender demographic questions for each country.

to be 30 years of age or younger (22.2%), and TMTs 51 years or older comprised only 12.4% of the total sample. However, there were some interesting details related to TMT age within countries not reported in Table 4.24. Azerbaijan reported 77.5% of the TMT members in the age group (31–50 years old). In comparison, four countries (Guatemala, Nigeria, India, and Turkey) reported approximately a third of their total sample under the age of 30. Among this group, Guatemala had the largest percentage (38.1%) of younger TMT members under the age of 30. Finally, the U.S. had the largest number of TMT members between 51 and 70 years of age (31.7%).

Table 4.25 indicates that the majority of TMT members were male (69.8%) with women representing 30.2% of the sample. Reviewing the country-specific data, there are differences in the distribution of TMT gender across countries that are worth noting. The countries of Azerbaijan, Mexico, India, and the Solomon Islands had 80% or more of their TMT members comprised of men. In contrast, five countries (Guatemala, Estonia, Slovenia, Romania, and Taiwan) showed that women constitute 40% or more of their TMT members. Of these, Romania reported a TMT sample of 44.9% women. As a region, the Eastern European sample (Estonia, Slovenia, Romania, and Russia) tended to have higher numbers of women among their TMT members, compared to other regions.

Table 4.24   Top Management Team Age

Age	N*	% n**
Under 30 years	1,365	22.2%
31 to 50 years	4,024	65.4%
51 to 70 years	756	12.3%
Over 70 years	6	0.1%
Total surveys completed	6,151	100.0%

Note: *N = number of TMT respondents completing survey. ** % n = percentage of respondents across countries.

Table 4.25   Top Management Team Gender

Gender	N*	% n**
Male	4,314	69.8%
Female	1,869	30.2%
Total	6,183	100.0%

Note: *N = number of TMT respondents completing surveys. ** % n = percentage of respondents across countries.

Finally, Table 4.26 reports the functional areas of jobs held by this overall group of TMT members. The majority of the total TMT respondents identified general administration as their organizational function area (19.3%), followed by jobs classified as other (11.7%). It may seem plausible that the majority of the TMT members report that their job functions are more wide-ranging (i.e., general administration) or more broad-spectrum (i.e., other) given the broad sample of firms included in this study. The next largest job functional area reported overall by this group of TMT members was sales or marketing (11%), followed by TMT members in production, manufacturing, or operations management (10.5%). Together, the job functions of finance and accounting comprised 16.1% of the sample. This relatively larger number of TMT members representing quantitative functional areas should be expected because firm performance information was required from each organization. Finally, the combined job functional areas of transportation, inventory management, and facilities management are reported by few TMT members across the firms.

Table 4.26   Top Management Team Job Functional Area

Job Functional Area	N*	% n**
General administration	1,145	19.3%
Other	693	11.7%
Sales or marketing	656	11.0%
Production, manufacturing, or operations management	623	10.5%
Finance	530	8.9%
Human resource management or personnel	490	8.2%
Accounting	429	7.2%
Staff support	271	4.6%
Purchasing	240	4.0%
Engineering	228	3.8%
Information technology management	199	3.3%
Research and development	178	3.0%
Transportation	108	1.8%
Facilities management	82	1.4%
Inventory management	70	1.2%
Total	5,942	100.0%

Note: *N = number of TMT respondents completing survey. ** % n = percentage of respondents across countries.

Reviewing the country-specific data, there are differences in the distribution of job functional areas reported by TMT respondents across countries that are worth highlighting. China, Fiji, India, and the Solomon Islands reported over 30% of their TMT members from the general administration functional area. The South Pacific nations of Fiji (36.4%) and the Solomon Islands (39.6%) identified this job classification for the preponderance of their sample. Within the combined job functional areas of finance and accounting, five countries identified over 20% of their TMT members worked in this area: (1) Romania, (2) Nigeria, (3) Russia, (4) Turkey, and (5) Tonga. The country of Turkey reported the most percentage of TMT members (25%) in this functional area. In the job functional area of production, manufacturing, or operations management, the countries of Romania and Turkey identified this classification for the largest percentage of their TMT members, reporting 23.9% and 20.3%, respectively. Further, the broad-spectrum job functional area labeled *other* identified three countries with over 20% of the TMT respondents in this classification: (1) Greece, (2) Taiwan, and (3) Vanuatu. Finally, the job functional area of sales or marketing identified two countries with over one fifth of their TMT members working in these areas: (1) Greece (23%) and (2) Slovenia (31%).

The previously stated information provides a number of interesting insights into this global sample of firms. The participating firms are mostly privately owned and managed, with the majority of firms from manufacturing industries. Almost half the sample of firms are 20 years or older, with the exceptions of Russia, Azerbaijan, and China, which had the majority of their firms in business less than 10 years. Over 80% of the overall sample reflected a domestically oriented focus (i.e., revenues below 40% from exports), with 10 countries reporting more than 90% focused on the domestic market. Turkey was the exception to this trend reporting well over half of the sample of firms export dominated. Firm CEOs in the sample were largely in their jobs for more than 6 years, with the majority between the ages of 41 and 50. Spain reported firm CEOs with longer tenure and firm CEOs from the South Pacific Island of Vanuatu tended to have shorter tenure. The TMT members overall were largely aged 50 or younger. The TMTs overall were largely aged between 31 and 50, with Guatemala having the largest percentage of TMT members under 30 years old and the United States having a larger percentage of TMT members between the ages of 51 and 70. The majority of the TMT members were men. Although no countries reported having the majority of women in the sample of firm TMT members, as a region the Eastern European sample tended to have higher numbers of women among their TMT members, compared to other regions. Regarding firm TMT members' organizational function area; almost 20% identified general administration as their job classification. However, there tended to be a significant assortment of organizational functional areas (i.e., finance and accounting, sales and marketing, operations management, other) among the TMT members probably due to the type of information requested.

Scale Development

As reported earlier, we collected data from TMTs and asked them to describe the actual behaviors of their CEOs. In short, our data represent the views of TMTs on how their CEOs behave. Throughout this book, we refer to our data as "observed CEO behavior," "actual CEO behavior," and "reported CEO behavior" interchangeably.

The leadership behavioral scales used in the current study were developed by the principal investigator (PI) through a multistep method. First, leader behavior items were generated based on the 21 primary leadership dimensions and associated CLTs identified in GLOBE 2004. All leader behavioral items were Q-sorted into categories. Second, outcome items were developed based on TMT internal processes, firm characteristics, and external firm performance. For all internal outcome items, Q-sorts were also conducted. Third, items were placed in three separate questionnaires. Fourth, items were subjected to a series of psychometric evaluations for evidence of constructs (i.e., evidence for aggregation, factor analysis, and measurement equivalence). Next, we will discuss the first three steps, with the final step thoroughly covered in Chapter 6.

Culturally Implicit Leader Behavioral Items

Phase 3 leadership behavior items were created largely on the basis of prior GLOBE studies of leadership prototypicality in multiple countries (Hanges & Dickson, 2004). Multilevel confirmatory factor analysis in Phase 2 provided support for the 21 first-order and 6 second-order dimensions of leadership (Dorfman, Hanges, & Brodbeck, 2004).

In the current GLOBE Phase 3, the survey items constituting these prototypical leadership behavior measures were written to reflect the actual leadership behavior of the 21 primary leadership dimensions. Based on extant corroborating studies as well as the empirical results of the CLTs, the PI diagramed each of the 21 primary CLT dimensions and then began mapping leadership behavioral items to describe the type of actions that would be associated with these constructs. To illustrate, considering the CLT dimension *inspirational,* the behavioral item of being "highly involved, energetic, enthused, motivated" was written based on the underlying behaviors stimulated by this CLT attribute. In another example, for the CLT dimension *administratively competent,* the behavioral item "is well-organized, methodical, and orderly" was created to reflect the action of the construct. This item generation process was repeated for all the 21 primary CLT dimensions.

Initially, a total of 142 leadership behavioral items were generated to assess the underlying 21 primary CLT constructs. From this initial pool of items, a modified Q-sort was conducted to determine the final set of items to be used for the leadership behavior scales (McKeown, 1988). Guided by the CLT theory, the items generated for the GLOBE Phase 3 study were Q-sorted into 21 categories: one category for each of the primary GLOBE CLT constructs and a not-applicable category (Sachs, 2000). Two raters, each with a PhD in management, classified leadership behavior items into the CLT dimensions. Initially, one researcher, who holds a PhD in international management, carefully read through the leadership behavior items. Based on her knowledge of leadership generally and the GLOBE CLT constructs specifically, she identified items that she believed to be related to the 21 CLT dimensions. Then, another researcher with expertise in leadership and cross-cultural research identified appropriate leader behavior items for the CLT categories. Having verified the themes that were associated with relevant leadership dimensions, these researchers categorized the leader behavior items into the CLT dimensions that they inferred reflected the themes. Any discrepancies were discussed, resulting in the exclusion of a pool of questionnaire items.

Leader behavior questionnaire items were excluded from the creation of scales when the coders could not unambiguously determine their meaning and intent. For instance, the item that stated the behavior descriptor "Is unique; has characteristics or behaviors that are different from most others" may have been theoretically related to our definition of Autonomous leadership. However, the researchers could not agree on the intent, so this item was excluded. In another example, the item that stated the behavior descriptor "Ritualistic, uses a prescribed order to carry out procedures" may have theoretically related to the definition of either administratively competent or bureaucratic. This was considered a double-barreled question, and such items were excluded when the distinctiveness of an item could not be determined. Following the Q-sort procedure, these items were then subjected to a series of statistical analyses, which are outlined in Chapter 5 and Chapter 6. Of the initial 142 leadership behavioral items that were generated to assess the underlying CLT constructs,[6] 118 items were retained. Table 4.27 shows an example list of leader behavior items and their related CLT constructs that were used in the GLOBE Phase 3 study. For each behavior item, there was a 7-point scale ranging from 1 (*strongly disagree*) to 7 (*strongly agree*). (All leadership survey items are presented in Appendix B.)

---

[6]The survey instrument included 171 total items, although only 118 were related to the CLT leader behavior dimensions to be used in the current research project.

Table 4.27   Examples of Six Global and Twenty-One Primary Culturally Endorsed Implicit Leadership Theory Dimensions With Phase 3 Leader Behaviors Questionnaire Items

Dimensions		CEO Behaviors
Global Leadership Dimension	**Primary Leadership Dimension**	
I. *Charismatic/Value-Based leadership*	Visionary	• Makes plans and takes actions based on future goals • Clearly articulates his/her vision of the future • Has a clear sense of where he/she wants this organization to be in 5 years
	Inspirational	• Gives courage, confidence, or hope through reassuring and advising • Highly involved, energetic, enthused, motivated • Increases morale of subordinates by offering encouragement, praise, and/or by being confident
	Self-Sacrificial	• Can be trusted to serve the interests of his/her subordinates rather than him/herself • Foregoes self-interests and makes personal sacrifices in the interest of a goal or vision • Views obstacles as challenges rather than threats
	Integrity	• Deserves trust, can be believed and relied upon to keep his/her word • Means what he/she says • Speaks and acts truthfully
	Decisive	• Makes decisions firmly and quickly • Has good intuition, insightful • Applies logic when thinking
	Performance oriented	• Strives for excellence in performance of self and subordinates • Sets high goals; works hard • Seeks continuous performance improvement
II. *Team-Oriented leadership*	Collaborative team orientation	• Concerned with the welfare of the group • Intervenes to solve conflicts between individuals • Stays with and supports friends even when they have substantial problems or difficulties

Dimensions		CEO Behaviors
Global Leadership Dimension	**Primary Leadership Dimension**	
	Team integrator	• Integrates people or things into cohesive, working whole • Knowledgeable, is aware of information • Works at getting members to work together
	Diplomatic	• Able to identify solutions which satisfy individuals with diverse and conflicting interests • Skilled at interpersonal relations • Interested in temporal events, has a world outlook
	Malevolent	• Is sly, deceitful, full of guile • Is actively unfriendly; acts negatively toward others • Pursues own best interests at the expense of others
	Administratively competent	• Has the ability to manage complex office work and administrative systems • Well-organized, methodical, orderly • Is able to plan, organize, coordinate, and control work of large numbers (over 30) of individuals
III. *Participative leadership*	Participative	• Seeks advice concerning organizational strategy from subordinates • Gives subordinates a high degree of discretion to perform their work • Shares critical information with subordinates
	Autocratic	• Is in charge and does not tolerate disagreement or questioning; gives orders • Forces his/her values and opinions on others • Expects unquestioning obedience of those who report to him/her
IV. *Humane-Oriented leadership*	Modesty	• Does not boast, presents self in a humble manner • Not easily distressed • Has and shows patience
	Humane orientation	• Has empathy for others, inclined to be helpful or show mercy

(Continued)

(Continued)

Dimensions		CEO Behaviors
Global Leadership Dimension	**Primary Leadership Dimension**	
		• Willing to give time, money, resources, and help to others • Is aware of slight changes in others' moods
V. *Autonomous leadership*	Autonomous	• Acts independently, does not rely on others • Does not rely on others; self-governing • Is individually oriented; places high value on preserving individual rather than group needs
VI. *Self-Protective leadership*	Self-Centered	• Self-absorbed, thoughts focus mostly on one's self • Is a loner, tends to work and act separately from others • Aloof, stands off from others, difficult to become friends with
	Status conscious	• Is conscious of class and status boundaries and acts accordingly • Believes that a small number of people with similar backgrounds are superior and should enjoy privileges • Aware of others' socially accepted status
	Internally competitive (formerly *conflict inducer*)	• Stimulates unrest • Tends to conceal information from others • Is unwilling to work jointly with others
	Face-Saver	• Refrains from making negative comments to maintain good relationships and save face • Avoids disputes with members of his/her group • Ensures that subordinates are not embarrassed or shamed
	Bureaucratic (formerly *procedural*)	• Tends to behave according to established norms, policies, and procedures • Administers rewards in a fair manner • Uses a common standard to evaluate all who report to him/her

Items for Outcome Measures

Next, the PI developed outcome measurement items to depict TMT internal processes, firm characteristics, and external firm performance. CEOs have arguably a strong ability to affect collective outcomes of their corporations (Mintzberg, 1973; Walsh & Seward, 1990; Westphal & Zajac, 1995). Generally, there is a positive relationship between leader behaviors and team performance outcomes (Burke et al., 2006). The focus on leadership at the top level of the organization was intentional because leaders affect both the top management group that directly reports to them but also the larger organization (Hambrick & Mason, 1984). Included in all top management groups, the CEOs and other executive members work together, although the way the group operates may vary greatly (Yukl, 2013). Scholars have proposed many theoretical reasons for team performance (Hambrick, 2007; Klein, Dansereau, & Hall, 1994; Kozlowski & Bell, 2003; Kozlowski & Ilgen, 2006; Zaccaro, Rittman, & Marks, 2001). Recent research has shown empirical evidence as to how CEO leadership behaviors impact organizational performance and employees' attitudes (Wang, Tsui, & Xin, 2011). Together, the outcomes of interest for this study focused on (1) the CEO leadership impact on TMT members and (2) the CEO leadership impact on overall competitive performance of the firm.

Outcome Measures: Top Management Team Internally Oriented Items

Reviewing the literature on the effects of leadership on team performance, the PI identified several themes that led to the formation of TMT internal outcome constructs. Related to leader influence on teams, the themes of motivation and commitment, social identification, and trust and cooperation emerged as most pertinent (Yukl, 2001), especially when studying the influence of leadership on TMT members. From the theory-based theme of motivation and commitment, the underlying concepts of *making personal sacrifices to achieve the organization objectives* and *being committed to one's future in the company* emerged. From the theory-based theme of social identification, the underlying concepts of *having greater team cohesion* and *identifying with the future of the organization* surfaced. From the theory-based theme of trust and cooperation, the underlying concept of *experiencing cooperation increased by inspiring vision* emerged.

Based on these three broader theory-driven themes, the PI developed items to illustrate each of the underlying concepts. For example, to describe the social identification theme, the item "I am willing to make serious personal sacrifices to contribute to the success of this organization" was developed. To illustrate the motivation and commitment theme, the item "I expect to be with this organization three years from now" was created. To depict the trust and cooperation theme, the item "The top managers work as an effective team" was developed.

In total, 11 items were generated to assess the stated underlying themes. To formulate the TMT outcome measures to be used in this study, a multistep process was used. First, two formal Q-sort processes were conducted by separate groups of scholars, to formulate the internally oriented outcome measures (Sachs, 2000). The second author of this book and two of his colleagues with PhDs in management[7] conducted a Q-sort of the items, resulting in the formulation of the three outcome variable measures. Additionally, another of the book authors and her colleague, holding a PhD in management,[8] performed a separate Q-sort of the pool of items. As a result of this item identification process, across the two Q-sort procedures we obtained adequate inter-rater agreement for three outcome measures. In total, 10 items were retained as a result of the Q-sort process. This process led to the formation of three measures of TMT internal outcomes: (1) extra Effort, (2) Commitment, and (3) Team Solidarity.

The first internally oriented outcome measure was that of individual extra Effort. This relationship between follower perceptions and their willingness to work hard and sacrifice for the organization lies at the heart of decades of leadership research (Bass, 1985; Conger & Kanungo, 1998; House, 1977;). We sought to extend prior measures of individual extra Effort, which traditionally ask followers to indicate if the leader stimulates them to put forth extra Effort (Bass, 1985). Because the wording in Bass's (1985) measure solicits perceptions of how *the leader* may stimulate extra Effort in followers, this confounds the rating of leadership with the rating of extra Effort of the followers. In the instructions for our participants, we instead asked them to assess their "reactions to, and views of, this organization" rather than asking about their Effort in relation to the leader. The internally oriented measure of extra Effort was assessed with four items, as shown in Table 4.28. For ease of discussion in the remainder of the book, we will use the term *Effort* rather than *extra effort*; however, the previously stated logic for choosing to use the term *extra effort* in the survey rather than *Effort* remains. Associated with each item, there was a 7-point scale ranging from 1 (*strongly disagree*) to 7 (*strongly agree*).

The second internally oriented outcome measure was that of Commitment. Again, focusing more on the organization than on the leader, we

---

[7]Jon Howell, PhD, and Leonel Prieto, PhD, assisted in conducting this Q-sort.

[8]Narda Quigley, PhD, assisted in conducting this Q-sort.

Table 4.28   Top Management Team Internal Outcome—Extra Effort Items

Extra effort	I contribute to this organization 100% of my ability.
	I am willing to make serious personal sacrifices to contribute to the success of this organization.
	My effort is above and beyond that which is required.
	The CEO stimulates others to put forth efforts above and beyond the call of duty and make personal sacrifices.

were interested in the extent to which the TMT follower's Commitment is associated with the effect of leader's behaviors in the organization. Commitment is often thought of as the degree to which individuals believe they have a strong relationship with the organization (Kanter, 1968; Mowday, Porter, & Steers, 1982). Extending this, we conceptualized TMT Commitment consistent with Meyer and Allen's (1991) notion of affective commitment. Affective commitment is described as the positive emotional attachment an employee has to the organization (Klein, Becker, & Meyer, 2009). An affectively committed employee deeply identifies with the organization goals and wants to continue with the organization (Meyer & Allen, 1997). Employees commit to the organization because they desire to be part of it (Morrow, 1993). In turn, follower commitment has been shown to be impacted by CEO's transformational leadership behaviors creating a motivational environment (Fu, Tsui, Lui, & Li, 2010). The internally oriented measure of Commitment was assessed with three items, as shown in Table 4.29. Associated with each item, there was a 7-point scale ranging from 1 (*strongly disagree*) to 7 (*strongly agree*).

The third internally oriented outcome measure was that of Team Solidarity. In addition to increasing TMT Commitment, CEO leadership may also impact TMT members' Team Solidarity. Team performance is contingent on how the interdependent activities of the various members are mutually reliable and coordinated (Yukl, 2013). If followers are compelled to identify with that leaders' vision and the values (House & Shamir, 1993), then this belief and identification increases motivation

Table 4.29   Top Management Team Internal Outcome—Commitment Items

Commitment	I expect to be with this organization 3 years from now.
	I am optimistic about my future with this organization.
	I expect this organization to have an excellent future.

and effort. Thus, team members become more willing to take action to realize the vision. Identifying more with the collective cause, they also revel in being part of the group generating those outcomes (Shamir, House, & Arthur, 1993). Where members' roles are highly interdependent, mutual trust and cooperation are significant contributors to group performance. When team members are cohesive, appreciate their membership, and connect with the team, higher levels of trust and cooperation develop (Barrick, Stewart, Neubert, & Mount, 1998). Collective team identification has been found to be important to learning and performance in teams (Van der Vegt & Bunderson, 2005). The theory-based theme of social identification supports the notion of collective identification (Reicher, Haslam, & Hopkins, 2005) and other social identity theories that advocate cohesiveness in teams. Together, these theories coalesce in a construct we have labeled *Team Solidarity*. The internally oriented measure of Team Solidarity was assessed with three items as shown in Table 4.30. Associated with each item, there was a 7-point scale ranging from 1 (*strongly disagree*) to 7 (*strongly agree*).

The three separate internally oriented outcomes of Effort, Commitment, and Team Solidarity were measured by the previously given items. They were then combined as a broader measure, which we labeled TMT Dedication. The psychometric processes used to confirm these scales will be discussed in Chapter 6.

Use of Perceptual Outcome Measures

Perceptual outcome measures were obtained from the TMT members. For the internally oriented outcome measures, assessing the influence of CEO leadership behavior on TMT members' attitudes and beliefs are important in their own right. We also used perceptual measures to assess external outcome measures. The reasons for using perceptual measures for the externally oriented outcome measures are more complex. As noted by Wang and colleagues (2011), perceptual measures have been used extensively to assess firm performance due to the lack of reliable and objective financial performance data. This issue is especially pertinent in emerging economies (Peng & Luo, 2000), which comprise many of the societies in our sample. Even in more developed economies procuring

Table 4.30   Top Management Team Internal Outcome—Team Solidarity Items

Team solidarity	People at my level work well together.
	The top managers work as an effective team.
	I agree with the chief executive's vision of this organization.

objective data from private small-scale businesses is difficult, which is often due to issues of authentic self-disclosure by the owners (Sapienza, Smith, & Gannon, 1988). Additionally, the majority of our 24-nation sample is comprised of organizations that are not publicly traded, hence obtaining annual reports and other conventionally available financial disclosure information is problematic.

Further complicating the issue, baseline measures of firm performance may be different across nations (Baer & Frese, 2003). Past researchers have noted that in some countries firms reporting profit rates of 5% may be seen as high profit firms. While in other countries, profit rates of 5% may be seen as too low, and firm owners would consider selling the firm if it is appreciably below 10%. Thus, even one's expectations of what constitutes adequate profit rate is culturally contingent.

Outcome Measures: Firm Financial Performance Items

When providing a comprehensive understanding of the performance relationship with the leader behavior constructs, it is important to look at multiple indicators, because performance is a multidimensional construct (Chakravarthy, 1986). To formulate the measures of externally oriented outcomes measuring competitive firm performance, a separate process for the selection of outcome items was employed.

Assessing the firm's performance relative to other firms in its industry, the PI adopted several perceptual performance-based items from Tan and Litschert (1994). Thus, we used two measures of externally oriented outcomes measuring Firm Competitive Performance: (1) Competitive Sales Performance and (2) Competitive Industry Dominance. Because the information we require for these measures demands the TMT members to have acumen of—and access to specific firm information—we used responses from executives who identified either finance or accounting as their job functional area. During the distribution of the surveys, the CCIs were to seek out TMT members who have knowledge about the firm's strategy formulation process, environment, and economic performance. Many of the respondents were from a variety of job functional areas (i.e., general administration—27%; other—18%), so for these external outcome measures we targeted only TMT members in relevant positions to obtain this information.

For the externally oriented outcome competitive sales, the targeted TMT members were asked to indicate the number on a 7-point scale that best reflects their organization's sales performance compared to their major competitors. Table 4.31 shows the item that comprises the externally oriented outcome item for Competitive Sales Performance.

For Competitive Industry Dominance, the targeted TMT members were asked to determine the number on a 5-point scale representing their view of the extent that the organization dominated its industry, ranging from *very little or not at all* to *almost completely*. Table 4.32 shows the item that comprises the externally oriented outcome item for Competitive Industry Dominance.

The two separate externally oriented outcomes of Competitive Sales Performance and Competitive Industry Dominance were measured separately and then combined as a broader measure that we labeled *Firm Competitive Performance*. The process used to develop our scales will be explained in detail in Chapter 5. Table 4.33 reports the total numbers of firms reporting the internally and externally oriented measures across the country sample.

This table shows that approximately 94% of the firms in this study reported internally oriented data. However, only approximately 32% of the firms were able to provide usable externally oriented data. The last column in this table shows the percentage of firms providing both usable internally and externally oriented outcome measures.

To summarize, the GLOBE Phase 3 scale development process used a multistep method, theory-driven item creation procedure. As such, the

Table 4.31   Externally Oriented Outcome—Competitive Sales Performance Item

Sales performance: Please indicate the number that best reflects this organization's performance compared to your major competitors.

1. ____ About 30% or more below major competitors

2. ____ Between 20 and 30% below major competitors

3. ____ Between 10 and 20% below major competitors

4. ____ About the same

5. ____ Between 10 and 20% above major competitors

6. ____ Between 20 and 30% above major competitors

7. ____ Above 30% more than major competitors

Table 4.32   Externally Oriented Outcome—Competitive Industry Dominance Item

To what extent does this organization dominate its industry?

1. very little or not at all

2. modestly

3. moderately

4. to a great extent

5. almost completely

Table 4.33   Number of Firms Reporting Internal and External Performance Measures

Country	Total Firms in Sample	Firms Reporting Internally Oriented Performance Measures—*Extra Effort, Commitment, and Team Solidarity*	Firms Reporting Externally Oriented Performance Measure—*Firm Competitive Performance*	Percentage of Firms Providing Both Measures
Austria	40	40	20	50.0%
Azerbaijan	40	40	17	42.5%
Brazil	37	34	06	16.2%
China	97	93	12	12.4%
Estonia	49	46	15	30.6%
Fiji	24	11	03	12.5%
Germany	29	29	16	55.2%
Greece	51	49	20	39.2%
Guatemala	40	39	13	32.5%
India	113	113	24	21.2%
Mexico	42	42	09	21.4%
Netherlands	53	46	07	13.2%
Nigeria	47	46	24	51.1%
Peru	29	25	11	37.9%
Romania	44	44	25	56.8%
Russia	40	40	22	55.0%
Slovenia	40	39	13	32.5%
Solomon Islands	20	13	00	0.0%
Spaln	35	35	13	37.1%
Taiwan	40	38	08	20.0%
Turkey	39	37	15	38.5%
Tonga	16	02	02	12.9%
United States	44	43	26	59.1%
Vanuatu	06	07	00	0.0%
Total	**1015**	**951**	**321**	

Note: More firms reported the externally oriented outcome measures. However, this table provides the number of firms that provided externally oriented financial measures from only TMT members associated with the accounting and finance departments.

leadership behavioral scales used in the current study were developed through a multistep method. Initially, leader behavior items were generated based on the 21 CLT primary leadership dimensions. All leader behavioral items were Q-sorted into categories. Then, outcome items were developed based on TMT internal processes, firm characteristics, and external firm performance. For all internal outcome items, Q-sorts were also conducted. Next, all the items generated from the process were placed in three separate questionnaires, as explained earlier. The project was made possible through the participation of the CCIs, who represented 24 countries and their diligent work interviewing CEOs and gathering data from their TMT members. The next two chapters will discuss the psychometric development and statistical analysis of the data.

5

Strategy for Measuring Constructs and Testing Relationships

I n this chapter, we discuss the statistical methods used to test the viability of our conceptual models as well as the methods used to test our hypotheses. We first discuss the justification for aggregating our measures to the CEO level of analysis. Next, we present the strategies used to assess the psychometric properties of our scales. We include a discussion of the critical issue of measurement equivalence that assesses whether our scales were interpreted similarity across countries. In this chapter, we also describe a new measure, Gestalt Fit, which we used to test our theoretical proposition that the match between country-level leadership expectations (culturally endorsed implicit leadership theory, or CLT) and actual CEO behavior leads to critical outcomes. This new measure assesses the fit between CLTs and CEO behavior across all dimensions and is theoretically driven from and consistent with the GLOBE conceptual model presented in Chapter 1.

Finally, we also discuss the rationale for the particular statistical techniques used to test our hypotheses. In order for hypotheses to be fairly and accurately tested, we have to be confident that the statistical techniques were used appropriately and did not introduce statistical conclusion errors (Hanges & Wang, 2012). These errors occur when the empirical findings lead researchers to false conclusions and are caused by inappropriate choice of statistical analysis or violations of statistical assumptions required for a particular statistical technique (e.g., violation of the independence of errors and assumption observations). Specifically, we used hierarchical linear modeling (HLM) to test the GLOBE hypotheses because of the nested nature of the data.

There are several statistical techniques that we used to help us test the viability of our conceptual models and hypotheses. For example, we hypothesized that members of a top management team (TMT) would agree in their description of the leadership behaviors of their CEO. That is, we hypothesized that because of sufficient shared experience with the CEO, the average leader behavior rating would be more reflective of the CEO than the individual perceptions of the TMT members. How do we demonstrate this? We will discuss that in this chapter.

Next, we discuss the evidence that we collected to assess the extent to which we have valid scales measuring each construct. For our purposes, this involves demonstrating not only that our scales are internally consistent within a country but that they are equivalent across various countries. Thus, we will discuss the methodology that we developed and used to assess cross-culture measurement equivalence.

Following this discussion, we present the methodology used to test the hypotheses concerning the relationships among culture, leadership expectations (i.e., CLTs), and leadership behavior. Subsequent to this, we present the methodology used to test the effectiveness of specific leadership behaviors such as Charismatic leadership. Following this discussion, we describe our fit hypotheses that reflect our belief regarding the importance of the match between the CEO behavior and the country-specific CLTs. Finally, we will review the methodology used to separate particularly effective from particularly ineffective CEOs.

It should be noted that the purpose of this chapter is only to describe the logic and relevant mathematical aspects underlying these statistical procedures. We leave the presentation, interpretation, and discussion of results to the subsequent chapters in this book. The intent of this chapter is to provide a framework to aid the reader's understanding and interpretation of the subsequent chapters.

Aggregation

The constructs that we are measuring in this study are what Kozlowski and Klein (2000) called convergent-emergent constructs. Our constructs start as a function of the individual psychological processes (i.e., cognition, affect) of our TMT respondents. However, even though the responses are a function of the individual TMT's psychological processes, their responses *converge* to a single value, represented by an average. This convergence occurs because the scale items are assessing some shared reality (e.g., employees' experience of organizational culture or TMT members' interactions with the CEO). For example, TMT members have their own unique impression of the CEO's participative leadership behavior. However, the TMT members' perceptions tend to converge because they are describing the same external reality, namely, the CEO's participative behavior. In addition to being convergent, the constructs are said to be *emergent* because the psychometric properties of these scales only operate or are only valid at the aggregate- or group-level of analysis (Hanges & Dickson, 2004). For instance, one can only have a valid discussion of Team Solidarity by measuring this variable at the team level of analysis.

Given that we hypothesized that TMT members' responses to our items supposedly measuring a particular construct should converge, we need to demonstrate that this is actually occurring. Similar to our prior quantitative work (House, Hanges, Javidan, Dorfman, & Gupta, 2004), we mainly relied on the intraclass correlation coefficients (ICC[1]) and one-way analyses of variance (Bliese, 2000; Shrout & Fleiss, 1979) to demonstrate that convergence was occurring, and thus, aggregation of individual responses to the mean response for a construct was justified. Median values of ICC(1) of .12 are reported in the organizational literature (James, 1982). As will be presented in Chapter 6, our ICCs for each scale compare very favorably to the literature. We also computed $r_{WG(J)}$ (James, Demaree, & Wolf, 1984) to demonstrate that aggregation of individual scores was justified. The $r_{WG(J)}$ analysis is an index that assesses the degree to which there is within-group agreement. Finally, we also examined the reliability of the TMT managers' average estimate (ICC[2]) for each scale. Our findings were very good for each scale thereby indicating that aggregation was appropriate. The $r_{WG(J)}$ analyses are reported for each scale and are presented in Chapter 6.

Creating Psychometrically Sound Scales

The following procedures were used to create our scales. First, we aggregated the responses from the TMT members to the CEO/organization level of analysis. Recall that the CEO and the organization level of analysis are equivalent because there is one to one correspondence for CEOs and organizations. TMT responses had to be aggregated to develop our scales because no TMT member responded to every leadership item for a particular scale. As discussed in Chapter 4, items for leadership dimensions (e.g., Charismatic: visionary) were separated across Surveys A and B. Each TMT member only completed one of these surveys. Thus, the covariance between the items on Survey A and those items on Survey B could not be estimated at the individual TMT member level of analysis. This covariance could only be estimated at the CEO/organization level of analysis and that is why we used aggregated data for this analysis and for all subsequent analyses. That is, because of the choice in our research design minimize same source error, individual TMT respondents only completed selected items for our constructs—thus, the necessary psychometric analyses for our scales could not be performed at the individual TMT respondent level.

We then standardized the average item responses within each country to remove country-level differences. Country-level differences are eliminated by this standardization procedure because the standardized scores for each scale will have a mean of zero within each country. Subsequent to this standardization, we performed a maximum likelihood exploratory factor analysis for each scale on the data pooled across all countries. This exploratory factor analysis is called a pooled within-country factor analysis and reflects the factor structure of the scales at the CEO/organization level of analysis across all countries. Recall that the CEO and organizational level of analysis are identical because there is only one CEO per organization. We also computed Cronbach's coefficient alpha to assess the degree of internal consistency reliability for these factors. The results of these analyses are also presented in Chapter 6.

Measurement Equivalence_____

While the prior factor analysis established the average within-country factor structure of our scales, we also need to establish the measurement equivalence of these scales prior to testing our GLOBE hypotheses. That is, we need to demonstrate that a similar factor structure actually exists in every country. Measurement equivalence can exist at several levels, and one does not have to attain the highest level in order to use a particular scale (Steenkamp & Baumgartner, 1998).

The first and lowest level of equivalence is called *construct equivalence,* and it is demonstrated by showing that the same number of factors emerges among a set of items and that the same items "load" on the same factors across countries. The second and next level of equivalence is called *metric or measurement unit equivalence.* Metric equivalence is demonstrated by determining whether the factor loadings are equivalent across countries. If this level of equivalence is demonstrated, there is evidence that the scale has equal scale intervals across countries and thus, assessment of statistical relationships (e.g., correlation, regression) is meaningful. The third and next level of measurement equivalence is *scalar equivalence.* This level assesses whether the items are either upwardly or downwardly biased between countries. That is, the true score for two countries on a particular scale (e.g., Team-Oriented leadership) could be truly equal but because of response bias, the average scale scores for these two countries would be different (if the scale lacked scalar equivalence). Scalar equivalence is assessed by examining the equivalence of the intercepts across countries. This level of equivalence is important for meaningful comparison of scale means or averages across countries.

The fourth and final level is labeled *full equivalence* in which the equivalence of the latent variance/covariance matrix and the error variance/covariance matrix across countries are examined. If the error variance/covariance matrix is equivalent across countries, then that means that the construct is measured with equal reliability across countries. This final level of measurement equivalence is an extremely difficult criterion and rarely obtained but provides a more complete understanding of the extent to which country-level variables have little or no effect on responses to survey items.

For the present project, we are primarily interested in assessing relationships among constructs. In order to meaningfully interpret these relationships among constructs (e.g., Participative leadership and Firm Competitive Performance), it is important that the metric level of equivalence exists for our scales. For example, participative leadership may relate to certain outcomes in the United States such as higher motivation for TMTs under a participative CEO, but not in Japan. This could be due to people interpreting the scale of participation differently in the United States and Japan—a relatively uninteresting finding. Conversely, the different relationships may be due to the fact that people in both cultures are interpreting the scale the same, but the effects of participatory leadership are different across countries. This latter finding is more theoretically and practically interesting.

Usually all four levels of measurement equivalence are assessed by using structural equation modeling. In particular, a multigroup structural equation model is performed in which each country's data is used and progressively more constraints are placed on the model as the lower levels of measurement equivalence are met. Minimal sample size for these types of analyses is 100 observations per group. Unfortunately we could not use this approach because our sample size was approximately 40 observations per country. Therefore, we developed an alternative protocol. This protocol was based on a meta-analytic perspective and assessed the extent to which our data had both construct and metric equivalence.

To demonstrate the first level of measurement equivalence (i.e., construct equivalence), we first conducted principal components analysis separately in each country and examined the eigenvalues for each scale. We computed the average eigenvalue across countries and computed a 95% confidence interval across countries for the extracted factors. Construct equivalence was declared if the lower bound of the confidence interval for a particular factor exceeded the eigenvalue > 1 rule. Therefore, the number of factors extracted for a set of items was determined by the number of factors whose lower bound of the confidence interval was higher than 1. In almost all cases, a single factor was adequate to represent the scale thus demonstrating the first level of measurement equivalence—construct equivalence. For example, in Table 6.6, the first factor for the visionary scale (Survey C items) had an eigenvalue that ranged from 2.91 to 4.62 across the 24 countries in our sample. That means that, across the 24 countries, this single factor explained anywhere from 48.5% to 77% of the original item variance. In other words, a single factor was extracted in all of our countries (i.e., construct equivalence) for this scale and that this single factor did a very good job summarizing the single visionary leadership construct among these items in all countries.

Metric Equivalence

To demonstrate metric equivalence, we conducted a series of within country exploratory factor analyses. It should be noted that when performing exploratory analyses, the resultant factor structure is a function of the population factor structure as well as some unique characteristics of the sample. Thus, when initially examining the factor structure across two countries, it might appear that there are meaningful differences in the factor structure across countries. Therefore, after obtaining each country's factor structure, we performed a Procrustes rotation to compare the similarity of each country's factor loadings. Procrustes rotation compares the factor structure of a pair of countries (or the factor structure between one country and some comparison sample's factor structure) and determines the degree to which the two country factor structures can be rotated to achieve total similarity. In other words, Procrustes rotation seeks to determine the extent to which the country differences in factor structure are more apparent than real.

The procedure to compute a Procrustes rotation was as follows. We first created a comparison sample that we used to compare the similarity of each country's factor structure for a particular scale. We used the pooled within-country data set, described earlier, as our comparison sample and obtained the factor loadings from this data set. Following the work of other cross-cultural researchers, the pooled within-country data set was created by obtaining the correlation matrix for a set of items within each country, converting these correlations to the Fisher Z equivalents, averaging the transformed correlations across countries and then reconverting these average values back into correlations to obtain a pooled within-country correlation matrix. We then performed a factor analysis on this pooled within-country correlation matrix, and the resultant factor structure was used as the comparison structure for all of our Procrustes rotations for a particular scale.

The specific results of this comparison for each scale are presented in Chapter 6. In general, our findings supported the metric equivalence of our scales—that is, factor loadings were equivalent across countries. This indicates that the relationships among our variables can be meaningfully interpreted across countries.

Statistical Analyses Testing GLOBE Hypotheses

As indicated in Chapter 4, we collected data from several different sources and across multiple levels of analysis in this study. Specifically, TMT members (Level 1: Individual TMT members) provided information about the CEO's leadership behavior as well as the organizational performance (Level 2: CEO/organization level of analysis). We sampled an average of 40 organizations per country with TMT members only appearing in our sample for a single organization (i.e., TMT members were nested within organizations). Further, these organizations were nested within countries (Level 3: Country). As indicated previously, we used the country-level CLT information presented in House and colleagues (2004) to provide information about leadership expectations for each country. Thus, statistical analyses used in this study were chosen in order to handle the nested data structure.

Research designs that have variables at multiple levels of analysis have been referred to as multilevel (Kozlowski & Klein, 2000), cross-level (Rousseau, 1985), meso (House, Rousseau, & Thomas, 1995), or mixed-determinant (Klein, Dansereau, & Hall, 1994) models or theories. As previously indicated, our research design and our hypotheses are multilevel and therefore require appropriate statistical analysis for this kind of data. We tested many of our hypotheses using a technique known to be an effective tool for analyzing multilevel conceptual models and nested data—HLM (Hofmann, 1997; Hofmann, Griffin, & Gavin, 2000). HLM, also referred to as multilevel linear models in the sociological research (Goldstein, 1995), mixed effects and random effects models in the biometrics literature, random coefficient regression models in the econometrics literature, and as covariance components models in the statistical literature (Bryk & Raudenbush, 1992). We choose this analysis because of the nature of our variables, the nature of our hypotheses, and the structure of our data. We should note that due to the nature of our research design, we could not run a three level HLM analysis. As discussed earlier, the data at Level 1 (i.e., TMT member level) were averaged to the CEO/Organization level of analysis before our analyses. Thus, we performed a 2 level HLM (CEO/Organization level and Country level).

HLM can be conceptualized as a multistep process designed to test relationships between independent and dependent variables at multiple levels. The following example is used to explain how the analysis was conducted. One hypothesis that was tested was that CEO leadership behavior (e.g., Charismatic) would predict TMT Effort and Firm Competitive Performance. This involves multilevel analysis because even though the independent variable (CEO leadership behavior) and the dependent variables (TMT Effort and Firm Competitive Performance) are at the same level of analysis (i.e., Level 1: CEO/organization), we need to account for the fact that the organizational data is nested within countries (i.e., Level 2: Country).

The first step of our HLM analysis can be thought of as producing an equation for each country between CEO Charismatic leadership and one of our dependent measures (e.g., TMT Effort). Equation 5.1 shows the Level 1 (i.e., within-country) equation regressing TMT Effort onto Charismatic leadership.

$$\text{TMT Effort}_{ij} = \beta_{oj} + \beta_{1j} \text{ Charisma}_{ij} + r_{ij} \qquad (5.1)$$

In this equation, β_{oj} refers to the intercept for country j. It represents the unadjusted mean TMT effort in country j. In Equation 5.1 above, β_{1j} represents the unstandardized slope for the relationship between Charismatic leadership and TMT effort in country j. Finally, r_{ij} represents the error associated with estimating this equation.

It is possible that Equation 5.1 varies across countries. For example, perhaps the unadjusted mean TMT Effort might be higher in some countries (e.g., Peru, Austria) than another (e.g., Russia, Estonia). It is also possible that the slopes of Charismatic leadership–TMT Effort relationship might vary across countries. In other words, perhaps this relationship is stronger in some countries than in others. To test these possibilities, one has to conduct a Level 2 (between country) analysis.

To test whether there are significant differences in the equation 5.1 regression coefficients, the following two equations would be computed:

$$\beta_{oj} = \gamma_{oo} + U_{oj} \qquad (5.2)$$

$$\beta_{1j} = \gamma_{10} + U_{1j} \qquad (5.3)$$

In equation 5.2, γ_{00} represents the grand intercept averaged across all countries and U_{oj} represents the between country variability among the intercepts. There is a χ^2 test that assesses whether U_{oj} is significantly larger than would be expected if there were no real differences in intercepts among the countries. This type of analysis is referred to as a random intercepts model (Bryk & Raudenbush, 1992; Kreft & Leeuw, 1998). In random intercept models, only the means of the dependent variable (i.e., the intercept in equation 5.1) are allowed to vary across countries and the focus of such analyses are usually to predict why this country-level variation is occurring.

In Equation 5.3, γ_{10} represents the grand slope averaged across all countries. U_{1j} represents the between country variability among the slopes. As with the random intercept model, there is a χ^2 test that assesses whether U_{1j} is significantly larger than would be expected if there were no real slope differences among the countries. This kind of analysis is called a random slopes model (Bryk & Raudenbush, 1992; Kreft & Leeuw, 1998). In random slope models, if there are significant country-level differences in the slope, some country-level variable is identified to help explain why the slopes vary. Basically, random slopes models can roughly be thought of as similar to traditional moderated multiple regression analysis in which some variable (e.g., culture) is believed to moderate the relationship between two other variables (e.g., Charismatic leadership–TMT Effort relationship).

Before closing this section, there are two final points. First, we used grand-mean centering in our HLM analysis. We choose grand-mean centering in this study because it enables more meaningful tests of interactions (Kreft & Leeuw, 1998) as well as tests for incremental variance of subsequent predictors in the analysis. Second, when we report percentage of variance explained (R^2) from our HLM analyses, we are reporting R^2s for the specific level at which the analysis was being conducted. Therefore, if we tested a predictor at Level 1, the R^2 associated with that predictor is the percentage of Level 1 variance explained by that predictor.

Assessment of Culturally Endorsed Implicit Leadership Theory–Behavior Fit

As shown in Figure 1.1, one of the major hypotheses in this study is that the fit between culturally endorsed implicit leadership theory (CLT) and CEO leadership behavior affects leader acceptance and effectiveness. The question that will be addressed in this section is how to assess fit so that this hypothesis can be empirically verified. We first considered using the response surface methodology recommended by Edwards (1995, 2002). However, it became clear that this approach would focus on each leadership dimension separately, and thus, it is not consistent with our current conceptual understanding of how schemas and CLTs actually operate (i.e., in a gestalt manner; Hanges,

Dorfman, Shteynberg, & Bates, 2006).[1] As these new cognitive models suggest, when people think of their ideal or prototypical leaders, an entire picture emerges as opposed to a dimension-by-dimension conceptualization. Thus, we develop a new fit index that is consistent with this current and more Gestalt approach to cognitive thinking.

To test our hypothesis we developed a new fit index. Our definition of *fit* is formally defined as the degree of similarity between a CEO's leadership behavior and the country-level leadership expectations (CLT scores) across the 21 primary leadership dimensions. This definition is operationalized by capturing two aspects of the match between CEO leader behavior and CLTs. The first aspect, hereafter referred to as profile pattern similarity, assesses the linear pattern between individual CEO's leadership profile and the CEO's cultural leadership profile (across the 21 leadership dimensions). The second aspect, hereafter referred to as the absolute behavioral match, assesses the overall similarity in the absolute level or magnitude between each CEO's behavior and the CLT dimensions (across the 21 leadership dimensions). These two aspects of fit, profile pattern similarity, and absolute behavioral match, were combined into a single fit index. The advantage of using this new method over previous methods is that it is consistent with current cognitive models and directly incorporates culture into the statistical analysis in a fashion consistent with our conceptual model.

Regression analyses were performed by first reformatting the GLOBE database so that for each CEO the reformatted data matrix consisted of 21 rows and 6 columns. The columns of this converted matrix represented variables specifying (1) the leadership dimension contained in each row of the data, (2) a country code variable, (3) the CLT variable ratings, the CEO leadership behavior variable, and (4) a CEO identification variable.

Because the fit index is new, we provide the following example to aid the reader's understanding of how it was computed. Table 5.1 presents simulated data for both country-level CLTs and CEO behaviors for five primary leadership behaviors. As can be seen in this table, CEO behaviors and the country specific CLTs are presented in each row for a single leadership dimension.

---

[1]We considered using the Edwards (1995, 2002) response surface methodology to test the fit between the CLT and CEO behavior. However, it soon became clear that the Edwards procedure was inconsistent with the underlying theory driving our project. Specifically, "fit" in Edwards' procedure is assessed element by element and would involve interaction terms between each of the 21 primary leadership dimensions with their respective country-level CLT dimensions. For example, for the Autonomous leadership scale, Edwards procedure requires the use of five predictors: autonomous behavior ($x1$), autonomous CLT ($x2$), autonomous behavior squared ($x1^2$), autonomous CLT squared ($x2^2$), and the interaction between autonomous behavior and CLT ($x1x2$). This procedure is then repeated for each of the remaining 20 primary leadership dimensions. Rather, as discussed in Chapter 9, we believe that the theoretical mechanism is a gestalt matching of all 21 leadership dimensions to the CLTs rather than a dimension-to-dimension analysis. Furthermore, using this procedure would require 105 predictors for each of the eight dependent variables (i.e., five predictors for each of the 21 primary leadership dimensions). A meaningful understanding of the results of such analyses, along with a visual depiction, would be virtually impossible.

Table 5.1   Illustrative Database Demonstrating Calculation of Profile Fit

	Country	CLT 2004	CEO Behavior	CEO ID
Admin. competence	1	6	5	A
Autocratic	1	5	3	A
Autonomous	1	4	2	A
Visionary	1	6	4	A
Inspirational	1	5	3	A
Admin. competence	1	6	5	B
Autocratic	1	5	3	B
Autonomous	1	4	3	B
Visionary	1	6	6	B
Inspirational	1	5	7	B
Admin. competence	2	2	2	C
Autocratic	2	1	2	C
Autonomous	2	2	3	C
Visionary	2	5	4	C
Inspirational	2	5	4	C

(While not shown in Table 5.1, in actuality, there were 21 rows of data for each CEO's data where each row provides the corresponding ratings for the 21 first-order GLOBE leadership scales.) Our example continues by considering a single country (labeled as country 1). For each primary leadership dimension such as "administratively competent," Table 5.1 presents this country's CLT score, a single CEO's rating on this dimension, and the identification of this CEO (e.g., ID for the first CEO in country 1 is labeled as CEO A). The first 5 rows of this table represent data for this specific CEO in country 1 (i.e., CEO A). The second five rows represent CEO B for the same five leadership behaviors. The last five rows show the data for CEO C for the same leadership behaviors along with the CLT for another country (denoted as country 2 in the first column in Table 5.1).

Pattern Similarity Fit

To assess the pattern similarity fit between each CEO's leadership behavioral profile and the CLT leadership profile, we conducted separate simple linear regressions for each CEO using the House and colleagues' (2004) 21 CLT leadership dimensions as the predictor and the measured (i.e., actual) 21 CEO leadership behaviors for the same dimensions as the dependent variable. The unstandardized regression coefficient for the slope between these variables was our measure of pattern similarity fit between the CLT leadership dimensions and the CEO behavioral dimensions. In other words, the following unstandardized regression equation was computed separately for *each* CEO:

$$Behavior = b_{0i} + b_{y_i \cdot x_i} CLT \tag{5.4}$$

In this equation, $b_{y_i \cdot x_i}$ represents the unstandardized slope between leadership CLT and leader behavior for the ith CEO. Greater linear pattern fit is indicated by larger positive $b_{y_i \cdot x_i}$. We used the unstandardized slopes, as opposed to the standardized slopes, because the unstandardized slopes are unaffected by differential variances in the ratings of the 21 primary leadership dimensions across CEOs.

In our Table 5.1 example, the pattern similarity fit is measured by the within CEO linear regression slopes for each CEO. These calculated slopes indicate that CEO A has an unstandardized regression weight of 1.29, CEO B has a weight of 1.14, and the weight for CEO C is .50. The larger the b weight, the greater the pattern similarity fit between the CLT and CEO behavior. Therefore, the closest pattern fit occurred for CEO A, CEO C had the worst fit, and CEO B, is pretty good as this CEO had an in-between level of fit but closer to A than C.

Absolute Behavioral Fit

The second aspect of fit was an assessment of absolute level of agreement between CLTs and behavior. This aspect of fit was conceptualized and measured as the square root of the absolute reliability coefficient (ρ_i) discussed in generalizability theory. The absolute reliability coefficient indicates the ability of the CLT ratings to exactly predict the level of the CEO's leadership behaviors.

The absolute reliability coefficient was computed by conducting a completely randomized factorial ANOVA for each CEO. In this factorial ANOVA, one facet was the attribute of leadership being rated (i.e., 21 primary leadership dimensions) and the other facet was "leadership CLTs versus leader behavior." The dependent variable for this analysis was a newly created variable we labeled "rating." This variable consisted of 42 lines of data for each CEO with the first 21 being the House and colleagues' (2004) country-level 21 CLT dimension ratings and the second 21 lines being the 21 average behavior ratings for that CEO. A source table was calculated for each CEO and the variance components of the design were computed. This analysis enabled us to calculate the absolute reliability coefficient (ρ_i) as follows:

$$\rho_i = \frac{\sigma^2_{Leader\,Profile}}{\sigma^2_{Leader\,Profile} + \sigma^2_{CLT} + \sigma^2_{Leader\,Profile*CLT}} \tag{5.5}$$

Where $\sigma^2_{Leader\,Profile}$ is the variance estimate for the effect of the leadership profile; σ^2_{CLT} represents the variance for the CLT prediction, and $\sigma^2_{Leader\,Profile*CLT}$ is the interaction between the leadership profile and the CLTs. The higher the ρ_i, the better the agreement between CLTs and CEO behavior. Mathematically, ρ_i is a variance estimate and so we took the square root of this estimate to yield the reliability index. This reliability index is basically a correlation, but it is important to remember that it expresses the relationship between the CLT to perfectly capture the CEO behavior.

Returning to our simulated example in Table 5.1, our calculation for the absolute behavioral fit index showed the closest square root absolute fit occurred for CEO C (.92), followed by CEO B (.67). The absolute behavior fit index was .39 for CEO A. Note, the rank order of fit according to this absolute behavior fit agreement is C, followed by B then A. This ranking is in contrast to the rank order of fit as provided by the pattern fit index (i.e., A was the highest, followed by B, then C).

To obtain a single measure of fit, we combined these two pieces of information into a single composite measure of fit. We created this single composite fit measure by first standardizing the pattern fit index and the square root of the absolute reliability coefficient and then averaging these two standardized indices into a single index. This standardization process allows us to create a composite measure of fit that equally weights both aspects of fit. The rank order for this combined index for the simulated data (assuming a mean and standard deviation [SD] of this simulated data of .6 and .4, respectively, for both aspects of fit) are .60, .76, and .28. On the basis of these scores, the best order of overall fit is CEO B, CEO A, and then CEO C. The reason CEO B had the highest fit was that this CEO was in the middle position for pattern fit and absolute behavioral fit. On the other hand, CEOs A and C had substantially poorer fit with at least one aspect of the Gestalt Fit measure thereby pulling their position on the overall fit score down. Further examples, explanation, and illustrations of pattern, behavioral similarity, and Gestalt Fit will be provided in Chapter 9.

In summary, in this chapter we discussed the rationale and procedure for developing scales and testing our hypotheses. We accomplished the following:

- Indicated which statistical methods would be used to test the viability of our conceptual models as well as the methods that would be used to test our hypotheses
- Discussed the necessity of justifying aggregation to the CEO level of analysis
- Indicated the various psychometric analyses that would be performed and included a discussion of measurement equivalence issues and analysis that would be performed to develop our measures
- Explained what HLM statistical analysis is and why we used it to test our hypotheses.
- Described our new measure of Gestalt Fit, which we used in this study to test our theoretical proposition that the match between country-level leadership expectations (CLT) and actual CEO behavior leads to critical outcomes
- Presented an example of Gestalt Fit, providing an illustration of how the two constituent components combine into a single overall fit index

6 Psychometric Evidence for Leadership and Outcome Constructs

The previous chapter discussed our rationale for choosing specific statistical methods to test our hypotheses in this project. In this chapter, we present the evidence for aggregating the top management team (TMT) member responses to the CEO/organization level of analysis. We also present the psychometric and measurement equivalence evidence for our scales. Overall, the information provided in this chapter indicates that our leadership and outcome scales generally either meet or exceed psychometric standards. They perform in a fashion consistent with our expectations.

Convergence Evidence

As discussed in the previous chapter, the constructs that are measured in this study are what Kozlowski and Klein (2000) referred to as convergent–emergent constructs. They are said to be convergent because even though we collect individual perceptions of phenomena from our TMT respondents, they are describing a shared reality. Thus, if the scale is working properly, their responses should *converge* onto a single value, usually represented by an average. The constructs have the *emergent* property because the psychometric properties of these scales only operate at the aggregate- or group-level of analysis (Hanges & Dickson, 2004). In this section, we discuss the evidence regarding the convergent property of the TMT responses. We first focus on the leadership scales and then discuss the convergence evidence for the three outcome measures.

Convergence Evidence for Leadership Scales

As discussed in Chapter 5, we used $r_{WG(J)}$; intraclass correlation coefficient, or ICC (ICC[1]); and ICC(2) to assess the extent to which the individual responses of the TMT respondents converged. The $r_{WG(J)}$ values for our 21 primary leadership scales are shown in Table 6.1. The $r_{WG(J)}$ values ranged from .78 to .93 with an average of .85. In general, $r_{WG(J)}$ values of .70 or greater are considered as evidence of sufficient convergence among the respondents. Thus, the $r_{WG(J)}$ statistic indicates that there is considerable agreement within TMT members who describe the leadership behaviors of the same CEO.

Table 6.1　Convergence Evidence for Leadership Behavior Scales Separated by Survey Version

Leadership Behavior Scale	$r_{WG(J)}$	ICC(1)	ICC(2)
Visionary—Survey A	.93	.35	.61
Visionary—Survey B	.90	.20	.42
Inspirational—Survey A	.89	.26	.51
Inspirational—Survey B	.90	.17	.38
Self-Sacrificial—Survey A	.86	.15	.35
Self-Sacrificial—Survey B	.83	.10	.25
Integrity—Survey A	.89	.24	.49
Integrity—Survey B	.89	.27	.53
Decisive	.88	.16	.37
Performance oriented—Survey A	.89	.15	.35
Performance oriented—Survey B	.89	.20	.43
Collaborative team orientation	.87	.20	.43
Team integrator—Survey A	.89	.20	.44
Team integrator—Survey B	.87	.20	.43
Diplomatic—Survey A	.86	.12	.29
Diplomatic—Survey B	.89	.16	.37
Malevolent—Survey A	.87	.24	.49
Malevolent—Survey B	.81	.19	.41
Administratively competent—Survey A	.88	.22	.46
Administratively competent—Survey B	.87	.18	.39
Participative	.88	.27	.53
Autocratic—Survey A	.82	.29	.55
Autocratic—Survey B	.81	.17	.38

Leadership Behavior Scale	$r_{WG(J)}$	ICC(1)	ICC(2)
Modesty—Survey A	.81	.10	.24
Modesty—Survey B	.81	.16	.37
Humane orientation—Survey A	.83	.13	.31
Humane orientation—Survey B	.84	.13	.31
Autonomous—Survey A	.78	.11	.27
Autonomous—Survey B	.79	.04	.12
Self-Centered	.83	.19	.41
Status conscious—Survey A	.78	.06	.17
Status conscious—Survey B	.79	.04	.12
Internally competitive	.81	.16	.36
Face-Saver—Survey A	.78	.11	.26
Face-Saver—Survey B	.81	.06	.16
Bureaucratic—Survey A	.83	.13	.30
Bureaucratic—Survey B	.85	.17	.38

Note: All ICC(1)s are significant.

Next, we examined the ICC(1) to provide additional convergence evidence. Table 6.1 provides the ICC(1) results for the 21 primary leadership scales. The average ICC(1) for our leadership scales was .17. The average value obtained in the organizational literature is .12 (James, 1982) with ICC(1) values typically reported between .05 and .20 with the higher numbers providing stronger evidence of convergence (Bliese, 2000). Thus, as can be seen from Table 6.1, our leadership scales are well within the typical ICC(1) range reported in this literature. Once again, we have evidence supportive of convergence in their description of CEO leadership behavior.

Finally, Table 6.1 also provides ICC(2) values for our leadership scales. As noted in Chapter 5, ICC(2) indicates the reliability of our estimate of the various TMT's convergence point (i.e., average score) for each leadership scale. In the present study, reliable measurement of the TMT average responses is primarily a function of the number of TMT members available to average a particular leadership scale for the CEO. In general, the literature typically looks for a value of .70 to indicate a minimum reliability value. As can be seen in this table, our ICC(2) values are lower than this desired level. This is due to the fact that we only had two or three TMT members providing survey responses per CEO. Our ICC(2) values would have been greater if we had more TMT members respond to each survey version. Unfortunately, that is impractical given the level of the people in the organization that were completing our survey as well as the research design decision discussed in Chapter 4 to control for same source bias by using multiple surveys. The consequence of having the level of reliability that we have is that any results reported concerning relationships with these variables would be *conservative* estimates. It has been known since the early days of classical test theory that unreliability suppresses the maximum correlation that can be found between two variables.

In summary, the results support the belief that the TMT members converge in their description of the leadership behavior of the CEO. Thus, there is support for aggregating the individual TMT responses to obtain an average CEO score for each leadership scale. While the reliability of these averages for some of these scales may be less than desired, we noted that the lower reliability causes a conservative bias when we test our hypotheses. In the next section, we focus on the convergence evidence for the outcome measures.

Convergence Evidence for Outcome Measures (Top Management Team Dedication and Firm Competitive Performance)

As with the leadership behavior scales, we examined the same three statistics (i.e., $r_{WG(J)}$, ICC[1], ICC[2]) to determine if the TMT member responses regarding the organizational outcomes were converging to a common answer. Table 6.2 shows the results of our analysis for all outcome measures, for each survey version, collected in this study. As can be seen, across all survey versions, the range of $r_{WG(J)}$s for our outcome measures was between .86 and .97 with an average $r_{WG(J)}$ of .89. Thus, there is substantial evidence of convergence in the responses of TMT members when describing the outcome variables.

We next examined the ICC(1)s for each outcome scale and these values are reported in Table 6.2. The average ICC(1) for the outcome scales is .48, which compares extremely favorably with the typically obtained ICC(1)'s reported in the organizational literature (Bliese, 2000; James, 1982).

Finally, the reliability of these average outcome scores (i.e., ICC[2]) are also shown in Table 6.2. The reliability of the average responses for the outcome measures were at professionally accepted levels regardless of survey version. It should be noted that the reliability of the financial outcomes measures could not be computed because this information was usually obtained from the one TMT member who was explicitly chosen because s/he had an accounting or financial background.

In summary, there was substantial support for the convergent nature of our outcome measures. This supports averaging the individual TMT responses on these scales to the CEO/organization level. In the next section of this chapter, we will examine the emergent psychometric properties of our scales.

Table 6.2   Convergence Evidence for the CEO Outcome Measures Separated by Survey Version

Outcome Measures	$r_{WG(J)}$	ICC(1)	ICC(2)
Survey A			
Commitment	.88	.55	.79
Effort	.86	.35	.69
Team Solidarity	.86	.52	.76
Survey B			
Commitment	.89	.61	.83
Effort	.86	.38	.71
Team Solidarity	.87	.47	.73
Survey C			
Commitment	.90	.52	.78
Effort	.90	.35	.68
Team Solidarity	.90	.41	.67
Financial Outcomes			
Competitive Sales Performance	.97	.44	NA
Competitive Industry Domination	.94	.66	NA

Note: All ICC(1)s are significant.

Emergent Psychometric Property: Internal Consistency and Factor Analysis

As discussed in Chapter 5, we conducted a series of analyses to assess the psychometric soundness of our leadership and outcome scales. These analyses consisted of factor analyses as well as assessment of the internal consistency (i.e., Cronbach's coefficient alpha) of the scales. However, before providing the results of these analyses, it is important to note that the structure of our data as well as the level of our constructs required a careful application of these statistical tools to our TMT manager database.

Specifically, recall that the leadership measures were designed to measure leadership at the CEO level. Further, the outcome measures were designed to measure properties of the organization (i.e., profitability of the entire organization, Commitment of the TMT). Thus, for each organization, any difference among the responses of individual TMT members when completing our scale is considered variability in which we were not interested. This variability for our analyses can be considered noise or error. Further, as discussed in Chapter 4, the leadership items were randomly distributed between two survey versions. While this design choice was useful in terms of minimizing common source bias when measuring constructs, the downside of this choice is that it eliminated the use of certain analytic tools when trying to interpret the psychometric properties of the data. The bottom line to these issues is that the psychometric analyses cannot be conducted at the individual TMT member level. Instead, we are only able to assess the psychometric properties at the CEO level of analysis. Because there is a single CEO per firm, the CEO level of analysis also represents the firm or organizational level of analysis. This is the appropriate level of analysis for our leadership scales. This analytic consequence is also true for the outcome measures in this study because, as noted earlier, they were designed to measure organizational level phenomena (i.e., TMT Dedication and Firm Competitive Performance).[1]

Before showing the results for our scales, it is important to recall that, as indicated in Chapter 5, we had to restructure our database before we could assess the emergent properties of our scales. This new database was created by averaging the individual TMT responses for each item to the CEO/ organization level. This new CEO/organization level database eliminated the systematic missing data that was present at the individual TMT level. The systematic missing data was due to the use of two different survey versions to collect leadership information from the individual TMT members. For example, visionary leadership was measured with nine items—some of which were on survey version 1 and the remaining of which were on survey version 2. Different TMT members completed the two survey versions. Thus, a complete correlation matrix for all nine visionary items could not be obtained using the individual TMT database because no one TMT member answered all nine items. A complete correlation matrix could only be obtained using the average CEO/organization database because each CEO had averaged responses for all

---

[1]Unlike our prior work, we could not use multilevel confirmatory factor analysis (e.g., Dyer, Hanges, & Hall, 2005; Hanges & Dickson, 2004) to confirm our factor scales. Multilevel confirmatory factor analysis would require us to have data at the individual respondent level of analysis (i.e., individual TMT members) and specify which CEOs the TMT members reported to (i.e., the CEO/organization level of analysis) as well as which countries the individual TMT members were citizens of (i.e., country level of analysis). Unfortunately, the present research design eliminated this possibility because a complete variance–covariance item matrix for our leadership scales could not be created at the individual TMT member level of analysis.

For example, the visionary leadership scale was measured by a total of nine items. As shown in Appendix B, six of the items measuring this construct were included in Survey A and the remaining three items of the scale were included in the other survey. Thus, no TMT member completed all nine items of the visionary leadership scale. This research design forces the estimated correlation between items on different surveys to be inappropriately estimated to be zero at the individual TMT level of analysis. Thus, the way the surveys were constructed prevents us from conducting a multilevel confirmatory factor analysis.

nine visionary items. Thus, the psychometric properties of the complete vision-ary scale could be determined using the CEO/organization database.

Emergent Psychometric Properties of the Leadership Measures

We first assessed the psychometric properties of our leadership scales by conducting pooled within-country factor analyses. To conduct this analy-sis, we standardized the averaged CEO/organization database for each country. This standardization removed country-level differences on the scales from influencing our factor analyses. This process created what can be called a pooled within-country CEO/organization database of aggre-gated leadership items.

We next conducted a series of maximum likelihood exploratory factor analyses on the entire pooled within-country CEO/organization database sepa-rately for each leadership scale. In this factor analysis, we followed the Kaiser rule (i.e., factors are retained if their eigenvalue is greater than one) to deter-mine the number of factors to retain. In this preliminary analysis, we included all items that measure a particular leadership construct into the factor analysis. The results of the pooled within-country factor analyses are shown in Table 6.3.

Table 6.3   Preliminary Exploratory Factor Analysis for the Leadership Scales

Leadership Behavior Scale	Number of Factors (Percentage Variance Explained)	Correlation Between Factors
1. Visionary	2 (53.1%)	.46
2. Inspirational	2 (47.1%)	.49
3. Self-Sacrificial	2 (71.6%)	.23
4. Integrity	2 (51.0%)	.53
5. Decisive	1 (46.4%)	NA
6. Performance oriented	2 (45.4%)	.49
7. Collaborative team orientation	1 (43.9%)	NA

(Continued)

(Continued)

Leadership Behavior Scale	Number of Factors (Percentage Variance Explained)	Correlation Between Factors
8. Team integrator	2 (46.2%)	.44
9. Diplomatic	2 (53.7%)	.33
10. Malevolent	2 (48.3%)	.36
11. Administratively competent	2 (55.7%)	.49
12. Participative	1 (50.0%)	NA
13. Autocratic	2 (42.8%)	.46
14. Modesty	1 (21.7%)	NA
15. Humane orientation	2 (51.5%)	.39
16. Autonomous	1 (47.6%)	NA
17. Self-Centered	1 (39.1%)	NA
18. Status conscious	2 (52.8%)	.06
19. Internally competitive	1 (28.0%)	NA
20. Face-Saver	2 (63.7%)	.03
21. Bureaucratic	2 (44.8%)	.34

As can be seen from this table, while we do have evidence of unidimensionality for some of our scales, many of the leadership scales separated into two dimensions. Examination of the structure matrices for the scales that separated into two dimensions revealed that these scales were affected by this study's research design. For example, the items loading on the first factor of the visionary leadership scale were all asked on survey version 1 whereas the visionary items loading on the second factor were all asked on survey version 2. In other words, our factor analyses yielded evidence of a "survey method" effect for some of our leadership scales. While disappointing to find evidence for a survey method effect, it is important to note the two factors obtained for any scale that split apart in the factor analysis were highly correlated (see the last column in Table 6.3). In other words, a single leadership construct, such as visionary leadership, split into two visionary leadership factors—one for each survey. However, they were highly correlated indicating that once the research method factor is taken into account, the two survey version-specific leadership scales basically converged in their depiction of the CEO leadership behavior.[2]

We next assessed the internal consistency reliability (i.e., Cronbach's alpha coefficient) for all the leadership scales. For these analyses, we computed the internal consistency reliability separately for each survey and for each construct. Table 6.4 shows Cronbach's alpha coefficients for each of the leadership scales. It also shows the final linear composite internal consistency estimate for the leadership scale created by combining the two survey version-specific leadership scales. As can be seen from this table, 16 of the 21 leadership scales exhibit acceptable levels of internal consistency. The only exceptions were modesty, autonomous, status conscious, internally competitive, and face-saver. As noted earlier, unreliability results in an underestimated relationship between two variables. Thus, we decided to continue using these scales and note the conservative bias introduced in our results by using these scales.

In summary, the pooled within-country maximum likelihood exploratory factor analysis provided initial information about the dimensionality of our scales. Specifically, it clearly showed that our research design created a substantial survey method effect that split some of our leadership scales. Fortunately, the relatively high intercorrelations among the two version specific scales indicated convergence of the information provided by the different TMT members regarding a particular leadership dimension. Further, our analyses also indicated that, for the most part, our scales exhibited acceptable levels of internal consistency.

Emergent Psychometric Properties of Outcome Measures

Similar to the leadership scale analyses, we started the analysis of the outcome measures by conducting a series of pooled within-country maximum likelihood exploratory factor analyses. The Kaiser rule was used once again to determine the number of factors to retain for each set of items. In this preliminary analysis, we included all items that measure a particular leadership construct into the factor analysis. The results of the factor

---

[2]We performed a secondary set of analyses testing our hypotheses in which we kept our leadership scales separate as a function of the survey (i.e., Survey A: visionary is treated as a separate construct from Survey B: visionary). We correlated these survey version-specific leadership scales with the outcome measures from Survey A and Survey B TMT members. While the magnitude of the relationships reported in Chapter 8 differ somewhat, the conclusions between the reported results and the results that would have been reached by keeping the survey-specific leadership scales were highly similar.

Table 6.4   Cronbach's Alpha Coefficient for the Leadership Scales

Leadership Behavior Scale	Cronbach's Alpha	
	Scale	Linear Composite
• Visionary—Survey A	0.88	0.91
• Visionary—Survey B	0.73	
• Inspirational—Survey A	0.82	0.88
• Inspirational—Survey B	0.64	
• Self-Sacrificial—Survey A	0.55	0.68
• Self-Sacrificial—Survey B	0.65	
• Integrity—Survey A	0.83	0.88
• Integrity—Survey B	0.81	
• Decisive	0.71	NA
• Performance oriented—Survey A	0.70	0.80
• Performance oriented—Survey B	0.76	
• Collaborative team orientation	0.76	NA
• Team integrator—Survey A	0.78	0.83
• Team integrator—Survey B	0.77	
• Diplomatic—Survey A	0.65	0.76
• Diplomatic—Survey B	0.72	
• Malevolent—Survey A	0.79	0.81
• Malevolent—Survey B	0.72	
• Administratively competent—Survey A	0.75	0.83
• Administratively competent—Survey B	0.77	
• Participative	0.82	NA
• Autocratic—Survey A	0.82	0.84
• Autocratic—Survey B	0.72	
• Modesty—Survey A	0.46	0.58
• Modesty—Survey B	0.58	
• Humane orientation—Survey A	0.68	0.75
• Humane orientation—Survey B	0.68	
• Autonomous	0.41	NA
• Self-Centered	0.72	NA

| | Cronbach's Alpha | |
Leadership Behavior Scale	Scale	Linear Composite
• Status conscious—Survey A	0.27	0.31
• Status conscious—Survey B	0.41	
• Internally competitive	0.22	NA
• Face-Saver	0.42	NA
• Bureaucratic—Survey A	0.62	0.72
• Bureaucratic—Survey B	0.70	

analysis are shown in Table 6.5. As can be seen in this table, all the outcome measures exhibited unidimensionality.

We also computed the internal consistency reliability for the outcome measures. This information is also contained in Table 6.5. All of the outcome measures exhibited acceptable levels of internal consistency reliability. It should be noted that the outcome measures collected using the third survey

Table 6.5   Preliminary Exploratory Factor Analysis and Cronbach's Alpha for the Outcome Measures

Leadership Behavior Scale	Number of Factors (Percentage Variance Explained)	Cronbach's Alpha	
		Scale	Linear Composite
Commitment			
Survey A	1 (67.1%)	0.75	0.83
Survey B	1 (73.7%)	0.78	
Survey C	1 (67.6%)	0.76	NA
Effort			
Survey A	1 (50.3%)	0.66	0.76
Survey B	1 (51.2%)	0.68	
Survey C	1 (51.8%)	0.69	NA

(Continued)

(Continued)

Leadership Behavior Scale	Number of Factors (Percentage Variance Explained)	Cronbach's Alpha	
		Scale	Linear Composite
Team Solidarity			
Survey A	1 (66.9%)	0.75	0.81
Survey B	1 (64.2%)	0.72	
Survey C	1 (66.7%)	0.75	NA

(Survey A) were used to test our hypotheses regarding Firm Competitive Performance. However, we also performed an analysis to determine the extent to which same source bias might affect our results. To do these analyses, we averaged the outcome scales obtained using survey versions 1 and 2 together. The linear composite internal consistency reliability estimate for the combined versions 1 and 2 outcome measures are also shown in this table.

In summary, the results of this analysis revealed that the outcome measures were unidimensional and internally consistent. In the next section of this chapter, we continue to explore the properties of our leadership and outcome scales. We will focus on whether the scales were being interpreted similarly in all of the countries.

Measurement Equivalence: Similarity in Meaning_____

In this section of the chapter, we discuss the analyses that we performed to establish the measurement equivalence of our scales. Measurement equivalence means that our scales were being interpreted similarly across countries. As noted previously, measurement equivalence is not an absolute property of a scale because it actually exists at various degrees or gradients. One can still meaningfully use a scale even though the scale does not meet the most stringent criterion regarding measurement equivalence. Further, measurement equivalence is important because we want to ensure that the meaning of the constructs themselves are being interpreted similarly before determining the relationships between constructs.

The first level of equivalence that we sought to establish in our scales is *construct equivalence*. Basically, construct equivalence is demonstrated when the same number of factors for a set of items is extracted in each country. In other words, construct equivalence indicates that a set of items "hang together" in the same manner for all countries from which data were collected. The second level of equivalence that we assessed for our scales was *metric or measurement unit equivalence*. Metric equivalence is demonstrated by assessing whether the strength of the connection between each item and its latent construct is the same in each country from which data was collected. In other words, the similarity of the factor loadings is assessed across countries for metric equivalence. Metric equivalence establishes that the scales have equal intervals in each country and thus, assessment of statistical relationships (e.g., correlation, regression) is meaningful. It is this level of scale equivalence that is important to demonstrate in order to properly interpret relationships between constructs.

Measurement Equivalence for Leadership Scales

We assessed the construct equivalence of our leadership scales by conducting a maximum likelihood exploratory factor analysis for a set of items for each country. Table 6.6 shows the range of eigenvalues for the first

Table 6.6   Construct Equivalence Results for Leadership Scales

Leader Behavior Scales	Within-Country Analysis		
	Eigenvalue Range for First Factor (Across 24 Countries)	Average Eigenvalue for First Factor (Across 24 Countries)	Number of Countries Extracting Second Factor
• Visionary—Survey A	2.91–4.62 (48.5%–77.0%)	3.59 (59.8%)	4
• Visionary—Survey B	1.42–2.45 (47.3%–81.7%)	1.88 (62.7%)	0
• Inspirational—Survey A	1.95–3.18 (48.8%–81.7%)	2.49 (62.3%)	0
• Inspirational—Survey B	1.28–2.22 (42.7%–74.0%)	1.73 (57.7%)	0
• Self-Sacrificial—Survey A	1.02–1.61 (51.0%–80.5%)	1.29 (64.5%)	0
• Self-Sacrificial—Survey B	1.08–1.76 (54.0%–88.0%)	1.47 (73.5%)	0
• Integrity—Survey A	2.03–3.46 (40.6%–69.2%)	2.67 (53.4%)	8
• Integrity—Survey B	1.75–3.02 (43.8%–75.5%)	2.49 (62.3%)	0

(Continued)

(Continued)

Leader Behavior Scales	Within-Country Analysis		
	Eigenvalue Range for First Factor (Across 24 Countries)	Average Eigenvalue for First Factor (Across 24 Countries)	Number of Countries Extracting Second Factor
• Decisive	1.41–2.23 (47.0%–74.3%)	1.82 (60.7%)	0
• Performance oriented— Survey A	1.31–2.15 (43.7%–71.7%)	1.77 (59.0%)	0
• Performance oriented— Survey B	1.57–2.81 (39.3%–70.3%)	2.21 (55.3%)	0
• Collaborative team orientation	1.76–2.62 (44.0%–65.5%)	2.23 (55.8%)	0
• Team integrator—Survey A	1.85–2.97 (37.0%–59.4%)	2.48 (49.6%)	5
• Team integrator—Survey B	1.60–2.33 (53.3%–77.7%)	1.98 (66.0%)	0
• Diplomatic—Survey A	1.23–1.81 (61.5%–90.5%)	1.45 (72.5%)	0
• Diplomatic—Survey B	1.34–2.42 (44.7% - 80.7%)	1.82 (60.7%)	0
• Malevolent—Survey A	1.69–3.37 (42.3%–84.3%)	2.37 (59.3%)	1
• Malevolent—Survey B	1.43–2.23 (47.7%–74.3%)	1.83 (61.0%)	0
• Administratively competent—Survey A	1.33–2.31 (44.3%–77.0%)	1.97 (65.7%)	0
• Administratively competent—Survey B	1.53–2.21 (51.0%–73.7%)	1.90 (63.3%)	0
• Participative	2.03–3.48 (40.6%–69.6%)	2.76 (55.2%)	2
• Autocratic—Survey A	2.23–4.32 (37.2%–72.0%)	3.16 (52.7%)	10
• Autocratic—Survey B	1.34–2.80 (33.5%–70.0%)	2.06 (51.5%)	0
• Modesty—Survey A	1.12–1.74 (37.3%–58.0%)	1.42 (47.3%)	0

Leader Behavior Scales	Within-Country Analysis		
	Eigenvalue Range for First Factor (Across 24 Countries)	Average Eigenvalue for First Factor (Across 24 Countries)	Number of Countries Extracting Second Factor
• Modesty—Survey B	1.05–1.58 (52.5%–79.0%)	1.31 (65.5%)	0
• Humane orientation— Survey A	1.12–1.67 (56.0%–83.5%)	1.44 (72.0%)	0
• Humane orientation— Survey B	1.10–2.16 (36.7%–72.0%)	1.75 (58.3%)	0
• Autonomous	1.03–1.60 (34.3%–53.3%)	1.36 (45.3%)	0
• Self-Centered	1.55–2.61 (38.8%–65.3%)	2.05 (51.3%)	0
• Status conscious—Survey A	1.08–1.88 (54.0% - 94.0%)	1.40 (70.0%)	0
• Status conscious—Survey B	1.0–1.42 (33.3%–47.3%)	1.20 (40.0%)	0
• Internally competitive	1.46–2.49 (29.2%–49.8%)	2.04 (40.8%)	13
• Face-Saver	1.09–1.99 (27.3%–49.8%)	1.52 (38.0%)	0
• Bureaucratic—Survey A	1.15–2.55 (38.3%–85.0%)	1.65 (55.0%)	0
• Bureaucratic—Survey B	1.19–1.83 (59.5%–91.5%)	1.52 (76.0%)	0

factor extracted in each country for each leadership scale. Eigenvalues can be converted into the percentage of variance accounted for by a factor. Table 6.6 shows both the range of the country eigenvalues for the first factor as well as the country percentage of variance accounted by that factor. Further, we also show the average eigenvalue and average percentage of variance accounted for by that factor in this table. Our results showed that the first factor for each leadership scale explained a substantial percentage of variance although for some leadership scales there was a substantial range across countries. In general, however, the average explained variance for the first factor was quite substantial. Further, while not shown in this table, for the primary leadership scales, the majority of countries only had one factor that had an eigenvalue greater than one.

Only three scales had a substantial number of countries that yielded a second factor with an eigenvalue greater than one. Further investigation showed that integrity and autocratic only had one or two problematic items whereas internally competitive had four. In summary, because the vast majority of countries and leadership scales showed only one factor that met the Kaiser rule, we determined that there was substantial support for the construct equivalence of our leadership scales.

We next performed Procrustes rotation to determine whether the factor loadings for the leadership scales were equivalent across countries (Van de Vijver & Leung, 1997). As discussed earlier, metric equivalence is established when the strength of the connection between each item and its latent construct (i.e., factor loadings) are the same across countries. We assessed the similarity of the factor loadings for a particular scale by examining the double-scaled Euclidean distance (DSED) fit measure and the kernel smooth distance fit measure (Barrett, 2006). Both of these measures range from a low of 0 to a maximum of 1 with perfect factor loading fit being represented by 1.0. Table 6.7 shows the average country results of these two fit indices for our leadership scales. As can be seen in this table, all but one of the primary leadership scales exhibited a substantial degree of metric equivalence. The only problematic scale was the scale labeled "status conscious." An examination of the items revealed that the factor loadings for a few of the items on this scale changed over countries. However, as discussed by Steenkamp and Baumgartner (1998), it is possible to still use a scale when it has partial metric equivalence. Thus, our results revealed that 20 of the 21 primary leadership scales exhibited metric equivalence and one scale exhibited partial metric equivalence. In other words, there is evidence that our leadership scales were being interpreted similarly at a sufficient level across countries to test computation of relationships. Table 6.8 shows the intercorrelation among the leadership behavior scales.

Table 6.7 Metric Measurement Equivalence Results for Leadership Scales

Leadership Scale	Average Fit Index	
	DSED	Kernel
• Visionary	0.94	0.94
• Inspirational	0.91	0.90
• Self-Sacrificial	0.93	0.90
• Integrity	0.93	0.92
• Decisive	0.92	0.91
• Performance oriented	0.92	0.92
• Collaborative team orientation	0.93	0.92

| Leadership Scale | Average Fit Index | |
	DSED	Kernel
• Team integrator	0.93	0.92
• Diplomatic	0.92	0.92
• Malevolent	0.93	0.92
• Administratively competent	0.92	0.91
• Participative	0.93	0.92
• Autocratic	0.93	0.91
• Modesty	0.87	0.81
• Humane orientation	0.93	0.91
• Autonomous	0.87	0.81
• Self-Centered	0.90	0.87
• Status conscious	0.62	0.50
• Internally competitive	0.89	0.84
• Face-Saver	0.88	0.81
• Bureaucratic	0.91	0.87

Table 6.8   Correlations Among the Six Global Leadership Dimensions

	Charismatic	Team Oriented	Participative	Humane Oriented	Autonomous	Self-Protective
Charismatic	1.00					
Team Oriented	.90**	1.00				
Participative	.56**	.60**	1.00			
Humane Oriented	.71**	.76**	.64**	1.00		
Autonomous	−.21**	−.30**	−.40**	−.30**	1.00	
Self-Protective	.12**	.08*	−.11**	.16**	.21**	1.00

Note: Sample size for these correlations is 1,010.

* p < .05, ** p < .01

Measurement Equivalence for the Outcome Measures

Table 6.9 shows the range of the eigenvalues for the first factor obtained from a maximum likelihood exploratory factor analysis performed for each country for each outcome measure. As can be seen in this table, there is strong evidence for construct equivalence of our outcome measures. Table 6.10 shows the results of the Procrustes rotation to determine the metric equivalence of our outcome measures. As can be seen from this table, there is very strong support for the metric equivalence of these scales. Thus, these analyses show that the outcome scales were being interpreted similarly at a sufficient level to allow meaningful testing of our hypotheses. Table 6.11 shows the intercorrelation among the outcome measures.

Table 6.9   Construct Measurement Equivalence for Outcome Measures

Outcome Measures	Within-Country Analysis		
	Eigenvalue Range for First Factor	Average Eigenvalue for First Factor	Number of Countries Extracting Second Factor
Commitment			
Survey A	1.45–2.62 (48.3%–87.3%)	2.00 (66.6%)	0
Survey B	1.50–2.48 (50.0%–82.7%)	2.09 (69.6%)	0
Survey C	1.50–2.45 (50.0%–81.7%)	2.02 (67.3%)	0
Effort			
Survey A	1.31–2.43 (32.8%–60.8%)	1.95 (48.6%)	1
Survey B	1.30–2.42 (32.5%–60.5%)	1.94 (48.4%)	1
Survey C	1.51–2.52 (37.8%–63.0%)	2.00 (49.9%)	1
Team Solidarity			
Survey A	1.55–2.26 (51.7%–75.3%)	1.93 (64.2%)	0
Survey B	1.41–2.25 (47.0%–75.0%)	1.87 (62.2%)	0
Survey C	1.35–2.31 (45.0%–77.0%)	1.99 (66.2%)	0

Table 6.10   Metric Equivalence Results for Outcome Measures

Outcome Measures	Average Fit Index	
	DSED	Kernel
• Commitment	0.93	0.90
• Effort	0.90	0.84
• Team Solidarity	0.93	0.91

Table 6.11   Correlations Among the Outcome Measures

Outcome Variables		Outcome Variables					
		1	2	3	4	5	6
1	Commitment						
2	Effort	.52**					
3	Team Solidarity	.66**	.45**				
4	Dedication	.87**	.78**	.84**			
5	Sales Performance	.23**	.15*	.17**	.21**		
6	Industry Dominance	.10	.10	.08	.12*	.35**	
7	Firm Competitive Performance	.20**	.11	.14*	.18**	.81**	.52**

Note: Firm level, standardized within countries to remove between-country variance in the correlations.

$N = 950$. *$p < .05$. **$p < .01$.

Response Bias: Leadership Scales

Cross-cultural researchers have noted that people from different cultures respond to questionnaire items in characteristic patterns (Triandis, 1994). For example, respondents from Asian cultures tend to avoid the extreme ends of a scale whereas respondents from Mediterranean cultures tend to avoid the midpoint of a scale (Hanges, 2004). Our final set of analyses assessed the extent to which our leadership and outcome scales were subject to this cultural response pattern bias.

A statistical standardization procedure that reportedly removes cultural response patterns from survey data has been developed in the cross-cultural literature. In this procedure, each TMT respondent's average response to all the items in a survey as well as their standard deviation (*SD*) to these items are first computed. Then the individual TMT member's responses to each item are standardized in an ipsative manner by subtracting that TMT member's survey mean from the item response and dividing this difference by the TMT member's survey *SD*. After computing the ipsatively corrected responses for the items, the cultural response-bias corrected scales are computed and aggregated to the cultural level of analysis. A large correlation between the ipsatively response-bias corrected scales and the original uncorrected scales is interpreted as indicating that the uncorrected scores were relatively free from cultural response bias.

We performed this cultural response bias in the present study. After ipsatively correcting each TMT member's responses, we aggregated the data to the CEO/organization level. We then correlated the response-bias corrected scores with their corresponding non-corrected scale scores. Table 6.12 shows the results for our leadership scales, and Table 6.13 shows the results for the outcome measures. As can be seen, almost all leadership scales correlated highly with their response-bias corrected versions. The only exceptions were the integrity scale and the team

Table 6.12 Correlations Between Nonresponse-Bias Corrected and Response-Bias Corrected Leadership Scales

	Correlation With Response-Bias Corrected Scale
1. Visionary	.85*
2. Inspirational	.85*
3. Self-Sacrificial	.88*
4. Integrity	.46*
5. Decisive	.84*
6. Performance oriented	.81*
7. Collaborative team orientation	.85*
8. Team integrator	.41*
9. Diplomatic	.81*
10. Malevolent	.89*
11. Administratively competent	.87*

	Correlation With Response-Bias Corrected Scale
12. Participative	.87*
13. Autocratic	.92*
14. Modesty	.85*
15. Humane orientation	.87*
16. Autonomous	.92*
17. Self-Centered	.90*
18. Status conscious	.79*
19. Internally competitive	.92*
20. Face-Saver	.89*
21. Bureaucratic	.88*

Note: N = 1,010.

*p < .05.

Table 6.13 Correlations Between Nonresponse-Bias Corrected and Response-Bias Corrected Outcome Measures

	Correlation With Response-Bias Corrected Scale
1. Commitment	.86*
2. Effort	.81*
3. Team Solidarity	.88*

Note: N = 1,012.

*p < .05 + p < .10.

integrator scale. It should be noted, however, that the same conclusions were reached when we reexamined our results with the response-biased corrected versions of these scales. The results for the three outcome measures were quite high. In summary, these results indicate that, with the exception of two leadership scales, our original leadership and outcome measures are relatively free from cultural response bias.

Summary

In this chapter, we described the results of the statistical analyses assessing the properties of our leadership and outcome scales. The results show that the TMT members' responses tended to converge when they rated the CEO's leadership behaviors as well as when they described organizational outcomes. These results are consistent with our intentions for the leadership and outcome scales and the results justify aggregating the individual TMT members' responses to the CEO/organization level of analysis.

The results described in this chapter also demonstrated that the emergent properties of our scales were operating as we had hoped. While the responses to the leadership scales were sometimes affected by the survey method factor, we were able to develop meaningful scales for our leadership and outcome dimensions. These scales exhibited respectable levels of internal consistency reliability as well as measurement equivalence across cultures. Finally, we showed that cultural response bias was not a major factor in our leadership and outcome measures. It is these leadership and outcome scales that are used to test our hypotheses, the results of which are presented in the remainder of this book.

7

CEO Leadership Behavior Across Cultures

The Linkage With Cultural Values and Culturally Endorsed Implicit Leadership Theory

Chapter 2 provided a review of the literature on executive leadership. It concluded that rigorous empirical research on CEOs seems to be in its infancy. Only a few studies have focused on how CEOs can influence firm outcomes and have found rather conflicting results. With minor exceptions, the extant literature is all based in North America and with North American executives. Furthermore, the existing literature examines how and what aspects of CEOs' behaviors and styles can result in positive or negative outcomes. But there is little study of *why* CEOs behave the way they do. The focus has so far been on the consequences of CEO behavior and not on drivers of CEO behavior. As noted by Yukl (2013), what empirical research that does exist is largely focused on the effects of a limited number of leadership behaviors such as charismatic and transformational (C/T) leadership (e.g., Jung, Wu, & Chow, 2008; Ling, Simsek, Lubatkin & Veiga, 2008a; Makri & Scandura, 2010; Peterson, Walumbwa, Byron, & Myrowitz, 2009). Completely absent are cross-cultural studies with large country samples, rigorous psychometric analyses, and a more complete examination of the wide variety of leadership behaviors exhibited by CEOs.

In this chapter, we will provide detailed empirical information about how CEOs in different countries act as leaders. We will also explain the drivers of CEO leadership behavior by examining the relationship between a country's cultural values, culturally endorsed implicit leadership theory (CLT), and CEO leadership behavior. As explained in Chapter 4, our findings are based on a survey of over 5,000 senior executives (TMT members) directly reporting to over 1,000 CEOs in 24 countries.

There are two streams of research that inform our work here. The upper echelon theory has been concerned with top-level managers and their effects on firm performance. Child's (1972) initial notion that top management's decisions and choices impact firm performance later evolved in the work of Hambrick and Mason (1984), and it has further expanded under the rubric of strategic leadership (Cannella & Monroe, 1997; Hambrick & Finkelstein, 1987).

In its earlier development, Hambrick and Mason (1984) focused on background and demographic characteristics of CEOs. These included such variables as age, functional track, formal education, and socioeconomic background. However, the relationship between CEO demographic variables and firm performance has found only limited support (Finkelstein & Hambrick, 1996; Waldman, Javidan, & Varella, 2004). Priem, Lyon, and Dess (1999) were critical about the use of such data in strategic leadership research, raising questions about their meaning and construct validity. Boal and Hooijberg (2001) went so far as to "call a moratorium on the use of demographic variables as surrogates for psychosocial constructs" (p. 523).

Finkelstein's (1992) research moved the upper echelon perspective closer to understanding the actual role of CEO leadership qualities and behavior. He suggested that the upper echelon perspective should be expanded to take into account how managerial power affects the association between top managers and organizational outcomes. He pointed out how "power may emanate from a manager's personality" (Finkelstein, 1992, p. 510). This argument is in line with others who have claimed that simple demographic or background factors (e.g., age and functional track) do not go far enough in assessing relevant upper management characteristics. A consideration of other characteristics is necessary for a more complete test of upper echelon theory (Hambrick & Mason, 1984; Hitt & Tyler, 1991). In short, the upper echelon theory's attempt to provide a description and explanation of CEO behavior and firm performance through the use of demographic variables has found limited success.

Another stream of research associated with upper echelon theory focuses on the behavior of CEOs. Generally referred to as the strategic leadership theory, it explores the way that CEOs and other senior executives make decisions. Hambrick and Finkelstein (1987) introduced the notion of managerial discretion to examine the extent to which CEOs and other senior executives make a difference for the success of the corporation: "Depending on how much discretion exists, an organization's form and fate may lie totally outside the control of its top management, completely within their control, or more typically, somewhere in between" (Finkelstein, Hambrick, & Cannella, 2009, p. 27).

They identified three sources of managerial discretion: (1) the degree to which the environment allows variety and change, (2) the degree to which the organization itself is amenable to an array of possible action, and (3) the degree to which the CEO himself is personally able to create multiple courses of action (Finkelstein et al., 2009). They further identified the environmental determinants of discretion as industry and legal forces.

Quite separate from the literature that was previously stated, another stream of research is focused on the impact of national culture on leadership behavior and effectiveness. The most common theme in cross-cultural research is the study of cross-cultural differences in leadership behavior driven by differences in cultural values (Yukl, 2013). The theoretical framework underpinning this line of research is that national culture impacts leaders' behavior because managers who grow up in that country internalize the country's values. These internalized values in turn shape leaders' attitudes and behaviors (Adler, 1997; Dorfman et al., 1997; Fu & Yukl, 2000; Hanges & Dickson, 2004; Peng, Peterson, & Shyi, 1991). For instance, the heavy emphasis placed by Asian managers on paternalism (Dorfman & Howell, 1988) and group maintenance activities (Bolon & Crain, 1985; Ivancevich, Schweiger, & Ragan, 1986) is consistent with countries that are culturally highly collective. McClelland (1961) found that achievement motivation reflected in grammar school books was predictive of entrepreneurial behavior 25 years later.

In individualistic societies, people prefer individual rather than group-based compensation practices and exhibit greater willingness to take risks (Erez, 1997). They are also focused on their own personal goals (Jung & Avolio, 1999) whereas in collectivistic cultures people are more likely to volunteer their time and engage in organizational citizenship behaviors (Jackson, Colquitt, Wesson, & Zapata-Phelan, 2006). In high Power Distance countries, managers make decisions in less consultation with their direct reports (Smith, Peterson, & Schwartz, 2002) while in low Power Distance countries, Participative leadership is practiced more often (Dorfman, Hanges, & Brodbeck, 2004). German managers, accustomed to a culture of high Uncertainty Avoidance (House, Hanges, Javidan, Dorfman, & Gupta, 2004), expect high levels of reliability and punctuality from their subordinates (Stewart, Barsoux, Kieser, Ganter, & Walgenbach, 1994).

In our earlier GLOBE work (House et al., 2004; Javidan & Dastmalchian, 2009; Javidan, House, Dorfman, Hanges, & Sully de Luque, 2006; Javidan, Dorfman, Sully de Luque, & House, 2006; Javidan & House, 2001), we built on the implicit leadership theory (ILT) to propose another link between national culture and leadership behavior.

ILT postulates that people have general ideas about leaders and leadership that include the personal qualities and behaviors necessary to be an effective leader. These general ideas can be further described in terms of implicit beliefs, convictions, and assumptions concerning attributes and behaviors that distinguish leaders from followers and effective leaders from ineffective leaders. From these abstract notions, individuals develop a mental representation (i.e., prototype) typical of leaders in various contexts (e.g., what constitutes excellent leadership in voluntary organizations versus leadership in military contexts). The mental process is thought to involve the match between the ideal leadership (i.e., the leadership prototype) and the characteristics and behaviors of the leader in this comparison. Epitropaki and Martin (2005) found the closer the match between an employee's endorsement of specific ILTs to their manager's ILT profile, the better the quality of interactions with the leader. In short, one's image of an *ideal* leader is a fundamental aspect of ILT and is critical to perceptions of leadership effectiveness (van Quaquebeke, van Knippenberg, & Brodbeck, 2011).

Shaw (1990) suggested three effects that culture can have on leadership schemas. He hypothesized that culture affects (1) the attributes believed to be typical of leaders (i.e., schema content), (2) the cognitive complexity and differentiation among the schema content (i.e., schema structure), and (3) the level of automaticity involved in processing a leadership encounter. There is general empirical support for the impact of culture on ILT. O'Connell, Lord, and O'Connell (1990) found that national culture plays a role in influencing the content of leader attributes and behaviors perceived as desirable and effective by individuals in that culture. Similarly, Gerstner and Day (1997) found that the prototypicality of specific leader attributes varied across cultures for university students from eight nations. Mehra and Krishnan (2005) found that the Indian cultural orientation of *Svadharma* (following one's own duty) is related to conceptions of successful leadership. Recht and Wilderom (1998) asserted that autocratic and paternalistic leadership styles are the most common among Latin American countries. Davila and Elvira (2012) argued further that existing literature portrays the Latin American leader as an authoritarian-benevolent paternalistic figure. Casimir and Waldman (2007) reported significant differences among white-collar employees from China and Australia regarding traits important for effective leadership.

As explained in Chapter 2, a major part of the GLOBE research program (House et al., 2004) was designed to capture the ILTs of societies and empirically determine the degree of commonality and differences within and among nations. GLOBE's 2004 extension of ILT to the cultural level of analysis (labeled *CLT*) found support for Shaw's hypothesized relationship between culture and leadership schema content. GLOBE researchers found a high and significant within-society agreement with respect to questions concerning the effectiveness of leader attributes and behavior. We showed strong empirical evidence that cultural values are associated with specific leadership prototypes. For instance, high Performance Orientation values were positively associated with Participative leadership as a component of respondents' CLT profile of outstanding leaders (Javidan, 2004). We also determined that culturally similar societies could be clustered together (Gupta & Hanges, 2004), and meaningful differences exist in the content of the CLT profiles of different clusters (Dorfman et al., 2004). For example, the Anglo (or English-speaking) cluster of countries particularly value Charismatic leadership, whereas the Latin American cluster most highly value Team-Oriented leadership. Furthermore, using a different subset of GLOBE data for European cultures, Brodbeck and colleagues (2000) presented convincing evidence that clusters of European cultures sharing similar cultural values also share similar leadership concepts.

In the following pages, we will show comparative information about how CEOs behave in each of the 24 countries in our sample. We will also provide comparative information on the CLTs of the surveyed countries. As a reminder, CLTs were measured in GLOBE 2004. Furthermore, we provide statistical analyses examining the relationship among CEO leadership behavior, cultural values, and CLT.

Describing CEO Leadership Behavior

Our measures of CEO behavior are based on our notion of CLTs. As explained in Chapters 1, 2, and 4, a CLT is a country's profile of outstanding leadership, or a country's expectations from its leaders. It consists of a set of leadership dimensions that a society expects from leaders in that country. There are two levels of CLTs: (1) the 6 global leadership dimensions and the 21 primary leadership dimensions that comprise them. As explained in Chapter 4, we created measures of CEO behavior consistent with the 6 global leadership and the 21 primary leadership dimensions of CLTs. In other words, we have two distinct but related profiles: First, there is the CLT, which is the desirable or ideal profile. Second is the CEO leadership behavioral profile, which is a set of leadership behaviors commensurate with the dimensions of the CLT. As an example, a primary dimension of the CLT profile is "visionary"; to measure a CEO's visionary behavior, each direct report was asked several questions to assess his/her CEO on a 7-point scale—the extent to which the CEO exhibits the following behaviors:

- Makes plans and takes actions based on future goals
- Clearly articulates his/her vision of the future
- Has a clear sense of where he/she wants this organization to be in 5 years

In this chapter, we show CLTs and behaviors both at the 6 global levels and the 21 primary levels to provide overall high level information as well as detailed fine grained findings showing what CEOs are expected to do and what they actually do.

Overall CEO Leadership Behavioral Profiles

Table 7.1 shows the overall CEO leadership behavior findings across 24 countries. The scores for all the CEOs in each country were aggregated to the country level and then averaged across the 24 countries.

In Table 7.1, the first numeric column shows the average scores for each behavior across the 24 countries. The scales range from 1 (*strongly disagree*) to 7 (*strongly agree*). The overall behavioral profile of over 1,000 CEOs in Table 7.2 shows that they are reported to be typically Charismatic (5.59 out

Table 7.1 Descriptive Statistics for Six and Twenty-One CEO Leadership Behaviors (Average Across Twenty-Four Countries)

	Mean	SD	Range	Min.	25th Percentile	Median	75th Percentile	Max.
Charismatic	**5.59**	**0.32**	**1.53**	**4.63**	**5.49**	**5.65**	**5.77**	**6.17**
Visionary	5.70	0.37	1.56	4.69	5.50	5.80	5.95	6.25
Inspirational	5.62	0.35	1.71	4.65	5.55	5.68	5.79	6.37
Self-Sacrificial	5.21	0.39	1.75	3.91	5.03	5.31	5.47	5.66
Integrity	5.62	0.38	1.71	4.51	5.41	5.60	5.88	6.22
Decisive	5.64	0.34	1.25	5.05	5.36	5.57	5.96	6.30
Performance oriented	5.75	0.31	1.34	4.99	5.66	5.79	5.95	6.33
Team Oriented	**5.43**	**0.28**	**1.25**	**4.65**	**5.29**	**5.43**	**5.62**	**5.90**
Collaborative team orientation	5.25	0.37	1.62	4.16	5.07	5.25	5.51	5.77
Team integrator	5.08	0.23	0.92	4.54	4.92	5.12	5.24	5.46
Diplomatic	5.64	0.33	1.36	4.86	5.45	5.68	5.83	6.22
Malevolent	2.35	0.55	1.77	1.68	1.90	2.24	2.53	3.45
Administratively competent	5.52	0.43	1.50	4.63	5.18	5.56	5.92	6.13
Participative	**4.84**	**0.37**	**1.57**	**3.95**	**4.71**	**4.79**	**5.15**	**5.52**
Participative	5.21	0.39	1.71	4.29	4.96	5.27	5.49	6.00
Autocratic	3.51	0.52	1.94	2.71	3.10	3.51	3.79	4.64
Humane Oriented	**5.00**	**0.35**	**1.51**	**3.97**	**4.83**	**5.10**	**5.21**	**5.48**
Modesty	4.92	0.37	1.56	3.86	4.76	5.01	5.15	5.42
Humane orientation	5.08	0.37	1.44	4.18	4.85	5.15	5.35	5.62
Autonomous	**4.11**	**0.55**	**2.37**	**2.72**	**3.86**	**4.12**	**4.47**	**5.09**
Self-Protective	**3.94**	**0.22**	**0.81**	**3.61**	**3.75**	**3.93**	**4.11**	**4.42**
Self-Centered	2.86	0.49	1.55	2.23	2.47	2.87	3.05	3.79
Status conscious	4.54	0.23	0.94	4.06	4.41	4.55	4.68	5.00
Internally competitive	2.92	0.46	1.90	2.30	2.62	2.83	3.26	4.20
Face-Saver	4.30	0.45	1.63	3.33	3.86	4.46	4.67	4.96
Bureaucratic	5.06	0.38	1.25	4.39	4.79	5.19	5.30	5.64

Note: The six global leadership dimensions are in bold. The *autonomous* primary leadership dimension is the same as the global *Autonomous* leadership dimension.

SD = standard deviation.

of 7), acting as visionary individuals who are performance oriented, willing to sacrifice self-interest, decisive, and inspirational, with high levels of integrity.

Figure 7.1a shows that CEOs in almost all countries are reported to behave in generally charismatic ways, scoring above 5.

Figure 7.1a Enactment of Charismatic Leadership Behavior

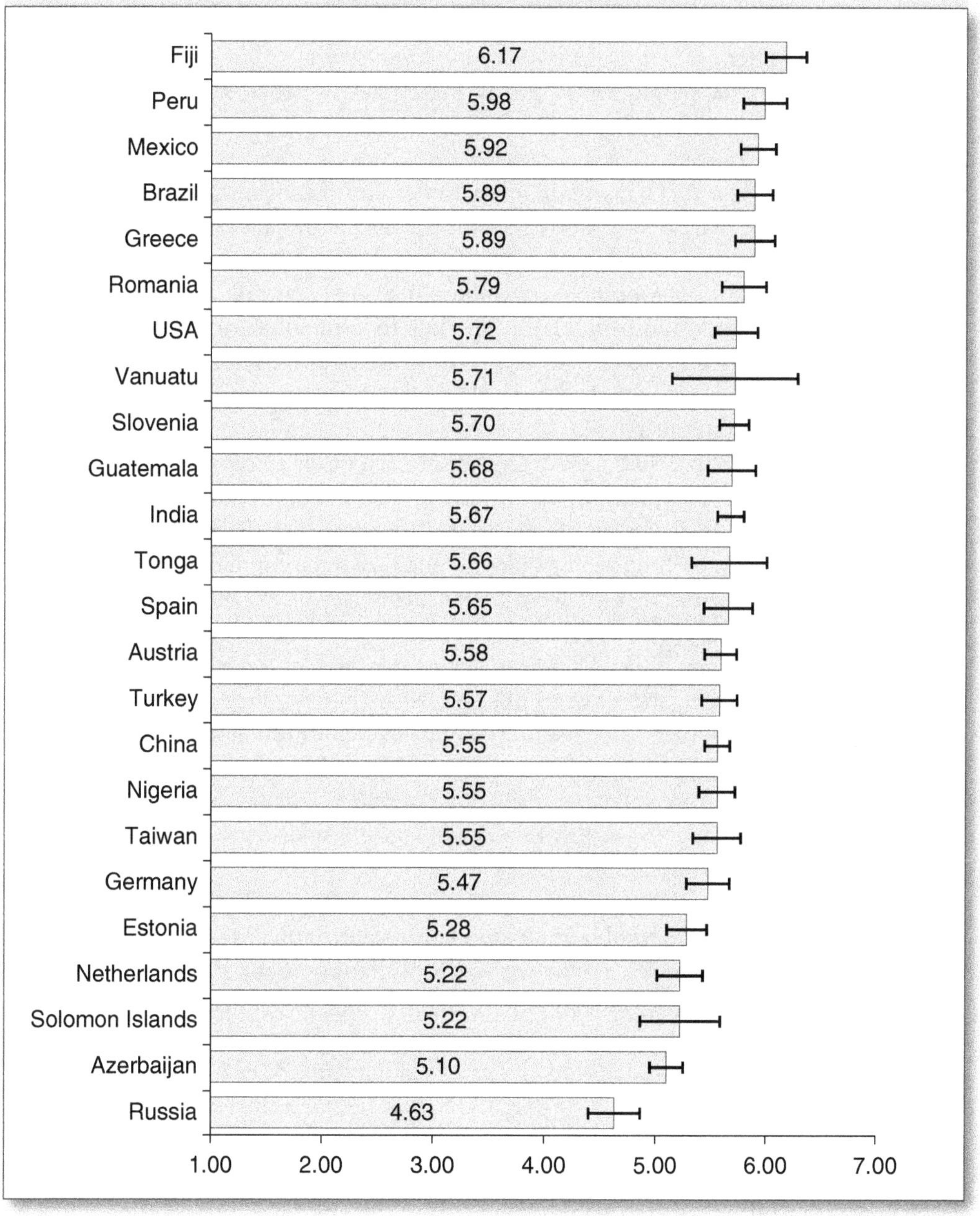
Fiji 6.17
Peru 5.98
Mexico 5.92
Brazil 5.89
Greece 5.89
Romania 5.79
USA 5.72
Vanuatu 5.71
Slovenia 5.70
Guatemala 5.68
India 5.67
Tonga 5.66
Spain 5.65
Austria 5.58
Turkey 5.57
China 5.55
Nigeria 5.55
Taiwan 5.55
Germany 5.47
Estonia 5.28
Netherlands 5.22
Solomon Islands 5.22
Azerbaijan 5.10
Russia 4.63
1.00
2.00
3.00
4.00
5.00
6.00
7.00

Note: The error bars around each mean depict the 95% confidence interval around that mean for each country. Thus, when countries' confidence intervals do not overlap, their means can be considered significantly different.

Here are a few quotes from a few CEOs in different countries during personal interviews:

> We have certainly visions for the future . . . we try to become and stay more independent, minimizing our risks. We try to develop different fields of activity with more and different groups of customers. . . . More over, employees are very important for us . . . but not only salary but quality of life, social objectives, that no one of our employees should suffer . . .

> One should set especially high goals in order to achieve what is required from him.. . . I learned that from my mentors in the course of my career.

> As a CEO, my main job is to develop the vision and to communicate that so everybody sees the bigger picture about who, what, and why. I visit each and every branch to communicate on one-to-one basis with everybody over here. I also try to talk to people in the factories and in the field. The key to communication of vision is to ensure consistency, what makes sense to the company, and in what it means to employee. In this company, there is no other way of going about it.

> I believe that in an organization, each of the employees, regardless of her/his post, she/he shall behave as shareholder, as owner of the company, so that each employee shall not feel that she/he is working for Company X, instead employees shall have the commitment and deeply believe that they are working for themselves. They will have such a feeling only if we relate to each other, and have the commitment to work, as people. If they have such feeling then they will put more effort, they will study and learn to improve what they do, they will work harder because they will feel the commitment to finish something because they are doing it for someone they know and they appreciate, they will be willing to go the extra mile for the Other. For me, that is the key for everything, to work with people as people, in order to achieve the goals of the company.

> In the '90s . . .they were looking for a flexible bank . . . they need a much more flexible bank especially oriented toward small and medium size businesses. Following the presentation of my project, my vision about such a bank and my ability to set up such a bank, I realized they share my proposal. . . . Our project got the approval. . . . It was a good idea, because our bank has grown along with SMEs dynamism. . . . My vision worked! It inspired the managerial team—the proof is the bank's quick success.

Table 7.1 also shows that CEOs are typically Team Oriented (5.43 out of 7) by being diplomatic, collaborative, and administratively competent and by avoiding malevolence (2.35 out of 7). Figure 7.1b shows

Figure 7.1b   Enactment of Team-Oriented Leadership Behavior

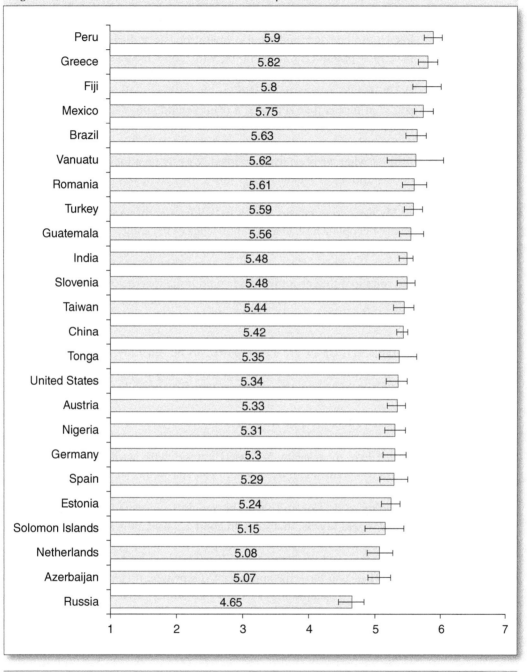

Peru	5.9
Greece	5.82
Fiji	5.8
Mexico	5.75
Brazil	5.63
Vanuatu	5.62
Romania	5.61
Turkey	5.59
Guatemala	5.56
India	5.48
Slovenia	5.48
Taiwan	5.44
China	5.42
Tonga	5.35
United States	5.34
Austria	5.33
Nigeria	5.31
Germany	5.3
Spain	5.29
Estonia	5.24
Solomon Islands	5.15
Netherlands	5.08
Azerbaijan	5.07
Russia	4.65

Note: The error bars around each mean depict the 95% confidence interval around that mean for each country. Thus, when countries' confidence intervals do not overlap, their means can be considered significantly different.

that CEOs in almost all countries (with the exception of Russia) are reported to behave in generally Team-Oriented ways, scoring above 5.

Following are a few quotes from the interviewed CEOs:

You as the management can develop the strategy, but you need a long-standing trust, and good cooperation, since they have to put the plan into practice. . . . I go home with good feelings every evening since I know there is good team who can do the job!

Ultimately, as a manager you can do nothing without your employees. That means that you need a team behind you, which you need to motivate.

I think our employees we have here are . . . team-oriented people. A lot of what we do is team oriented. We rely on a lot of meetings and understanding of where we are going as a company. And open communication helps a lot.

My basic strategy was always to build a usually small but functional team of people who had good knowledge of the subject and confidence in their ability to succeed.

My major strengths I would say are teambuilding as with my previous roles in different companies I could bring together a lot of different people from different backgrounds to help them achieve a common purpose, and I have achieved that to some extent.

In Table 7.1, CEOs are also reported to be generally Participative (4.84 out of 7) and Humane Oriented (5.00 out of 7). Figures 7.1c and 7.1d show that CEOs in most countries score around 5 on both dimensions.

Here are a few CEO quotes:

Well, I love to delegate, because I know I have weaknesses when it comes to details. I can drive well, I can sell well . . . There were many situations when I had to say, come on now, stop the discussion, and we are going to do this and this. This would be accepted by some while others would say no, that's not so good . . . Well, now I have the experience. If you are communicating well with the people, one will get better ideas, and the ideas will be better (easier) implemented. Only in case, when you have the support of the people, it can really function well. It is not functioning if I simply go and tell that we are going to do this and this. In order to discuss things and to convince each other, we are making these company meetings. Normally, these are a whole day meetings, where we sit from the morning till the evening in order to discuss all the details.

I think we have evolved into having a multilayer approach of both benevolent autocracy and we also have reasonable Participative management style. We are moving into complete empowerment. We would like to evolve management style which empowers all our senior managers to undertake complete control of activities.

Figure 7.1c   Enactment of Participative Leadership Behavior

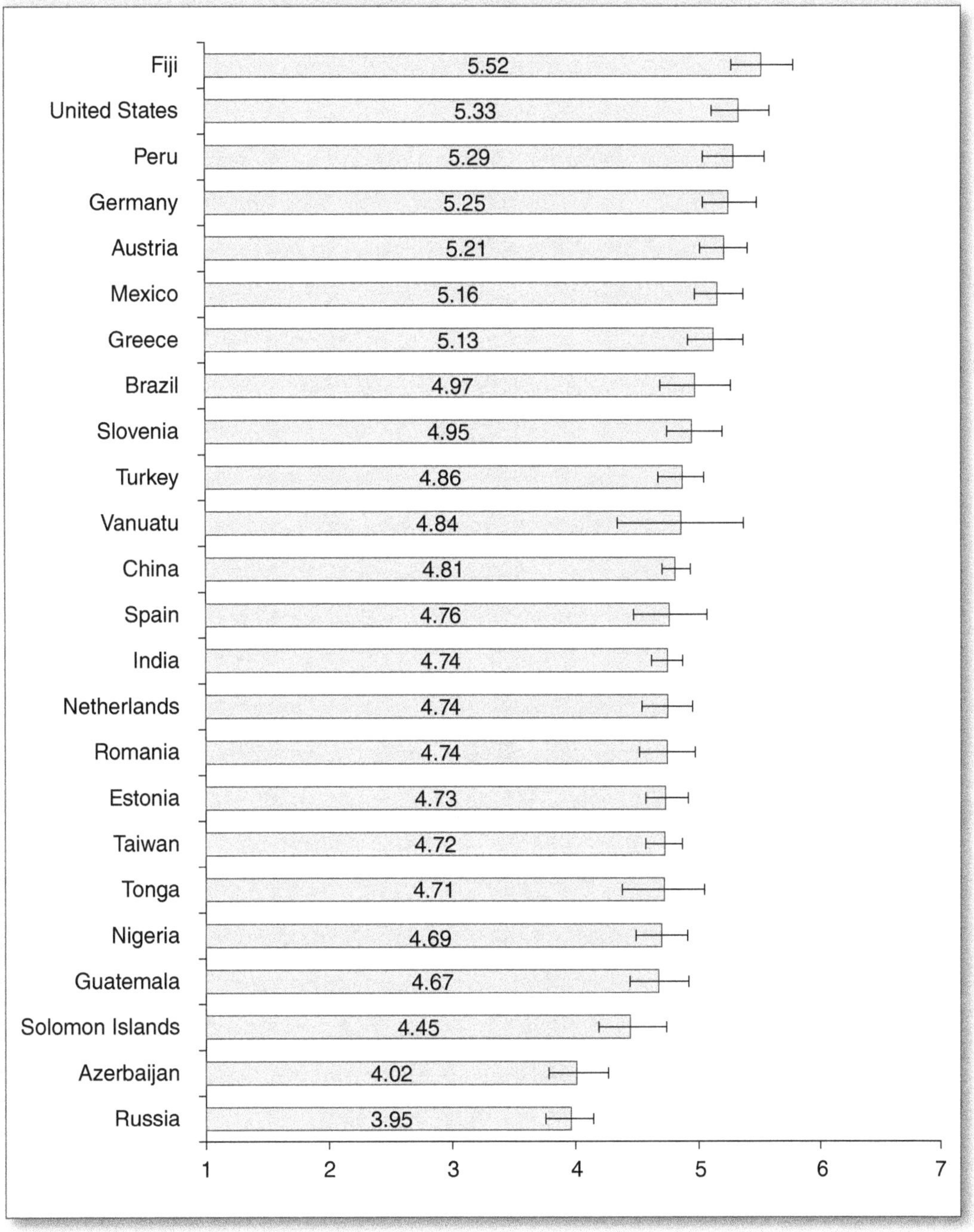

Fiji	5.52
United States	5.33
Peru	5.29
Germany	5.25
Austria	5.21
Mexico	5.16
Greece	5.13
Brazil	4.97
Slovenia	4.95
Turkey	4.86
Vanuatu	4.84
China	4.81
Spain	4.76
India	4.74
Netherlands	4.74
Romania	4.74
Estonia	4.73
Taiwan	4.72
Tonga	4.71
Nigeria	4.69
Guatemala	4.67
Solomon Islands	4.45
Azerbaijan	4.02
Russia	3.95

Note: The error bars around each mean depict the 95% confidence interval around that mean for each country. Thus, when countries' confidence intervals do not overlap, their means can be considered significantly different.

My philosophy is Participative style of management to motivate people with vision where we are going and trying to get everybody

Figure 7.1d Enactment of Humane-Oriented Leadership Behavior

Tonga	5.48
Fiji	5.47
Greece	5.4
Mexico	5.27
India	5.25
Peru	5.21
China	5.2
Nigeria	5.19
Guatemala	5.17
United States	5.15
Romania	5.14
Vanuatu	5.12
Turkey	5.08
Taiwan	5.03
Germany	4.95
Brazil	4.93
Slovenia	4.89
Austria	4.86
Spain	4.82
Netherlands	4.79
Solomon Islands	4.71
Estonia	4.55
Azerbaijan	4.34
Russia	3.97

Note: The error bars around each mean depict the 95% confidence interval around that mean for each country. Thus, when countries' confidence intervals do not overlap, their means can be considered significantly different.

on board of the train if you will. Where we are going and this is what we are going to do on that I am not fire brim stone type of leader I don't have many cross words with people. If I have to I can do that but it is very much the team concept. We succeed as a team rather than individually.

I don't have any issue with them (employees) making mistakes if they make mistakes for the right reasons . . . as long as I feel they do right thing, as long as their hearts are in the right place and effort is in the right place, I forgive them a lot and that gives them a lot of freedom to do what they need to do.

At first, I thought that if I didn't have control over everything, things wouldn't be done right. In time, this was diminished—not eliminated . . . I decided to switch this tactic and adopt a more Participative management approach . . . so I managed to relax and let myself make more informed decisions, based on many views . . . which led to better results for the unit.

I put special attention on good, even friendly, relationships with my subordinates. I consider that good relationships in the working environment create a positive, favorable atmosphere that fosters the creative development and progress of the firm.

Treat your subordinates' elders as VIPs.

Table 7.1 also shows that in general, CEOs are not particularly Autonomous (4.11 out of 7) or Self-Protective (3.94 out of 7). Figures 7.1e and 7.1f show that CEO scores in most countries on both dimensions hover around 4.

Lastly, Table 7.1 shows that CEOs are typically reported not to be self-centered (2.86 out of 7) or internally competitive (2.92 out of 7). Overall, they tend to be bureaucratic (5.06 out of 7) and somewhat status conscious (4.54) and face-saver (4.30).

In sum, CEOs are generally positively assessed by their direct reports across countries, pointing to the conclusion that while there are differences, overall, at the highest level of corporations, leaders tend to mobilize and engage their teams and are charismatic.

The diversity of CEO behavior across countries is presented in the second (standard deviation, or SD) and third (range) columns in Table 7.1. Among the six global leadership behaviors, Self-Protective has the smallest SD (0.22) and range (0.81 —minimum score 3.61 and maximum score 4.42) indicating relative similarity among all the CEOs in 24 countries. On the other hand, Autonomous has the largest SD (0.55) and range (2.37 —minimum score 2.72 and maximum score 5.09) indicating that CEOs are reported to be somewhat Autonomous in some countries and not Autonomous in other countries.

A further review of Figures 7.1a to 7.1f shows that CEOs in Estonia, Solomon Islands, Azerbaijan, and Russia show strong similarities: They tend to behave in less Charismatic, less Team Oriented, less Participative, less Humane Oriented, and more Autonomous ways than the CEOs in other countries. A few CEO quotes are offered here:

I want to see the faces of those who are against me. This helps me to know all the possible threats. Those, who attack, do it, staying behind. And I turn around to see everyone and everything (a Russian CEO).

Figure 7.1e Enactment of Autonomous Leadership Behavior

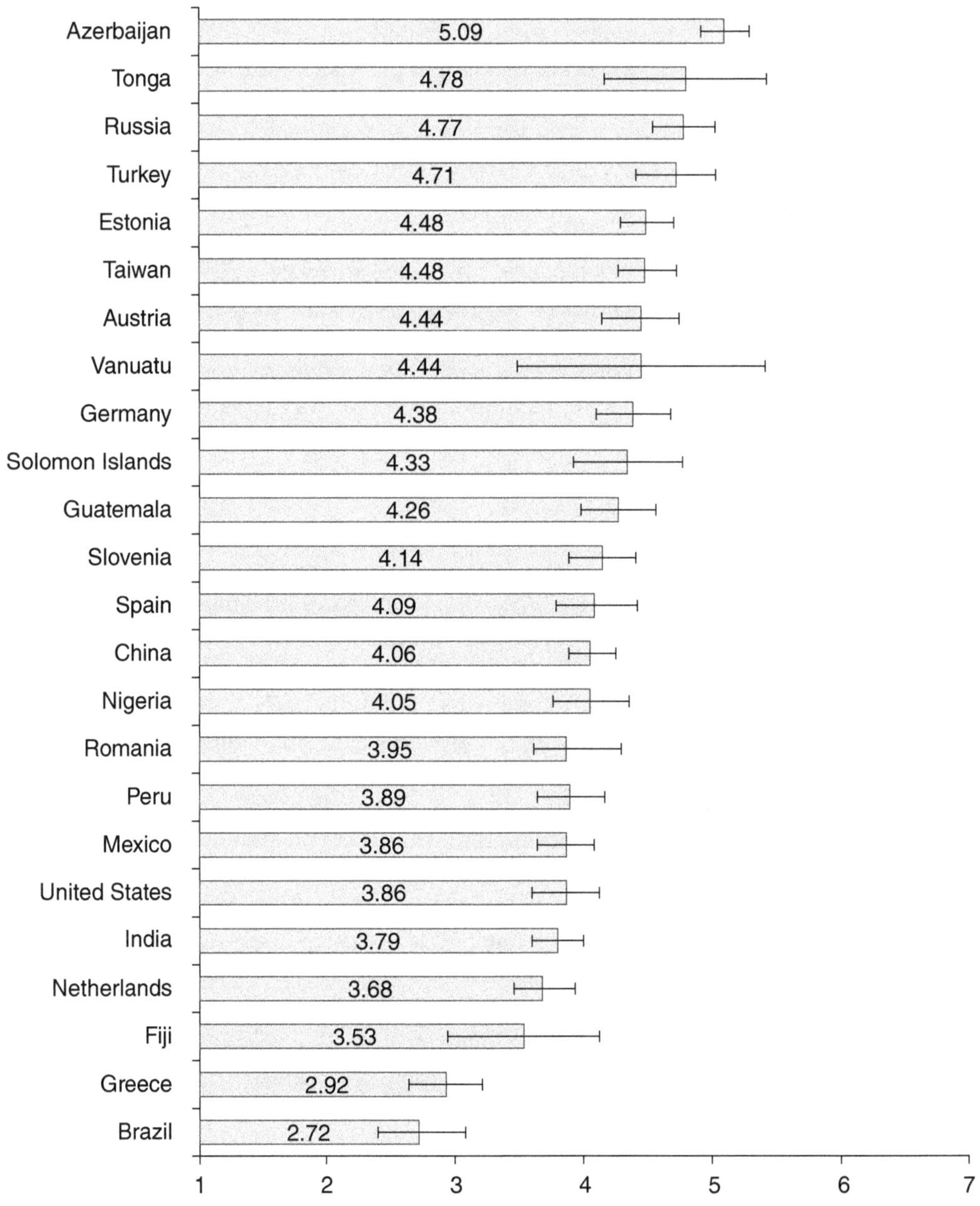

Azerbaijan	5.09
Tonga	4.78
Russia	4.77
Turkey	4.71
Estonia	4.48
Taiwan	4.48
Austria	4.44
Vanuatu	4.44
Germany	4.38
Solomon Islands	4.33
Guatemala	4.26
Slovenia	4.14
Spain	4.09
China	4.06
Nigeria	4.05
Romania	3.95
Peru	3.89
Mexico	3.86
United States	3.86
India	3.79
Netherlands	3.68
Fiji	3.53
Greece	2.92
Brazil	2.72

Note: The error bars around each mean depict the 95% confidence interval around that mean for each country. Thus, when countries' confidence intervals do not overlap, their means can be considered significantly different.

> I have always fought against the system. I have tried to find the better way. And that is why I became famous through fights, without help. Sometimes you really need help and support, but the only person you can depend on is yourself (a Russian CEO).

Figure 7.1f   Enactment of Self-Protective Leadership Behavior

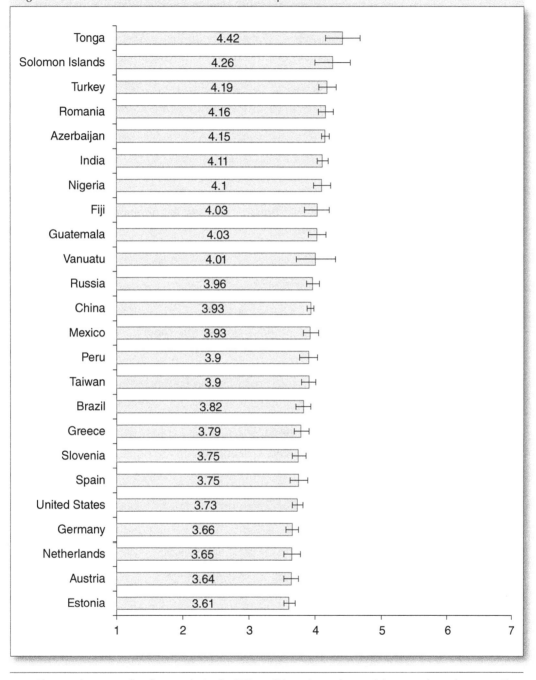

Note: The error bars around each mean depict the 95% confidence interval around that mean for each country. Thus, when countries' confidence intervals do not overlap, their means can be considered significantly different.

Russia is a unique country in terms of the fact that you are never sure of the next day. It is very hard to plan, to leave problems and the questions for the next day, you always have to wait for the unexpected and think of all the possible and not possible (a Russian CEO).

People who work in this company must share some basic principles that are essential for me and other chief managers. What are they? First of all, these are discipline, obedience, diligence, and loyalty. That's all. I need these qualities first. Only then I would ask them for their intelligence, knowledge and qualification (an Azerbaijani CEO).

I hold a responsibility for my company, for what we are doing. Our company should be strong enough to be able to function under all these obstacles. I have to be strong and sometimes even tight with personnel to avoid anarchy and mistakes. I think it is important to manage with strong hand (an Azerbaijani CEO).

In contrast, CEOs in Mexico, Peru, Fiji, Greece, and Brazil seem to behave in more Charismatic, more Team Oriented, more Participative and Humane Oriented (except Brazil), and less Autonomous ways than the CEOs in other countries.

Understanding CEO Leadership Behavior: Does National Culture Matter?

As explained in Chapter 2 and earlier in this chapter, there is substantial literature arguing for the effect of cultural values on leadership behavior. However, there is a lack of clear rigorous empirical evidence supporting this relationship. It is conventional wisdom that cultural values impact the way leaders behave, but clear empirical support is missing. This is the gap we will fill in this section. As explained in Chapter 1, we identified nine cultural dimensions in GLOBE 2004: Performance Orientation, Assertiveness, Future Orientation, Humane Orientation, Institutional Collectivism, In-Group Collectivism, Gender Egalitarianism, Power Distance, and Uncertainty Avoidance. The detailed information about each country's cultural values is provided in GLOBE 2004 and will not be repeated here. Table 7.2

Table 7.2   Correlations Among Six Global CEO Leader Behaviors and Cultural Values

CEO Leader Behavior Dimension	Cultural Values				
	Uncertainty Avoidance	Future Orientation	Power Distance	Institutional Collectivism	Humane Orientation
Charismatic	.17	.21	−.12	.56*	.05
Team Oriented	.23	.14	−.04	.59*	−.07
Participative	−.27	.04	−.13	.29	.10
Humane Oriented	.20	.25	−.12	.52*	.13
Autonomous	−.13	−.15	.23	−.43	−.11
Self-Protective	.47*	.38	−.02	.19	.10

Note: N = 18.

*p < .05.

CEO Leader Behavior Dimension	Cultural Values			
	Performance Orientation	In-Group Collectivism	Gender Egalitarianism	Assertiveness
Charismatic	.29	.15	.36	.24
Team Oriented	.16	.09	.20	.14
Participative	.25	.01	.58*	.06
Humane Oriented	.34	.19	.10	.27
Autonomous	−.24	.02	−.46	−.02
Self-Protective	.12	.30	−.47*	.08

Note: N = 18.

*p < .05.

shows the correlations between six global CEO leadership behaviors and the cultural values. A total of 18 countries participated both in GLOBE 2004 and in the current survey. Of the 54 possible correlation coefficients, only 6 are statistically significant (approximately 11%), leading to the conclusion that cultural values generally do not predict CEO leadership behavior. Of course, the fact that our sample consists of 18 countries need to be taken into consideration.

Table 7.3 presents the correlations among the nine cultural values and the 21 primary leadership behaviors and shows that out of a total of 189 possible correlation coefficients, only 15 are significant (approximately 8%)—further confirming that in general, cultural values do not predict leadership behavior. Again, it is important to note that the sample consists of only 18 countries.

Table 7.3   Correlations Among GLOBE Twenty-One Primary Leadership Behaviors and Cultural Values

Primary Leadership Behaviors	Cultural Values				
	Uncertainty Avoidance	Future Orientation	Power Distance	Institutional Collectivism	Humane Orientation
Visionary	.11	.24	−.17	.49*	.08
Inspirational	.20	.16	−.01	.53*	.03
Self-Sacrificial	.12	.03	.04	.44	.01
Integrity	.11	.22	−.13	.58*	.01
Decisive	.15	.04	−.02	.44	−.20
Performance oriented	.28	.42	−.35	.58*	.34

(Continued)

(Continued)

Primary Leadership Behaviors	Cultural Values				
	Uncertainty Avoidance	Future Orientation	Power Distance	Institutional Collectivism	Humane Orientation
Collaborative team orientation	.35	.20	−.04	.60**	−.10
Team integrator	.39	.18	−.01	.53*	−.02
Diplomatic	.09	.12	−.19	.60**	−.03
Malevolent	.31	.05	.14	−.40	.03
Administratively competent	.42	.14	.16	.37	−.13
Participative	.13	.21	−.20	.49*	.22
Autocratic	.52*	.16	.04	−.06	.03
Modesty	.12	.01	.09	.29	−.07
Humane orientation	.26	.43	−.29	.65**	.30
Autonomous	−.13	−.15	.23	−.43	−.10
Self-Centered	.24	.31	−.17	−.10	.23
Status conscious	.44	.35	−.14	.55*	.13
Internally competitive	−.38	−.04	−.11	−.36	.20
Face-Saver	.63**	.31	.05	.32	−.01
Bureaucratic	.25	.08	.24	.08	−.20

Note: $N = 18$.
*$p < .05$. **$p < .01$.

Primary Leadership Dimension	Cultural Values			
	Performance Orientation	In-Group Collectivism	Gender Egalitarianism	Assertiveness
Visionary	.32	.21	.46	.19
Inspirational	.26	.08	.20	.27
Self-Sacrificial	.17	−.06	.09	.45
Integrity	.22	.15	.45	.07
Decisive	.03	.02	.37	.14
Performance-Oriented	.58*	.38	.36	.17
Collaborative team orientation	.11	.09	.06	.17
Team integrator	.21	.13	−.01	.19

Primary Leadership Dimension	Cultural Values			
	Performance Orientation	In-Group Collectivism	Gender Egalitarianism	Assertiveness
Diplomatic	.17	.12	.41	.04
Malevolent	−.12	.07	−.61**	.10
Administratively competent	.07	.10	−.16	.25
Participative	.44	.21	.41	.24
Autocratic	−.04	.15	−.57*	.10
Modesty	.15	−.03	.06	.38
Humane orientation	.46	.37	.12	.13
Autonomous	−.24	.02	−.46	−.02
Self-Centered	.03	.32	−.45	−.14
Status conscious	.05	.26	−.27	−.28
Internally competitive	.13	−.01	−.01	−.27
Face-Saver	.18	.25	−.37	.35
Bureaucratic	−.04	.01	−.16	.37

Note: N = 18.

*p < .05. **p < .01.

The only possible exception is the cultural value of Institutional Collectivism, which according to Table 7.3, is significantly correlated with several primary leadership behaviors. Societies that value Institutional Collectivism tend to experience CEOs who are particularly Charismatic, Team Oriented, and Participative. In sum, our findings are counter to the conventional wisdom in cross-cultural research in two important ways: First, contrary to popular belief, cultural values do not predict leadership behavior. Second, the only cultural value that has some impact on leadership behavior is Institutional Collectivism, a cultural dimension that was introduced in GLOBE 2004 and has not received sufficient attention by other scholars.

Culturally Endorsed Implicit Leadership Theory Across Countries

Another possible explanation for CEO leadership behavior across countries is the CLT of the different countries. As explained previously, a country's CLT is its culturally endorsed leadership expectations. We identified a country's CLT in our earlier work (House et al., 2004) based on a survey of middle managers in that country. House and colleagues (2004) provided full details on what CLTs are and how they are measured. In this section, we will first provide descriptive information on the CLTs of the participating countries and then statistically test the relationship between the CLT and CEO leadership behavior.

Table 7.4 presents the average of the CLTs in the participating countries and shows what leaders are generally expected to do. As explained earlier, CLTs are the leadership attributes and behaviors that are expected in a society to lead to outstanding leadership. The table is sorted from the highest expectation (CLT) to lowest expectation. It also shows the average CEO score (across all countries) on corresponding leadership behaviors and the gap between the two (behavior minus CLT). Our statistical analyses show that the gap between CLTs and behaviors is statistically significant for all the six dimensions across the countries.

It is clear from the CLT scores in this table that across the countries in our sample, leaders are generally expected to be Charismatic, Team Oriented, and Participative and somewhat Humane Oriented. They are not expected to be Autonomous or Self-Protective. The table also shows that CEOs' overall behavioral profile is somewhat similar to the overall leadership expectations. They show less Charisma, Team-Oriented, and Participative leadership than expected but more Humane Oriented, Autonomous, and Self-Protective than expected.

Table 7.4   Overall Global Leadership Expectations Versus CEO Leadership Behavior–Six Global Leadership Dimensions

Leadership Dimension	Behavior	Overall CLT	Gap (Behavior–CLT)	Paired Sample t test[1]
Charismatic	5.58	5.81	−0.23	−9.96**
Team Oriented	5.41	5.74	−0.33	−15.46**
Participative	4.84	5.24	−0.40	−14.57**
Humane Oriented	5.02	4.94	0.08	3.02**
Autonomous	4.00	3.80	0.19	4.45**
Self-Protective	3.90	3.58	0.31	20.29**

Note: The values in the Behavior column and the Overall CLT column might differ from other tables (e.g., Table 7.2) because the values reported in this table represent only those CEO/organizations that have both leader behavior and CLT information. Other tables can include CEO/organizations with one but not both of these scales.

Degrees of freedom for the paired sample t test was 874 for all leadership dimensions.

**$p < .01$.

[1]A paired sample t test is a more powerful test for differences between two groups than a typical t test. Only CEOs who have both leadership behavior data and CLT data are included in the analysis (i.e., the two measures are paired at the CEO level of analysis) and thus controls for random error variance compared to the traditional t test.

Appendix 7.1, at the end of this chapter, shows the relationship between CLT and CEO behavior on the six global dimensions across the participating countries as well as in each country. Please note that Azerbaijan and a few other countries did not participate in GLOBE 2004 (House et al., 2004) and therefore do not have CLT information. Here are a few findings of note:

- Brazilian CEOs are as Humane Oriented as expected but not as Participative as desired.
- Chinese CEOs behave in almost perfect unison with their country's CLT.
- Dutch CEOs are much less Charismatic, Team Oriented, and Participative than expected.
- Estonia's CLT does not have very high expectations so Estonian CEOs are more Team Oriented and Participative than expected. They are as Self-Protective as expected but more Autonomous than desired.
- German CEOs are less Particiative and more Self-Protective than desired.
- Greek CEOs behave close to expectations but are less Paricipative and much less Autonomous than desired.
- Russian CEOs are much less Charismatic, Team Oriented, and Participative than expected.
- Taiwanese CEOs are the only group who are less Self-Protective than expected.
- Turkish CEOs are as Humane Oriented and Participative as expected.

Table 7.5 shows similar information in terms of the 21 primary leadership dimensions. It is also sorted in terms of the highest CLT score to lowest. It is clear that integrity is deemed to be the most important leadership expectation followed by inspiration and performance orientation. Leaders are also expected to have a vision and mobilize teams. Perhaps a surprising finding is

Table 7.5   Overall Global Leadership Expectations Versus CEO Leadership Behavior—Twenty-One Global Leadership Dimensions

Leadership Dimension	Behavior	Overall CLT	Gap (Behavior—CLT)	Paired Sample t test	Average Percentage of CEOs Across Countries Who Received 5.5 or Higher on Behavior Dimension
Integrity	5.59	6.11	−0.52	−19.69**	63%
Inspirational	5.63	6.03	−0.40	−14.22**	62%

(Continued)

(Continued)

Leadership Dimension	Behavior	Overall CLT	Gap (Behavior—CLT)	Paired Sample t test	Average Percentage of CEOs Across Countries Who Received 5.5 or Higher on Behavior Dimension
Performance oriented	5.71	6.00	−0.28	−11.39**	70%
Visionary	5.68	5.99	−0.31	−11.66**	66%
Administratively competent	5.48	5.88	−0.40	−13.99**	58%
Team integrator	5.04	5.85	−0.81	−36.11**	29%
Decisive	5.63	5.72	−0.08	−2.60**	61%
Collaborative team orientation	5.25	5.52	−0.26	−8.53**	46%
Diplomatic	5.61	5.47	0.14	5.22**	64%
Participative	5.20	5.14	0.05	1.54ns	44%
Self-Sacrificial	5.24	5.03	0.20	7.05**	42%
Modesty	4.95	5.03	−0.08	−2.58**	29%
Humane orientation	5.09	4.86	0.23	8.01**	34%
Status conscious	4.48	4.52	−0.03	−1.22 ns	11%
Internally competitive	2.87	4.05	−1.18	−32.93**	0%
Bureaucratic	5.00	3.98	1.02	35.07**	35%
Autonomous	4.00	3.80	0.19	5.54**	11%
Face-Saver	4.30	3.17	1.13	36.00**	13%
Autocratic	3.51	2.67	0.84	25.28**	0%
Self-Centered	2.82	2.21	0.61	15.85**	1%
Malevolent	2.30	2.01	0.29	8.20**	0%

Note: The values in the Behavior column and the Overall CLT column might differ from other tables (e.g., Table 7.2) because the values reported in this table represent only those CEO/organizations that have both leader behavior and CLT information. Other tables can include CEO/organizations with one but not both of these scales.

Degrees of freedom for the paired sample t test was ranged from 854 to 874.

**$p < .01$.

that leaders are also expected to be administratively competent. Particularly undesirable leadership attributes are those of being self-centered, autocratic, and malevolent.

The table also shows that CEOs in general tend to behave in accordance with CLTs. However, our statistical analyses show that the gap between the CLT and behavior for the 21 primary leadership dimensions is statistically significant across the countries with the exception of participative and status conscious. Of particular note in Table 7.5 is that for the highly desirable CLTs such as inspirational where the average CLT score is 5.5 or higher, the corresponding CEO average behavior scores, while high, tend to be lower than the CLT scores. In contrast, for the neutral or undesirable CLTs such as autocratic, where the average CLT score is below 4, the CEO average behavior scores tend to be higher than the CLT scores. In other words, while CEOs receive generally positive assessments across countries, they act below expectations on the desirable attributes and act excessively on the undesirable attributes. While they behave close to expectations, they do not fully match them.

The last column in Table 7.5 shows the average percentage of CEOs across countries whose behavior received a score of 5.5 or higher, indicating that the particular behavior is enacted at high levels. The table shows that across countries, 70% of CEOs are reported to be high performance oriented. Over 60% of CEOs are reported to be inspirational, visionary, decisive, and diplomatic. Over 60% are also believed to have high integrity. Furthermore, 58% of CEOs are reported to be administratively competent. A small percentage of CEOs—29%—are reported to be very modest or team integrator. Lastly, less than half are viewed as very collaborative, participative, and self-sacrificial.

Appendix 7.2 at the end of this chapter shows the CLT and leadership behavior profiles for each country for the 21 primary leadership dimensions. A few countries like Azerbaijan did not participate in GLOBE 2004 (House et al., 2004) and do not have country data for CLT.

Figures 7.2a to 7.2s show the contrast between each country's CLT and its average CEO behavior. Here are a few findings of note:

- In general, CEOs are as self-sacrificial, decisive, diplomatic, and participative as expected. They are also more humane, self-centered, autocratic, and face-saving than desired. Lastly, while CEOs are generally more bureaucratic than expected, they are less administratively competent than desired (Figure 7.2a).
- Austrians (Figure 7.2b), Germans (Figure 7.2f), and Americans (Figure 7.2s) have very high expectations from their leaders in terms of inspiration, integrity, and performance orientation (all above 6). Austrian, German, and American CEOs, while assessed reasonably highly, do fall short of these expectations.
- Austrian CEOs (Figure 7.2b) are less collaborative, team integrator, administratively competent, and participative than expected. They are also more autocratic and bureaucratic than desired.
- Brazilians (Figure 7.2c) have very high expectations from their leaders in terms of integrity, inspiration, and performance orientation. Brazilian

CEOs behave close to these expectations but fall a little short. They are also less Team Oriented, administratively competent, participative, and modest than desired. They are more humane, autocratic, and bureaucratic than expected.

- Chinese CEOs (Figure 7.2d) behave in general harmony with their country's CLT. The major exceptions are that they tend to be more self-sacrificial but show less integrity than desired. They are also less internally competitive and more bureaucratic than desired.
- German CEOs (Figure 7.2f) are far more bureaucratic and face-saver and more humane than desired. They are also more autocratic and less participative than expected.
- Greek CEOs (Figure 7.2g) behave close to their country's expectations. The major exceptions are that they are more autocratic, bureaucratic, and face-saver than desired. They are also less team integrator, autonomous, and internally competitive than expected.
- Indian CEOs (Figure 7.2i) act close to their country's CLT. The major exceptions are that they are more autocratic, bureaucratic, and face-saver than desired. They are less team integrator and internally competitive than expected.
- Mexican CEOs (Figure 7.2j) are more bureaucratic, participative, humane oriented, and face-saver than desired.
- Dutch CEOs (Figure 7.2k) fall short of their country's expectations in terms of vision, inspiration, integrity, decisiveness, performance orientation, team integration, administrative competence, and participation. They are more autocratic, self-centered, face-saver, and bureaucratic than desired.
- Russian CEOs (Figure 7.2n) behave very differently from their country's expectations on almost all the 21 primary dimensions. They fall short of the expectations on most dimensions. The major exceptions are that they are more bureaucratic, face-saver, self-centered, autocratic, and malevolent than desired.

Does Culturally Endorsed Implicit Leadership Theory Predict CEO Leadership Behavior?

As explained earlier in this chapter, our hypothesis is that a country's CLT impacts and drives the behavior of leaders by communicating what is expected of them. In this section, we will statistically test this relationship. Table 7.6 shows the correlations among the six CLT dimensions and their corresponding six global CEO leadership behavior dimensions. Four of the six global CLT dimensions are significantly correlated with their counterpart leadership behaviors. Another CLT dimension, Team Oriented, shows a trend toward significant correlation ($p < .1$), and only one, Charismatic leadership, is not correlated with its counterpart

Figure 7.2a   Average Culturally Endorsed Implicit Leadership Theory and CEO Leadership Behavior

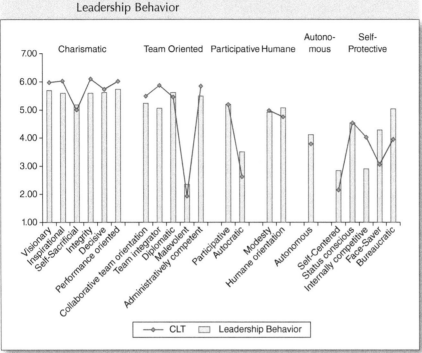

For Leadership Behavior: Indicate your level of agreement with the extent to which your CEO demonstrates the behavior.

1 = Strongly Disagree

2 = Moderately Disagree

3 = Slightly Disagree

4 = Neither Agree nor Disagree

5 = Slightly Agree

6 = Moderately Agree

7 = Strongly Agree

For CLT:

1 = This behavior or characteristic **greatly inhibits** a person from being an outstanding leader.

2 = This behavior or characteristic **somewhat inhibits** a person from being an outstanding leader.

3 = This behavior or characteristic **slightly inhibits** a person from being an outstanding leader.

4 = This behavior or characteristic **has no impact** on whether a person is an outstanding leader.

5 = This behavior or characteristic **contributes slightly** to a person being an outstanding leader.

6 = This behavior or characteristic **contributes somewhat** to a person being an outstanding leader.

7 = This behavior or characteristic **contributes greatly** to a person being an outstanding leader.

Figure 7.2b   Austria Culturally Endorsed Implicit Leadership Theory and CEO
                  Leadership Behavior

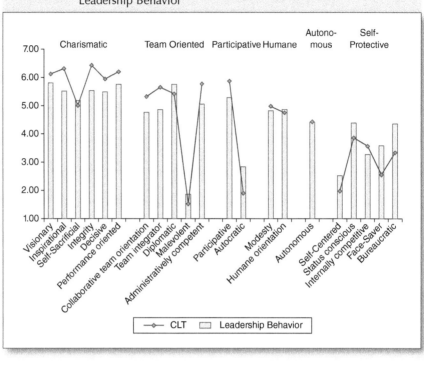

Figure 7.2c   Brazil Culturally Endorsed Implicit Leadership Theory and CEO
                  Leadership Behavior

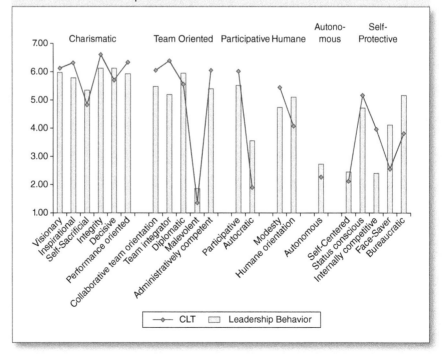

Figure 7.2d   China Culturally Endorsed Implicit Leadership Theory and CEO Leadership Behavior

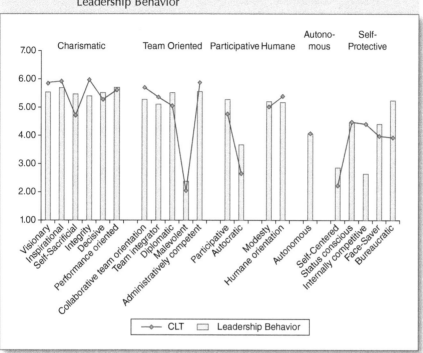

Figure 7.2e   Estonia Culturally Endorsed Implicit Leadership Theory and CEO Leadership Behavior

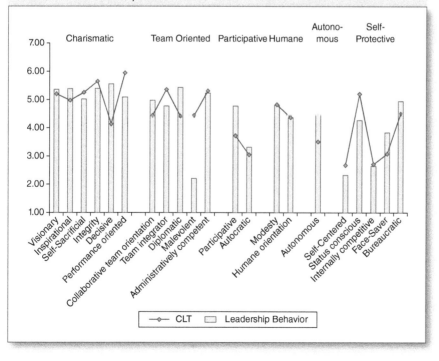

Figure 7.2f Germany Culturally Endorsed Implicit Leadership Theory and CEO Leadership Behavior

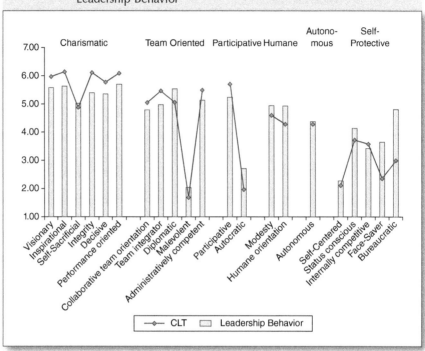

Figure 7.2g Greece Culturally Endorsed Implicit Leadership Theory and CEO Leadership Behavior

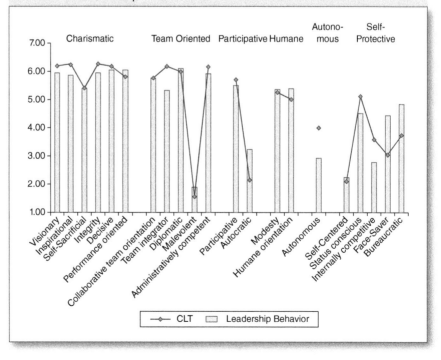

Figure 7.2h   Guatemala Culturally Endorsed Implicit Leadership Theory and CEO Leadership Behavior

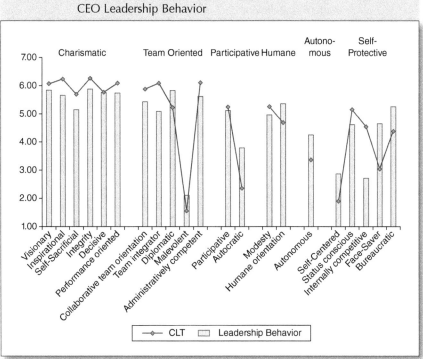

Figure 7.2i   India Culturally Endorsed Implicit Leadership Theory and CEO Leadership Behavior

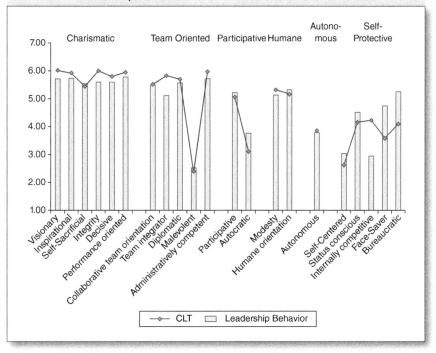

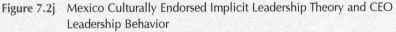

Figure 7.2j   Mexico Culturally Endorsed Implicit Leadership Theory and CEO Leadership Behavior

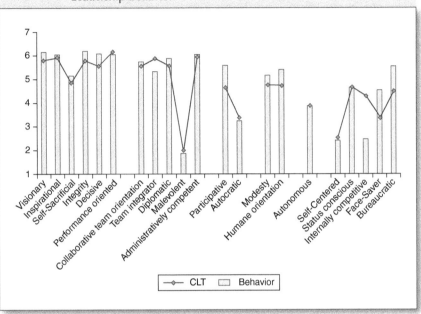

Figure 7.2k   Netherlands Culturally Endorsed Implicit Leadership Theory and CEO Leadership Behavior

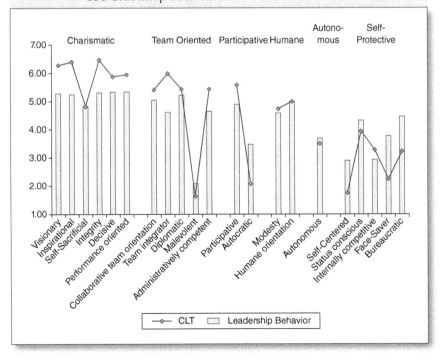

Figure 7.2l   Nigeria Culturally Endorsed Implicit Leadership Theory and CEO Leadership Behavior

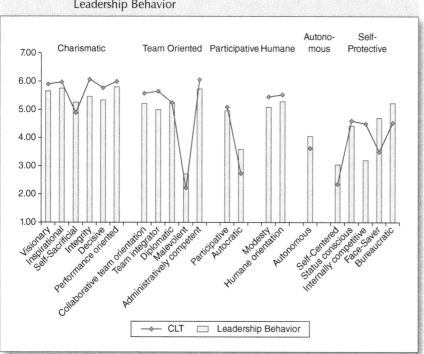

Figure 7.2m   Romania Culturally Endorsed Implicit Leadership Theory and CEO Leadership Behavior

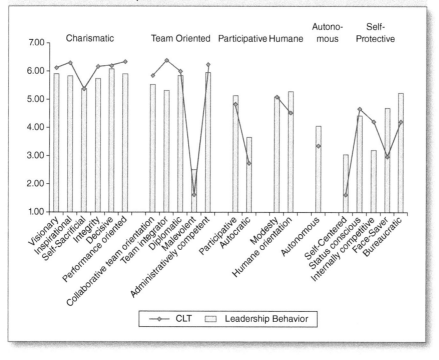

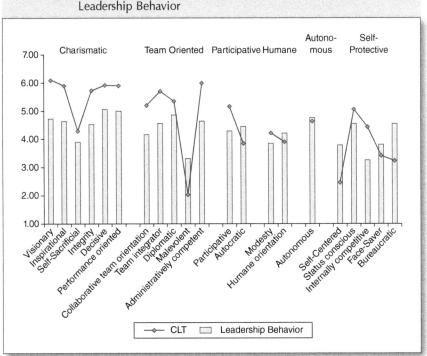

Figure 7.2n Russia Culturally Endorsed Implicit Leadership Theory and CEO Leadership Behavior

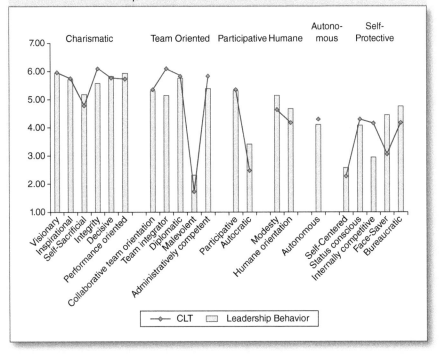

Figure 7.2o Solvenia Culturally Endorsed Implicit Leadership Theory and CEO Leadership Behavior

Figure 7.2p   Spain Culturally Endorsed Implicit Leadership Theory and CEO Leadership Behavior

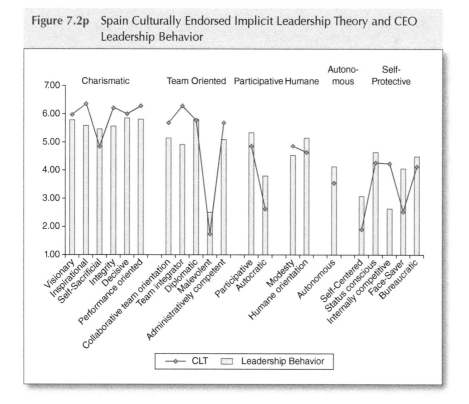

Figure 7.2q   Taiwan Culturally Endorsed Implicit Leadership Theory and CEO Leadership Behavior

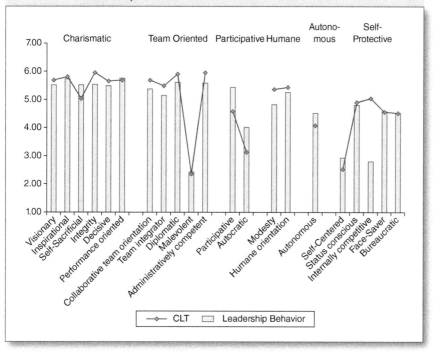

Figure 7.2r Turkey Culturally Endorsed Implicit Leadership Theory and CEO Leadership Behavior

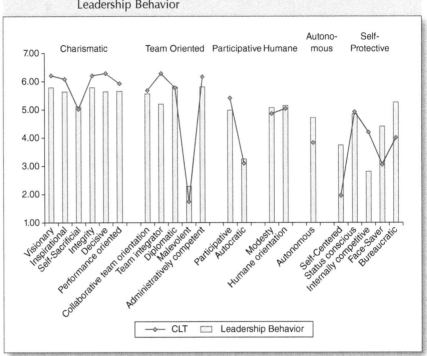

Figure 7.2s United States Culturally Endorsed Implicit Leadership Theory and CEO Leadership Behavior

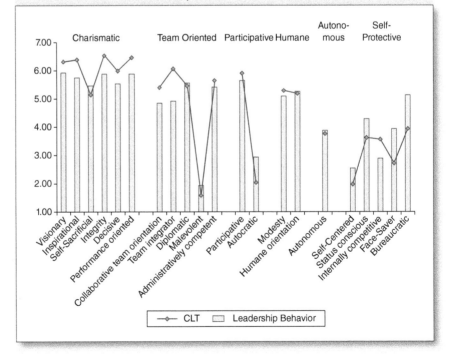

Table 7.6   Correlations Among Six Global Culturally Endorsed Implicit Leadership Theory Dimensions and CEO Leader Behaviors

Global CLT Dimension		Global CEO Leader Behavior Dimension					
		1	2	3	4	5	6
1	Charismatic	.377					
2	Team Oriented		.450†				
3	Participative			.576*			
4	Humane Oriented				.748**		
5	Autonomous					.598**	
6	Self-Protective						.587*

Note: N = 18.

† $p < .10$. * $p < .05$. ** $p < .01$.

behavior. These findings lead to the conclusion that CLTs are generally predictive of CEO leadership behavior.

To further examine the relationship, the following tables present the correlations between the 21 primary CLT dimensions and their counterpart behaviors. Table 7.7a shows that only one of the six primary dimensions of Charismatic leadership, self-sacrificial, is correlated with its corresponding leader behavior. In Table 7.7b, three of the five primary dimensions of Team Oriented are correlated with their counterpart

Table 7.7a   Correlations Among Primary Dimensions of Culturally Endorsed Implicit Leadership Theory and CEO Leader Behavior Dimensions

Global Dimension: Charismatic							
CLT Primary Dimension		Leader Behavior Dimension					
		1	2	3	4	5	6
1	Visionary	.18					
2	Inspirational		.17				
3	Self-Sacrificial			.53*			
4	Integrity				.42		
5	Decisive					.13	
6	Performance oriented						.24

Note: N = 18, *N*-Sample size.

* $p < .05$.

Table 7.7b   Correlations Among Primary Dimensions of Culturally Endorsed
Implicit Leadership Theory and CEO Leader Behavior Dimensions

Global Dimension: Team Oriented					
	CEO Primary Leader Behavior				
Primary Dimensions	1	2	3	4	5
1 Collaborative team orientation	.59*				
2 Team integrator		.36			
3 Diplomatic			.47*		
4 Malevolent				.20	
5 Administratively competent					.62**

Note: N = 18, N-Sample size.
*p < .05. **p < .01.

Table 7.7c   Correlations Among Primary Dimensions of Culturally Endorsed
Implicit Leadership Theory and CEO Leader Behavior Dimensions

Global Dimension: Participative		
	CEO Leader Behavior Dimension	
CLT Primary Dimension	1	2
1 Participative	.30	
2 Autocratic		.60**

Note: N = 18, N-Sample size.
**p < .01.

Table 7.7d   Correlations Among Primary Dimensions of Culturally Endorsed
Implicit Leadership Theory and CEO Leader Behavior Dimensions

Global Dimension: Humane Oriented		
	CEO Leader Behavior Dimension	
CLT Primary Dimension	1	2
1 Modesty	.55*	
2 Humane orientation		.66**

Note: N = 18, N-Sample size.
*p < .05. **p < .01.

Table 7.7e   Correlations Among Primary Dimensions of Culturally Endorsed Implicit Leadership Theory and CEO Leader Behavior Dimensions

Global Dimension: Autonomous		
		CEO Leader Behavior Dimension
CLT Primary Dimension		1
1	Autonomous	.60**

Note: $N = 18$, N-Sample size.

**$p < .01$.

Table 7.7f   Correlations Among Primary Dimensions of Culturally Endorsed Implicit Leadership Theory and CEO Leader Behavior Dimensions

Global Dimension: Self-Protective						
		CEO Leader Behavior Dimension				
CLT Primary Dimension		1	2	3	4	5
1	Self-Centered	−.08				
2	Status conscious		.55*			
3	Internally competitive			−.07		
4	Face-Saver				.59**	
5	Bureaucratic					.49*

Note: $N = 18$, N-Sample size.

*$p < .05$. **$p < .01$.

behaviors. Tables 7.7c to 7.7e show that the primary CLT dimensions of Participative, Humane Oriented, and Autonomous are correlated with their corresponding behaviors while Table 7.7f shows that three out of five Self-Protective primary dimensions are correlated with their counterpart behaviors.

Summary

In this chapter, we showed how and why CEOs behave as leaders. We provided detailed information on CEO behavior in each participating country and showed the results of our statistical analyses linking CEO behavior to cultural values and CLTs. Our results show that, contrary to popular opinion, cultural values do not predict CEO leadership behavior. We showed strong evidence that there is little direct relationship between cultural values and CEO leadership behavior. The only exception was the cultural value of Institutional Collectivism, which did predict a few of the CEO leadership behaviors. In contrast, we showed strong evidence that CLTs do indeed predict leadership behavior. What does this mean? In GLOBE 2004, we showed that cultural values of countries predict their CLTs. In other words, a society's expectations of its leaders are driven by its cultural values. For example, cultures that value Performance Orientation believe leaders need to be Charismatic in order to be outstanding. Our work shows that CLTs drive CEO leader behaviors. In other words, the way leaders behave in a society tends to be generally consistent with the society's leadership expectations. In short, cultural values do not directly predict leadership behavior. Instead, they drive the cultural expectations that in turn drive leader behaviors. So culture's impact on leadership behavior is mediated through its CLT, as shown here.

Cultural values → CLT → Leadership behavior

Our findings are also related to the literature on strategic leadership (Finkelstein et al., 2009). Finkelstein and Hambrick (1996) argued that CEOs operate under constraints, and their ability to influence the fate of the organization depends on how much managerial discretion they have. They further argued that environmental forces such as industry dynamics and legal frameworks could constrain the CEO's actions. Our findings point to another source of managerial discretion: the country's culturally endorsed implicit leadership theory (CLT). CEOs tend to act in accordance to their country's CLT. While, in theory, they may be free to act as they wish, in practice, they end up following the CLT of their country and are constrained in the way they can behave. Falling short of the country CLT can have performance implications for the CEO and for the firm.

To summarize, this chapter provided a detailed analysis of how CEOs in different countries behave and how their behavior compares to their countries' expectations. In Chapter 10, our purpose is to better understand the relationship between what a society expects from its leaders and how CEOs behave in that society. We compare two extreme groups of CEOs: The first group consists of CEOs who are extremely effective, whom we call "superior CEOs." These are CEOs associated with extremely high levels of Firm Competitive Performance or TMT Dedication. The second group consists of CEOs who are much less effective, whom we call "inferior CEOs."

Appendix 7.1. Country Culturally Endorsed Implicit Leadership Theories and CEO Leadership Behaviors: Six Global Dimensions

Average (Across All Countries) Culturally Endorsed Implicit Leadership Theory and CEO Behavior

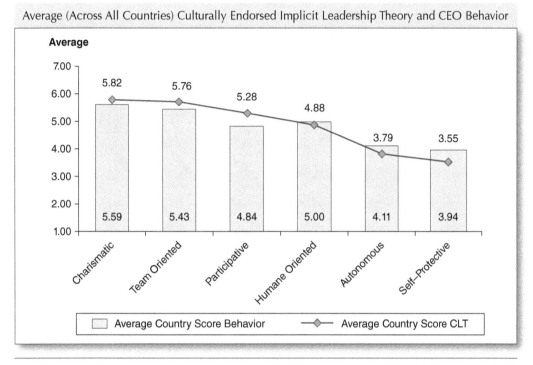

Note: There are slight discrepancies between the numbers in this figure and that of Table 7.4. The numbers in this figure represent data from all available CEO/organizations whereas data in Table 7.4 excluded any CEO/organizational data that did not have corresponding CLT   information.

Austria Culturally Endorsed Implicit Leadership Theory and CEO Behavior

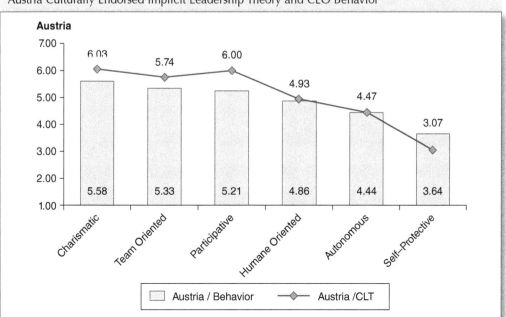

Brazil Culturally Endorsed Implicit Leadership Theory and CEO Behavior

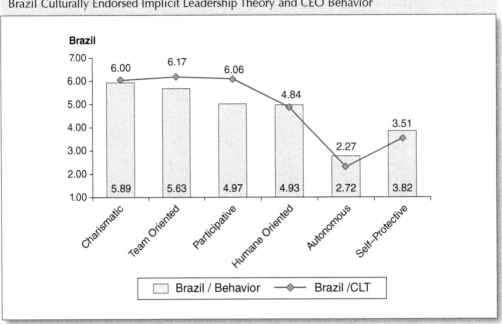

China Culturally Endorsed Implicit Leadership Theory and CEO Behavior

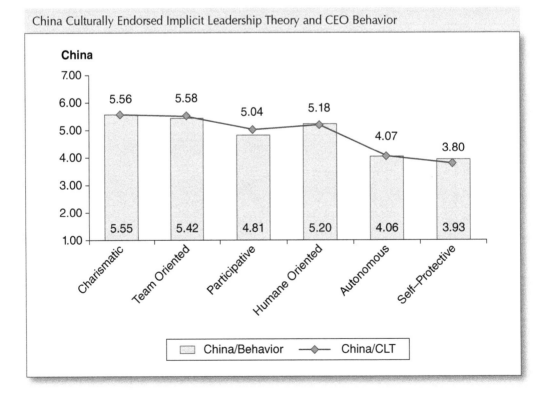

Estonia Culturally Endorsed Implicit Leadership Theory and CEO Behavior

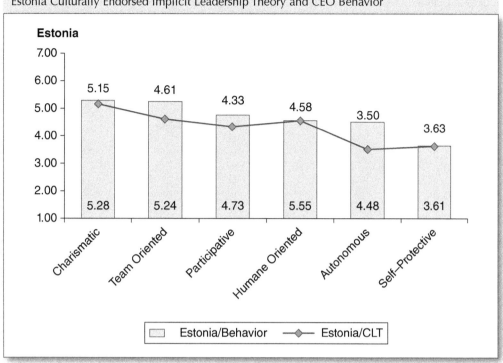

Germany Culturally Endorsed Implicit Leadership Theory and CEO Behavior

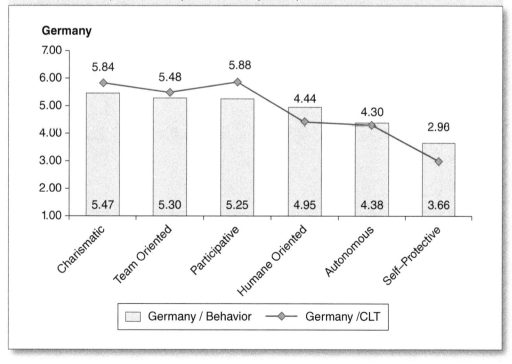

Greece Culturally Endorsed Implicit Leadership Theory and CEO Behavior

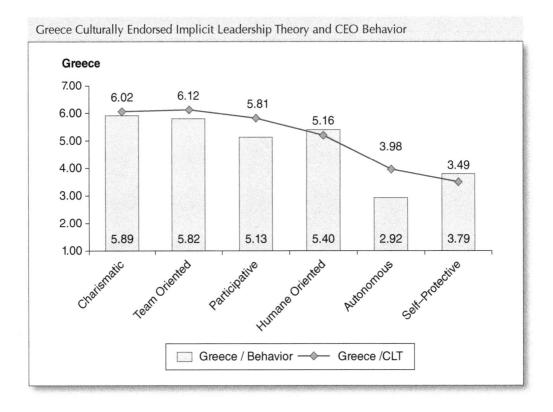

Guatemala Culturally Endorsed Implicit Leadership Theory and CEO Behavior

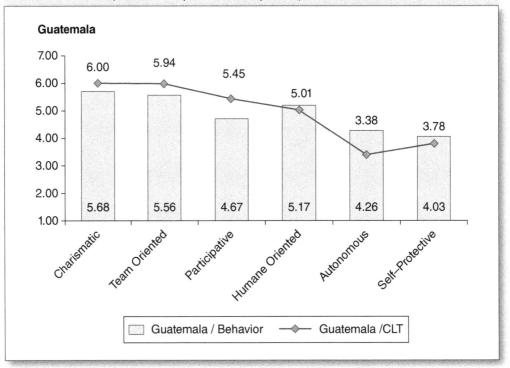

India Culturally Endorsed Implicit Leadership Theory and CEO Behavior

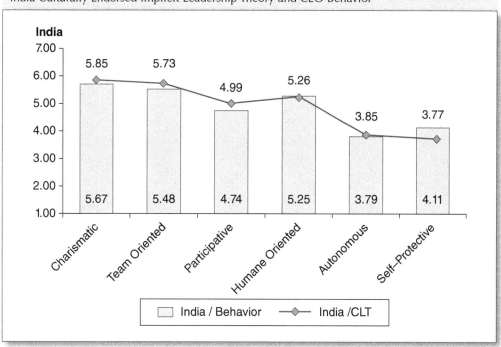

Mexico Culturally Endorsed Implicit Leadership Theory and CEO Behavior

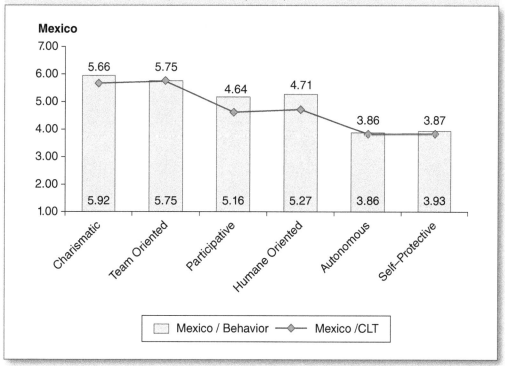

Netherlands Culturally Endorsed Implicit Leadership Theory and CEO Behavior

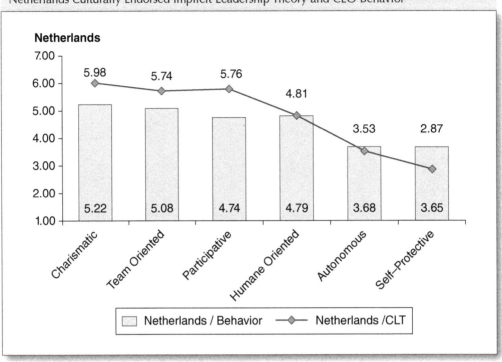

Nigeria Culturally Endorsed Implicit Leadership Theory and CEO Behavior

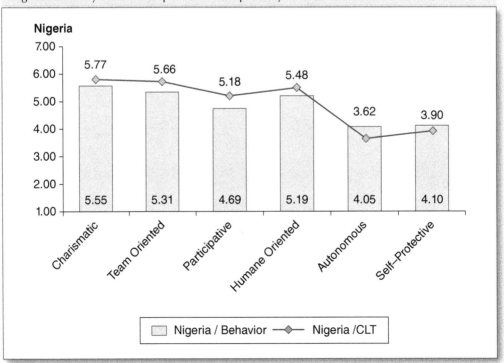

Romania Culturally Endorsed Implicit Leadership Theory and CEO Behavior

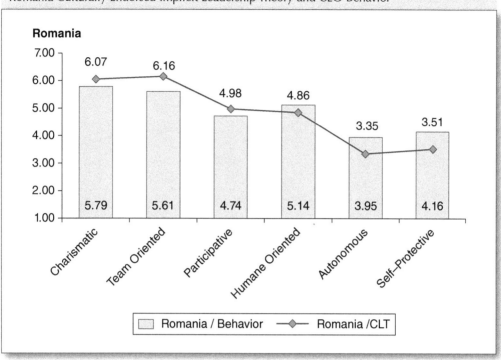

Russia Culturally Endorsed Implicit Leadership Theory and CEO Behavior

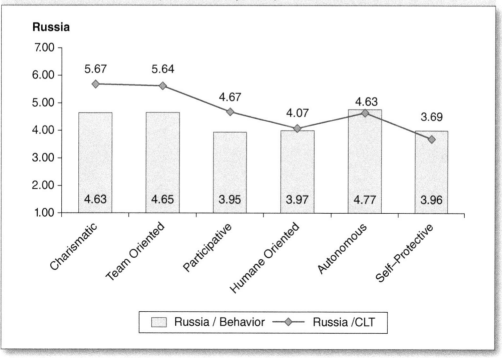

Slovenia Culturally Endorsed Implicit Leadership Theory and CEO Behavior

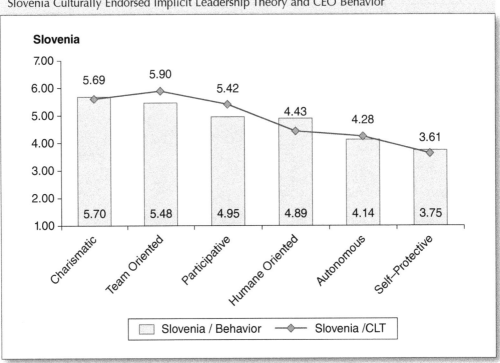

Spain Culturally Endorsed Implicit Leadership Theory and CEO Behavior

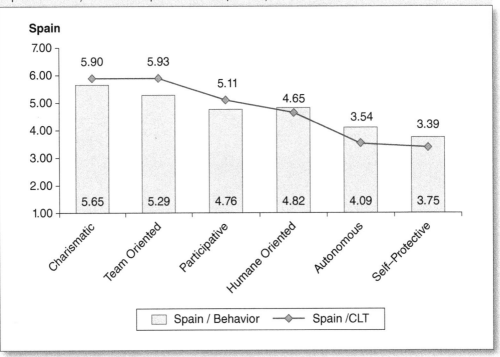

Taiwan Culturally Endorsed Implicit Leadership Theory and CEO Behavior

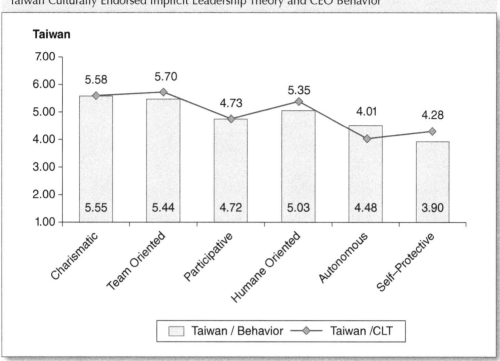

Turkey Culturally Endorsed Implicit Leadership Theory and CEO Behavior

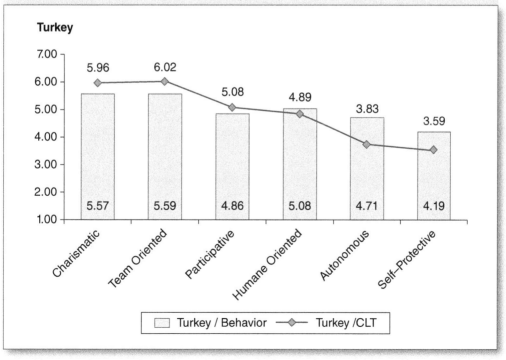

United States Culturally Endorsed Implicit Leadership Theory and CEO Behavior

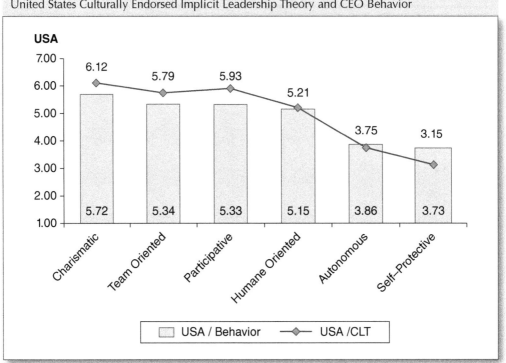

Appendix 7.2. Culturally Endorsed Implicit Leadership Theory and CEO Leader Behavior on Twenty-One Primary Leadership Dimensions by Country

Primary Leadership Dimension	Country Scores (Combined)		Azerbaijan		Austria		Brazil		China	
	Behavior*	CLT**	Behavior	CLT	Behavior	CLT	Behavior	CLT	Behavior	CLT
Visionary	5.70	5.99	5.12		5.83	6.13	5.98	6.15	5.54	5.85
Inspirational	5.62	6.05	4.91		5.55	6.34	5.80	6.35	5.69	5.92
Self-Sacrificial	5.21	5.01	4.50		5.21	5.03	5.35	4.84	5.48	4.70
Integrity	5.62	6.13	5.14		5.56	6.46	6.14	6.62	5.41	5.98
Decisive	5.64	5.75	5.25		5.52	5.96	6.14	5.70	5.52	5.29
Performance oriented	5.75	6.03	5.64		5.79	6.23	5.94	6.36	5.70	5.64
Collaborative team orientation	5.25	5.51	5.23		4.78	5.34	5.50	6.09	5.28	5.71
Team integrator	5.08	5.89	5.05		4.88	5.67	5.22	6.43	5.12	5.36
Diplomatic	5.64	5.48	5.07		5.78	5.43	5.97	5.57	5.51	5.05
Malevolent	2.35	1.95	3.45		1.88	1.54	1.86	1.33	2.38	2.04
Administratively competent	5.52	5.87	5.17		5.08	5.80	5.41	6.07	5.57	5.88
Participative	5.21	5.20	4.61		5.31	5.89	5.54	6.04	5.28	4.76
Autocratic	3.51	2.63	4.64		2.85	1.90	3.57	1.93	3.67	2.66
Modesty	4.92	5.00	4.22		4.85	5.05	4.75	5.44	5.21	5.03
Humane orientation	5.08	4.77	4.51		4.89	4.80	5.12	4.08	5.18	5.40
Autonomous	4.11	3.79	5.09		4.44	4.47	2.72	2.27	4.06	4.07
Self-Centered	2.86	2.16	3.54		2.54	1.99	2.45	2.12	2.86	2.22
Status conscious	4.54	4.54	4.53		4.41	3.86	4.73	5.17	4.46	4.47
Internally competitive	2.92	4.02	4.20		3.30	3.57	2.41	3.96	2.65	4.40
Face-Saver	4.30	3.07	3.33		3.61	2.56	4.13	2.53	4.42	3.97
Bureaucratic	5.06	3.96	5.27		4.39	3.36	5.18	3.85	5.24	3.94

Note: * N = 24. ** N = 18.

Country

Primary Leadership Dimension	Estonia		Fiji		Germany		Greece	
	Behavior	CLT	Behavior	CLT	Behavior	CLT	Behavior	CLT
Visionary	5.37	5.20	6.25		5.60	5.99	5.96	6.19
Inspirational	5.37	4.96	6.37		5.65	6.15	5.88	6.25
Self-Sacrificial	5.01	5.26	5.66		5.01	4.87	5.41	5.42
Integrity	5.39	5.63	6.22		5.42	6.12	5.95	6.27
Decisive	5.55	4.11	6.30		5.38	5.78	6.07	6.18
Performance oriented	5.08	5.96	6.33		5.71	6.11	6.07	5.82
Collaborative team orientation	4.97	4.42	5.75		4.80	5.05	5.77	5.76
Team integrator	4.78	5.33	5.32		4.98	5.48	5.34	6.19
Diplomatic	5.43	4.40	6.06		5.56	5.08	6.12	6.01
Malevolent	2.20	4.42	1.88		2.04	1.68	1.88	1.55
Administratively competent	5.23	5.30	6.06		5.14	5.51	5.93	6.18
Participative	4.78	3.73	6.00		5.25	5.72	5.52	5.75
Autocratic	3.31	3.05	2.82		2.71	1.95	3.23	2.14
Modesty	4.81	4.84	5.30		4.97	4.61	5.37	5.28
Humane orientation	4.35	4.29	5.58		4.93	4.27	5.40	5.02
Autonomous	4.48	3.50	3.53		4.38	4.30	2.92	3.98
Self-Centered	2.31	2.68	2.56		2.28	2.10	2.23	2.10
Status conscious	4.26	5.20	4.58		4.14	3.72	4.52	5.12
Internally competitive	2.64	2.71	2.36		3.44	3.59	2.77	3.62
Face-Saver	3.84	3.09	4.76		3.66	2.36	4.45	3.05
Bureaucratic	4.97	4.50	5.64		4.82	3.00	4.85	3.74

	Country							
	Guatemala		India		Mexico		Netherlands	
Primary Leadership Dimension	Behavior	CLT	Behavior	CLT	Behavior	CLT	Behavior	CLT
Visionary	5.84	6.06	5.72	6.02	6.13	5.78	5.27	6.30
Inspirational	5.66	6.25	5.74	5.93	6.00	5.91	5.24	6.38
Self-Sacrificial	5.15	5.71	5.57	5.45	5.13	4.80	4.84	4.79
Integrity	5.90	6.24	5.61	5.99	6.17	5.77	5.32	6.52
Decisive	5.76	5.77	5.61	5.83	6.04	5.54	5.35	5.87
Performance oriented	5.74	6.09	5.79	5.96	6.02	6.14	5.34	5.95
Collaborative team orientation	5.43	5.87	5.49	5.51	5.71	5.54	5.06	5.42
Team integrator	5.09	6.09	5.14	5.83	5.29	5.85	4.60	6.01
Diplomatic	5.83	5.23	5.58	5.70	5.85	5.55	5.21	5.43
Malevolent	2.10	1.59	2.53	2.35	1.95	2.09	2.08	1.62
Administratively competent	5.62	6.12	5.74	5.98	6.02	5.92	4.63	5.43
Participative	5.12	5.25	5.23	5.07	5.55	4.62	4.89	5.59
Autocratic	3.79	2.35	3.76	3.10	3.21	3.35	3.45	2.08
Modesty	4.97	5.27	5.15	5.33	5.14	4.74	4.58	4.71
Humane orientation	5.36	4.68	5.33	5.17	5.38	4.72	5.02	4.98
Autonomous	4.26	3.37	3.79	3.85	3.86	3.86	3.68	3.53
Self-Centered	2.87	1.87	3.05	2.63	2.39	2.52	2.90	1.75
Status conscious	4.62	5.17	4.53	4.18	4.64	4.64	4.32	3.93
Internally competitive	2.70	4.55	2.97	4.24	2.44	4.27	2.93	3.26
Face-Saver	4.66	3.05	4.75	3.57	4.51	3.34	3.75	2.23
Bureaucratic	5.26	4.38	5.28	4.10	5.52	4.48	4.44	3.22

	Country							
	Nigeria		Peru		Romania		Russia	
Primary Leadership Dimension	**Behavior**	CLT	Behavior	CLT	Behavior	CLT	Behavior	CLT
Visionary	5.66	5.89	6.14		5.89	6.11	4.69	6.07
Inspirational	5.75	5.98	5.93		5.82	6.30	4.65	5.93
Self-Sacrificial	5.27	4.92	5.66		5.36	5.34	3.91	4.28
Integrity	5.46	6.07	6.09		5.73	6.16	4.51	5.72
Decisive	5.35	5.75	6.02		6.07	6.18	5.06	5.95
Performance oriented	5.79	6.00	6.02		5.87	6.33	4.99	5.92
Collaborative team orientation	5.23	5.60	5.65		5.52	5.86	4.16	5.19
Team integrator	5.02	5.64	5.46		5.32	6.35	4.54	5.68
Diplomatic	5.24	5.22	6.22		5.81	5.98	4.86	5.35
Malevolent	2.70	2.15	1.78		2.53	1.63	3.32	2.02
Administratively competent	5.72	6.03	6.13		5.95	6.22	4.65	6.01
Participative	4.97	5.12	5.75		5.12	4.82	4.29	5.18
Autocratic	3.59	2.75	3.07		3.64	2.86	4.45	3.86
Modesty	5.10	5.46	4.96		5.04	5.12	3.86	4.25
Humane orientation	5.27	5.54	5.43		5.22	4.55	4.18	3.91
Autonomous	4.05	3.62	3.89		3.95	3.35	4.77	4.63
Self-Centered	3.02	2.35	2.32		3.01	1.63	3.79	2.48
Status conscious	4.42	4.61	4.69		4.63	4.66	4.54	5.06
Internally competitive	3.18	4.47	2.30		3.03	4.21	3.28	4.43
Face-Saver	4.72	3.47	4.48		4.69	2.95	3.82	3.40
Bureaucratic	5.21	4.53	5.45		5.39	4.19	4.55	3.21

Country								
	Slovenia		Solomon Islands		Spain		Taiwan	
Primary Leadership Dimension	Behavior	CLT	Behavior	CLT	Behavior	CLT	Behavior	CLT
Visionary	5.96	6.00	5.18		5.77	5.91	5.48	5.66
Inspirational	5.68	5.74	5.26		5.56	6.34	5.70	5.74
Self-Sacrificial	5.21	4.77	5.01		5.43	4.80	5.48	4.98
Integrity	5.59	6.08	5.22		5.54	6.11	5.48	5.89
Decisive	5.81	5.79	5.34		5.81	5.95	5.44	5.60
Performance oriented	5.96	5.76	5.33		5.80	6.25	5.70	5.67
Collaborative team orientation	5.35	5.35	5.13		5.12	5.72	5.35	5.66
Team integrator	5.15	6.11	5.16		4.89	6.26	5.12	5.44
Diplomatic	5.78	5.85	5.40		5.80	5.73	5.57	5.84
Malevolent	2.32	1.67	3.45		2.48	1.77	2.40	2.31
Administratively competent	5.42	5.85	5.23		5.06	5.66	5.55	5.92
Participative	5.32	5.33	5.21		5.31	4.83	5.42	4.53
Autocratic	3.41	2.49	4.36		3.79	2.60	4.00	3.07
Modesty	5.14	4.66	4.60		4.52	4.76	4.81	5.32
Humane orientation	4.67	4.18	4.84		5.12	4.57	5.24	5.40
Autonomous	4.14	4.28	4.33		4.09	3.54	4.48	4.01
Self-Centered	2.58	2.28	3.68		3.04	1.84	2.89	2.50
Status conscious	4.06	4.33	4.56		4.62	4.23	4.77	4.83
Internally competitive	2.95	4.15	3.71		2.62	4.24	2.78	5.01
Face-Saver	4.48	3.04	4.63		4.05	2.48	4.54	4.53
Bureaucratic	4.78	4.19	5.07		4.45	4.11	4.48	4.52

243

Primary Leadership Dimension	Tonga		Tonga		United States		Vanuatu	
	Behavior	CLT	Behavior	CLT	Behavior	CLT	Behavior	CLT
Visionary	5.89		5.75	6.25	5.91	6.28	5.92	
Inspirational	5.63		5.62	6.08	5.72	6.35	5.74	
Self-Sacrificial	5.48		5.08	5.03	5.45	5.16	5.37	
Integrity	5.72		5.76	6.16	5.84	6.51	5.64	
Decisive	5.05		5.59	6.29	5.50	5.96	5.78	
Performance oriented	5.95		5.63	5.91	5.86	6.46	5.83	
Collaborative team orientation	5.09		5.58	5.70	4.83	5.38	5.13	
Team integrator	5.10		5.18	6.28	4.90	6.03	5.25	
Diplomatic	5.82		5.78	5.74	5.54	5.46	5.52	
Malevolent	3.41		2.28	1.76	1.93	1.55	1.68	
Administratively competent	5.90		5.79	6.13	5.39	5.63	6.00	
Participative	5.28		4.95	5.38	5.63	5.90	4.61	
Autocratic	3.88		3.23	3.22	2.94	2.03	2.98	
Modesty	5.29		5.05	4.82	5.06	5.24	5.42	
Humane orientation	5.62		5.11	5.02	5.24	5.19	4.84	
Autonomous	4.78		4.71	3.83	3.86	3.75	4.44	
Self-Centered	3.48		3.71	1.93	2.52	1.97	2.54	
Status conscious	5.00		4.82	4.91	4.25	3.60	4.85	
Internally competitive	3.34		2.80	4.17	2.86	3.53	2.38	
Face-Saver	4.96		4.39	2.99	3.92	2.66	4.68	
Bureaucratic	5.50		5.25	4.02	5.12	3.90	5.31	

Country

8 Leadership Effectiveness across Cultures

The Linkage With CEO Behaviors

This chapter presents our empirical evidence regarding CEO leadership behavior and effectiveness across cultures. As indicated in Chapter 4, data were obtained from more than 1,000 CEOs and 5,000 top management team (TMT) members located in 24 countries across the world. The leadership behaviors are actual CEO behaviors that are reported by TMT members. The outcome measures were obtained from different TMT members than those reporting the CEO leadership behaviors (the exception is the presentation of same source results for comparison purposes in Table 8.2a). We present findings regarding a number of research questions posed in previous chapters regarding the similarities and differences of leadership behaviors and effectiveness found in very different cultural contexts. These questions were formed as a result of previous GLOBE research (GLOBE 2004 and GLOBE 2007), the cumulative research literature on cross-cultural leadership to date, and our model presented in Chapter 1. The following topics are of specific interest in this chapter:

- Understanding the general level of CEO effectiveness as perceived by TMT members across cultures
- Analyzing the *overall* impact of CEO leadership behaviors on TMT Dedication and Firm Performance
- Determining the specific impact of 6 global CEO leadership behaviors and 21 primary CEO leadership behaviors on TMT Dedication and Firm Performance
- Identifying leadership behaviors that are particularly effective, not effective, and ineffective in influencing outstanding leadership
- Investigating the similarities and differences in effective leadership across cultures and the meta-question of leadership universality versus cultural contingency.

The Measurement of CEO Effectiveness _____

The concept and metrics of measuring leadership and organizational effectiveness is complex. Leadership effectiveness may be reflected in a number of diverse indices, including financial success, meeting organizational objectives, the level of employee satisfaction, clients, and customers among many other indices. Measuring leadership effectiveness becomes far more problematic when considering the diversity of organizations and industries found across cultures.

In the present GLOBE project, we examined effectiveness from two different but related perspectives. First, we examined effectiveness from the standpoint of the CEOs' TMT motivation, commitment, and ability to work together as a team. We developed these measures of effectiveness from direct reports under the rubric of "Internally Oriented Measures of Effectiveness." As explained in Chapter 4, three separate outcomes of TMT individual Commitment, individual Effort, and Team Solidarity were measured independently and then combined as a gestalt, which we labeled *TMT Dedication* (this is a term that will be used throughout the remainder of the chapter). As a second main metric of effectiveness, we measured firm performance. As explained in Chapter 4, this approach was challenging as completely objective measures of firm performance such as return on investment (ROI) are notoriously difficult to reliably obtain even within a single country. They are even more problematic with respect to overall validity and comparability across countries. We chose to measure firm performance by asking TMT members who had access to financial information to report how competitive their firm is compared to their peers. Our *Firm Competitive Performance* measure consisted of two separate outcomes: (1) Competitive Sales Performance and (2) Competitive Industry Dominance.[1] These are our "Externally Oriented Measures of Effectiveness." Again, only TMT members who had access to financial information were included in the assessment of Firm Competitive Performance (see Chapter 4 for a complete description of the measurement properties of these variables).

In the sections to follow, we first describe our results pertaining to leadership effectiveness in general. Then we present a detailed discussion of effectiveness with respect to our internal and external measures of effectiveness (TMT Dedication and Firm Competitive Performance). We briefly present descriptive information regarding the perception of CEO effectiveness. This information is presented for two related reasons. First, we were interested in determining if the generally negative portrayal of CEOs in popular media outlets such as TV, movies, and

---

[1]We also developed a measure of perceived ROI, but this measure proved very problematic and was dropped from the analysis.

social media hold true in organizations around the world. That is, we were curious if this negative perception is the norm for TMT members or if the reality is that CEOs are generally held in a more positive light. Second, it would seem inappropriate for the present project to convey the impression that certain leadership behaviors are more (or less) effective if we find that CEO influence is generally negative. We will show in later chapters that not all CEOs are equally successful as demonstrated by their TMT Dedication and Firm Competitive Performance.

CEO Effectiveness Across Countries: Top Management Team Dedication and Firm Competitive Performance

We first computed a measure of TMT Dedication averaged across countries. The Dedication measure contains scores composed of TMT Commitment, Effort, and Team Solidarity. The average score across all countries is 5.61 on a 7-point Likert scale. We interpret this average score in a positive light. Overall, TMT members are reasonably committed, put forth significant work effort, and view each other as a team. Our measure of Firm Competitive Performance was composed of two constituent measures: Competitive Sales Performance and Competitive Industry Dominance. Each measure reflects the financial officer's perception of the extent to which the firm is competitive using two separate indices. The average Firm Competitive Performance score was 4.27 on a 7-point scale, demonstrating that the firms are perceived to be somewhat successful as indicated by their sales performance and competitive industry domination.

Effectiveness of Six Global CEO Leadership Behaviors Considered Together

The primary purpose of this chapter is to examine CEO effectiveness and determine what kinds of leadership behaviors lead to effectiveness. Before presenting evidence as to which CEO behaviors are most influential, it seems critical to us to first prove that leadership is important when viewed as a gestalt. Fortunately, an overall view is possible by computing a hierarchical linear modeling (HLM) analysis using the six GLOBE global leadership variables as predictors for the seven dependent variables employed in this project. Recall that TMT Dedication is comprised of three dependent measures and Firm Competitive Performance is comprised of two measures, hence a total of seven dependent measures: two overall and five constituent variables.

Table 8.1 provides an overall assessment of leadership effectiveness for the six global leadership dimensions considered together.[2] Admittedly, this analysis views leadership as an undifferentiated package where all six global leadership behaviors are considered simultaneously as predictors. This table shows the percentage variance accounted (R^2) for each dependent variable. For instance, our overall measure of TMT Dedication is significantly predicted by the six global leadership behaviors as the combined leadership variables account for 21% of the variance ($R^2 = 21\%$, $p < .01$). When examining each measure comprising TMT Dedication, we see a corresponding level of variance accounted for (Commitment $R^2 = 19\%$, Effort $R^2 = 17\%$, and Team Solidarity $R^2 = 15\%$). We believe this data is particularly impressive given the fact that as explained in Chapter 4, "same source bias" was ruled out since leadership behaviors

Table 8.1 Percentage Variance Accounted for by Leadership Behaviors Predicting Dependent Variables

Dependent Variable	Six Global Leadership Dimensions	Twenty-One Primary Leadership Dimensions
TMT Dedication	21%**	20%**
Commitment	19%**	19%**
Effort	17%**	17%**
Team Solidarity	15%**	15%**
Firm Competitive Performance	16%**	18%**
Competitive Sales Performance	12%**	14%**
Competitive Industry Dominance	18%**	20%**

Note: Analyses were conducted via random coefficient modeling using the R program.

$N = 998$ for TMT Dedication and $N = 320$ for Firm Competitive Performance.

**$p < .01$.

---

[2]The HLM regression analysis is performed in a normal manner. The amount of variance accounted for by the analysis is computed. We will call that R (preliminary). This figure is an underestimate because it includes variance that is not under the control of the leaders (i.e., between society differences in the dependent variable). The percentage of variance in the dependent variable due to society differences is computed and removed. The R^2 (preliminary) is then corrected by doing the following:

$$R^2_{corrected} = \frac{R^2_{pre\lim inary}}{(1 - R^2_{Society})}$$

were obtained from a separate sample from the assessment of each dependent variable.[3]

Similarly, we found that the gestalt effects of leadership behaviors considered simultaneously also predict Firm Competitive Performance. The amount of variance accounted for by employing the six global leadership dimensions was 16% ($p < .01$). The picture is also positive for predicting each of the two constituent measures of this variable. Leadership influence was significant when considering the dependent variables of Competitive Industry Dominance ($R^2 = 18\%$) and Competitive Sales Performance ($R^2 = 12\%$).

Effectiveness of Twenty-One Primary CEO Leadership Behaviors Considered Together

As expected, when viewing the same table (8.1) but this time examining the gestalt effect for the 21 primary leadership behaviors considered simultaneously, we see a very similar pattern to that of using the 6 global leadership behaviors. The results of using the 21 primary leadership behaviors considered as a unit is generally equally or more predictive of combining the primary leadership dimensions into the 6 global dimensions considered previously. That is, the level of variance accounted for is the same or larger. For example, the R^2 increases from 18% to 20% when predicting Competitive Industry Dominance. Competitive Sales Performance increases from 12% to 14% variance accounted for. Again, the major purpose of this section is to demonstrate that leadership in this worldwide sample has a significant impact on both internally (i.e., TMT Dedication) and externally oriented (i.e., Firm Competitive Performance) dependent measures. It is now up to us to provide a little more detail regarding which leadership behaviors result in greater effectiveness than others and whether effectiveness is moderated by national culture.

Which CEO Leadership Behaviors Predict Top Management Team Dedication?

For ease of discussion, this first section presents results concerning TMT Dedication, which then is followed by a discussion of leadership effectiveness regarding Firm Competitive Performance. Table 8.2a provides evidence regarding leadership effectiveness for the overall TMT Dedication measure, and Table 8.2b presents evidence of leadership effectiveness for

---

[3]The relationships between the independent and dependent variables, however, may still be inflated by attribution biases whereby the rating of CEO behaviors are inflated in firms with high performance.

Table 8.2a   CEO Leadership Behaviors Predicting Top Management Team
             Dedication: Comparison of Different Versus Common Sources

| | TMT Dedication | | | |
| | Different Source | | Common Source | |
Leadership Behavior	Correlation	χ² Slope	Correlation	χ² Slope
Charismatic	**.37****	**5.87†**	**.71****	**1.65**
Visionary	.35**	2.98	.68**	1.64
Inspirational	.36**	3.00	.59**	2.14
Self-Sacrificial	.29**	4.36	.56**	3.46
Integrity	.35**	1.67	.67**	3.60
Decisive	.23**	1.85	.47**	20.29**
Performance oriented	.33**	6.28*	.62**	8.68*
Team Oriented	**.32****	**5.62†**	**.64****	**0.16**
Collaborative team orientation	.18**	1.96	.46**	7.60*
Team integrator	.24**	3.37	.66**	4.66†
Diplomatic	.31**	3.97	.57**	5.65†
Malevolent	−.22**	0.00	−.39**	0.42
Administratively competent	.31**	6.20*	.57**	13.66**
Participative	**.21****	**0.29**	**.39****	**9.52†**
Participative	.22**	1.00	.42**	2.53
Autocratic	−.12**	1.20	−.21**	8.26*
Humane Oriented	**.25****	**5.99†**	**.52****	**14.97****
Modesty	.17**	4.20	.32**	20.74**
Humane orientation	.26**	2.83	.53**	13.34**
Autonomous	**−.07***	**3.05**	**−.12****	**7.21***
Self-Protective	**.05**	**0.41**	**.18****	**0.06**
Self-Centered	−.11**	1.08	−.22**	1.13
Status conscious	.11**	0.03	.23**	0.10
Internally competitive	−.19**	0.00	−.24**	8.13*
Face-Saver	.06	0.39	.21**	9.96**
Bureaucratic	.23**	0.12	.48**	7.17*

Note: The autonomous primary leadership dimension is the same as the global Autonomous leadership dimension.

$N = 998$ for different source. $N = 1,008$ for common source.

† $p < 0.10$. * $p < .05$. ** $p < .01$.

Table 8.2b CEO Leadership Behaviors Predicting Three Constituent Measures of TMT Dedication

TMT Dedication

Leadership Behavior	Commitment			Effort			Team Solidarity		
	HLM	SD	Corr	HLM	SD	Corr	HLM	SD	Corr
Charismatic	0.48	0.68ᵃ	.32**	0.34	0.68	.29**	0.47	0.68	.33**
	χ² Slope:	1.01ᵇ		χ² Slope:	0.8		χ² Slope:	0.96	
		9.20**			9.07*			3.31	
Visionary	0.41	0.77ᵃ	.31**	0.26	0.77	.25**	0.38	0.77	.30**
	χ² Slope:	1.01ᵇ		χ² Slope:	0.8		χ² Slope:	0.96	
		4.06			5.90+			0.75	
Inspirational	0.42	0.77	.32**	0.28	0.77	.27**	0.39	0.77	.31**
	χ² Slope:	1.01		χ² Slope:	0.8		χ² Slope:	0.96	
		4.83+			10.76**			2.20	
Self-Sacrificial	0.28	0.85	.24**	0.24	0.85	.26**	0.26	0.85	.23**
	χ² Slope:	1.01		χ² Slope:	0.8		χ² Slope:	0.96	
		5.14+			9.55**			1.94	
Integrity	0.37	0.79	.29**	0.27	0.79	.27**	0.37	0.79	.30**
	χ² Slope:	1.01		χ² Slope:	0.8		χ² Slope:	0.96	
		4.13			3.13			0.42	
Decisive	0.23	0.88	.20**	0.14	0.88	.15**	0.23	0.88	.21**
	χ² Slope:	1.01		χ² Slope:	0.8		χ² Slope:	0.96	
		1.73			4.87+			0.06	
Performance oriented	0.36	0.72	.26**	0.31	0.72	.28**	0.37	0.72	.28**
		1.01			0.8			0.96	

(Continued)

(Continued)

Leadership Behavior	TMT Dedication								
	Commitment			Effort			Team Solidarity		
	HLM	SD	Corr	HLM	SD	Corr	HLM	SD	Corr
Team Oriented	χ² Slope:	9.68**		χ² Slope:	10.03**		χ² Slope:	2.18	
	0.47	0.60	.28**	0.32	0.60	.24**	0.48	0.60	.30**
		1.01			0.8			0.96	
Collaborative team orientation	χ² Slope:	8.55*		χ² Slope:	6.91*		χ² Slope:	2.00	
	0.19	0.92	.17**	0.1	0.92	.11**	0.18	0.92	.17**
		1.01			0.8			0.96	
Team integrator	χ² Slope:	2.85		χ² Slope:	4.30		χ² Slope:	0.27	
	0.33	0.75	.25**	0.25	0.75	.23**	0.35	0.75	.28**
		1.01			0.8			0.96	
Diplomatic	χ² Slope:	7.30*		χ² Slope:	5.69+		χ² Slope:	1.32	
	0.36	0.78	.28**	0.23	0.78	.22**	0.33	0.78	.27**
		1.01			0.8			0.96	
Malevolent	χ² Slope:	5.36+		χ² Slope:	12.17**		χ² Slope:	0.24	
	−0.21	0.94	−.19**	−0.13	0.94	−.15**	−0.21	0.94	−.21**
		1.01			0.8			0.96	
Administratively competent	χ² Slope:	0.89		χ² Slope:	0.31		χ² Slope:	0.07	
	0.3	0.88	.26**	0.21	0.88	.24**	0.3	0.88	.28**
		1.01			0.8			0.96	
Participative	χ² Slope:	9.17**		χ² Slope:	7.96*		χ² Slope:	2.78	
	0.18	0.77	.14**	0.19	0.77	.18**	0.21	0.77	.17**
		1.01			0.8			0.96	

| Leadership Behavior | TMT Dedication | | | | | | | | |
| | Commitment | | | Effort | | | Team Solidarity | | |
	HLM	SD	Corr	HLM	SD	Corr	HLM	SD	Corr
Participative	χ^2 Slope:	1.99		χ^2 Slope:	2.62		χ^2 Slope:	0.14	
	0.18	0.95	.17**	0.17	0.95	.20**	0.17	0.95	.17**
		1.01			0.8			0.96	
Autocratic	χ^2 Slope:	7.14**		χ^2 Slope:	3.14		χ^2 Slope:	3.64	
	–0.11	0.99	–.11**	–0.07	0.99	–.09**	–0.13	0.99	–.13**
		1.01			0.8			0.96	
Humane Oriented	χ^2 Slope:	1.07		χ^2 Slope:	2.24		χ^2 Slope:	0.06	
	0.49	0.81	.39**	0.20	0.81	.20**	0.26	0.81	.22**
		1.01			0.8			0.96	
Modesty	χ^2 Slope:	6.14*		χ^2 Slope:	8.23*		χ^2 Slope:	1.95	
	0.13	0.75	.13**	0.19	0.75	.18**	0.19	0.75	.15**
		1.01			0.8			0.96	
Humane orientation	χ^2 Slope:	1.86		χ^2 Slope:	5.09+		χ^2 Slope:	2.95	
	0.23	0.85	.24**	0.18	0.85	.19**	0.27	0.85	.24**
		1.01			0.8			0.96	
Autonomous	χ^2 Slope:	3.91		χ^2 Slope:	7.69*		χ^2 Slope:	0.01	
	–0.03	1.05	–.09**	–0.02	1.05	–.03	–0.07	1.05	–.08
		1.01			0.8			0.96	
Self-Protective	χ^2 Slope:	1.88		χ^2 Slope:	4.85+		χ^2 Slope:	0.31	
	0.26	0.42	.11**	0.19	0.42	.10*	0.23	0.42	.10**
		1.01			0.8			0.96	
	χ^2 Slope:	0.72		χ^2 Slope:	6.82*		χ^2 Slope:	0.12	

(Continued)

(Continued)

Leadership Behavior	TMT Dedication								
	Commitment			Effort			Team Solidarity		
	HLM	SD	Corr	HLM	SD	Corr	HLM	SD	Corr
Self-Centered	−0.11	1.11	−.12**	−0.03	1.11	−.05	−0.11	1.11	−.12**
		1.01			0.8			0.96	
	χ² Slope:			χ² Slope:			χ² Slope:		
Status conscious	0.06	3.34	.05	0.04	0.89	.04	0.03	0.75	.02
		1.01			0.8			0.96	
	χ² Slope:			χ² Slope:			χ² Slope:		
Internally competitive	−0.13	0.77	−.10**	−0.12	0.77	−.11**	−0.16	0.77	−.12**
		1.01			0.8			0.96	
	χ² Slope:			χ² Slope:			χ² Slope:		
Face-Saver	0.14	0.91	.12**	0.05	0.09	.06	0.13	0.57	.12**
		1.01			0.8			0.96	
	χ² Slope:			χ² Slope:			χ² Slope:		
Bureaucratic	0.2	0.87	.17**	0.14	1.56	.15**	0.25	0.41	.23**
		1.01			0.8			0.96	
	χ² Slope:	4.55		χ² Slope:	0.40		χ² Slope:	6.73**	

Note: The *autonomous* primary leadership dimension is the same as the global *Autonomous* leadership dimension.

HLM = HLM coefficient; SD = standard deviation; Corr = correlation.

[a] Standard deviation for independent variable.

[b] Standard deviation for dependent variable.

N = 998.

*p < .05. **p < .01.

the *three constituent measures* of TMT Dedication. We also want to point out several aspects of Tables 8.2a and 8.2b, and Tables 8.4a and 8.4b. In Table 8.2a, we present the results of the 6 global leadership dimensions and 21 primary leadership dimensions predicting *overall* TMT Dedication. However, you will note that we present two sets of results for the TMT Dedication measure; one set is for the dependent measures obtained by different sources from those rating the CEO leadership behaviors; the other set is for dependent measures obtained from common sources that also rated the CEO leadership behavior. Subsequently, Table 8.2b shows the effectiveness of both the 6 global and 21 primary leadership behaviors for the *three constituent measures comprising* TMT Dedication. The same organization scheme is found for the Firm Competitive Performance measures in Tables 8.4a and 8.4b. Note that the outcome data for all analyses presented in this book were obtained *only* from different sources from those that rated the CEO leadership behavior (with the exception of results presented in Table 8.2a for "common sources").

A second point is that some of the tables include results that test for the moderating effect of culture (i.e., nations or countries). A χ^2 index indicates *slope* differences across countries between the leader behavior-outcome measure relationships. It provides evidence as to whether the relationship between the leadership behavior and the dependent measure varies across countries—a typical test for the moderating impact of culture. Table 8.2a presents the HLM correlations along with the slope index because the focus of this table is on leadership effectiveness, whether leadership effectiveness of each leadership dimension varies across cultures, and the extent to which results differ using different sources or common sources. We need to be cognizant, however, of assuming that *cross-national differences* truly reflect *cross-cultural differences*. This issue of cross-national versus cross-cultural differences has been referred to as the fundamental methodological issue stemming from the "rival hypothesis confound" (Brett, Tinsley, Janssens, Barsness, & Lytle, 1997). Essentially besides culture, a myriad of other cross-national factors including technological, political, economic, and organizational factors may influence organizational behavior (Dorfman, 2004). We will have more to say about "the rival hypothesis confound" later in the book. In this chapter, however, we are setting the stage to consider whether cross-national effects are evident regarding leadership-behavior outcomes. The complete HLM analyses for TMT Dedication with HLM coefficients, standard deviations (*SDs*), correlations, and χ^2 slopes are presented in Appendix 8.1.

Third, our primary analyses are very conservative indicators of leadership effectiveness as the data were collected and analyzed to completely eliminate common source variance i.e., separate TMT members rated CEO leadership behaviors from those whose ratings comprised the

Dedication and Firm Performance measure. It is however possible, and in fact, desirable to also provide results using data from the same source[4] (but possibly introducing common source biases). As previously indicated, Table 8.2a presents results from data obtained by both different source and common sources.

By examining the results in Table 8.2a, one is immediately struck by the obvious fact that leadership effectiveness clearly depends on the specific leadership behavior in question. For our discussion presented here, we rely on the data obtained from different sources—thereby eliminating the potential bias caused by same sources. (Note, however, that as a general approximation, the size of the correlations using common sources is approximately twice the size as compared to results with different sources.) With respect to TMT Dedication, the global leadership behaviors fall into identifiable groups of general effectiveness. The Charismatic and Team-Oriented behaviors are most predictive of TMT Dedication ($r = .37$ and $r = .32, p < .01$) followed by Humane-Oriented and Participative behaviors ($r = .25$ and $r = .21, p < .01$). Autonomous leadership has a weak but significant *negative* effect ($r = -.07, p < .05$) and the Self-Protective behavior seems to have no effect at all ($r = .05, p$ is ns). Table 8.3 lists the rank order of the primary leadership dimensions in predicting TMT Dedication.

Charismatic and Team-Oriented Leadership Predicting Top Management Team Dedication

Starting with the two most influential global leadership behaviors (i.e., Charismatic and Team-Oriented), Table 8.2a indicates that the more fine-tuned analysis of the 21 primary behaviors within the 6 global behaviors reveals some interesting facts. All six primary leadership behaviors of the

---

[4]Our rationale for analyzing and then presenting data taken from common sources includes the following: First, the findings with same sources show that the different source findings are clearly conservative estimates. The same source findings are approximately double that of our different source findings. However, the findings that we rely on (i.e., different source) are likely to reflect the lower bound of leadership influence. Second, and related to the first point, the correlations reported for different sources are conservative given that they have not been corrected for unreliability (i.e., intraclass correlation coefficients [ICC(2)] for the leadership and outcome variables). Third, we obtained additional information using common source regarding HLM moderation by culture. Considering both results, our findings support the impact of several leadership behaviors being moderated by culture. Fourth, we have explored the magnitude of common method and source variance in our study. Recent articles have suggested that common method bias may be overstated and go so far as to call it "an urban legend" (Spector, 2006). While in the present study, our results may initially look like common source bias had a large effect; Spector (2006) cautioned that using different sources might actually attenuate valid relationships.

Table 8.3 Rank Order of Primary CEO Leadership Behaviors Predicting TMT Dedication

TMT Dedication		
Rank	**Leadership Behavior**	**Correlation**
1	Inspirational	.36**
2.5	Visionary	.35**
2.5	Integrity	.35**
4	Performance oriented	.33**
5.5	Administratively competent	.31**
5.5	Diplomatic	.31**
7	Self-Sacrificial	.29**
8	Humane orientation	.26**
9	Team integrator	.24**
10.5	Decisive	.23**
10.5	Bureaucratic	.23**
12.5	Participative	.22**
12.5	Malevolent	−.22**
14	Internally competitive	−.19**
15	Collaborative team orientation	.18**
16	Modesty	.17**
17	Autocratic	−.12**
18.5	Status conscious	.11**
18.5	Self-Centered	−.11**
20	Autonomous	−.07*
21	Face-Saver	.06

Note: This table shows the bivariate correlations. Each leadership dimension predicts the dependent variable one at a time.

$N = 998$.

*$p < .05$. **$p < .01$.

Charismatic global dimension are influential. Visionary, inspirational, and integrity leadership dimensions lead this group in terms of effectiveness ($r = .35$ and $r = .36$, respectively, $p < .01$). If we examine the effects of these two most powerful leadership dimensions on each of the three constituent measures of TMT Dedication, perhaps not surprisingly, Charismatic leadership tops the list with Team-Oriented following closely behind (see Table 8.2b). The Charismatic CEO behavior had significant impacts on each of the three dependent measures and with only one exception: the size of the relationship was strongest among all leadership-outcome relationships. But, interestingly, there were differences among nations for the dependent variables of TMT Commitment and TMT Effort as evidenced by significant moderation (χ^2 slopes) for these two dependent measures.

For Team-Oriented leadership, two of the constituent leadership behaviors are as influential as the global Team-Oriented behavior (where $r = .32, p < .01$ for the global leadership behavior). But perhaps surprisingly, these two behaviors are likely not what one would expect; they are diplomatic and administratively competent ($r = .31, p < .01$ for both). We believe this is a very important finding as it reinforces Henry Mintzberg's (2004, 2009) admonition that managerial competence is as important as the current zeitgeist emphasizing *leadership*.

Another interesting finding emerges when considering the two primary dimensions of collaborative team orientation and team integrator within the global Team-Oriented dimension. The latter is considerably more impactful than the former and can be explained by examining the actual behaviors within each dimension. For collaborative team orientation ($r = .18, p < .01$), the behavioral items indicate a leader who is concerned with the welfare of the group, is collaborative, and loyal. For the team integrator dimension ($r = .24, p < .01$), this leader gets members to work together and integrates members into a cohesive and working whole. In a sense, the active nature of team integration is seen as being slightly more effective than the passive concern of team welfare. We further note that the dimension labeled *malevolent* is predictably negative in its effect ($r = -.22, p < .01$), demonstrating the negative effect of leaders who are deceitful, punitive, and believe the worst in people.

Participative, Humane-Oriented, Autonomous, and Self-Protective Leadership Predicting Top Management Team Dedication

The Participative global dimension holds no surprises when examining the constituent parts: Each primary dimension makes sense as the participative primary dimension is positive in its effects ($r = .22, p < .01$), and the autocratic dimension is significantly negative ($r = -.12, p < .01$). Participative leadership also had a positive effect for all three constituent measures, and its impact did not vary across countries.

The global Humane-Oriented dimension also holds no surprises when examining the constituent dimensions where both are positive in their influence. However, modesty ($r = .17, p < .01$) seems to be slightly less impactful than the humane-oriented ($r = .26, p < .01$) primary dimension. The Autonomous global dimension is identical to its primary dimension since they are one and the same. It has a small but significant negative effect on TMT Dedication ($r = -.07$, $p < .05$).

The Self-Protective global dimension is perhaps the most interesting when examining the effectiveness of its primary constituent parts. The over- all effectiveness of the global Self-Protective dimension is negligible ($r = .05$ ns). However, two of the primary dimensions within this global leadership dimension have a positive effect (status conscious and bureau- cratic, $r = .11$ and $r = .23$, $p < .01$, respectively). In contrast, the self-centered and internally competitive primary dimensions have a significant negative effect ($r = -.11$ and $r = -.19$, $p < .01$, respectively).

The primary dimension of face-saving has a negligible effect ($r = .06$ ns). Thus, a more fine-grained analysis of the Self-Protective global dimension yields meaningful differences where four of the five primary dimensions have signifi- cant effects but two are positive and two are negative. Perhaps surprisingly, we found a complete absence of HLM slope effects, which would have indicated different relationships among countries. Simply put, the negative effects of being self-centered and fomenting internally competitive conflict within the group is equal across cultures as is the positive effects of status conscious and bureaucratic across cultures. Explaining the positive effects of being status conscious and bureaucratic tendencies are difficult from a Western perspective, but it becomes more understandable when examining the actual behaviors within each leadership dimension (see Chapter 4 for leadership item examples and all items in Appendix A at the end of the book). For instance, "being aware of others' socially accepted status" and "acts accordingly to ones' status" can make social interactions less stressful. For the primary dimension of bureau- cratic, which anecdotal evidence has a generally negative connotation world- wide, the actual items for this dimension in our survey do not carry the same baggage as the term itself. As an example, the behavior "follows established rules and guidelines" would be characteristic of a bureaucratic organization. This CEO behavior might be perceived positively by TMT members since an overlooked positive aspect of bureaucracies is that rules and procedures are more likely to supersede personality differences and familial favoritism.

Interestingly, the strongest leadership-outcome relationship occurred for Humane-Oriented leadership when considering the TMT Commitment- dependent measure. The Autonomous global leadership behavior had a neutral or slightly negative impact. But the Self-Protective leadership behavior had a slight positive impact for each of the constituent measures. Yet if you recall from Table 8.2a, the overall Self-Protective had a negligi- ble effect for the overall TMT Dedication measure.[5]

---

[5]This might be due to the increase in variance attributable to more reliable compos- ite scores as opposed to the variance associated with the scores comprising the composite itself. If the relationship between the dependent variable and the compos- ite score is at the margin of significance, then a unique situation could occur in which a relationship is found to be significant with the constituent dependent vari- ables but not with their composite.

Summary of CEO Leadership Influence on Top Management Team Dedication

- As a group, CEOs worldwide are given moderately high marks in effectiveness in terms of TMT Dedication.
- The global CEO Charismatic leadership behavior is consistently the most impactful leadership behavior on TMT Dedication. CEO Team-Oriented behavior is the next most important and then followed by Humane-Oriented leadership behaviors. Participative leadership is moderately important.

  o With regard to Charismatic leadership, the most influential CEO behaviors were visionary, inspirational, integrity, and performance oriented.
  o With regard to Team-Oriented leadership, a leader who is active in developing an integrative team (i.e., team integrator) may be more effective than a leader who is simply well meaning and supportive of group welfare (collaborative orientation).
  o Humane-Oriented leadership was particularly important for TMT Commitment.
  o Autonomous leadership is generally ineffective as it has a small but negative relationship with TMT Dedication. Self-Protective leadership may be positive or negative depending on the constituent primary leadership behaviors (bureaucratic is positive whereas self-centered is negative).

Which CEO Leadership Behaviors Predict Firm Competitive Performance?

Recall that the Firm Competitive Performance measure was our summary externally oriented variable. Our results show that three global leadership behaviors predict Firm Competitive Performance (Charismatic, Team-Oriented, and Humane-Oriented global leadership; see Tables 8.4a and 8.4b). Charismatic leadership had the strongest overall positive effect of $r = .26$ ($p < .01$). Team-Oriented leadership also had a positive impact on Firm Competitive Performance ($r = .23$, $p < .01$). Humane Oriented had a significant but smaller impact on Firm Competitive Performance than the other two global factors ($r = .14$, $p < .05$). None of the other global leadership behaviors had an impact on Firm Competitive Performance.

Summary of CEO Leadership Influence on Firm Competitive Performance

- CEOs are perceived to be moderately successful in terms of Firm Competitive Performance.

Table 8.4a CEO Leadership Behaviors Predicting Firm Competitive Performance

Leadership Behaviors	Firm Competitive Performance			
	HLM	SD	Correlation	χ^2 Slope
Charismatic	**0.30**	**0.68** **0.80**	**.26****	**2.29**
Visionary	0.30	0.77 0.80	.29**	2.09
Inspirational	0.20	0.77 0.80	.19**	2.58
Self-Sacrificial	0.12	0.85 0.80	.13*	1.89
Integrity	0.16	0.79 0.80	.16*	1.23
Decisive	0.21	0.88 0.80	.23**	2.51
Performance oriented	0.18	0.72 0.80	.16*	1.96
Team Oriented	**0.30**	**0.60** **0.80**	**.23****	**3.06**
Collaborative team orientation	0.12	0.92 0.80	.14*	0.60
Team integrator	0.28	0.75 0.80	.26**	4.68†
Diplomatic	0.16	0.78 0.80	.16*	1.58
Malevolent	−0.09	0.94 0.80	−.11	1.27
Administratively competent	0.22	0.88 0.80	.24**	3.99
Participative	**0.05**	**0.77** **0.80**	**.05**	**0.05**
Participative	0.01	0.95 0.80	.01	0.57
Autocratic	−0.05	0.99 0.80	−.06	0.00
Humane Oriented	**0.14**	**0.81** **0.80**	**.14***	**3.33**
Modesty	0.14	0.75 0.80	.13†	6.12*

(Continued)

(Continued)

Leadership Behaviors	Firm Competitive Performance			
	HLM	SD	Correlation	χ^2 Slope
Humane orientation	0.09	0.85 0.80	.10	0.70
Autonomous	**−0.08**	**1.05 0.80**	**−.11**	**1.13**
Self-Protective	**−0.03**	**0.42 0.80**	**−.02**	**1.05**
Self-Centered	−0.04	1.11 0.80	−.06	0.13
Status conscious	0.04	0.75 0.80	.04	0.73
Internally competitive	−0.05	0.77 0.80	−.05	0.28
Face-Saver	0.01	0.91 0.80	.01	2.50
Bureaucratic	0.04	0.87 0.80	.04	5.59†

Note: The *autonomous* primary leadership dimension is the same as the global *Autonomous* leadership dimension.

HLM = HLM coefficient; *SD* = standard deviation.

[a] Standard deviation for independent variable.

[b] Standard deviation for dependent variable.

N = 255.

† $p < 0.10$. *$p < .05$. **$p < .01$.

Table 8.4b   CEO Leadership Behaviors Predicting Two Constituent Measures of Firm Competitive Performance

Leadership Behavior	Firm Competitive Performance					
	Competitive Sales Performance			Competitive Industry Dominance		
	HLM	SD	Corr	HLM	SD	Corr
Charismatic	0.46	0.68[a]	.20*	0.37	0.68	.16**
		1.64[b]			1.1	
	χ^2 Slope:	0.41		χ^2 Slope:	1.88	
Visionary	0.52	0.77 [a]	.24**	0.40	0.77	.28**
		1.64 [b]			1.10	
	χ^2 Slope:	0.82		χ^2 Slope:	2.44	

| Leadership Behavior | Firm Competitive Performance | | | | | |
| | Competitive Sales Performance | | | Competitive Industry Dominance | | |
	HLM	SD	Corr	HLM	SD	Corr
Inspirational	0.27	0.77	.13†	0.24	0.77	.17*
		1.64			1.10	
	χ^2 Slope:	0.43		χ^2 Slope:	1.91	
Self-Sacrificial	0.24	0.85	.12	0.13	0.85	.10
		1.64			1.10	
	χ^2 Slope:	1.44		χ^2 Slope:	2.79	
Integrity	0.32	0.79	.15*	0.17	0.79	.12†
		1.64			1.10	
	χ^2 Slope:	0.54		χ^2 Slope:	1.51	
Decisive	0.27	0.88	.14*	0.24	0.88	.19**
		1.64			1.10	
	χ^2 Slope:	0.26		χ^2 Slope:	1.54	
Performance oriented	0.22	0.72	.10	0.31	0.72	.20**
		1.64			1.10	
	χ^2 Slope:	0.05		χ^2 Slope:	1.64	
Team Oriented	0.42	0.60	.16*	0.40	0.60	.15**
		1.64			1.1	
	χ^2 Slope:	0.44		χ^2 Slope:	4.80+	
Collaborative team orientation	0.09	0.92	.05	0.21	0.92	.17*
		1.64			1.10	
	χ^2 Slope:	0.02		χ^2 Slope:	3.17	
Team integrator	0.35	0.75	.13*	0.35	0.75	.19*
		1.64			1.10	
	χ^2 Slope:	0.50		χ^2 Slope:	6.53	
Diplomatic	0.26	0.78	.12†	0.16	0.78	.12
		1.64			1.10	
	χ^2 Slope:	1.06		χ^2 Slope:	1.87	
Malevolent	−0.15	0.94	−.08	−0.11	0.94	−.10
		1.64			1.10	
	χ^2 Slope:	2.61		χ^2 Slope:	0.17	

(Continued)

(Continued)

Leadership Behavior	Firm Competitive Performance					
	Competitive Sales Performance			Competitive Industry Dominance		
	HLM	SD	Corr	HLM	SD	Corr
Administratively competent	0.31	0.88	.17*	0.24	0.88	.19*
		1.64			1.10	
	χ² Slope:	0.63		χ² Slope:	8.93*	
Participative	0.14	0.77	.07	0.06	0.77	.03
		1.64			1.1	
	χ² Slope:	0.00		χ² Slope:	0.54	
Participative	0.04	0.95	.02	0.04	0.95	.04
		1.64			1.10	
	χ² Slope:	0.54		χ² Slope:	1.27	
Autocratic	−0.09	0.99	−.06	−0.04	0.99	−.03
		1.64			1.10	
	χ² Slope:	0.30		χ² Slope:	0.10	
Humane Oriented	0.25	0.81	.13*	0.16	0.81	.08†
		1.64			1.1	
	χ² Slope:	0.71		χ² Slope:	2.82	
Modesty	0.21	0.75	.11†	0.14	0.75	.11
		1.64			1.10	
	χ² Slope:	1.10		χ² Slope:	3.92	
Humane orientation	0.16	0.85	.08	0.10	0.85	.07
		1.64			1.10	
	χ² Slope:	0.14		χ² Slope:	1.33	
Autonomous	−0.08	1.05	−.05	−0.10	1.05	−.10
		1.64			1.10	
	χ² Slope:	0.41		χ² Slope:	3.96	
Self-Protective	0.14	0.42	.04	−0.09	0.42	−.02
		1.64			1.1	
	χ² Slope:	1.23		χ² Slope:	6.79*	
Self-Centered	0.11	1.11	.07	−0.13	1.11	−.13*
		1.64			1.10	
	χ² Slope:	0.08		χ² Slope:	0.20	

| Leadership Behavior | Firm Competitive Performance | | | | | |
| | Competitive Sales Performance | | | Competitive Industry Dominance | | |
	HLM	SD	Corr	HLM	SD	Corr
Status conscious	0.04	0.75	.02	0.08	0.75	.05
		1.64			1.10	
	χ^2 Slope:	1.39		χ^2 Slope:	0.03	
Internally competitive	−0.10	0.77	−.06	−0.07	0.77	−.06
		1.64			1.10	
	χ^2 Slope:	2.67		χ^2 Slope:	0.29	
Face-Saver	−0.04	0.91	−.02	0.02	0.91	.02
		1.64			1.10	
	χ^2 Slope:	1.25		χ^2 Slope:	7.79*	
Bureaucratic	0.09	0.87	.05	0.00	0.87	.00
		1.64			1.10	
	χ^2 Slope:	0.18		χ^2 Slope:	6.05*	

Note: The *autonomous* primary leadership dimension is the same as the global *Autonomous* leadership dimension.

HLM = HLM Coefficient; *SD* = standard deviation; Corr = correlation.

[a] Standard deviation for independent variable.

[b] Standard deviation for dependent variable.

N = 255.

† $p < 0.10$. * $p < .05$. ** $p < .01$.

- CEO Charismatic leadership was the most impactful leadership behavior predicting Firm Competitive Performance. Team-Oriented behavior was also important.

  o With regard to Charismatic leadership, visionary leadership is the most critical aspect, but all primary dimensions of our Charismatic leadership factor were related to Firm Competitive Performance (see Table 8.5).
  o With regard to Team-Oriented leadership, team integrator and administratively competent were the most important primary leadership dimensions followed by diplomatic and collaborative.

- Humane-Oriented leadership was less predictive of Firm Competitive Performance compared to either Charismatic or Team-Oriented leadership.

○ Similar to the TMT Dedication findings, a leader who is active in developing an integrative team (i.e., team integrator) may have a more competitive firm than a leader who is just well-meaning and supportive of group welfare (i.e., collaborative).

- Participative, Autonomous, and Self-Protective leadership were not important behaviors predicting Firm Competitive Performance.

Table 8.5 Rank Order of Primary CEO Leadership Behaviors Predicting Firm Competitive Performance

Rank	Leadership Behavior	Correlation
1	Visionary	.29**
2	Team integrator	.26**
3	Administratively competent	.24**
4	Decisive	.23**
5	Inspirational	.19**
6	Performance oriented	.16*
7	Integrity	.16*
8	Diplomatic	.16*
9	Collaborative team orientation	.14*
10	Self-Sacrificial	.13*
11	Modesty	.13†

Note: $N = 255$.

† $p < .10$. * $p < .05$. ** $p < .01$.

This table shows the bivariate correlations. Each leadership dimension predicts the dependent variable one at a time.

Evidence of Leadership Impact Moderated by Culture

In Tables 8.2a and 8.2b, there is some evidence (i.e., a statistical trend) for differences among the three HLM slopes regarding the influence of the global Charismatic, Team-Oriented, and Humane-Oriented leadership behaviors on TMT Dedication ($p < .10$). Recall that a significant slope indicates that the leadership effects differ across countries, but cultural differences may only be partially responsible for cross-national differences. Part of our rationale for presenting the results using "common sources" in addition to the primary results using different source data was to provide additional evidence regarding cultural variability. Several findings stand out when comparing the dual results for common and different sources. First, the trend for the global Charismatic and Team-Oriented leadership dimensions to vary across cultures for different sources was not replicated using common source data (see Table 8.2a). However, moderator effects for the Humane-Oriented dimension increased in significance from a trend ($p < .10$) to being significant ($p < .01$). In addition, moderator effects for the two primary leadership dimensions of performance oriented and administratively competent were significant for both common and different source analyses. These replicated findings lend additional credence to earlier findings regarding differential leadership impact across cultures.

Even though we generally conclude that the impact of Charismatic leadership does not vary across cultures, we find intriguing results when examining the six primary dimensions comprising the global Charismatic leadership behavior. Only the primary dimension of performance oriented varied in impact across cultures for both data sources (see Table 8.2a). However, there were differential impacts of the primary Charismatic leadership behaviors for each of the three TMT Dedication measures. Considering TMT Effort, five of the six Charismatic leadership-outcome relationships were moderated by national culture (all but integrity). Considering TMT Commitment, three of the six leadership-outcome relationships were moderated by national culture (a trend for inspirational and self-sacrificial and statistical significance for performance oriented). Considering TMT Team Solidarity, none of the leadership-outcome relationships were moderated by national culture for the dependent measure of TMT Team Solidarity—that is, all Charismatic primary leadership behavior impacts Team Solidarity equally across countries.

Integrating GLOBE Empirical Findings With Previous Literature

GLOBE Insights Into Charismatic Leadership

Popular business trade magazines often promote the notion that charismatic and transformational (C/T) leadership is universally desirable. The management research literature is more nuanced in pointing out that there are dark sides to Charismatic leadership as well as the often-portrayed bright side (Conger, 1990). Nevertheless, as reviewed in Chapter 2, the totality of findings indicates that charismatic and transformational (C/T) leadership are routinely endorsed, and leaders who enact these qualities tend to be more successful than those who don't. Alternatively, the dark side of charismatic leadership can be found in notorious cult leaders such as Jim Jones (leader of the People's temple) or David Koresh (leaders of the Branch Davidians). The real-life example of Steve Jobs, the late founder and CEO of Apple, also is relevant to both sides of charismatic leadership. His great successes at Apple through visionary leadership are legendary, but less well known was his aggressive and demanding leadership style where he accepted nothing less than perfection. His searingly intense personality frequently instilled fear in his employees accompanied with an intense eagerness to please (Isaacson, 2011).

Before this GLOBE project, we simply didn't have enough evidence to determine if CEO Charismatic leadership is universally effective or varies in importance and impact across cultures. Nor did we know if the same set of leadership behaviors could capture the essence of Charismatic leadership. The measurement equivalence results presented in Chapter 6 shows that our measure of Charismatic leadership is meaningfully interpreted the same way across countries. Further, our results conclusively show that considering TMT Dedication and Firm Competitive Performance together, it was an extremely effective leadership behavior. Furthermore, as discussed previously, each of the six primary leadership dimensions comprising Charismatic leadership were almost equally effective as the global Charismatic dimension when predicting TMT Dedication. The primary Charismatic factors of visionary and inspirational leadership were very important for both TMT Dedication and Firm Competitive Performance. As shown in Table 8.3 and Table 8.5, inspirational and visionary leadership behaviors were among the top five ranked CEO leadership behaviors impacting both TMT Dedication and Firm Competitive Performance. The other primary leadership behaviors were also important for TMT Dedication and Firm Competitive Performance but varied in leadership impact.

Our conclusion is that Charismatic leadership likely constitutes a "nearly universal" leadership behavior (i.e., universally important but varies somewhat as to its effectiveness depending on culture). Recall that our results show that it is universally effective for both internally oriented dependent measures of TMT Dedication as well as externally oriented measures of Firm Competitive Performance. Interestingly, as indicated in Table 8.2b, the global Charismatic dimension varies in impact for the TMT Commitment and Effort dependent variables but not the TMT Team Solidarity variable. Thus, the global Charismatic dimension is likely at least a variform functional universal (always important but varies in importance across cultures). The additional secondary analyses conducted on TMT Dedication—but using same-source evidence—provides further information regarding the near universality of this leadership behavior (i.e., it is not moderated greatly by culture).

However, it is very important for us to point out that our view of Charismatic leadership is very different from the use of this term in the popular press. A charismatic leader has become synonymous with a leader who is flamboyant, showy, and captivating and who often exists within the political arena. For GLOBE, Charismatic leadership embodies the leadership characteristics of vision, inspiration, performance oriented, decisive, and high integrity. This person may be exemplary but does not have to be superman nor exemplify a flashy and over-the-top demeanor. According to our criteria, both Bill Gates of Microsoft fame and Warren Buffett of Berkshire Hathaway qualify as outstanding charismatic leaders; neither is flashy and showy yet both embody many of the qualities found in the GLOBE Charismatic leadership behavior (i.e., visionary, performance oriented, integrity, and decisive). Both have achieved success as business leaders and philanthropists but neither considers themself charismatic.

For the primary leadership dimensions constituting Charismatic leadership, we can also ask and answer the same question regarding cross-cultural variability as we did for the global Charismatic dimension in the previous paragraph. Are the constituent leadership dimensions equally important across all cultures? Results presented in Table 8.2b reveal that almost all of the primary Charismatic dimensions vary across cultures but only for the TMT Effort dependent variable, somewhat for the TMT Commitment dependent variable, and not at all for the TMT Team Solidarity dependent variable. Again, we now feel confident that Charismatic leadership should be considered a nearly universal effective leadership dimension. It is universally effective for both internally oriented dependent measures of TMT Dedication as well as externally oriented measures of Firm Competitive Performance.

Thus, one can be confident that leaders who engage in a variety of charismatic behaviors will have TMT team members who work well together, in any culture. We should note that when viewing the actual behaviors in the GLOBE survey, our findings regarding Charismatic leadership is close to the concept of transformational leadership in the literature. This literature indicates that leaders should aspire to inspire, motivate, and expect high performance outcomes from their TMT. GLOBE researchers also portray Charismatic leadership including additional leadership behaviors constituting high integrity and decisiveness.

GLOBE Insights Into Team-Oriented Leadership

The variety of teams prevalent in modern organizations precludes a simplistic perspective when reviewing the literature with regards to successful team leadership. Leadership that works best for cross-functional teams, self-managed teams, top-level executive teams, and virtual teams certainly may differ. Our prior literature review was made more difficult because of this variety. In addition, to best understand the prior literature review of Team-Oriented leadership from a cross-cultural perspective (in Chapter 2), we should remain cognizant that most empirical studies of team leadership employ leadership measures not specifically designed to directly test the importance of Team-Oriented leader behaviors but instead use commonly found measures in the leadership literature. For instance, the Wendt, Euwema, and Van Emmerik (2009) study employs measures of supportive and directive leadership in their study of team cohesiveness. Similarly,

Jung, Butler, and Baik (1998) found that transformational leadership in Korea was highly correlated with group cohesiveness. To muddy the concept further, team leadership functions may include planning, organizing, networking, representing, and engaging in team development.

It should be obvious by now that the present GLOBE study differs from previous cross-cultural studies in that GLOBE researchers developed new measures of Team-Oriented leadership instead of employing leadership measures found in the literature that are more tangential to team effectiveness (e.g., supportive leadership). Second, we developed separate measures for each facet of Team-Oriented leadership to match the fivefold dimension structure of this leadership dimension found in GLOBE 2004. That structure included the following primary dimensions of Team-Oriented behaviors: collaborative team orientation, team integration, diplomatic management of teams, malevolent team leadership (reverse scored), and administratively competent management.

According to country-level ratings regarding leadership expectations across countries (House, Hanges, Javidan, Dorfman, & Gupta, 2004), the global Team-Oriented dimension is perceived to be at least *somewhat important* in enhancing effective leadership. Its moderately positive ratings and country variability for the GLOBE culturally endorsed implicit leadership theories (CLTs), however, begs the question as to its universality. That is, all cultures had absolute scores exceeding 5.00, and most exceeded 5.60 of the GLOBE 7-point scale of qualities leading to outstanding leadership. When examining the results, the Southern Asia, Confucian Asia, Eastern Europe, and Latin America clusters reported Team-Oriented leadership to be particularly critical for effective leadership. This comports with the generally believed contributions of collectivist values for these parts of the world. Nevertheless, extensive teamwork is the norm in organizations worldwide whether it is in manufacturing (e.g., all major automobile manufacturers use cross-functional teams including Honda, Toyota, Nissan, BMW, GM, Ford, Chrysler [Robbins & Judge, 2011]) or service organizations (e.g., a Merrill Lynch team reduced the number of days to open a cash management account [Bodinson & Bunch, 2003]).

Considering our overall measure of TMT Dedication (presented in Table 8.2a), the global Team-Oriented behaviors were the second most impactful CEO behavior following that of Charismatic leadership. The Team-Oriented global measure also predicted our externally oriented dependent measure of Firm Competitive Performance. Administratively competent and diplomatic primary behaviors were important for both TMT Dedication and Firm Competitive Performance. They were ranked evenly (rank = 5.5), predicting TMT Dedication and third and seventh predicting Firm Competitive Performance. Our finding on the importance of administrative competence supports Mintzberg's (2006) suggestion that "separating leadership from management is part of the problem. . . Does anyone want to work for a manager who lacks the

qualities of leadership . . . ? Well, how about a leader who doesn't practice management?"

Furthermore, there is little evidence that this global dimension, like that
of the global Charismatic dimension, varies in impact across cultures. Table
8.2a indicates that only the primary dimension of administratively competent of the Team-Oriented dimension varies across cultures. Interestingly,
statistical findings regarding cultural variability are much stronger in Table
8.2b when examining the more specific dependent measures making up the
overall TMT Dedication measure. In this table, the Team-Oriented dimension varies in influence for predicting TMT Commitment and Effort, but
not for Team Solidarity. The universal impact of Team-Orientation to create
team solidarity makes conceptual sense. Recall that in the previous section
concerning Charismatic leadership, similar results were found for the universal positive effect considering the specific dependent measure of TMT
Team Solidarity.

Another important finding related to the Team-Oriented factor is that of
the two primary dimensions of collaborative team orientation and team
integrator (within the global Team-Oriented dimension). As pointed out
earlier, the latter is more impactful than the former. In fact, the team integrator dimension ranked second in terms of impact on Firm Competitive Performance. Thus, what is most critical is the active component of team
leadership—that of getting members to work together, communicating and
explaining what is expected, and integrating members into a cohesive and
working whole. While a leader who is concerned with the welfare of the
group is collaborative and loyal is also important, these "feel-good" behaviors are a little less important to creating an effective team than the hands-
on effort to generate a working team.

While the team integrator and collaborative dimensions are intuitively
obvious aspects of a Team-Oriented leadership dimension, there are two
others that require an explanation as they are less intuitively obvious primary dimensions of the global Team-Oriented leadership dimension. The
"diplomatic" primary dimension describes leaders who are diplomatic and
skilled at interpersonal relations. The survey items asked about leaders who
identify solutions that satisfy individuals with conflicting interests, and can
also maintain good relationships with others. Clearly, these are important
in developing and maintaining effective teams. The reverse scored "malevolent" dimension refers to leaders who are not dishonest, deceitful or punitive and vengeful. It would be hard to envision a leader who can effectively
manage teams with negative traits characteristic of malevolent leadership.

Earlier in the book, we stated that while teams are ubiquitous in modern
organizations worldwide, we are ignorant of potential cultural influences in
how leadership processes vary in successfully directing team members. The
results of our CEO study presented so far clarifies our knowledge regarding
critical leadership processes for team success. This is true whether we are
considering the outcomes important to employees (e.g., TMT Commitment)

as well as those leading to successful firm performance (i.e., Firm Competitive Performance). We now know that Team-Oriented leadership is critical to personal outcomes as well as company effectiveness. The actual impact may, however, vary across cultures, particularly with respect to employee commitment and effort but steady with regard to team solidarity.

GLOBE Insights Into Participative Leadership

Employees in the United States typically desire to have an input in the management decision-making process. The extent to which leaders ask for, receive answers to, and make use of employee input is often a topic of considerable discussion around the proverbial office watercooler. Yet supervisors often struggle with the extent to which subordinates should participate and become involved in organizational decisions. Conversely, employees often complain about leaders who either ignore their ideas or alternatively hold lengthy meetings seeking extensive discussion and input even for trivial matters. Is this desire for input for many organizational decisions similar in all countries? Anecdotal evidence suggests that it does not have the same cache in all cultures nor for all problem situations even within a single culture that treasures participative leadership such as in the United States.

We noted in Chapter 2 that participatory leadership is often described in terms of a continua, where extremes are characterized from decisions made by supervisors without asking for input by others (i.e., autocratic and/or directive leadership) to subordinates being given complete authority and responsibility (i.e., delegation). Participation falls somewhere in between and may take the form of consultation and/or joint decisions to arrive at a conclusive decision. Notable leaders such as Nelson Mandela (showing a participative governing style as president of South Africa), Abraham Lincoln (demonstrating a participative approach to problem solving with cabinet members during the Civil War), and Mary Kay Ash (using extensive participation with directors in her cosmetics company) have all been described as demonstrating high levels of participatory decision making (Howell, 2013).

Much of the early research in participation and decision making uses the conceptualization of participation being a continuum (cf. Heller & Wilpert, 1981; Vroom & Jago, 1988). Contemporary studies of participatory leadership have extended the conceptualization of participation noting that differing "species" of participation exist even in countries that highly espouse participatory management (Brodbeck & Eisenbeiss, in press). Depending on how participation is manifested, it may be prescribed in national labor laws regarding the structural organization of labor and management or more linked to actual participatory leadership that is contrasted from autocratic and directive leadership.

The effects of participative leadership have been the object of hundreds, if not thousands, of studies, but as noted by Yukl (2013), "the results from research on the effects of participative leadership are not sufficiently strong and consistent enough to draw any firm conclusions . . . [it] sometimes results in higher satisfaction, effort, and performance, and at other times it does not" (p. 111). The difficulty of developing conclusions regarding the effectiveness of participatory leadership is compounded when considering it from a cross-cultural perspective. We can look at the GLOBE project to further examine the complexity of this leadership behavior.

Early on in the GLOBE project, we demonstrated that culture clusters varied considerably in the *endorsement* of these leadership dimensions. Participative leadership was highly desired in societies that value Performance Orientation, Gender Egalitarianism, and Humane Orientation but less so for societies with high cultural values for Power Distance, Uncertainty Avoidance, and Assertiveness. Thus, the Germanic European and Anglo cultures were strong supporters of Participative leadership whereas the Confucian Asian and Eastern European cultures were less supportive of this leadership style.

Similar to GLOBE 2004 (House et al., 2004), the participatory leadership dimension in the present project reflected our two primary leadership dimensions: participative and autocratic (reverse scored). Our leadership behavior measures in the present project were carefully crafted and closely reflected the degree to which managers involve others in making and implementing decisions. The survey items for the participatory dimension were straightforward (see Appendix B), asking respondents to rate the degree to which their CEO shared critical information with subordinates, sought advice, and reconsidered decisions given subordinate input, among others. The reverse-scored autocratic leadership dimension asked respondents whether the CEO made decisions in a dictatorial way, forced his/her values on others, and told subordinates what to do in a commanding way, among others.

The Participative global dimension was predictive of the overall TMT Dedication dependent measure ($r = .21, p < .01$) but not the Firm Competitive Performance measure ($r = .05, p > .05$). Overall, it was ranked fourth of the six global leadership dimensions predicting TMT Dedication following Charismatic, Team-Oriented, and Humane-Oriented global leadership dimensions. In addition, the primary CEO Participative behavior dimension was only ranked 12.5 out of 20 significant dimensions, which places it a little lower than half of the primary dimensions in predictability for TMT Dedication; it did not appear in the ranking for Firm Competitive Performance. The autocratic primary dimension was among the lowest ranking of dimensions predicting TMT Dedication (rank = 17 out of 20 significant dimensions). What was most surprising to us, however, was the very limited evidence that the effects of Participative leadership are culturally contingent. General comments by scholars often point out the fact that Participative leadership is most often required in individualistic nations typically found in the United States and Europe. In fact, our research findings presented so far only indicate variability across nations for when the Participative CEO behavior predicts TMT Commitment. We will return to the evidence of cultural moderation for participation in Chapter 9.

Earlier in this chapter and in Chapter 2 we noted that it is very difficult to make firm conclusions with regard to participatory leadership since studies have shown that its effectiveness is not consistent. Combining earlier research, both conducted in single Western countries as well as research conducted in multiple countries, we might argue that (1) managers at all levels talk a good game with regards to participatory leadership. In fact, in our interviews with CEOs, they almost without exception endorse the importance of participation with TMT members. However, as Haire, Ghiselli, and Porter (1966) concluded that while managers from all countries espoused democratic management styles and favored participatory leadership, managers from most countries held a low opinion of whether subordinates had the capacity for leadership and initiative; (2) the actual influence of participatory leadership is moderately significant and positive but perhaps more so with respect to employee attitudes such as TMT Dedication (TMT Commitment, Effort, and Team Solidarity) but not so much for Firm Competitive Performance; (3) the influence of participatory leadership was not culturally contingent, as its effects were positive but moderate in all countries. This finding, however, may be premature and simplistic given (4) the many forms of participative leadership found around the world. This fact should bring us back to the research drawing board and reinforces the general research consensus that the construct itself varies greatly across cultures. Chapter 9 presents additional evidence regarding cultural influences on participatory leadership.

GLOBE Insights Into Humane-Oriented Leadership

In Chapter 2, we noted that in general, GLOBE societal cultures and "culture clusters" (House et al., 2004) perceived Humane-Oriented leadership as being slightly important but certainly not critical in contributing to effective leadership. The average Humane-Oriented CLT score for this dimension was 4.88, with a country range of 3.80 to 5.60 (on a 7-point scale). Four culture clusters were singled out as particularly endorsing this characteristic in enhancing effective leadership: Southern Asia, Anglo, Sub-Saharan Africa, and Confucian Asia. The GLOBE Humane-Oriented global leadership dimension actually was comprised of two primary dimensions: (1) humane orientation and (2) modesty. The humane orientation primary dimension emphasizes empathy for others by giving time, resources, and assistance when needed and showing concern for follower's personal welfare. The modesty primary dimension reflects leaders who do not boast, are modest, and present themselves in a humble manner. The development of the

Humane-Oriented leadership dimension can be found in GLOBE 2004 (House et al., 2004).

Relying on past research complementary to Humane-Oriented leadership, we expected that it would have a positive outcome but generally not be as impactful as Charismatic leadership or perhaps Team-Oriented leadership. The closest we might come to prior research informing the GLOBE construct are the earlier studies examining "relationship behaviors," which were part of The Ohio State University (e.g., Fleishman, 1953; Fleishman, Harris, & Burtt, 1955) and University of Michigan research programs (Bowers & Seashore, 1966; Likert, 1961, 1967). As noted by Yukl (2013), relations-oriented behaviors include a variety of behaviors that demonstrate empathy and a concern for the needs and feelings of followers. Some of the Humane-Oriented behaviors in the present GLOBE project are very similar and include general helpfulness; looking out for personal welfare of followers; and willingness to give time, money, and resources to help others. Also, by definition and construction of the global Humane-Oriented dimension, which includes modesty as a second primary dimension, the current CEO project includes leadership qualities of being modest and not boastful such as presenting self in a humble manner. These qualities and behaviors related to modesty are likely to be most important in Asian countries but not typically considered in Western leadership research. Both qualities of humane leadership carried out in a modest manner were characteristic of Mother Teresa, who ministered to the poorest of the poor in India. She gave time and resources to the sisters of her convent and supported them by teaching them how to handle administrative issues and problems they would face (Howell, 2013). Mohandas Gandhi also portrayed these qualities in his lifetime struggle for Indian independence. He was tireless in his service to the poor and provided for his follower's needs by giving away his possessions; supporting ashrams; and exhibiting personal characteristics of empathy, openness, and humility (Howell, 2013). Both leaders clearly exhibited humane-oriented leadership.

Recent cross-cultural studies continue to support previous findings (Dorfman, 2004) that worldwide, considerate and supportive leadership behaviors will increase subordinates' satisfaction with both their job and their supervisor (Agarwal, DeCarlo, & Vyas, 1999; Bass & Bass, 2008; Euwema, Wendt, & van Emmerik, 2007; Lok & Crawford, 2004; Wendt et al., 2009). The near universality of positive effects for leader supportiveness with respect to employee attitudes should not be surprising since supportive leaders show concern for followers and are considerate and available to listen to followers' problems.

The evidence regarding a "people-oriented" leadership dimension for individual job and firm performance is not nearly so clear. An empirical study of top-level Chinese managers found that showing benevolence (i.e., showing love and care for subordinates) was related to both employee attitudes and firm performance (the latter through employee attitudes such as organizational commitment) (Wang, Tsui, & Xin, 2011). Dorfman and colleagues (1997) found that supportive leadership had a direct impact on job performance in Mexico, an indirect impact on job performance through reducing role ambiguity in South Korea, and no impact on job performance for the U.S. samples.

GLOBE results support the prediction that Humane-Oriented leadership will have a significant effect on the overall TMT Dedication measure as well as for all three dependent measures comprising the TMT Dedication measure. The global Humane-Oriented leadership dimension predicted TMT Dedication ($r = .25$, $p < .01$) *and* Firm Competitive Performance ($r = .14$, $p < .05$). Interestingly, there were important distinctions when examining the effectiveness of this leadership behavior on TMT Commitment, Effort, and Team Solidarity. As seen in Table 8.2b, Humane-Oriented leadership had its largest impact on TMT Commitment ($r = .39$, $p < .01$), which, in fact, was the *largest* relationship among all leadership behaviors and dependent variables. Its effectiveness was also apparent with regard to TMT Effort and Team Solidarity. Perhaps we should not be surprised that TMT Commitment was substantially elevated when CEOs looked out for the direct report's welfare, willingness to give resources to them, as well as behaving empathetically.

The two primary dimensions comprising the global Humane-Oriented dimension, modesty and humane orientation, were likewise predictive of TMT Dedication ($r = .17$, $p < .01$ and $r = .26$, $p < .01$, respectively) but only the former was somewhat predictive of Firm Competitive Performance ($r = .13$, $p < .10$). For the TMT Dedication dependent measure, humane orientation was more impactful than modesty and was ranked higher (i.e., 9th versus 16th out of 20 significant dimensions). Our results suggest moderately positive outcomes from CEOs who do not boast and are humble and modest. It might be worthwhile to recall that the humane behaviors included statements such as "being willing to help others," "looks out for 'my' personal welfare," and "inclined to be helpful." Supporting others and looking out for their welfare is a more action-oriented leadership behavior and, hence, appears to be even more influential than acting modestly.

Given that the Humane-Oriented leadership had quite an impact, what is the evidence regarding differential effectiveness of this leadership dimension cross-culturally? The answer is that it appears to have differential effects across cultures. The moderating effect of culture for the global Humane-Oriented dimension was marginally significant using the TMT Dedication variable obtained from different sources. However, moderating effects of culture were highly significant considering common source data for TMT Dedication. Further evidence regarding cultural moderation effects on this CEO leadership behavior will be presented in Chapter 9.

GLOBE Insights Into Autonomous Leadership

As part of the GLOBE (2004) project, we found evidence that many countries around the world respected leaders who were independent, individualistic, and self-governing. This idea led to the formulation and operationalization of the GLOBE (global) leadership dimension labeled *Autonomous*. This newly defined global leadership dimension refers to leadership that is independent and individualistic. GLOBE's concept of Autonomous leadership is associated with the tendency to be and act as an independent agent with little interest in interdependent relations (House et al., 1999). It reflects a tendency to prefer to work alone and be self-reliant rather than working with others. Autonomous leaders tend to be suspicious of others' actions and intents and avoid interpersonal relations because they believe they take too much energy and time. They therefore prefer to build and protect their independence.

The Autonomous leadership dimension in GLOBE 2004 was measured as a single primary leadership dimension that contained the following attributes: individualistic, independent, autonomous, and unique. Survey respondents indicated the extent to which each attribute contributed to or hindered outstanding leadership. Because this primary leadership dimension was statistically independent from the other 20 GLOBE primary dimensions, it was labeled a *global* leadership dimension (i.e., second-order dimension) in addition to being a primary leadership dimension. This is the only leadership dimension in GLOBE that is both a primary and secondary leadership dimension.

The corresponding Autonomous CEO behaviors in the present study include acting independently, self-governing and not relying on others, and being individually oriented. As noted in Chapter 2, this leadership style familiar to U.S. moviegoers might be that of John Wayne if he were to head up a major corporation. Extreme examples of this style can be found in Mike Davis (the past CEO of Tiger Oil in the United States, now defunct). His independent leadership style is best exemplified in his (now humorous) memos whereby among other things, he stated the following:

> In case anyone does not know who owns Tiger Oil company, it is me, Edward Mike Davis. . . . Do not let anyone think that they are the owner but me. There is one thing that differentiates me from my employees, I am a known son-of-a-bitch, do not speak to me when you see me, if I want to speak to you, I will do so.

In contrast to this extreme, the independent prototype in Germany is represented by Alfred Herrhausen, former president of Deutsche Bank, who was described as an individualist, an outsider, often reserved and distanced but with a high need for recognition (Brodbeck, Frese, & Javidan, 2002). The real-life example of Steve Jobs, the late founder and CEO of Apple, also is relevant to Autonomous leadership since his personality quirks included being solitary, self absorbed, and independent (Young & Simon, 2005).

In the GLOBE 2004 project, Autonomous leadership attributes were generally viewed across cultures as being culturally contingent. Scores ranged from negative, to neutral, to slightly positive across cultures with respect to contributing to or impeding effective leadership. The average Autonomous score for this dimension was 3.79, with a country range of 2.30 to 4.70 (on a 7-point scale). The country rating scores portray the Sub-Saharan Africa, Middle East, Latin Europe, and Latin America clusters as rejecting this dimension whereas the Eastern Europe and Germanic Europe clusters were the two highest ranking clusters for this leadership dimension. Brodbeck and colleagues' (2000) study of cultural variation of leadership prototypes across 22 European countries found that autonomy was one of three primary dimensions differentiating European cultures. They also clarified how an individualistic leadership prototype can be viewed positively in Germany (Brodbeck et al., 2002). Autonomous German leaders may be seen as unique, independent, and individualistic, and they generally stay apart from the crowd.

Two GLOBE cultural dimensions were related to the endorsement of Autonomous leadership (Javidan, Dorfman, Howell, & Hanges, 2010). As predicted, collectivism values (specifically, Institutional Collectivism) were negatively related to the Autonomous leadership dimension. But, perhaps unexpectedly, Performance Orientation cultural values were positively related to Autonomous leadership. In sum, members of societies and organizations with high performance-oriented and individualistic values will likely have autonomous attributes as part of their effective CLT leadership prototype. We know of no empirical behavioral research, however, actually investigating the effectiveness of Autonomous leadership behaviors.

As shown earlier, Autonomous leadership behavior had a small but significant negative relationship with the TMT Dedication measure ($r = -.07, p < .05$) but had no impact with respect to Firm Competitive Performance. Examining this leadership behavior with respect to the three dependent measures comprising TMT Dedication provides little additional information, but the negative relationship with Team Solidarity was the strongest negative relationship.

GLOBE Insights Into Self-Protective Leadership

This newly defined GLOBE global leadership dimension focuses on ensuring the safety and security of the individual and group through status enhancement and face-saving. This leadership dimension includes five primary leadership dimensions, labeled (1) status conscious, (2) internally competitive, (3) face-saver, (4) bureaucratic, and (5) self-centered. In GLOBE 2004, the mean CLT score for the Self-Protective global leadership dimension was 3.55 with a range of 2.5 to 4.6 (on a 7-point scale). These scores clearly indicate that it was culturally contingent regarding its perceived impact leading to outstanding leadership. Because the primary dimensions within the global Self-Protective leadership dimension are new to the literature, it is useful to define each before summarizing the GLOBE results (complete definitions are found in Appendix A).

Status conscious: reflects a consciousness of one's own and others' social position, holding an elitist belief that some individuals deserve more privileges than others.

Internally competitive (formerly labeled *conflict inducer*, GLOBE 2004): reflects the tendency to encourage competition within a group and may include concealing information in a secretive manner and unwillingness to work jointly with others.

Face-saver: reflects the tendency to ensure followers are not embarrassed or shamed; maintains good relationships by refraining from making negative comments; instead uses metaphors and examples.

Bureaucratic (formerly labeled *procedural*, GLOBE 2004): emphasize following established norms, rules, policies, and procedures and habitually follow regular routines.

Self-Centered: characterized by a leader who is self-absorbed, is a loner, is aloof and stands off from others.

Earlier in the chapter, we noted that the Self-Protective leadership dimension is perhaps the most interesting of all global dimensions as the effectiveness of its primary constituent parts varied greatly. The overall effectiveness of the global Self-Protective dimension is negligible ($r = .05$) influencing TMT Dedication. However, two of the primary dimensions within this global leadership dimension have a positive effect (status conscious and bureaucratic, $r = .11$ and $r = .23$, $p < .01$, respectively) and two have a negative effect (self-centered and internally competitive primary dimensions, $r = -.11$ and $r = -.19$, $p < .01$, respectively). The primary dimension of face-saver has a negligible effect ($r = .06$ ns).

Regarding the rank order of the primary dimensions in terms of impact, as shown in Table 8.3, bureaucratic was near the middle ranking (rank = 10.5, positive) and actually equal to the Charismatic dimension labeled *decisive*. Internally competitive was ranked 14th and was a negative dimension in terms of TMT Dedication. This global factor had no impact with respect to Firm Competitive Performance.

Perhaps, surprisingly, we found almost a complete absence of results indicating a difference across cultures on this leadership dimension. As indicated in Tables 8.2a and 8.2b, neither the global Self-Protective leadership dimension nor any of the primary dimensions comprising the global dimension varied significantly across cultures when predicting TMT Dedication. While we found a few cross-cultural differences, there only was a limited amount of evidence showing cultural differences for this leadership behavior. Further evidence regarding cultural moderating effects will also be presented in the following chapter.

The positive results for status conscious and bureaucratic leadership from a Western perspective is seemingly difficult to explain but becomes understandable when examining the *actual* behaviors within each leadership dimension (see Appendix B). For instance, "being aware of others' socially accepted status" and "acts accordingly to one's status" can make social interactions less stressful. For the primary dimension of bureaucratic, which anecdotal evidence has a generally negative connotation worldwide, the actual items for this dimension do not carry the same baggage as the term itself. For instance, a positive aspect of bureaucracies is that rules and procedures are more likely to supersede personality differences and familial favoritism.

Summary of Overall Findings

We started this chapter by posing a number of questions, including the following: What is the *overall* impact of CEO leadership on TMT Dedication and Firm Performance? What are the specific impacts of 6 global CEO leadership behaviors and 21 primary CEO leadership behaviors on TMT Dedication and Firm Performance? Which leadership behaviors are most effective, which are ineffective, and which are countereffective? What are the the similarities and differences in effective leadership across cultures addressing the meta-question about leadership universality versus cultural contingency? We also wanted to integrate the GLOBE 2004 findings and the extant literature with the findings from the present project.

We first noted that overall, CEO leadership across cultures is perceived as being reasonably effective as TMT members worldwide are reasonably satisfied—they are committed, put forth significant work effort, and view each other as a functioning team. Our results provide strong support for leadership effectiveness when considering the combined impact of leadership on our TMT dependent measures and on Firm Competitive Performance. This CEO sample of more than 1,000 CEOs undoubtedly had significant influence on their organizations, which generally comports with the research literature.

Perhaps it should be of no surprise that Charismatic leadership in particular was a critical leadership behavior. Leaders who are visionary, inspirational, self-sacrificial, decisive, and performance oriented when acting with integrity can expect superior TMT outcomes and firm performance. In particular, visionary leadership has positive impacts on TMT Dedication and firm performance. Team-Oriented and Humane-Oriented leadership are also important. Similar to Charismatic leadership, Team-Oriented leadership had positive impacts on both TMT Dedication and Firm Competitive Performance. Perhaps surprisingly, so did Humane-Oriented leadership. It had a strong effect on TMT Dedication and also a smaller but still significant impact on firm performance. Furthermore,

Humane-Oriented leadership is *most* predictive of all leadership behaviors when TMT Commitment is the dependent variable. And Humane-Oriented leadership is a stronger predictor than Participative leadership for all three dependent variables (Commitment, Effort, and Team Solidarity). Surprisingly, elements of Self-Protective leadership also had positive impacts, but Autonomous leadership was generally ineffective.

Evidence for leadership effectiveness being culturally contingent was more limited. Overall, we conclude that Charismatic and Team-Oriented leadership are nearly universal in their impacts. At a minimum they might be classified as at least a variform functional universal (i.e., universally important but vary somewhat as to its effectiveness depending on culture). Humane-Oriented leadership also showed some cultural moderation. We should not forget, however, that the impact of leadership on one particular dependent variable in this research, TMT Effort, was almost always culturally contingent. Nonetheless, as discussed earlier in the chapter, our findings regarding societal differences only allude to potential differences due to national culture. The following chapter investigating leadership/cultural fit directly investigates this issue that cross-national differences are directly the result of cultural differences.

9

CEO Leadership Effectiveness Across Cultures

The Effect of Fit and Behavior

T his chapter presents our findings on CEO leadership effectiveness. We examine the effect of two possible sources: (1) the fit between CEO leadership behavior and societal expectations (culturally endorsed implicit leadership theories, or CLTs) and (2) the combined effect of fit and leadership behavior. The chapter has three sections. The first section summarizes our Chapter 8 findings demonstrating how CEO leadership behaviors impact CEO effectiveness. The second section provides evidence that the fit between societal leadership expectations and CEO leadership behavior impact CEO leadership effectiveness. The third section provides a simultaneous comparison of the two contrasting sources of leadership effectiveness—observed CEO behavior and fit.

CEO Leadership Behavior as a Source of CEO Effectiveness

We started the previous chapter by posing the following questions: What is the evidence that CEO leadership behavior matters? Which leadership behaviors are most effective? Is the effectiveness of specific CEO leadership behaviors constant across cultures, or do they vary in effectiveness across cultures? A summary of our findings regarding the effectiveness of specific CEO leadership behaviors is presented in Table 9.1.

Perhaps it should be of no surprise that Charismatic leadership in particular was a critical global leadership behavior (see Table 9.1). Leaders who are visionary, inspirational, self-sacrificial, decisive, and performance oriented when acting with integrity can expect superior outcomes. In particular,

Table 9.1 Summary of CEO Leadership Behaviors Predicting Top Management Team Dedication and Firm Competitive Performance

Leadership Behavior	TMT Dedication		Firm Competitive Performance	
	Global Dimension	Primary Dimension	Global Dimension	Primary Dimension
Charismatic	✓✓		✓✓	
Visionary		✓✓		✓✓
Inspirational		✓✓		✓✓
Self-Sacrificial		✓✓		✓
Integrity		✓✓		✓
Decisive		✓✓		✓✓
Performance oriented		✓✓		✓
Team Oriented	✓✓		✓✓	
Collaborative team orientation		✓✓		✓
Team integrator		✓✓		✓✓
Diplomatic		✓✓		✓
Malevolent		✓✓ (negative)		
Administratively competent		✓✓		✓✓
Participative	✓✓			
Participative		✓✓		
Autocratic		✓✓ (negative)		
Humane Oriented	✓✓		✓	
Modesty		✓✓		† (trend)
Humane orientation		✓✓		
Autonomous	✓ (negative)			
Self-Protective				
Self-Centered		✓✓ (negative)		
Status conscious		✓✓		
Internally competitive		✓✓ (negative)		
Face-Saver				
Bureaucratic		✓✓		

Note: N = 998 for TMT Dedication. N = 255 for Firm Competitive Performance.

† $p < 0.10$. ✓ $p < .05$. ✓✓ $p < .01$.

the primary leadership variables of visionary and inspirational leadership are in particular very impactful considering both criteria of Top Management Team (TMT) Dedication and Firm Competitive Performance together. Team-Oriented leadership was a second important global leadership behavior. Similar to Charismatic leadership, Team-Oriented leadership predicted TMT Dedication and Firm Competitive Performance. The primary Team-Oriented behaviors that stand out for both TMT Dedication and Firm Competitive Performance are team integrator, administratively competent, and diplomatic when considering both criteria.

The global Humane-Oriented leadership behavior also had an impact on both TMT Dedication and Firm Competitive Performance, but its impact on Firm Competitive Performance is not quite as strong as the Charismatic and Team-Oriented CEO leadership behaviors. An interesting observation for us regarding Humane-Oriented leadership is that in earlier GLOBE (2004) findings, the Humane-Oriented leadership expectations (i.e., CLTs) were rated as being only slightly important for outstanding leadership. However, our empirical results found that Humane-Oriented leadership behavior has a huge impact on TMT Dedication and is the *most* predictive of all leadership behaviors for TMT Commitment (see Table 8.2b).

The three other global leadership behaviors had a more complex and nuanced relationship to effectiveness than Charismatic, Team-Oriented, and Humane-Oriented leadership. Participative CEO leadership was predictive of TMT Dedication, but not Firm Competitive Performance. In addition, its predictive power for TMT Dedication was less than that of Charismatic, Team-Oriented, and Humane-Oriented leadership. The final two global leadership behaviors—Autonomous and Self-Protective—were interesting in several regards. Autonomous leadership had a small but significant *negative* relationship with TMT Dedication but had no impact with respect to Firm Competitive Performance. Lastly, Self-Protective leadership was interesting as its overall impact was minimal, but surprisingly, two of the primary behaviors (status conscious and bureaucratic) had positive effects whereas two had negative effects (i.e., self-centered and internally competitive).

Before discussing the importance of "fit" for leadership effectiveness, we present our view on two complementary methods to determine the influence of culture on leadership. In Chapter 8, we highlighted the specific leadership-outcome relationships that were moderated by culture. The extant cross-cultural literature generally posits that a major means to empirically demonstrate a cultural effect, the variable of culture (or nation) should have a statistically moderating effect—that is, the relationships between behavior and outcomes should be affected by culture. Absent a moderating effect of culture, the usual interpretation would be that CEO behaviors have a constant impact in every culture—culture doesn't matter. Using the example of Charismatic leadership in the present research, an absence of specific moderating effects of societal culture would lead one to assert that this leadership behavior should result in higher TMT Dedication and Firm Competitive Performance irrespective of country. But we previously have shown in Chapter 7 that culture doesn't directly impact leadership; rather, it has an indirect impact through culturally based leadership expectations. Therefore, we reject the assertion that an absence of a statistical interaction (i.e., moderation effect between leadership behavior and outcome relationships) *automatically* implies that culture doesn't matter. Rather, we assert that culture has an effect by changing the nature of the leadership expectations (CLTs), which in turn indirectly affect leadership effectiveness. We will demonstrate this through our new fit perspective and analysis.

For GLOBE, using our new fit perspective, we will empirically demonstrate that CEO effectiveness is predicated on a match between cultural leadership expectations and observed CEO behaviors. Thus, there are at least two complementary perspectives regarding cultural impact: (1) demonstrating a statistical hierarchical linear modeling (HLM) moderating effect of culture, which we tested for and reported in Chapter 8, and (2) demonstrating that fit is important, which we will demonstrate in this chapter. These approaches are complementary and are not inconsistent.

Definition of *Fit*: The Match Between CEO Behavior and Expectations

This section presents a short recapitulation from Chapter 2 as to why we believe that leadership effectiveness is predicated on the match between leadership expectations within a culture and observed CEO behavior. We then define *fit* and present a conceptual understanding of the measurement of fit. Chapter 5 presented the detailed statistical formula to calculate fit and it is summarized in an endnote of this chapter.[1]

Recall that much of the cross-cultural leadership literature presented in Chapter 2 refers to the importance of leaders being sensitive to societal culture to be effective. Chapter 7 showed our assessment of the mechanisms by which culture influences leadership—that is, through cultural expectations embodied in leadership CLTs. Cognitive psychology, through implicit leadership theory, suggests that people consider their own leadership schema against a specific

---

[1]Fit index: Recall that the fit index was described in Chapter 5. This index enabled us to test hypotheses concerning the consequences of CEOs behaving similarly to a country's cultural leadership expectations (i.e., CLTs). This newly created fit index assesses two aspects of the fit between CEO leader behavior and CLTs. First, the index assesses the similarity in pattern between individual CEO's leadership profile and the CEO's cultural leadership profile as measured by the CLT dimensions. Second, the new fit index also reflects the overall similarity in level or magnitude between each CEO's behavior and the CLT dimensions. These two aspects of fit, profile pattern similarity, and absolute behavioral level match were combined into a single fit index.

target leader as a whole to assess their leader. From this theoretical perspective, fit can be considered the extent to which an individual's leadership schema (i.e., the expected personality, skills, and behaviors of leaders) or in short, a person's leadership prototype matches a target leader (e.g., the CEO). This matching process is thought to be an automatic process, one that takes place with little or no active conscious personal awareness of the match (Hanges, Dorfman, Shteynberg, & Bates, 2006).

As a result of this matching process, there may be a perfect match between one's schema and the leaders' characteristics and behaviors, somewhat of a match, or none at all. Current thinking is that people likely don't isolate or analyze specific aspects of this schema but assess this match as a gestalt (Lord & Brown, 2004). We therefore define *fit* as the match between all 21 GLOBE CLT primary dimensions of leadership and the observed CEO behavior on these same dimensions (e.g., visionary leadership expectations and visionary leadership behaviors). As explained earlier, we specifically concentrate on the relationship between the overall fit across the 21 dimensions and outcome measures because our theory of leadership schema views it as a holistic concept.

In Chapter 5, we presented our statistical methodology for developing a fit index. As explained earlier, it became apparent to us that there are two separate and complementary aspects of fit (i.e., pattern or profile similarity and absolute behavioral similarity). We needed to design a fit index that assesses these two aspects of the fit between CEO leader behavior and cultural expectations (i.e. CLTs). The first aspect of fit assesses the similarity in *patterns* or *profiles* between a CEO's leadership behavior profile and the country's expected leadership profile—that is, CLTs measured for each of the global leadership dimensions. This fit measure is described in Chapter 5 as a *profile pattern similarity*, which is defined and measured as a within person slope between their societal CLT and their corresponding 21 leadership behaviors. The second aspect of fit was an assessment of absolute level of agreement between CLTs and behavior—that is, absolute behavioral similarity. This second measure of fit calculates the *distance* between each of the CEO's behaviors and its corresponding CLT dimension.

To provide a clear explanation, in Figure 9.1, we show a hypothetical country's CLT for a few leadership dimensions (the dark blue solid line). We also show the behavioral *profile* of two CEOs in terms of these dimensions. We can see that the behavioral profile of the first CEO is more similar to the CLT compared to the behavioral profile of the second CEO—that is, CEO 1 has a higher fit. In other words, CEO 1 generally behaves in a way that follows the CLT profile of the country. In contrast, the second CEO behaves in ways that are quite different from the CLT. For example, she or he is much more administratively competent than expected but less autocratic than expected. Clearly, the pattern of CEO 2's behavior is different from the country's CLT.

The second measure of fit calculates the *distance* between each of the CEO's behaviors and its corresponding CLT dimension. It reflects the overall

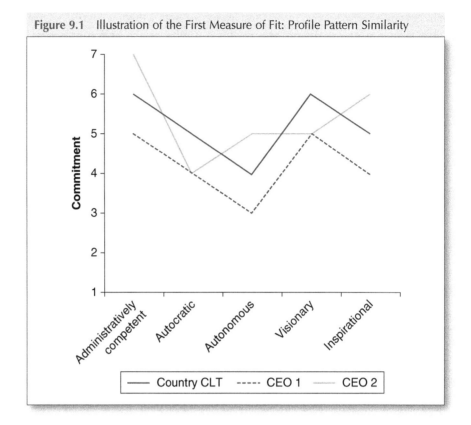

Figure 9.1 Illustration of the First Measure of Fit: Profile Pattern Similarity

similarity in *level* or magnitude between each CEO's observed behavior and the CLT dimensions. Previously in Chapter 7 we showed how CEOs in different countries behave in comparison to the country's CLT. We label the distance between the average score for each dimension of CEO leadership behavior in a country and the country's CLT on that dimension as the "gap." It is measured as the difference between the CEO leadership behavior score minus its corresponding country CLT score.

In Figure 9.2, we show a hypothetical country's CLT in terms of a few dimensions, as well as the behavioral profiles of two CEOs. It shows that the overall gap between CLT and CEO 1's dimensions (sum of absolute value of the gaps) is smaller than that of CEO 2. Therefore, using the second measure of fit, CEO 1 also has a higher level of fit.

Statistically, this absolute behavioral similarity measure was described in Chapter 5 as a within person "absolute consistency reliability" estimate. It is based on the sum of the squared deviation between the CLT and corresponding 21 leadership behaviors. These two aspects of fit, profile pattern similarity, and absolute behavioral level match were combined into a single fit index. The single fit measure captured two somewhat independent aspects of the behavioral match. It is a composite score that is computed by averaging the standardized profile similarity and absolute behavioral similarity scores across all 21 primary leadership behaviors.

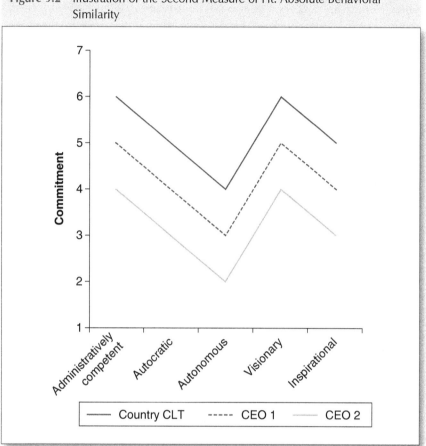

Figure 9.2   Illustration of the Second Measure of Fit: Absolute Behavioral Similarity

Together, these two complementary aspects of fit should present interesting comparisons among CEOs: Some leaders may follow the country's CLT profile, but their behavioral similarity may be low; others may have a high behavioral similarity, but their profiles do not match the CLT. In Figure 9.1, the absolute behavioral similarity between the two CEOs is the same, but the profile similarity is different (CEO 1 has perfect profile pattern similarity, whereas CEO 2's profile pattern similarity is substantially lower). In Figure 9.2, CEO 1 and CEO 2 identically match the pattern of country CLTs for the five primary leadership behaviors, but the absolute behavioral similarity is low for CEO 2. The possibility of both indices matching—or not matching—are also potential outcomes.

Importance of Fit: The Match Between CEO Behavior and Leadership Expectations

In this section, we present findings regarding the importance of fit for leadership effectiveness. Table 9.2 presents the results of CEO fit for predicting

TMT Dedication and Firm Competitive Performance. For this analysis, each outcome measure was regressed against our fit measure using HLM. In this table, fit is calculated using all 21 primary leadership dimensions—using both country-defined CLTs and CEO behavior. Note that our results indicate that fit predicts the overall TMT Dedication measure and each of the three constituent measures of TMT Dedication (i.e., statistically significant t values are found for the overall TMT Dedication measure as well as for each of the three constituent measures comprising TMT Dedication). In short, as the fit increases between the CEO behavior and leadership expectations for a country, so does TMT Dedication as well as TMT Effort, Commitment, and Team Solidarity. The importance of fit for Firm Competitive Performance is also strong, but its significance is carried by the Competitive Industry Dominance, not the Competitive Sales Performance measure. For purposes of clarity, we will subsequently refer to the fit using all 21 primary leadership CLTs and behaviors as Gestalt Fit because we are using all 21 primary leadership dimensions in our analysis.

In the previous paragraph, we showed that the overall discrepancies between CLTs and leadership behaviors (i.e., Gestalt Fit) had important consequences for the CEO and the organization. We now examine whether all discrepancies

Table 9.2   The Impact of Gestalt Fit Between All Twenty-One Dimensions of Culturally Endorsed Implicit Leadership Theories (Societal Leadership Expectations) and Twenty-One CEO Behaviors on Outcome Variables

Gestalt Fit: All Twenty-One Culturally Endorsed Implicit Leadership Theories and All Twenty-One Leadership Behaviors				
	Predictor	**Coefficient**	**Degree of Freedom**	**t Value**
Dedication[a]	Fit	0.66	833	7.55**
Commitment	Fit	0.23	833	6.63**
Effort	Fit	0.16	833	5.67**
Team Solidarity	Fit	0.22	833	6.42**
Firm Competitive Performance[b]	Fit	0.13	269	2.45*
Competitive Sales Performance	Fit	0.15	228	1.31
Competitive Industry Dominance	Fit	0.22	258	3.32**

Note: [a] Dedication is a composite of the Commitment, Effort, and Team Solidarity items.

[b] Firm Competitive Performance is a composite of the Competitive Sales Performance, and Competitive Industry Dominance items.

*$p < .05$. **$p < .01$.

between CLTs and each individual global leadership behavior are equally important. Specifically, we test the importance of fit for each global leadership dimension independently. In short, the following analyses test whether there are certain discrepancies that are more or less salient than others.

For this analysis, a fit measure is calculated for each of the six global leadership dimensions one at a time (e.g., Charismatic leadership). We use the primary leadership behaviors within each dimension for our analysis in order to suggest whether the fit for one particular global leadership dimension is the most important for our Gestalt Fit findings. The issue concerns the saliency of fit measures for each leadership dimension in impacting the Gestalt Fit results. That is, while we believe that the Gestalt Fit is critical to assess, it may be possible to determine the extent to which the Gestalt Fit is driven by the fit for each *specific* leadership behavior. For example, results presented in Table 9.3 indicate that the fit between Charismatic leadership CLT and the Charismatic CEO behavior across all CEOs is only slightly important for TMT Dedication and not important for Firm Competitive Performance. Specifically, fit predicts Team Solidarity at the normal significance level but only predicts the overall TMT Dedication measure and the constituent measure of TMT Commitment as a trend. The fit measure for Charismatic leadership does not predict any of the Firm Competitive Performance measures. The following discussion continues to present the results for the fit analysis considering each leadership dimension separately.

Table 9.3   The Impact of Fit Between Charismatic Societal Leadership Expectations (Culturally Endorsed Implicit Leadership Theories) and Charismatic CEO Behaviors on Outcome Variables

	Predictor	Coefficient	Degree of Freedom	t Value
Dedication[a]	Fit	0.19	833	1.91[†]
Commitment	Fit	0.07	833	1.69[†]
Effort	Fit	0.02	833	0.64
Team Solidarity	Fit	0.09	833	2.23*
Firm Competitive Performance[b]	Fit	0.06	269	1.12
Competitive Sales Performance	Fit	0.08	228	0.67
Competitive Industry Dominance	Fit	0.11	258	1.45

Note: [a] Dedication is a composite of the Commitment, Effort, and Team Solidarity items.

[b] Firm Competitive Performance is a composite of the Competitive Sales Performance and Competitive Industry Dominance items.

[†] $p < .10$. *$p < .05$.

The results for fit regarding the leadership dimension of Team Oriented are particularly strong as fit significantly predicts the overall measures of Dedication and Firm Competitive Performance (see Table 9.4). In fact, all the constituent measures in both variables are also significant (except Competitive Sales Performance). Again, the closer the fit between the leadership expectations and leadership behavior, the more effective the leader.

As shown in Table 9.5, the impact of CEO fit for Participative leadership is significant for TMT Dedication but not Competitive Firm Performance. All three constituent measures of TMT Dedication are predicted by fit in Participative leadership—the higher the fit, the more dedicated the TMT. The findings for Humane-Oriented leadership indicate that fit is irrelevant for effective leadership, and in fact, we found a negative relationship between Humane-Oriented fit and Competitive Sales Performance (see Table 9.6).

The impact of fit for the Self-Protective global factor is only moderate as there are significant effects for TMT Solidarity and Competitive Industry Dominance (and trends for TMT Dedication and TMT Commitment; see Table 9.7). It was not possible to calculate a fit index for the Autonomous leadership dimension as this dimension has only one primary dimension (i.e., also labeled *autonomous*).

Modern cognitive categorizations theory suggests that the schema matching process occurs in a gestalt-like fashion where each node of the schemas net activates all the subsequent attributes in the schema (Hanges et al., 2006; Lord, Hanges, & Godfrey, 2003). Second, as shown by the correlation among the

Table 9.4 The Impact of Fit Between Team-Oriented Societal Leadership Expectations (Culturally Endorsed Implicit Leadership Theories) and Team-Oriented CEO Behaviors on Outcome Variables

	Predictor	Coefficient	Degree of Freedom	t Value
Dedication[a]	Fit	0.73	833	7.94**
Commitment	Fit	0.25	833	6.71**
Effort	Fit	0.18	833	5.84**
Team Solidarity	Fit	0.25	833	7.06**
Firm Competitive Performance[b]	Fit	0.14	269	2.67**
Competitive Sales Performance	Fit	0.16	228	1.40
Competitive Industry Dominance	Fit	0.22	258	3.14**

Note: [a] Dedication is a composite of the Commitment, Effort, and Team Solidarity items.

[b] Firm Competitive Performance is a composite of the Competitive Sales Performance and Competitive Industry Dominance items.

**$p < .01$.

Table 9.5   The Impact of Fit Between Participative Societal Leadership Expectations (Culturally Endorsed Implicit Leadership Theories) and Participative CEO Behaviors on Outcome Variables

	Predictor	Coefficient	Degree of Freedom	t Value
Dedication[a]	Fit	0.35	819	3.46**
Commitment	Fit	0.13	819	3.17**
Effort	Fit	0.10	819	2.97**
Team Solidarity	Fit	0.10	819	2.62**
Firm Competitive Performance[b]	Fit	0.03	263	0.50
Competitive Sales Performance	Fit	0.13	222	1.01
Competitive Industry Dominance	Fit	0.03	253	0.44

Note: [a] Dedication is a composite of the Commitment, Effort, and Team Solidarity items.

[b] Firm Competitive Performance is a composite of the Competitive Sales Performance and Competitive Industry Dominance items.

**$p < .01$.

Table 9.6   The Impact of Fit Between Humane-Oriented Societal Leadership Expectations (Culturally Endorsed Implicit Leadership Theories) and Humane CEO Behaviors on Outcome Variables

	Predictor	Coefficient	Degree of Freedom	t Value
Dedication[a]	Fit	−0.07	833	−0.66
Commitment	Fit	−0.01	833	−0.20
Effort	Fit	−0.01	833	−0.39
Team Solidarity	Fit	−0.04	833	−0.98
Firm Competitive Performance[b]	Fit	−0.06	269	−0.77
Competitive Sales Performance	Fit	−0.36	228	−2.13*
Competitive Industry Dominance	Fit	0.02	258	0.23

Note: [a] Dedication is a composite of the Commitment, Effort, and Team Solidarity items.

[b] Firm Competitive Performance is a composite of the Competitive Sales Performance and Competitive Industry Dominance items.

*$p < .05$.

Table 9.7 The Impact of Fit Between Self-Protective Societal Leadership Expectations (Culturally Endorsed Implicit Leadership Theories) and Self-Protective CEO Behaviors on Outcome Variables

	Predictor	Coefficient	Degree of Freedom	t Value
Dedication[a]	Fit	0.16	833	1.80 [†]
Commitment	Fit	0.06	833	1.76 [†]
Effort	Fit	0.02	833	0.66
Team Solidarity	Fit	0.07	833	2.13*
Firm Competitive Performance[b]	Fit	0.03	269	0.59
Competitive Sales Performance	Fit	−0.14	228	−1.19
Competitive Industry Dominance	Fit	0.14	258	1.98*

Note: [a] Dedication is a composite of the Commitment, Effort, and Team Solidarity items.

[b] Firm Competitive Performance is a composite of the Competitive Sales Performance and Competitive Industry Dominance items.

[†] $p < .10$. *$p < .05$.

global leadership behaviors in Chapter 6, they do not operate in isolation but instead covary. Considering these two points, it is unlikely that only one global dimension would be salient in exclusion of the others. Therefore, we believe that the gestalt using all the 21 primary dimensions together most clearly represents our view as to how cognitive mental processing works in reality. For the Gestalt Fit, higher fit results in higher TMT Dedication (TMT Effort, Commitment, and Team Solidarity) and higher Firm Competitive Performance (for Competitive Industry Dominance). CEOs who enact their nation's leadership expectations, in general, tend to be more effective than those who don't.

We can summarize these findings by pointing out that Gestalt Fit across all 21 primary leadership factors is particularly important for leadership effectiveness. Our analysis of fit for each of the leadership dimensions suggests that the fit for Team-Oriented and Participative leadership are important drivers of the Gestalt Fit findings. The fit for Charismatic and Self-Protective leadership are less important. The fit for Humane-Oriented leadership is not important.

CEO Behavioral Enactment and Fit: A Simultaneous Comparison of Effects?

In Chapter 9, we showed that CEO leadership behaviors predict CEO effectiveness. In this chapter, we showed that the fit between CEO behavior and CLT also predicts CEO effectiveness. A next logical and intuitively appealing question now is as follows: Which one has stronger explanatory power when it comes to CEO effectiveness: CEO behavior or the fit between CEO behavior and CLT? This is obviously an important question from both a research and a practical point of view.

However, one has to be careful when testing this hypothesis. For example, it may seem obvious to test this hypothesis by using all 21 primary leadership measures in a regression along with Gestalt Fit to predict our dependent variables. Unfortunately, this method will not work due to the multicollinearity between Gestalt Fit and the 21 primary leadership dimensions. As shown in classical test theory, a composite score (i.e., Gestalt Fit) is highly correlated (multicollinear) with the items used to create that composite (i.e., 21 primary leadership dimensions). Further, readers should conceptualize the regression using the 21 primary leadership dimensions as a profile approach (not a dimensional approach), which is exactly what the Gestalt Fit measure does. In other words, there is both empirical overlap as well as conceptual overlap between the behavior and fit approach if one were to conduct this analysis.

Rather than using the regression approach described previously, we tested the behavior versus fit hypothesis by performing a regression equation using the Gestalt Fit measure along with a single measure of leadership behavior. The single leadership measure, hereafter called Gestalt Leadership score, was created by averaging all the 21 leadership dimensions together for each CEO. This single composite leadership score can be thought of as the overall leadership behavioral level shown by the CEOs. This approach is consistent with how subscales are typically combined into higher order scales. For example, the four transformational leadership scales (i.e., individualized consideration, intellectual stimulation, inspirational motivation, idealized influence) are often combined into a single transformation leadership factor. This is what we accomplished by creating our new Gestalt Leadership measure. However, it should be noted that we did not reverse code any of the 21 leadership scales when creating Gestalt Leadership. Reverse coding of a leadership scale implies that the researcher has an a priori implicit leadership theory about what "good leadership is." For example, should the Autonomous leadership scale be combined with the other leadership scales as is, or should it be reverse coded before being combined to form the Gestalt Leadership scale? The answer depends upon which cultural CLT one is considering (Dorfman, Javidan, Hanges, Dastmalchian, & House, 2012). This would be true for all of our 21 leadership scales that we previously found to be culturally contingent (e.g., bureaucratic, face-saver, humane orientation, self-sacrificial, status conscious). In short, whether or not these scales should be reverse coded depends upon the CLT and the societal cultural values that the researcher is assuming as true. Thus, we did not reverse code any of our 21 leadership behavior scales when creating this Gestalt Leadership measure.

We then ran an HLM using the Gestalt Fit measure along with this new Gestalt Leadership behavior score. The results showed that for the internally oriented outcome measure (i.e., TMT Dedication), both Gestalt Fit and Gestalt Leadership behavior added uniquely to this equation (Gestalt Fit: $b = 0.35$, $t(832) = 3.59$, $p < .01$; Gestalt Leadership: $b = 1.64$, $t(832) = 6.16$, $p < .01$). However, for the externally oriented outcome measure (i.e., Firm Competitive Performance) neither Gestalt Fit nor the Gestalt Leadership behavior measures added unique amounts of variance (Gestalt Fit: $b = 0.07$, $t(268) = 1.33$, $p > .10$; Gestalt Leadership: $b = 0.25$, $t(268) = 1.61$, $p > .10$).

A Country-Level Assessment of Fit

One can look in Chapter 7 to see the same country's gap score—that is, the gap between the CLT and CEO behavior within each country. As explained in Chapter 6, the gap scores and the fit indices are not equal as the gap does not measure profile fit. Recall that in the present chapter, our fit index is composed of two indices: (1) the absolute behavior index and (2) the relative pattern index. Chapter 7 provided empirical information about how CEOs in different countries act as leaders within each culture. It presented the average of the CLTs for each global leadership behavior thus showing what leaders are generally expected to do. In fact, Table 7.5 showed the average CEO score (in and across all countries) on corresponding leadership behaviors and the *gap* between the two (CLT–behavior). Statistical analyses in Chapter 7 showed that the gap between CLTs and behaviors is statistically significant for all the six leadership dimensions across the countries.

In the present chapter, we go beyond measuring the gap index (which is akin to the behavioral, not the pattern part of our fit index) in our analyses. All the analyses so far presented in this chapter show that the Gestalt Fit index predicts effective leadership. Table 9.8 presents the overall Gestalt Fit (across 21 primary leadership dimensions) for the CEOs in each country in our sample. The Gestalt Fit scores can be interpreted in the following manner. The higher and more positive the fit scores, the better the fit between the CLT and the behavior. The more negative the number, the worse CLT/behavior fit. We want to point out that the average Gestalt Fit for the entire sample is represented by a Gestalt Fit score of zero because both the "absolute behavior" and "behavioral pattern" fit were first standardized before being combined into a single composite Gestalt Fit measure. Mexico, Greece, and the United States have leaders with the highest Gestalt Fit scores and Spain, Netherlands, and Russia have the lowest Gestalt Fit scores. The tables show that among the CEOs in our 24-country sample, Russian CEOs behave in a way that is quite

Table 9.8 Average Gestalt Fit for Each Country

Average Gestalt Fit	Country	Sample Size
0.83	Mexico	42
0.40	Greece	51
0.17	United States	44
0.17	Slovenia	40
0.13	Austria	40
0.09	India	113
0.06	China	97
0.02	Germany	29
0.00	Brazil	37
−0.01	Taiwan	40
−0.10	Nigeria	47
−0.14	Estonia	49
−0.21	Romania	44
−0.21	Turkey	39
−0.27	Guatemala	40
−0.31	Spain	35
−0.33	Netherlands	53
−1.20	Russia	40

Note: Average Gestalt Fit indicates the average Gestalt Fit scores for CEOs within each country.

different from what is expected of them. Mexican CEOs, however, tend to behave very close to what is expected.[2]

_____

[2]We are showing the average amount of fit between CLT and leadership behaviors because we think it provides interesting descriptive information of the extent to which people in various societies are getting the kinds of leadership they desire. The present study, however, was not designed to assess the antecedents and consequences of societal level fit—only instead to assess the relationship between fit and organizational outcomes. While we could also aggregate the dependent variables in our present study such as TMT Dedication to the society level, those variables do not have any conceptual meaning at the societal level. Further, any attempt to correlate the average level of CLT behaviors' fit with our societal level aggregated variable would yield meaningless data (i.e., ecological fallacy—relationships at one level of analysis may provide confusing and incorrect understanding applied to another level of analysis).

Summary

In this chapter, we switched our conceptual lens several times. We first summarized evidence from Chapter 8 indicating the effectiveness of specific CEO leadership behaviors. Then we presented evidence showing that CEO effectiveness also results from matching CEO leadership to cultural requisites (i.e., fit). We conducted this analysis in several stages. The first time we analyzed Gestalt Fit for all 21 CEO behaviors considered together (CEO behavior compared with the leadership expectations for the 21 same primary behaviors). Second, we analyzed the fit of each global leadership behavior separately (using the primary leadership dimensions within the global leadership behavior—e.g., the five primary Team-Oriented behaviors were used for the global Team-Oriented dimension). For both these fit analyses, our perspective views leadership from the cultural contingency viewpoint instead of suggesting that effectiveness may be simply related to the level or amount of CEO behaviors enacted. Our analyses supported the case that the Gestalt Fit was important for TMT outcomes and Firm Competitive Performance. The importance of fit for each global leadership dimension yielded particularly interesting results with respect to Team-Oriented and Participative leadership. Cultural leadership expectations as represented by fit are especially important for these two leadership behaviors. The importance of fit is less so for Charismatic and Self-Protective leadership and not at all for Humane-Oriented leadership.

In summary, we presented evidence regarding a simultaneous comparison of the relative importance of cultural fit with that of the previously found nearly universally effective behaviors discussed in this and earlier chapters. In a sense, employing a simultaneous prediction from Gestalt Fit and behavior gives us a more complete and nuanced view of leadership effectiveness of global CEO leadership.

10

CEO Leadership
Effectiveness
Across Cultures

Superior and Inferior CEOs

In Chapters 5 and 9, we presented a methodology to measure the fit between CLT and CEO behavior in each country. The methodology used two different but related aspects of fit and created a fit index. We then showed the relationship between the fit index and CEO effectiveness. We showed that the Gestalt Fit between CEO behavior and culturally endorsed implicit leadership theory (CLT) predicts CEO effectiveness in terms of Top Management Team (TMT) Dedication and in terms of the firm's competitive performance. In sum, our findings are quite clear that how a CEO behaves and how his/her behavior compares to the societal expectations are both important. For example, being Team Oriented is important, but it is also important to be as Team Oriented as that expected by the society.

Given that both behavior and fit are important, we need to understand what this means and how to explain it. To this end, we compare two extreme groups of CEOs: The first group consists of CEOs who are extremely effective, whom we call "superior CEOs." These are CEOs associated with extremely high levels of Firm Competitive Performance or TMT Dedication. The second group is called "inferior CEOs" who are CEOs with extremely low TMT Dedication or Firm Competitive Performance. In other words, we identified the group of superior and inferior CEOs separately for the two aggregate dependent variables—(1) TMT Dedication and (2) Firm Competitive Performance.

Superior and Inferior CEOs: Top Management Team Dedication

With respect to TMT Dedication, we computed the means and standard deviations (SDs) for each country and initially split our samples within country into three groups using the following rule: Inferior CEOs were one SD ($SD_{Country}$) below the mean in each country ($\overline{X}_{Country} - SD_{Country}$) whereas superior CEOs were one SD above the mean in each country ($\overline{X}_{Country} + SD_{Country}$). Examining the number of people within these various classified groups revealed that this initial rule was too strict a criterion with fewer than desired CEOs in each group. We could have used a median split on each criterion to greatly increase the sample size of each group, but this would not result in clear conceptual and statistical distinctions between the groups. A compromise was reached whereby we changed our general statistical rule to permit more CEOs into the superior and inferior categories. However, no single overall rule could be found that classified sufficient numbers of CEOs into the two categories for all countries. Thus, given that this analysis was descriptive in nature, we took the additional step of slightly adjusting the cutoffs for some countries if the slight change in the cutoff resulted in a sufficient sample size of either superior or inferior CEOs. In short, these extremes defined the superior and inferior CEOs within each country in terms of TMT Dedication.

Superior and Inferior CEOs: Firm Competitive Performance

Determination of superior and inferior CEOs in terms of Firm Competitive Performance variable was easier. The distribution of this variable only permitted a dichotomous split of this variable within each country. Thus, we split each country's sample based upon each country's median. Specifically, the inferior CEOs were below the median in each country whereas the superior CEOs were equal to and/or above the median on Firm Competitive Performance. Please note that as described in Chapter 4, while we have a very large number of firms reporting on TMT Dedication, we have a smaller number of firms reporting on Firm Competitive Performance. The analyses resulted in the identification of the following groups:

- 263 CEOs with superior and 215 CEOs with inferior TMT Dedication
- 99 CEOs with superior and 86 CEOs with inferior Firm Competitive Performance
- 42 CEOs with superior and 29 CEOs with inferior TMT Dedication *and* Firm Competitive Performance. These CEOs are at the high end or low end on both measures of effectiveness.

Profile Similarity for Gestalt Fit

As explained in Chapter 5 and 9, our measure of fit has two components: (1) profile similarity and (2) the behavioral similarity or gap between each behavioral dimension and its corresponding CLT dimension. We first examined the profile similarity of Gestalt Fit—our label for the fit considering all leadership behaviors and CLTs simultaneously. Specifically, we averaged our measure of profile similarity (i.e., the unstandardized regression coefficient for the regression of the 21 leadership behaviors onto the complete range of CLT dimensions) for the superior and inferior CEO groups. Superior CEOs had a higher average unstandardized regression coefficient (0.74) than inferior CEOs (0.58). In other words, superior CEOs exhibited a stronger profile similarity to each society's overall CLT than the inferior CEOs did. Simply stated, their overall leadership behavior profile is more in tune with that expected by the society.

Behavioral Similarity for Gestalt Fit

We next focused on the second component of the Gestalt Fit: the absolute consistency measure between each dimension of the CEO behavioral profile and its corresponding CLT dimension. It is the gap or the distance between each behavior dimension and its corresponding CLT dimension. In this chapter, we present a series of graphs that show the gap between each of the leadership behavior scales and the corresponding CLT dimension. To help interpret the magnitude of the gaps, we standardized these gaps within each country. These standardized scores can now be interpreted as a distance measure. The standardized gap basically indicates how far a leader's behavior is from the country's CLT in SD units. For example, a z score of +1.5 on the visionary leadership scale for the superior CEO group indicates that the average superior CEO is 1.5 SDs more visionary than the level specified by the CLT. An average z score of –0.5 on this scale for the superior CEO group would be interpreted as the average superior CEO is 0.5 SDs below the visionary behavior specified in the CLT.

To compare the superior and the inferior groups in terms of their gap with the CLT, we conducted the following analyses:

- A comparison of the superior and the inferior groups based on TMT Dedication in terms of the gap between their behavior and the CLT
- A comparison of the superior and the inferior groups based on Firm Competitive Performance in terms of the gap between their behavior and the CLT
- A comparison of the superior and the inferior groups based on both criteria: TMT Dedication and Firm Competitive Performance in terms of the gap between their behavior and the CLT

Gap Between Superior and Inferior CEOs' Leadership Behavior and Culturally Endorsed Implicit Leadership Theory

Figure 10.1a compares the gap between superior CEOs' behavior and CLT with the gap between inferior CEOs' behavior and CLT with regard to the six global leadership dimensions. As explained earlier, the vertical axis is the standardized distance between CEO leadership behavior and the corresponding CLT dimension rating.

As shown in the figure, the superior and inferior CEOs are quite distinct. The CEOs who generate extremely high levels of TMT Dedication substantially exceed their countries' leadership expectations (i.e.,

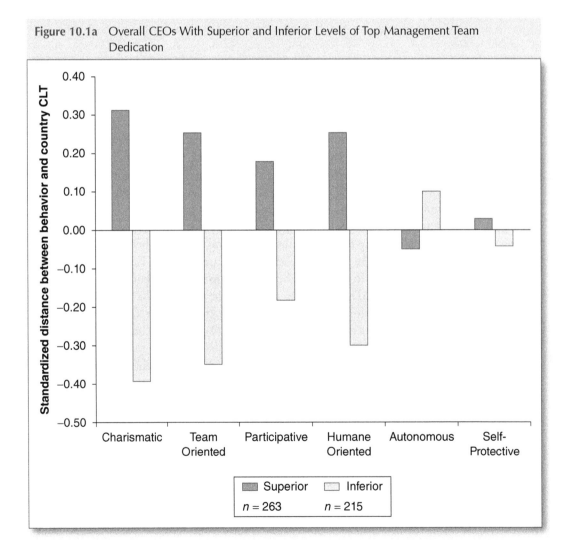

Figure 10.1a Overall CEOs With Superior and Inferior Levels of Top Management Team Dedication

CLTs) in terms of Charismatic, Team-Oriented, Humane-Oriented, and Participative leadership. They match the CLT in terms of Autonomous and Self-Protective leadership. In contrast, the CEOs who generate extremely low levels of TMT Dedication seem to present a mirror image: They fall substantially short of their countries' leadership expectations (i.e., CLTs) in terms of Charismatic, Team-Oriented, Participative, and Humane-Oriented leadership. The findings are quite similar when comparing CEOs with superior and inferior Firm Competitive Performance. The only difference is that the gaps between superior CEOs' behavior and CLT are somewhat smaller for Firm Competitive Performance than for TMT Dedication. Figure 10.1b shows the same relationships for the 21 primary leadership dimensions. It confirms that the superior CEOs and inferior CEOs do present a mirror image. The former substantially exceed their country CLTs on all dimensions of Charismatic, Team-Oriented, Humane-Oriented, and Participative leadership. The inferior CEOs' behavior as a group is almost the exact opposite of the superior CEOs.

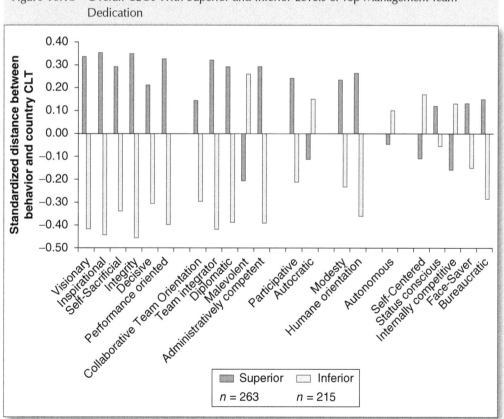

Figure 10.1b Overall CEOs With Superior and Inferior Levels of Top Management Team Dedication

Super Superior and Super Inferior CEOs _____

Figure 10.2a shows a comparison of the CEOs with superior and inferior performance on *both* TMT Dedication and Firm Competitive Performance. Again, the superior CEOs profile seems to be a mirror image of the inferior CEOs. The former exceed their societies' expectations on five of the six global dimensions, especially in terms of Charismatic and Team-Oriented leadership. Inferior CEOs fall short of expectations on four of the six dimensions. They substantially exceed expectations on Autonomous leadership. Inferior CEOs are more autonomous than expected.

Figure 10.2b shows a comparison of the two groups of CEOs in terms of the 21 dimensions. While showing generally similar results, the figure highlights important findings. While there is a large difference between superior and inferior CEOs regarding global leadership dimensions of Charismatic and Team-Oriented leadership, three primary dimensions seem to be distinguishing the two groups: (1) visionary, (2) performance oriented, and (3) administratively competent leadership. The differences between the two groups are particularly large. CEOs who lead extremely dedicated TMTs and extremely competitive firms are substantially more visionary,

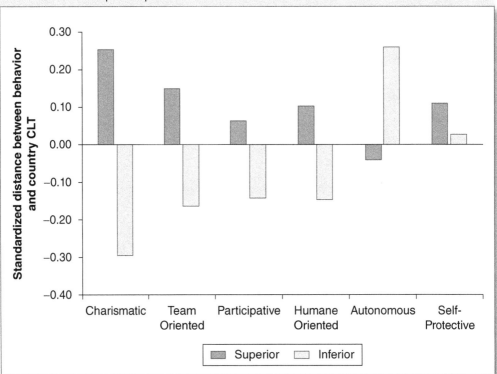

Figure 10.2a Overall CEOs with Superior and Inferior Levels of TMT Dedication and Firm Competitive performance

performance oriented, and administratively competent than expected by their societies. In contrast, CEOs with extremely low levels of TMT Dedication and Firm Competitive Performance are substantially less visionary, performance oriented, and administratively competent than expected by their societies.

In sum, in Chapter 9, we focused on the size of the fit between behavior and CLT. We showed that the better the fit between the combined 21 primary CEO behaviors and their counterpart CLTs, the higher the TMT Dedication and Firm Competitive Performance. In this chapter, we show that consistent with these findings, the extremely low-performing CEOs clearly fall short of their societies' leadership expectations. However, we also show here that superstar CEOs do not just fit their countries' leadership expectations; they substantially exceed them. Our findings lead to important conclusions. To produce superior outcomes, CEOs across countries need to exceed their societies' expectations in terms of many of the 21 primary and 6 global dimensions of leadership. However, while exceeding expectations, they need to also be cognizant of the overall profile of the CLT. In other words, the CLT of a society acts as a constraint on leaders not in terms of the individual dimensions but in terms of the overall profile of the 6 or 21 dimensions. To succeed, CEOs need to exceed expectations on several key dimensions (e.g., visionary) but in a way that their overall behavioral profile does not drastically deviate from the CLT.

Figure 10.2b   Overall CEOs With Superior and Inferior Levels of Top Management Team Dedication and Firm Competitive Performance

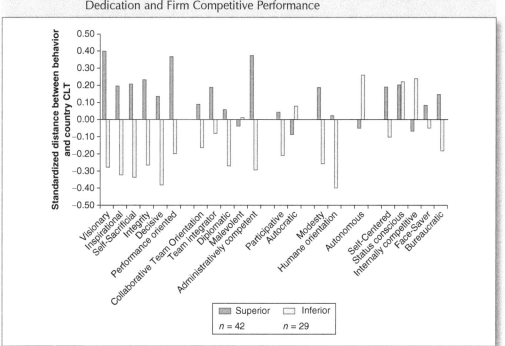

Profiles of Superior and Inferior CEOs _____

In the following pages, we present the profiles of inferior CEOs and superior CEOs in each of the 18 countries in terms of the 21 primary dimensions. We can only focus on TMT Dedication as the criterion measure because of insufficient numbers of firms reporting on Firm Competitive Performance in each country.

Austria

Figure 10.3 contrasts inferior CEOs and superior CEOs in Austria. It shows that inferior CEOs and superior CEOs differ substantially on vision, inspiration, integrity, diplomacy, modesty, and bureaucracy. Superior CEOs substantially exceed expectations while inferior CEOs fall short of expectations. Austrian star CEOs show very high levels of integrity, diplomacy, participation, and face-saving behavior. Inferior Austrian CEOs, in contrast, fall short of expectations, particularly in terms of vision, inspiration, integrity, team integration, diplomacy, administrative competence, modesty, humane orientation, and bureaucracy.

Figure 10.3　Austria CEOs With Superior and Inferior Levels of Top Management Team Dedication

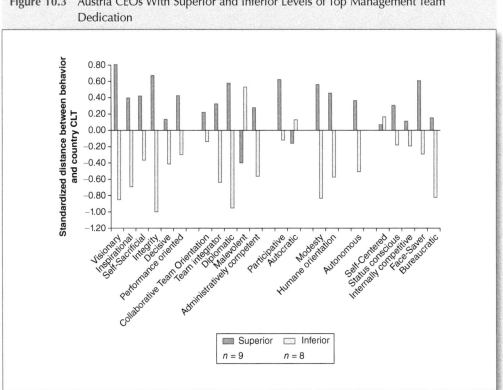

China

Figure 10.4 contrasts the inferior CEOs and superior CEOs in China. While Chinese superior CEOs exceed expectations on all dimensions, what is even more important is that Chinese inferior CEOs fall very substantially short of expectations. The only exceptions are that the inferior CEOs are more malevolent, autocratic, self-centered, and status conscious than desired.

Estonia

Figure 10.5 contrasts the inferior CEOs and superior CEOs in Estonia. Star CEOs exceed the country's expectations on dimensions of Charismatic leadership (visionary, inspirational, self-sacrificial, integrity, decisive, performance oriented) and Team-Oriented leadership (collaborative team orientation, team integrator, diplomatic, malevolent, administratively competent). They are, however, less modest and less self-centered than expected. Estonian underperforming CEOs fall substantially short of expectations. They are particularly indecisive and are less visionary, inspirational, performance oriented, and humane oriented than desired. They are, however, more modest and self-centered than desired.

Figure 10.4   China CEOs With Superior and Inferior Levels of Top Management Team Dedication

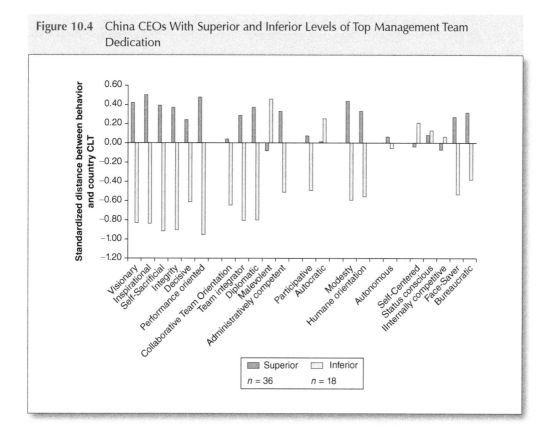

Figure 10.5   Estonia CEOs With Superior and Inferior Levels of Top Management Team Dedication

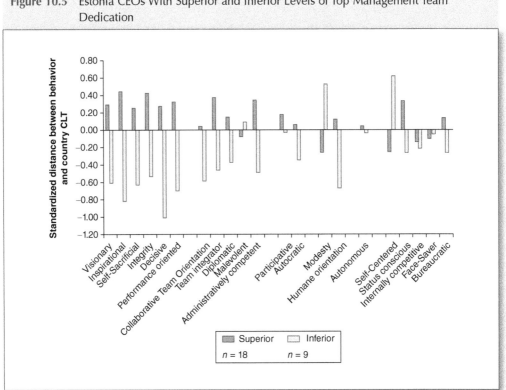

Germany

Figure 10.6 contrasts the superior CEOs and inferior CEOs in Germany. Inferior German CEOs basically meet their societies' expectations. Their behavioral profile is very close to the country's CLT, although they are less inspirational, collaborative, and modest and more autonomous than desired. The star CEOs exceed their country's expectations on most dimensions—especially vision, inspiration, participation, modesty, and humane orientation.

Greece

Figure 10.7 contrasts the inferior CEOs and superior CEOs in Greece. It shows that Greek star CEOs exceed expectations on most dimensions. The exceptions are that they are less autonomous and less self-centered than expected. Underperforming Greek CEOs fall short of expectations in all dimensions except that they are more malevolent, autonomous, and self-centered than desired.

Figure 10.6   Germany CEOs With Superior and Inferior Levels of Top Management Team Dedication

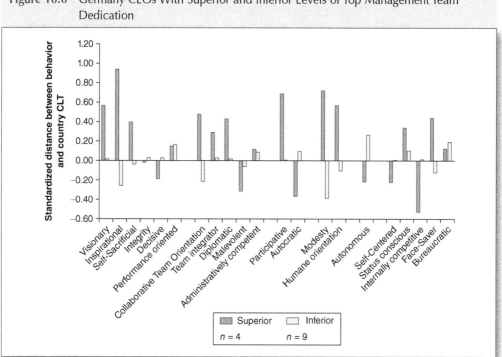

Figure 10.7   Greece CEOs With Superior and Inferior Levels of Top Management Team Dedication

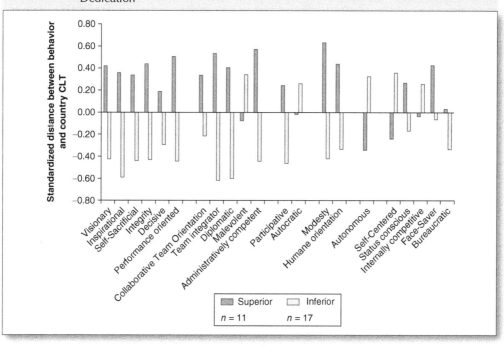

Guatemala

Figure 10.8 contrasts the inferior CEOs and superior CEOs in Guatemala. Underperforming CEOs fall substantially short on most dimensions except that they are more malevolent, autocratic, and internally competitive than desired. Superior CEOs are distinct from the inferior CEOs in that they have more integrity and are more performance oriented, collaborative, diplomatic, and humane oriented than expected. They are also less autocratic and status conscious than expected.

India

Figure 10.9 contrasts the inferior CEOs and superior CEOs in India. Superior Indian CEOs are less malevolent, autocratic, autonomous, self-centered, and internally competitive than expected. They exceed the CLT on all other dimensions. Inferior CEOs are substantially below expectations in all primary dimensions of the two global dimensions of Charismatic and Team-Oriented leadership. They are particularly less humane-oriented than desired and are more autocratic and self-centered than expected.

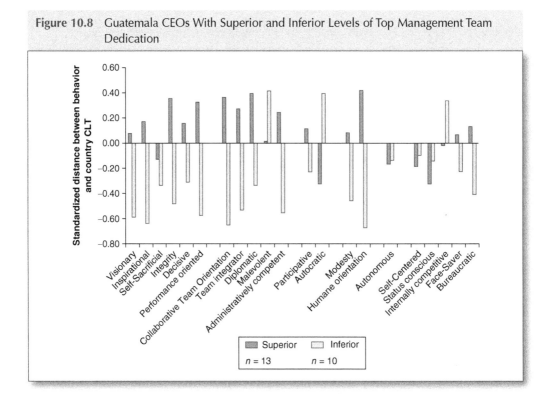

Figure 10.8 Guatemala CEOs With Superior and Inferior Levels of Top Management Team Dedication

Figure 10.9   India CEOs With Superior and Inferior Levels of Top Management Team Dedication

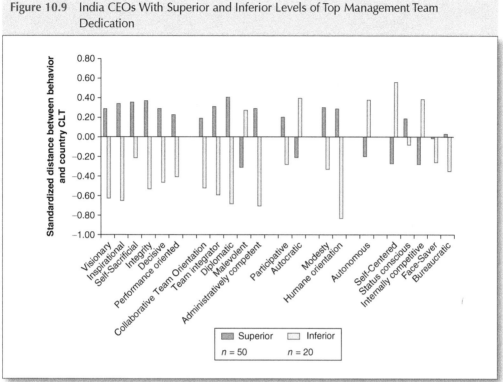

Mexico

Figure 10.10 contrasts the inferior CEOs and superior CEOs in Mexico. Superior Mexican CEOs are substantially more modest and autonomous than expected. They are also more inspirational and have more integrity than the CLT. They are less malevolent, autocratic, internally competitive, bureaucratic, and self-centered than expected. Inferior Mexican CEOs' overall profile for many dimensions seems to be close to the CLT (i.e., the zero point line) with the two exceptions that they are less diplomatic and less humane oriented.

Netherlands

Figure 10.11 contrasts the inferior CEOs and superior CEOs in the Netherlands. Dutch superior CEOs match the CLT in terms of autocratic leadership, autonomy, and self-centeredness. They exceed the CLT on all other dimensions. Inferior Dutch CEOs present an almost-mirror image with particularly lower levels of Charismatic and Team-Oriented dimensions.

Figure 10.10   Mexico CEOs With Superior and Inferior Levels of Top Management Team Dedication

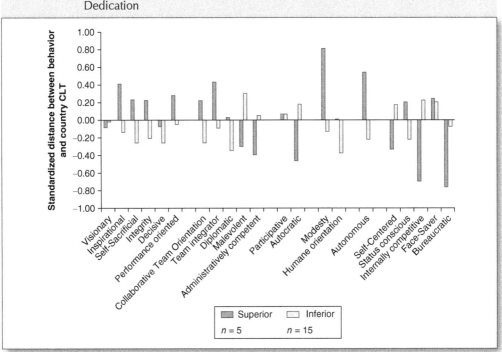

Figure 10.11   Netherlands CEOs With Superior and Inferior Levels of Top Management Team Dedication

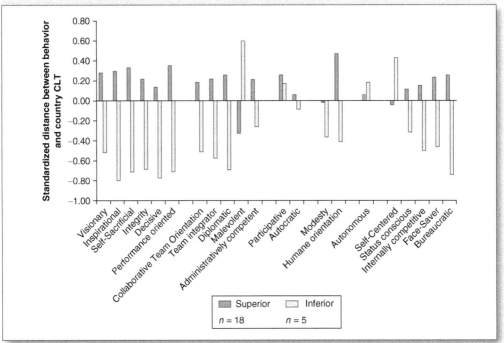

Nigeria

Figure 10.12 contrasts the inferior CEOs and superior CEOs in Nigeria. Superior Nigerian CEOs are substantially less malevolent, autocratic, and autonomous than expected. They are also less internally competitive and self-centered than expected. They exceed the CLT on almost all the other dimensions. Inferior Nigerian CEOs particularly fall short of expectations in terms of vision, self-sacrifice, performance orientation, administrative competence, and participation.

Romania

Figure 10.13 contrasts the inferior CEOs and superior CEOs in Romania. Superior and inferior Romanian CEOs present an almost-perfect mirror image. Superior CEOs exceed expectations on almost all dimensions while inferior CEOs fall considerably short.

Russia

Figure 10.14 contrasts the inferior CEOs and superior CEOs in Russia. The findings in this table are quite unusual in the sense that superior

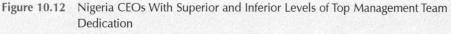

Figure 10.12   Nigeria CEOs With Superior and Inferior Levels of Top Management Team Dedication

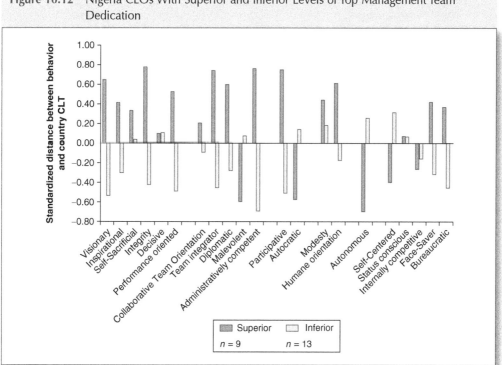

Figure 10.13   Romania CEOs With Superior and Inferior Levels of Top Management Team
Dedication

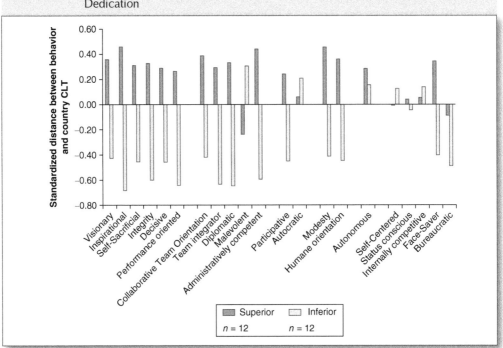

Figure 10.14   Russia CEOs With Superior and Inferior Levels of Top Management Team
Dedication

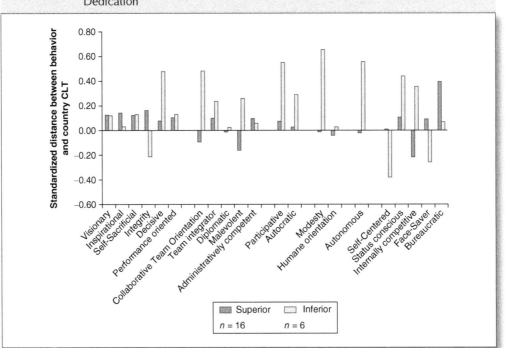

Russian CEOs match the CLT. They behave very much as expected. However, inferior Russian CEOs actually exceed several CLT dimensions. On Charismatic leadership, the only difference between the superior and inferior CEOs is that the latter group has less integrity but is more decisive. Inferior CEOs are also more Team Oriented than the superior group. Lastly, inferior Russian CEOs are more participative, more modest, more autonomous, and more status conscious than expected.

Slovenia

Figure 10.15 contrasts the inferior CEOs and superior CEOs in Slovenia. Inferior Slovenian CEOs are more malevolent, more autocratic, more autonomous, and more internally competitive than expected. They are less inspirational, less performance oriented, less team integrator, less participative, and less performance oriented than expected. They also show less integrity than desired. Superior Slovenian CEOs are less autonomous than expected and show higher profiles in terms of the dimensions of Charismatic, Team-Oriented, and Participative leadership.

Figure 10.15   Slovenia CEOs With Superior and Inferior Levels of Top Management Team Dedication

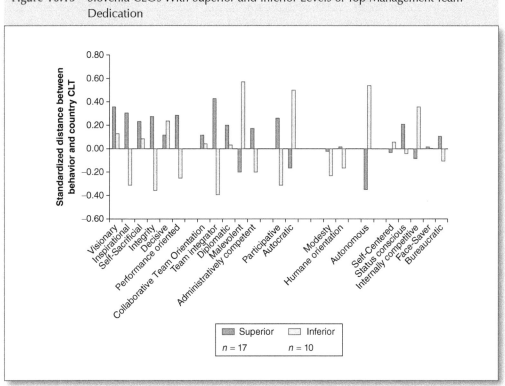

Spain

Figure 10.16 contrasts the inferior CEOs and superior CEOs in Spain. Superior and inferior Spanish CEOs have an almost-perfect mirror image in terms of the dimensions of Charismatic and Team-Oriented leadership. With the exception of modesty, they show almost no differences in terms of Participative and Humane-Oriented leadership. Inferior CEOs are less autonomous than expected while superior CEOs are more status conscious and less internally competitive than desired.

Taiwan

Figure 10.17 contrasts the inferior CEOs and superior CEOs in Taiwan. The two groups show an almost-perfect mirror image in terms of the dimensions of Charismatic, Team-Oriented, Participative, and Autonomous leadership. Their profiles are reasonably close on Humane-Oriented and Self-Protective leadership with the exception that they are more self-centered and less humane oriented than expected.

Figure 10.16 Spain CEOs With Superior and Inferior Levels of Top Management Team Dedication

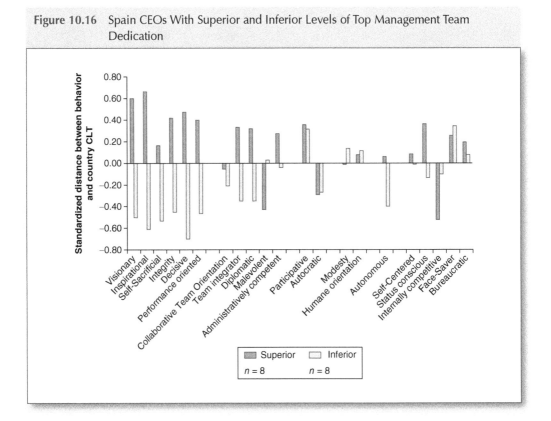

Figure 10.17   Taiwan CEOs With Superior and Inferior Levels of Top Management Team Dedication

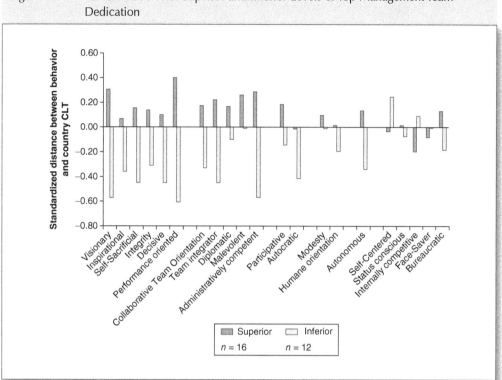

Turkey

Figure 10.18 contrasts the inferior CEOs and superior CEOs in Turkey. Inferior Turkish CEOs tend to match the CLT in most cases. Three major exceptions are that they are less collaborative, less team integrative, and less status conscious than expected. Superior Turkish CEOs exceed the CLT on almost all dimensions of CLT, with the exception of being autocratic, autonomous, self-centered, and face-saving where they match the CLT.

United States

Figure 10.19 contrasts the inferior CEOs and superior CEOs in the United States. The two groups present a mirror image on dimensions of Charismatic, Team-Oriented, Participative, and Self-Protective leadership. Superior CEOs greatly exceed expectations on all six Charismatic dimensions and also the Participative dimensions (i.e., more participative and less autocratic). They also are much less malevolent, status conscious, and internally competitive than expected. Superior and inferior CEOs have a similar profile on autonomy.

Figure 10.18   Turkey CEOs With Superior and Inferior Levels of Top Management Team
Dedication

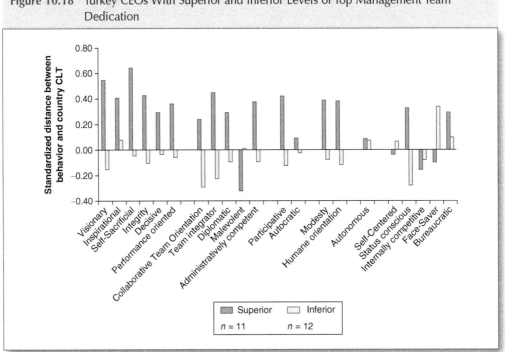

Figure 10.19   United States CEOs With Superior and Inferior Levels of Top Management
Dedication

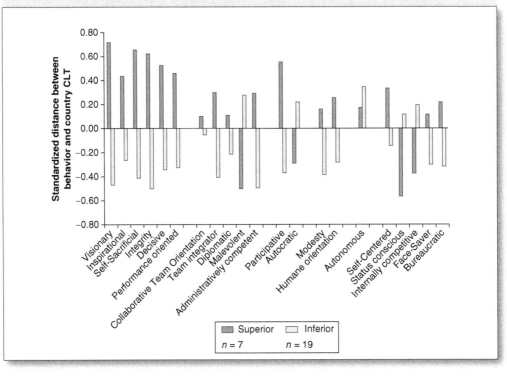

_____**Summary**

To conclude, the findings that were given shed light on how to be a superior or inferior CEO in different countries and leads to several important lessons:

- Higher than expected levels on the dimensions of Charismatic and Team-Oriented leadership clearly produce more effective leadership results in all countries in our sample except Russia.
- Higher than expected levels of participation can produce effective results in all countries in our sample except Estonia, Russia, the Netherlands, and Spain. In Estonia, superior CEOs match the CLT on Participative leadership, but inferior CEOs are less autocratic than the CLT. In Russia, inferior CEOs are actually considerably more participative as leaders than superior CEOs. In the Netherlands, inferior and superior CEOs have similar profiles on Participative leadership and are both close to the CLT. In Spain, inferior and superior CEOs have almost the same profile on Participative leadership, and they both differ from the CLT.
- Higher than expected levels of Humane-Oriented leadership can produce effective results in all countries in our sample except Estonia, Spain, and Slovenia. However, higher than expected levels of humane orientation can produce ineffective results in Russia.
- Higher than expected levels of autonomous leadership can produce effective results in countries like Austria, neutral results in countries like China, and negative results in countries like the United States.
- The global dimension of Self-Protective leadership does not generally distinguish between superior and inferior CEOs across countries. Among its constituent dimensions, face-saver and bureaucratic leadership tend to distinguish between superior and inferior CEOs in about half of the countries. Perhaps surprisingly, where it does make a difference, superior CEOs often exceed the inferior CEOs on these two dimensions.

11

Conclusions, Implications, and Future Research

The current GLOBE research project is an attempt to bridge across two separate streams of research—(1) cross-cultural leadership and (2) strategic leadership. Our overall objective is to understand the drivers and consequences of leadership at the highest level of organizations. Specifically, we examined the impact of societal cultural values and leadership expectations on how CEOs behave as leaders and the consequences of their behavior in terms of Top Management Team (TMT) Dedication and Firm Competitive Performance.

Our research has several distinct features. First, it is the first large-scale study of CEOs and TMTs across cultures and countries. We worked with almost 70 researchers to collect data from over 1,000 CEOs and over 5,000 senior executives in corporations in a variety of industries in 24 countries. Our sample of countries represents cultures in almost all cultural regions of the world. Second, the current research project is a continuation of the 20-year programmatic GLOBE research project that started in the early 1990s. The measures of leadership behavior used in the current project are based on earlier GLOBE findings of leadership expectations (culturally endorsed implicit leadership theories, or CLTs) across 62 societies (House, Hanges, Javidan, Dorfman, & Gupta, 2004). Each country CLT consists of 6 global and 21 primary dimensions of leadership behavior. Measures of leadership behavior were created based on the constituent leadership expectations in each society (see GLOBE 2004, for details). While some of these leadership behaviors (e.g., visionary) exist in the current leadership literature, others (e.g., self-protective leadership) are new additions to the extant literature.

Third, we used a multimethod, multiphase, and multisample approach including quantitative and qualitative research methods. For example, in addition to using survey research, our team of researchers held personal interviews with CEOs in their countries. This helps us triangulate our results so that we minimize the chance that our findings are due to methodological biases. Fourth, we controlled for common source bias by collecting data for different constructs from different sources. That is, we collected

CEO leadership behavior data from two groups of senior executives in the corporation and collected data regarding CEO effectiveness from a third group of executives. Fifth, we developed and used psychometrically sound leadership behavior and effectiveness scales, which are unidimensional, metrically equivalent across countries, and can be aggregated, to the CEO/ organization level.

Sixth, this is the first large-scale research project to directly and empirically examine the relationship between culture, leadership behavior, and societal leadership expectations. We created a new methodology and measure to assess the match (i.e., Gestalt Fit) between the actual leader behavior and societal leadership expectations. This fit measure assessed both the profile similarity and absolute behavioral similarity between leadership behavior and societal leadership expectations. We used a hierarchical linear modeling (HLM) statistical technique to test our hypotheses in a fashion consistent with the nested structure of our data. That is, recall that we collected data from multiple CEOs and multiple TMT members within each society. HLM provides unbiased assessment of our hypotheses by controlling for commonality of respondents in each society (Bliese & Hanges, 2004).

In this chapter, we provide a summary of our key findings and conclusions, as well as their academic and managerial applications. We also offer suggestions for future research on this important topic.

Summary of Key Findings

We define leadership as "the ability of an individual to influence, motivate, and enable others to contribute towards the effectiveness and success of the organizations in which they are members" (GLOBE 2004). Table 11.1 shows a summary of the six global leadership dimensions, which were identified in GLOBE 2004. Combined, they represent the ingredients of what we refer to as culturally endorsed implicit leadership theories (CLTs) across societies. They are the criteria that members of different societies use to assess their leaders. The following is a brief summary of findings reported in previous chapters.

Drivers of CEO Leadership Behavior

- Cultural values do not directly predict CEO leadership behavior. Using the nine GLOBE cultural dimensions, we found very few significant relationships between cultural values and the 6 global and 21 primary leadership behaviors. This is an important finding and one that is contrary to the conventional wisdom in the literature. While it is intuitively appealing to presume that leaders behave in accordance with the values of their society (Hofstede, 2001), our empirical findings pointed to a different direction.

Table 11.1 Culturally Endorsed Implicit Leadership Theory

Charismatic Leadership

Charismatic leaders inspire their followers with a desirable and realistic vision that is developed based on appropriate analysis and high performance expectations. They are viewed as sincere, decisive, and credible because of their integrity and willingness to sacrifice their own self-interest.

Team-Oriented Leadership

Team-Oriented leaders are loyal to their teams and care for the welfare of their team members. They use their administrative and interpersonal skills to manage the team's internal dynamics and to create a cohesive working group.

Participative Leadership

Participative leaders believe that employees can contribute to decision making and should be engaged in the process of decision making and implementation. They also believe that debate, discussion, and disagreement are a natural part of good decision making and should not be suppressed.

Humane-Oriented Leadership

Humane-Oriented leaders are unpretentious, show humility, and are reticent to boast. They are empathetic and likely to help and support team members in a humane manner by offering resources and other forms of assistance.

Autonomous Leadership

Autonomous leaders have extreme confidence in their own abilities and lack respect for others' abilities and ideas. They view themselves as unique and superior to others and as a result prefer to work independently and without much collaboration with colleagues or direct reports.

Self-Protective Leadership

Self-Protective leaders have a deep desire to succeed among a group of colleagues and direct reports who may act as competitors for the leaders' position and success. To protect themselves, they defer to positions of power, hide information that might advantage potential competitors, follow rules and policies to avoid risk, and interact carefully with others to ensure they leave a positive impression.

- Societal leadership expectations (i.e., CLTs) predict CEO leadership behavior. Our findings strongly suggest that leaders behave in accordance with their societies' leadership expectations. One possible explanation is that as individuals grow up, they learn what it means to be an effective leader in their society. They learn the criteria that are used, implicitly or explicitly, in their society to assess leaders. In GLOBE 2004, we showed that societal expectations of leadership are driven by cultural values. For example, societies that value performance orientation expect their leaders to be performance oriented (Dorfman, Hanges, & Brodbeck, 2004). Therefore, our current findings clarify the relationship between cultural values, societal leadership expectations, and leadership behavior. Specifically, leaders behave in a particular way not because of cultural values but because of what they believe will be effective in their society. Of course, as shown in GLOBE 2004, what leaders believe to be effective in their society is driven by the society's cultural values and aspirations. To summarize:

Cultural values → leadership expectations (CLTs) → leadership behavior.

Drivers of CEO Leadership Effectiveness—The Impact of Leadership Behavior

We used two measures of CEO effectiveness. The first measure was labeled *TMT Dedication*, which consisted of TMT Effort, Commitment, and Team Solidarity. The second measure was labeled *Firm Competitive Performance* and consisted of Competitive Sales Performance and Competitive Industry Dominance. As explained in Chapters 4 and 8, we controlled for common source bias by obtaining leadership behavior and outcome measures from different sources. Using HLM, we found that leadership behaviors represented by the six global leadership dimensions or the 21 primary leadership dimensions predict effectiveness. We then examined the relationship between each of the six global and 21 primary leadership dimensions on our two measures of CEO effectiveness and found the following:

CEO Leadership Behavior and Top Management Team Dedication

- Among the six global dimensions of CEO leadership behavior, Charismatic leadership behavior is consistently the most impactful leadership behavior on TMT Dedication. All six of the constituent dimensions of Charismatic leadership are important—in particular the most influential primary behaviors are visionary, inspirational, integrity, and performance-oriented leadership.

- CEO Team-Oriented behavior is the next most important global leadership behavior. Among the five constituent primary dimensions, being administratively competent and diplomatic are the most influential dimensions followed by team integrative leadership. Well-organized leaders who can plan and monitor the work of their teams and use their diplomatic and interpersonal skills to create synergy and cohesion tend to be more effective. While it is important to be a well-meaning leader who is supportive of group welfare (collaborative orientation), it is not as important as the aforementioned behaviors.
- Humane-Oriented leadership is also positively related to TMT Dedication. This global leadership dimension has a particularly strong and positive relationship with TMT Commitment.
- Participative leadership is moderately related to TMT Dedication as it is fourth most important in predicting TMT Dedication.
- Autonomous leadership is generally ineffective as it has a small but negative relationship with TMT Dedication.
- Self-Protective leadership does not have a significant relationship with TMT Dedication because some of its constituent primary dimensions (i.e., bureaucratic) have a significant and positive relationship with TMT Dedication while other constituent primary leadership behaviors (i.e., self-centered) have a negative relationship.

CEO Leadership Behavior and Firm Competitive Performance

- Our results show that three global leadership behaviors predict Firm Competitive Performance (Charismatic, Team-Oriented, and Humane-Oriented). None of the other global leadership behaviors had an impact on Firm Competitive Performance.
- Charismatic leadership had the strongest overall positive effect. All primary dimensions of Charismatic leadership predicted Firm Competitive Performance although visionary leadership is the most critical behavior.
- Team-Oriented leadership also had a positive impact on Firm Competitive Performance. Among the five constituent primary leadership behaviors, team integrator and administratively competent behaviors were the most important followed by diplomatic and collaborative behaviors. Similar to the TMT Dedication findings, leaders who are active in developing integrative teams (i.e., team integrator) tend to have more competitive firms than leaders who are simply well-meaning and supportive of group welfare (i.e., collaborative).
- Humane-Oriented leadership had a significant but smaller impact on Firm Competitive Performance than the other two global behaviors of Charismatic and Team-Oriented leadership.
- Participative, Autonomous, and Self-Protective leadership did not predict Firm Competitive Performance.

Table 11.2 provides a list of the primary leadership behaviors that predict both TMT Dedication and Firm Competitive Performance. It shows that four primary behaviors of inspirational, visionary, administratively competent, and performance oriented are among the top six behaviors predicting both outcome measures. CEOs who inspire their followers with a highly ambitious vision, set high performance expectations and goals, are well organized and effectively manage complex systems are likely to lead highly dedicated TMTs and produce successful results for their corporation.

Drivers of CEO Leadership Effectiveness—The Effect of Fit Between Behavior and Culturally Endorsed Implicit Leadership Theory

Our findings show that CEO leadership behavior is not the only predictor of CEO effectiveness. While CEOs need to behave in particular ways described previously (e.g., visionary), they also need to be cognizant of and sensitive to societal expectations of leaders. We created a measure of the extent to which CEO behavior matches societal leadership expectations (CLTs) and called it *fit*. Our measure of fit consists of two distinct elements—(1) the extent to which the CEO's overall behavioral profile matches the country CLT profile and (2) the gap between each CEO leadership behavior score and its corresponding CLT dimension score.

Our analyses showed that the overall fit between the entire set of 21 primary leadership behaviors and the entire set of country CLTs (i.e., Gestalt Fit) predicts CEO success in terms of TMT Dedication and Firm Competitive Performance. In other words, CEOs who behave in accordance with their country's leadership expectations are more likely to lead dedicated TMTs and successful corporations.

We conducted further analyses and found that among the six global leadership dimensions, Team-Oriented leadership is most sensitive to societal expectations. We previously defined Team-Oriented leadership as being loyal to the team, caring for the welfare of the team members, and using administrative and interpersonal skills to manage the team's internal dynamics and to create a cohesive working group. As explained earlier in this chapter, Team-Oriented leadership results in CEO effectiveness. However, our analyses in GLOBE 2004 show that societies differ in the extent to which they want leaders to be team oriented. Our current fit analysis shows that CEOs need to behave accordingly to be successful.

We found similar, although more limited, findings regarding Participative leadership. Our fit analyses showed that the fit between CEO Participative behavior and the country's Participative CLT predicts CEO effectiveness in terms of TMT Dedication but not in terms of Firm Competitive Performance. Those CEOs whose participative leadership style matches their country's leadership expectations tend to lead dedicated TMTs. GLOBE 2004 showed that societies differ in the extent to which they want leaders

Table 11.2   Rank Order of Primary CEO Leadership Behaviors Predicting Top Management Team Dedication and Firm Competitive Performance

	TMT Dedication		Firm Competitive Performance		
Highest	**Leadership Behavior**	**Correlation**	**Leadership Behavior**	**Correlation**	Highest
	Inspirational (C)	.36**	Visionary (C)	.29**	
	Visionary (C)	.35**	Team integrator (TO)	.26**	
	Integrity (C)	.35**	Administratively competent (TO)	.24**	
	Performance oriented (C)	.33**	Decisive (C)	.23**	
	Administratively competent (TO)	.31**	Inspirational (C)	.19**	
	Diplomatic (TO)	.31**	Performance oriented (C)	.16*	
	Self-Sacrificial (C)	.29**	Integrity (C)	.16*	
	Humane orientation (HO)	.26**	Diplomatic (TO)	.16*	
	Team integrator (TO)	.24**	Collaborative team orientation (TO)	.14*	
	Decisive (C)	.23**	Self-Sacrificial (C)	.13*	
	Bureaucratic (SP)	.23**	Modesty (HO)	.13†	Lowest
	Participative (P)	.22**			
	Malevolent (TO)	−.22**			
	Internally competitive (SP)	−.19**			
	Collaborative team orientation (TO)	.18**			
	Modesty (HO)	.17**			
	Autocratic (P)	−.12**			
	Status conscious (SP)	.11**			
Lowest	Self-centered (SP)	−.11**			
	Autonomous (A)	−.07*			

Note: The primary leadership dimension is contained in the global leadership behavior dimension shown in the parentheses: C = Charismatic; TO = Team Oriented; P = Participative; HO = Humane Oriented; A = Autonomous; SP = Self-Protective.

$N = 998$ for TMT Dedication. $N = 255$ for Firm Competitive Performance.

† $p < .10$. * $p < .05$. ** $p < .01$.

to be participative. Our fit analysis shows that CEOs need to behave accordingly to be successful.

The findings that were just summarized show that to be effective CEOs need to behave in particular ways and at the same time, need to act according to the leadership expectations in their societies. To further understand the impact of behavior and fit, in Chapter 10, we compared the superior and inferior CEOs in each country and across countries. We compared the extent to which their behavior matches the CLT in their countries. Superior CEOs are those who are extremely effective in creating highly dedicated teams of senior executives or high-performing firms. Inferior CEOs are those who are extremely ineffective in creating highly dedicated teams of senior executives or high-performing firms.

Our results showed that superior CEOs and inferior CEOs present mirror images in the sense that the former exceed their countries' CLT in terms of Charismatic, Team-Oriented, Humane-Oriented, and Participative leadership while the latter fall substantially short of CLT. To produce superior outcomes, CEOs across countries need to exceed their societies' expectations in terms of many of the 21 primary and 6 global dimensions of leadership. However, while exceeding expectations, they need to also be cognizant of the overall profile of the CLT. In other words, the CLT of a society acts as a constraint on leaders not in terms of the individual dimensions but in terms of the overall profile of the 6 or 21 dimensions. To succeed, CEOs need to exceed expectations on several key dimensions (e.g., visionary) but in a way that their overall behavioral profile does not drastically deviate from the CLT profile across 21 leadership dimensions.

Theoretical Contributions and Implications for Theory Development

Our research offers important contributions to several streams of scholarly work. In the following sections, we will highlight our key contributions.

Cultural Context and Culturally Endorsed Leadership: The Development of Implicit Leadership Theories and Culturally Endorsed Implicit Leadership Theories

As noted earlier in the book, GLOBE built on the foundation of *implicit leadership theory* (ILT) (Lord & Maher, 1991) to develop our culturally endorsed implicit leadership theory (CLT) (House et al., 2004). The theoretical basis of ILTs originated from the work by Rosch (1975) and Lord and colleagues (Lord, Foti, & De Vader, 1984; Lord & Maher, 1990). They argued that beliefs about the characteristics, attributes, and behaviors typical of a leader are clustered in memory structures called schemas. According to ILT, leadership is an attribution process that occurs when there is substantial overlap between a particular person's schema of leadership and that of the person they are assessing (i.e., a possible leader) (Fiske & Taylor, 1991; Hanges, Dorfman, Shteynberg, & Bates, 2006; House, Wright, & Aditya, 1997; Shaw, 1990). We believe that the findings from the current GLOBE project have important theoretical implications for both ILT and CLT theories.

First, we can conclusively point to a societal culture's impact on the development of the society's leadership expectations. GLOBE 2004 presented empirical evidence that societal CLTs are related to societal cultural values (e.g., societal Performance-Oriented cultural values are related to the desirability of Participative leadership). Numerous examples demonstrate how societal and organizational cultures can shape the ILT of their members. For example, in countries with relatively low Power Distance values, such as Denmark, family decisions are made with extensive discussion and debate with the participation of all family members. It is therefore not surprising that the predominant ILT in such societies reflects consensus building and participation rather than autocratic decision making. As adults, employees in organizations in such societies are not accepting of high Power Distance values and autocratic leadership styles in their organizations. Instead, they prefer a more participative and egalitarian approach to leadership.

Another example can be seen in countries with relatively high family oriented values, such as Mexico. In such countries, respect for the family and trust among family members tilts the country's ILT toward paternalism and nepotism. The radius of trust tends to be short, and the notion of trust takes a personal context. People trust only those whom they spend much time with and get to know deeply. As a result, the ILTs in these societies tend to emphasize that effective leaders are those that support in-groups and cliques who can be trusted to get the work done.

Second, societal leadership expectations (CLTs) have real-world consequences on leadership behaviors—they are not imaginary constructs lacking in important outcomes. As shown in the current project, leaders generally enact behaviors consistent with societal leadership expectations. An important question that therefore needs to be answered concerns the development of ILTs: How do people come to understand the nature of leadership and relationships to authority figures? Research findings point out the importance of personal experience, social relationships, and personality factors in the formation of ILTs (Keller, 2003, Shondrick, Dinh, & Lord, 2010). That is, experience with role models, such as parents and caregivers, provide an early understanding of typical relationships with authority figures. Further experiences with teachers, coaches, siblings, friends, and authority relations with managers as well as political leaders help individuals encode specific attributes being important for leadership effectiveness. The findings from the GLOBE 2004 project provided rigorous empirical evidence that societal culture influences the development of societal expectations (CLTs). Furthermore, the current project provides empirical evidence that CLTs subsequently influence leadership behaviors. This should not be surprising in that leaders are socialized into and internalize the cultural values and practices of the culture they grow up in. They learn over time what are the desirable and undesirable modes of leadership behavior—what works and what is counterproductive in leading others and being led themselves.

Third, societal leadership expectations through CLTs have significant implications for leadership effectiveness. The totality of evidence in the current project points to the importance of enacting many leadership behaviors that are linked to ILT and CLTs. The results of the Gestalt Fit analysis empirically showed that the style of leadership exhibited by a CEO needs to be consistent with societal expectations. Recall that fit is composed of two linked constructs—(1) the absolute amount of behavioral and (2) pattern similarity. In sum, superior leaders tend to follow the societal expectations as determined by the pattern of leadership expectations required in their society, but these superior leaders need to enact (and exceed) the expected level of these behaviors.

In summary, although ILT was developed with interindividual variation in mind, strong evidence exists that it can be extended to the organizational and national cultural level of analysis (GLOBE 2004). A society's culture reflects some collective agreement on meanings and interpretations of events. Such agreements turn into social influences by producing "a set of compelling behavioural, affective, and attitudinal orientations and values for the members" (House et al., 1997, p. 538). We agree with Triandis's (1993) assertion that the cultural value orientations in a country will determine the optimum leadership profile for that country. He went on to suggest that while there are some universal attributes of management systems, each distinct culture may have a distinct management style that is both moderated and directly influenced by culture. GLOBE supports his conclusion.

Leadership Taxonomies and GLOBE Leadership Theory

The two layers of GLOBE leadership dimensions (i.e., the 6 global and 21 primary dimensions) were created as the result of a combination of theory development and rigorous and systematic empirical research. These leadership dimensions are a critical part of the GLOBE culturally endorsed implicit leadership theory (CLT). In the 20-plus years of the project, we endeavored to systematically proceed through several stages of understanding and measuring dimensions of culture, providing an explanation for societal leadership expectations (i.e., CLTs), linking cultural dimension values to CLTs, and finally examining the link between CLTs and behavior and effectiveness. The GLOBE taxonomy of 6 global and 21 primary dimensions of leadership has remained constant throughout the project.

We have strived to maintain consistency in constructs, definitions, and behavioral manifestations of variables comprising the GLOBE model. There are several aspects of the GLOBE leadership taxonomy and behavioral constructs that bear mention.

First, we do not claim to have developed a comprehensive and exhaustive set of leadership behaviors encompassing all possible leadership behaviors and sets of leadership behaviors found in the literature. Taxonomies may be more or less inclusive depending on the particular leadership theory (e.g., transformational leadership vs. flexible leadership theory [FLT]), purpose (e.g., facilitate research or suggest practitioner implications), level of abstraction (e.g., meta-categories vs. specific behavior categories), or focus of influence (motivate subordinates or leading groups). In other words, taxonomies are diverse and "no absolute set of 'correct' behavior categories can be established" (Yukl, 2013, p. 49). Yukl (2012) further noted that "to be highly useful for designing research and formulating theories, leader behavior categories should be observable, distinct, measurable, and relevant for many types of leaders . . . " (p. 66). He went on to note that some taxonomies include other constructs in addition to behaviors such as leadership knowledge, skills, roles, and personality constructs in addition to leadership behaviors.

The GLOBE leadership taxonomy is an example of the latter. While our research survey is behaviorally based, we included a wide variety of constructs that are important for leadership effectiveness at multiple organizational levels—mid-level and upper echelon leaders. We did not limit ourselves to using only the leadership behaviors and theories found in existing Western leadership literature in the 1990s (e.g., task-oriented behaviors vs. relationship-oriented behaviors) or in recent theories emphasizing charismatic and transformational (C/T) leadership. Instead, the GLOBE set of leadership behaviors is comprised of previous behavioral constructs (e.g., relationships and interactions with subordinates) but also included traits (e.g., integrity) and personality characteristics (e.g., modesty) that were empirically developed (see GLOBE 2004). An examination of Table 11.1 shows the inclusive nature of constructs within the definitions of our six global leadership behaviors.

Including a wide range of attributes allows a more comprehensive understanding of leadership behavior and effectiveness at the highest levels of organizations. Yukl (2012) noted that observable leadership behaviors are not the same as skills, values, personality traits, or roles even though these are important constructs and useful for understanding effective leadership. We agree, but the GLOBE set of 21 primary leadership behaviors define each construct in terms of observable behaviors. For instance, while integrity is a trait and modesty is a personality characteristic, multiple behavioral items were used in our study to measure each. Specifically, nine behavioral items were developed to measure CEO integrity (e.g., speaks and acts truthfully) and four behavioral items were developed to measure modesty (e.g., does not boast, presents self in a humble manner). See Appendix B for a list of all leadership items. Given the more than satisfactory psychometric properties of these scales, we feel confident that respondents could respond intelligently about their CEO in describing his/her behavior without being confused as to the meaning of the behaviors.

Another important aspect of our approach is that the GLOBE taxonomy sufficiently covers relevant task behaviors commonly classified as managerial rather than leadership (e.g., planning and problem solving). For instance, the administratively competent primary dimension of leadership contains several task behaviors related to planning, coordinating, and organizing individuals. This is due to our belief that separating leadership from management may be intuitively appealing but does not represent the realities of executives in senior positions. Of course, the GLOBE taxonomy also included relationship-oriented behaviors (e.g., collaborative, team integrator, and participative). Change-oriented behaviors are more than adequately covered in the visionary primary dimension of leadership. In short, the GLOBE taxonomy includes a variety of leadership behaviors, traits, and personality characteristics, all of which were behaviorally defined and measured.

GLOBE's Culturally Endorsed Implicit Leadership Theory: Support for Hypothesized Relationships and Remaining Theoretical Relationships to Be Studied

GLOBE 2004 presented a model linking societal culture to various societal outcomes, leadership processes, behaviors, and effectiveness. The central proposition in GLOBE's research continues to be that the attributes and characteristics that differentiate societal cultures from each other lead to organizational practices and leader attributes/behaviors that will be frequently enacted and effective in that culture. The current version of the GLOBE model, which we presented in Chapters 1 (Figure 1.1) and 3 (Figure 3.1) and reproduced in this chapter (see Figure 11.1), is coded in the following way. Constructs and relationships shown by solid lines refer to relationships among constructs tested in the previous phases of GLOBE. Relationships shown by dashed lines were tested in the present study. As stated in the previous chapters and summarized previously, we now are in a better position to understand how societal leadership expectations relate to CEO leadership behavior and effectiveness.

Findings from the current GLOBE CEO study support a number of hypothesized relationships in the GLOBE theoretical model (Figure 11.1). First, we provide strong empirical evidence that societal leadership expectations (i.e., CLTs) influence the kind and amount of leadership enacted by CEOs. That is, the desirability of CLTs found in a society has a direct link to the level of leadership behavior enacted on almost all leadership dimensions (e.g., level of country CLTs for Participative leadership predicts CEO

Participative behavior). Second, leadership effectiveness is predicted by the enactment of many but not all leadership behaviors. For example, we found that our Charismatic leadership dimension positively predicted both TMT Dedication and Firm Competitive Performance. In contrast, Autonomous leadership had a slight negative impact. Third, we found that useful information was obtained when we examined the primary leadership dimensions in addition to the global leadership dimension. For instance, while the global Self-Protective leadership behavior had essentially no direct effect on effectiveness, two of the constituent dimensions had positive effects (i.e., status conscious and bureaucratic) and two had negative effects (i.e., internally competitive and self-centered). Fourth, the Gestalt Fit analysis demonstrated that leadership effectiveness depends on the match between CEO leadership behavior and societal leadership expectations. Simply put, *Gestalt Fit* predicted CEO effectiveness for both TMT Dedication and Firm Competitive Performance. Fifth, in contrast to commonly held views in the cross-cultural literature, we did not find a direct relationship between societal culture and leadership enactment. As indicated previously, the impact of societal culture on leadership behavior was indirect—through societal leadership expectations.

Figure 11.1   Modified GLOBE Theoretical Model 2013

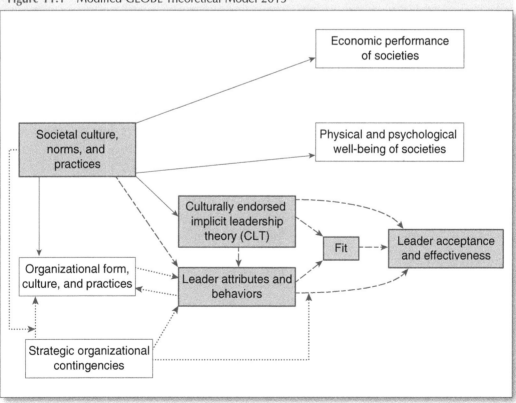

Before leaving our discussion of the GLOBE model, we want to point out that relationships shown by dotted lines will be examined in future research. These include understanding the interaction between societal *and* organizational culture as they impact leadership behavior and effectiveness. Recall that GLOBE 2004 showed that societal culture has a direct impact on organizational culture, and this generally occurred in an isomorphic manner (e.g., performance-oriented societal cultures spawn performance-oriented organizations). These relationships studied in GLOBE 2004 only focused on the GLOBE cultural dimensions for *both* societal and organizational culture. Clearly, however, many other dimensions of organizational culture have been found to be important (e.g., culture for innovation, aggression, team orientation, and decisiveness; O'Reilly, Chatman, & Caldwell, 1991). A more comprehensive understanding of how societal culture affects these and other aspects of organizational culture and practices remains to be understood.

We know that a CEO's values are influenced by societal culture, and these values are often imbued in an organizational culture over time. As a result, organizational practices such as reward structures likely reflect CEO values such that an increased level of entrepreneurial activity and creativity can be expected in organizations where the CEOs value innovation and risk-taking. However, the conversion process by which CEO values are enacted into executive action and the all-encompassing influence of societal culture process on this conversion is wide open for research (Finkelstein, Hambrick, & Cannella, 2009). As a concrete example, one can envision the following strategic leadership question linking societal culture to CEO values and organizational practices: To what extent will the societal cultural dimension of Power Distance affect a CEO's vision, selective perception, and interpretation of information? Many such research questions can be subsumed under the meta-question related to the role of societal culture in shaping the leadership functions in influencing organizational culture and practices.

In addition, the other main construct in the model yet to be studied concerns how strategic organizational contingencies (e.g., size, organizational environment, technological sophistication) affect organizational form, culture, and practices that in turn impact leadership behavior and effectiveness. The central proposition of structural contingency theory is that there is a set of demands that are imposed on organizations that must be met for them to ensure survival and guarantee effectiveness. These demands are referred to as organizational contingencies. It is asserted that these contingencies influence organizational form and practice and that congruence between the demands of the contingencies and organizational form and practice is associated with organizational effectiveness. While some have asserted that the propositions of structural contingency theory are universal and culturally transcendent (cf. Hickson, Hinings, McMillan, and Schwitter, 1974), its empirical verification is very limited to small sample studies of organizations in industrialized countries (House et al., 1997).

It seems reasonable that to remain viable, organizational practices need to be directed toward meeting requirements imposed by organizational contingencies such as rapidly changing technology (Donaldson, 1993; Lawrence & Lorsch, 1967). Societal culture is expected to influence a number of relationships between strategic organizational contingencies and organizational forms and practices. Future GLOBE research should strive to untangle the role of culture and strategic organizational contingencies in influencing leadership behavior and effectiveness.

Integrating the GLOBE Study Findings Into the Leadership and Cross-Cultural Literature

As described in the previous chapters, our findings support the conclusion that CEO leadership behavior has an impressive impact on TMT Dedication and Firm Competitive Performance. This part of the conclusions chapter provides a closer look at our findings in relation to the existing leadership literature and more specifically to the cross-cultural leadership literature. While it is informative to review the linkage between GLOBE's 21 primary leadership dimensions and the corresponding literature, for ease of discussion, this review is organized according to the 6 global leadership dimensions.

Do GLOBE's Findings Support the Existing Charismatic and Transformational Leadership Literature?

GLOBE's definition of Charismatic leadership provided earlier in the book indicates that *charismatic leaders inspire their followers with a desirable and realistic vision that is developed based on appropriate analysis and high performance expectations. They are viewed as sincere, decisive, and credible because of their integrity and willingness to sacrifice their own self-interest.*

The research from hundreds of non-GLOBE research studies, including those completed in Western and non-Western countries, clearly supports many of the key propositions of charismatic and transformational (C/T) leadership (Yukl, 2013). In fact, charisma was initially identified as a key factor in transformational leadership, but it was later relabeled as idealized influence "because of the popular meaning of charisma in the public mind as being celebrated, flamboyant, exciting and arousing" (Bass, 2008, p. 620). The relabeling of constructs is emblematic of a major problem in reviewing the effectiveness of C/T leadership in the literature. Unfortunately, there are many versions of C/T leadership in the literature with each having a set of behaviors that vary among and within theories. Nevertheless, GLOBE's definition and measurement of Charismatic leadership is consistent with the core set of behaviors (e.g., visionary) and motivational effects (e.g., meeting challenging expectations) of charismatic theories. Leaders who embody charismatic qualities and associated behaviors are more likely to be successful than those who don't (DeGroot, Kiker, & Cross, 2000). Bass (1997) provided evidence regarding the universality of transformational leadership leading to leadership effectiveness worldwide. Our present findings support the positive assessment found in most previous studies of Charismatic leadership.

GLOBE's Insights Into Charismatic and Transformational Leadership

Because there are many versions of charismatic theories, there is great difficulty in teasing out which elements are most critical. This is particularly true when trying to understand effects of charismatic leadership in cross-cultural studies. Our findings speak to this issue.

Before presenting our insights, we need to again point out that there is an unfortunate use of the terms charisma and charismatic leadership in the popular press. The terms have come to stand for a leader with a flamboyant, showy, and flashy demeanor and are used haphazardly when discussing favorite media personalities (e.g., Donald Trump). Recall that this was the reason Bass and Avolio (1990) changed their charismatic leadership behavioral dimension to "idealized influence" so as not to confuse the popular media hype with actual leadership behaviors. As it is quite clear from our primary leadership dimensions within our global Charismatic leadership dimension, our concept of charismatic leadership has nothing to do with the media version of flamboyance, showiness, and grandiosity. While we do not offer a new charismatic theory, GLOBE findings can point to several new discoveries and conclusions.

First, across all the countries in our study, we found that CEOs are reported to show a high level of Charismatic leadership behavior—it was the highest level among the six GLOBE leadership behaviors (see Chapter 7, Table 7.2). Second, because our cross-cultural CEO sample covers a wide range of countries, we have evidence supporting the universal effectiveness of Charismatic leadership. While Bass (1997) provided evidence from a variety of studies regarding the effectiveness of transformational leadership, none included the variety of countries nor the numbers of senior level executives as does the current CEO study. Considering both dependent variables in tandem, it was the most effective leadership behavior of all leadership dimensions when contrasted with our other global leadership behaviors. That is, our results show that Charismatic leadership is universally effective for both internally oriented dependent measures of TMT Dedication as well as externally oriented measures of Firm Competitive Performance.

Third, the GLOBE Charismatic leadership construct introduces additional leadership behaviors not explicitly found and measured in existing charismatic or transformational theories (i.e., decisiveness, integrity, and performance orientation). For example, for a long time integrity was not an explicit component of charismatic/transformational leadership. Only recently has this been changed with the introduction of the concept of authenticity. Transformational leaders who have integrity are labeled authentic whereas transformational leaders who lack integrity are inauthentic (Bass & Steidlmeier, 1999). Furthermore, high performance orientation is associated with charismatic and transformational (C/T) leadership but previously has not been explicitly incorporated in measures of C/T leadership. Similarly, decisiveness has not been incorporated in measures of C/T leadership. In sum, our research supports the inclusion of these new charismatic and transformational constructs.

Fourth, while all six GLOBE primary leadership behaviors in our Charismatic construct predicted TMT Dedication, four stand out in importance. They are visionary, inspirational, integrity, and performance-oriented leadership. For the other dependent variable, Firm Competitive Performance, visionary leadership tops the list even though the remaining five also significantly predict firm performance.

Fifth, the general lack of statistically significant moderating effects using "nation" as a surrogate of culture indicates that Charismatic leadership should be considered a universally effective leadership dimension in all cultures. However, societal expectations (i.e., CLTs) are important even for this universally effective leadership behavior. Recall that *superior CEOs in terms of TMT Dedication and Firm Competitive Performance enact Charismatic behaviors that exceed the society's leadership expectations (i.e., CLTs) whereas inferior CEOs fall short of their society's expectations.* Thus, the CLT appears to be the dividing line distinguishing superior from inferior CEOs. This is particularly true for the primary Charismatic behaviors of visionary, inspirational, integrity, and performance-oriented behaviors. Going one step further, in examining CEOs whose outcomes include *both* high TMT Dedication and high Firm Competitive Performance, we find that Charismatic leadership behavior is critical—again particularly with respect to the primary leadership dimensions of visionary and performance oriented behaviors.

Lastly, while most if not all charismatic theories include the personal identification with an extraordinary leader as a central component, we should point out that none of the GLOBE primary dimensions reflect the actual personal identification with their CEO. The omission of personal identification was deliberate as we intended to separate CEO Charismatic behaviors from the confounding aspect of "attributed charisma." The notion of leadership as an attribution, or as "a romantic figment of the imagination," created problems in interpreting early charismatic theories (Bass, 2008). In the present study, we behaviorally defined all the Charismatic dimensions so as to minimize the influence of attributions into our survey. We believe that for leaders to effectively use GLOBE findings regarding Charismatic leadership, they should pay attention to the six primary leadership behaviors found in the GLOBE Charismatic dimension.

Do GLOBE's Findings Support the Existing Team-Oriented Leadership Literature?

Many competent reviews of leadership in groups and teams are available (Aguinis & Kraiger, 2009; Burke et al., 2006), and in fact, we do know a good deal about creating effective teams (cf. Hackman, 2002). What we do not know very much about, however, is team leadership from a cross-cultural perspective because there simply are not many cross-cultural studies of Team-Oriented leadership. Furthermore, what studies exist typically employ leadership measures not specifically designed to directly test the importance of Team-Oriented leader behaviors but instead use commonly found measures in the leadership literature. For example, the Wendt, Euwema, and Van Emmerik (2009) study using a large cross-cultural database from the Hay Group (mentioned in Chapter 2) employs measures of supportive and directive leadership in their study of team cohesiveness. As another example, the study of transformational leadership in Korea by Jung, Butler, and Baik (1998) found that this leadership style was highly correlated with group cohesiveness.

The GLOBE Team-Oriented leadership dimension is defined in terms of effective team-building and implementation of a common purpose and goal among team members.

GLOBE's Team-Oriented leadership behavior indicates that *Team-Oriented leaders are loyal to their teams and care for the welfare of their team members. They use their administrative and interpersonal skills to manage the team's internal dynamics and to create a cohesive working group.*

To start with, the GLOBE Team-Oriented leadership behavior supports the somewhat obvious conclusion that the leadership of teams is important given the ubiquitous use of teams in modern organizations. Consider that the initial GLOBE analysis of CLT data reported in 2004 revealed that Team-Oriented leadership is perceived globally to be at least somewhat important in enhancing effective leadership—all cultures had absolute scores exceeding 5.0, and most exceeded 5.6 of the GLOBE 7-point scale of qualities leading to outstanding leadership. When examining the results, the Southern Asia, Confucian Asia, Eastern Europe, and Latin America clusters reported Team-Oriented leadership to be particularly critical for effective leadership. While this data provides evidence regarding the perceived importance of Team-Oriented leadership, it does not speak to the issue of actual CEO behaviors. For this information, we have to point to the current CEO study. Here we find that it was the second highest level of CEO behavioral enactment for all the GLOBE leadership behaviors (see Chapter 7, Table 7.2). As discussed next, our current study provides a wealth of new information regarding the enactment and effectiveness of Team-Oriented leadership.

GLOBE's Insights Into Team-Oriented Leadership

As indicated previously, this GLOBE study differs from previous cross-cultural studies in several ways. First, GLOBE researchers developed new measures of Team-Oriented leadership instead of employing leadership measures found in the literature that are more tangential to team effectiveness (e.g., supportive leadership). GLOBE researchers developed a new way of thinking about team-oriented leadership and subsequently created behavioral indicators of this construct that were used in the current study. Initially, the Team-Oriented leadership dimension resulted from a factor analysis of GLOBE 2004 data on societal leadership expectations (i.e., CLTs). This analysis also generated separate facets of Team-Oriented leadership, providing a five-dimension structure of this leadership construct. Two of these five dimensions—collaborative team orientation and team integration—are easily envisioned as important for a construct labeled team orientation. The remaining three constructs (i.e., diplomatic, malevolent (reverse scored) and administratively competent) were also determined to be part of this leadership dimension. Effective leaders should be skilled at interpersonal relations (i.e., diplomatic), not interpersonally destructive (i.e., not malevolent), and effective in managing complex teams (i.e., administratively competent). We further note that the dimension labeled *malevolent* is conceptually connected to the popular term *toxic leadership,* and these types of leaders have been predicted to be particularly destructive to the team morale (Schmidt, 2013). Thus, despite the variety of constructs in the Team-Oriented dimension, they are conceptually linked through a common thread of understanding how a leader manages team dynamics and promotes teamwork.

Second, in terms of predicting our overall measure of TMT Dedication, Team-Oriented behaviors were the second most impactful following that of Charismatic leadership. In addition, the Team-Oriented global measure also impacted our externally oriented dependent measure of Firm Competitive Performance.

Third, the current literature on team leadership is mostly silent on whether its requisite competencies are similar across cultures. Our fit analysis findings presented in Chapter 9 demonstrated that matching societal expectations for the profile of Team-Oriented dimensions significantly predicts the overall effectiveness for TMT Dedication and Firm Competitive Performance. As expected, the closer the fit between the leadership expectations and leadership behavior, the more effective the leader.

Finally, our findings related to administrative competence is consistent with Mintzberg (2006), who, while agreeing with other researchers that strategic management roles such as developing a vision and inspiring followers are critical, asserted that being a competent manager is also critical to effective leadership—good management and leadership cannot be separated. Administratively competent leaders embody management skills of being well-organized and able to coordinate and control the efforts of many individuals. In short, they can manage complex administrative systems by being orderly and methodical. Mintzberg (2006) went so far as to suggest that "separating leadership from management is part of the problem . . . Does anyone want to work for a manager who lacks the qualities of leadership . . . ? Well, how about a leader who doesn't practice management?"

Do GLOBE's Findings Support the Existing Participatory Leadership Literature?

GLOBE 2004 found that participative leadership does not have the same cache in all cultures as it does in Western cultures. For instance, while employees in the United States typically desire to have an input in the management decision-making process, the same may not be true for employees in high Power Distance cultures (GLOBE 2004). We noted in Chapter 2 that participatory leadership is often described in terms of a continua (cf. Heller & Wilpert, 1981; Vroom & Jago, 1988) where extremes are characterized from decisions made by supervisors without asking for input by others (i.e., autocratic and/or directive leadership) to subordinates being given complete authority and responsibility (i.e., delegation). Participation falls somewhere in between and may take the form of consultation and/or joint decisions to arrive at a conclusive decision.

The effects of participative leadership have been the object of hundreds, if not thousands, of studies, but as noted by Yukl (2013), "the results from research on the effects of participative leadership are not sufficiently strong and consistent enough to draw any firm conclusions . . . [it] sometimes results in higher satisfaction, effort, and performance, and at other times it does not" (p. 111).

GLOBE's Insights Into Participative Leadership

Early on in the GLOBE project (2004), researchers determined that cultures varied considerably in the *endorsement* of the Participative leadership dimension. Participative leadership was highly desired in societies that value

Performance Orientation, Gender Egalitarianism, and Humane Orientation but less so for societies with high cultural values for Power Distance, Uncertainty Avoidance, and Assertiveness.

To our knowledge, there are no studies that have explored the level of participatory leadership around the world. The importance of culture regarding CEO participatory leadership effectiveness has never been empirically demonstrated before. Our study is the first that shows that CEOs across all cultures were moderately participative (see Chapter 7, Table 7.2). Further, the Participative global dimension was predictive of TMT Dedication but not Firm Competitive Performance. Overall it was the fourth most positive global leadership dimension predicting Dedication following Charismatic, Team-Oriented, and Humane-Oriented global leadership dimensions.

The global dimension of Participative leadership consists of two primary behaviors: (1) participation and (2) autocratic (reverse coded). Consistent with the idea that participation varies across cultures, we found that the primary dimension of participation significantly varies across cultures when predicting TMT Commitment. Further, when examining the results for the superior and inferior CEOs, the role of culture emerged again. CEOs who exceed their society's expectations for Participative leadership can expect more dedicated TMT members.

Do GLOBE's Findings Support the Existing Humane-Oriented Leadership Literature?

Because the GLOBE Humane-Oriented leadership dimension is new, it is impossible to directly compare the GLOBE findings to the previous research. Given this fact, it follows that we know of no cross-cultural behavioral research investigating the cross-cultural effectiveness of Humane-Oriented leadership. The closest we might come to prior research informing the GLOBE construct are earlier studies examining "relationship behaviors," which were part of The Ohio State University (e.g., Fleishman, 1953; Fleishman, Harris, & Burtt, 1955) and University of Michigan research programs (Bowers & Seashore, 1966; Likert, 1961, 1967). As noted by Yukl (2013), relations-oriented behaviors include a variety of behaviors that demonstrate empathy and a concern for the needs and feelings of followers.

Recent cross-cultural studies continue to support previous findings (Dorfman, 2004) that worldwide, considerate and supportive leadership behaviors will increase subordinates' satisfaction with both their job and their supervisor (Agarwal, DeCarlo, & Vyas, 1999; Bass, 2008; Euwema, Wendt, & van Emmerik, 2007; Lok & Crawford, 2004; Wendt, Euwema, & Van Emmerik, 2009). The near universality of positive effects for leader supportiveness with respect to employee attitudes should not be surprising since supportive leaders show concern for followers and are considerate and available to listen to followers' problems.

The current leadership literature evidence regarding a "people-oriented" leadership dimension for firm performance is not nearly so clear. As indicated in Bass (2008), supportive and considerate leadership behaviors are not consistently related to group productivity. Contrary findings have occasionally been found. For example, an empirical study of top-level Chinese managers found that showing benevolence (i.e., showing love and care for subordinates) was related to both employee attitudes and firm performance (the latter through employee attitudes such as organizational commitment) (Wang, Tsui, & Xin, 2011). Consistent with the past literature on supportive and considerate leadership, we found that CEO Humane-Oriented leadership impacts TMT Dedication. In contrast to the majority of leadership studies on the supportive–performance relationship, we also found humane orientation predicting firm performance.

GLOBE's Insights Into Humane-Oriented Leadership

The GLOBE Humane-Oriented leadership dimension was comprised of two primary dimensions: (1) modesty and (2) humane orientation. We again point this out because while one aspect of Humane-Oriented leadership—humane orientation—is related to supportive leadership, the modesty dimension is entirely new. The humane orientation primary dimension emphasizes empathy for others by giving time, resources, and assistance when needed and showing concern for follower's personal welfare. The modesty primary dimension reflects leaders who do not boast, are modest, and present themselves in a humble manner. These qualities and behaviors related to modesty are likely to be most important in Asian countries but not typically considered in Western leadership research. The development of the Humane-Oriented leadership dimension can be found in GLOBE 2004 (House et al., 2004).

According to GLOBE's definition, *Humane-Oriented leaders are unpretentious, show humility, and are reticent to boast. They are empathetic and likely to help and support team members in a humane manner by offering resources and other forms of assistance.* Relying on past research complementary to Humane-Oriented leadership, we anticipated that this dimension will have some positive outcomes because of its similarity to supportive leadership. In the current study, the CEOs exhibited a moderate level of Humane-Oriented Leadership (see Chapter 7, Table 7.2).

Humane-Oriented leadership had its largest impact on TMT Commitment. In fact, it had the *highest* correlation among all leadership behaviors and dependent variables! Its effectiveness was also apparent with regard to TMT Effort and Team Solidarity. Perhaps we should not be surprised that TMT Commitment was substantially elevated when CEOs looked out for direct reports' welfare, were willing to give resources to them, and behaved empathetically.

What is the evidence regarding the effectiveness of this leadership dimension differing across cultures? At first glance, we have a somewhat mixed picture as "culture" was a marginally significant moderator for the global Humane-Oriented dimension. However, a more informative picture appears when examining the impact of this dimension on the three separate dependent variables. There are significant cultural differences for the TMT Commitment and Effort variables but not for Team Solidarity.

However, when we examine evidence related to results for superior and inferior CEOs, the role of culture becomes more apparent. CEOs who exceed their society's expectations for the global Humane-Oriented behavior and for the two primary behaviors of modesty and humane orientation have more dedicated TMTs and higher Firm Competitive Performance than those CEOs who fall short of their society's leadership expectations.

Do GLOBE's Findings Support the Existing Autonomous Leadership Literature?

Because Autonomous leadership is also a newly defined global leadership dimension developed in GLOBE 2004 research, it obviously is not possible to relate the current GLOBE findings directly to any cross-cultural leadership literature. In fact, we know of no research to compare our findings except for the GLOBE 2004 research project. However, we can provide new information regarding the effectiveness, or lack of effectiveness, for this behavior. The construct itself refers to leadership that is independent and individualistic. As currently defined in GLOBE, *Autonomous leaders have extreme confidence in their own abilities and lack respect for others' abilities and ideas. They view themselves as unique and superior to others and as a result, prefer to work independently and without much collaboration with colleagues or direct reports.*

GLOBE's Insights Into Autonomous Leadership

The Autonomous CEO behaviors assessed in the present study include acting independently, being self-governing, not relying on others, and being individualistic by behaving in a manner different from peers. We would like to point out several aspects of this leadership dimension. At first glance, one might conclude that Autonomous leadership is simply the inverse of Participative leadership. The GLOBE constructs of Autonomous and Participative leadership are indeed negatively correlated ($r = -.40$, thus sharing 16% of the variance). However, the Autonomous survey items stress independent thinking and action whereas the Participative survey items indicate various levels of interaction with subordinates. Thus, the inverse of Autonomous does not translate into Participative leadership. Secondly, this leadership dimension should not be confused with "laissez-faire leadership" (Bradford & Lippitt,

1945). Autonomous leaders do not necessarily abdicate their responsibilities and may not be inactive and indifferent to what is happening, which are characteristics of laissez-faire leaders.

Because we know of no empirical behavioral research investigating the effectiveness of Autonomous leadership behaviors, our findings—by definition—have to be considered new. First, the overall level of enactment across countries is not high thus indicating they are not particularly autonomous (see Chapter 7, Table 7.2). However, there is considerable variability in the enactment of this behavior.

Second, the findings regarding leadership effectiveness generally indicate that this behavior is somewhat counterproductive. As already indicated, this type of leadership behavior has previously been ignored. Autonomous leadership behavior had a small but significant negative relationship with the TMT Dedication measure but had no impact with respect to Firm Competitive Performance. As might be expected, the negative relationship with the dependent measure of Team Solidarity was the strongest negative relationship. In other words, most of the leadership literature ignores behaviors that are counterproductive and assume that bad leadership is simply the absence of good leadership. We show otherwise. The Autonomous dimension has not been discussed in the literature, and this set of behaviors decrease effectiveness. Societal expectations are also important for Autonomous leadership. CEOs whose Autonomous leadership exceeds the societal leadership expectations can expect to have less dedicated TMT members and less successful firms.

Do GLOBE's Findings Support the Existing Self-Protective Leadership Literature?

Similar to the GLOBE leadership dimensions of Humane Oriented and Autonomous, we know of no behavioral research investigating GLOBE's Self-Protective leadership behaviors. The Self-Protective leadership dimension mainly came about from the explicit attempt at an early meeting of GLOBE researchers to extend our leadership attributes to include non-Western style of leadership, which also included potentially negative attributes (e.g., malevolent).

Despite the absence of cross-cultural behavioral research with regards to Self-Protective leadership, several constructs in this GLOBE dimension are well represented in various literatures. Weber (1947) delineated bureaucratic leaders as one of three types of legitimate authority in organizations (charismatic and patrimonial were the other two types of legitimate authority). The concept of status and status consciousness has a long history within the leadership literature (cf. Barnard, 1951). In addition, the construct of saving face, is a well-established construct within Asian societies (Earley, 1993).

GLOBE's Insights to Self-Protective Leadership

Our current study found that CEOs are not particularly Self-Protective (see Chapter 7, Table 7.2). However, in considering the primary dimensions, bureaucratic, status-conscious, and face-saving leadership were enacted more than self-centered and internally competitive leadership. Regarding the effectiveness of Self-Protective leadership, it is perhaps the most interesting of all global dimensions as the effectiveness of its primary constituent parts varied greatly. The primary dimensions of status conscious and bureaucratic had positive effects whereas self-centered and internally competitive dimensions had negative effects.

We were surprised by the complete absence of findings indicating cultural differences for this leadership dimension. Recall, these behaviors and dimensions arose from an explicit attempt to obtain non-Western leadership behaviors in our survey such as face-saving and status conscious. Despite this effort, culture was not a significant moderating factor in the HLM analysis nor did we find evidence for leadership cultural fit as being important for predicting CEO effectiveness (again specifically for the fit across the five primary leadership dimensions for Self-Protective leadership). We did, however, find some effects for the importance of societal expectations in the analysis of superior CEOs in contrast to inferior CEOs. In sum, the results are complex, but in general, the inferior CEOs exceed their society's expectations and the superior CEOs just match their society's expectations.

Implications of Our Findings for the Strategic Leadership Literature

Our findings have clear implications for the strategic leadership literature. To begin with, we found that CEOs do matter—and they matter greatly. Our results support the view in the literature that CEOs do have an impact on the performance of their firms. Using both internally oriented and externally oriented measures of performance, we found that CEO behavior is significantly correlated with firm performance. Meindl, Ehrlich, and Dukerich (1985) argued that the leadership literature is romanticizing leadership by attributing success or failure of groups and organizations to leaders while in fact leaders may have no real impact. The ideal research design to address this issue would use objective financial metrics for firm performance and use a longitudinal approach to directly test whether reported CEO behavior predicts future firm performance or whether past firm performance predicts reports of CEO behavior. To our knowledge, Waldman, Javidan, and Varella (2004) conducted the only such study with a group of American and Canadian CEOs and found that CEO charismatic behavior predicted future firm performance, but past firm performance did not predict reports of CEO charismatic behavior.

We designed our current research in a way that can best address this issue in a cross-cultural setting. As explained earlier in the book, it is not possible to use financial measures of firm performance across cultures due to lack of availability or consistency of such data in many countries. It is also extremely difficult to conduct longitudinal studies across a large number of countries. In this research, we collected firm performance data from senior executives in the participating firms with the expertise and access to the relevant financial information. We did not inform them about our plans to correlate their information with their CEO's behavior to avoid biased firm performance data. We then collected CEO behavior data from other senior executives without informing them of our plans to correlate the results with firm performance. Therefore, our research design is a viable method in a cross-cultural setting and still shows that CEOs matter and matter greatly. Our design also avoided the methodological bias due to common sources of information.

The extant strategic leadership theory suggests that CEO behavior is mostly driven by his/her personality, values, and beliefs, as well as the constraints imposed by the industry in which the firm is competing. Some industries allow a greater level of discretion to CEOs while others impose more strict constraints on their actions. CEOs adjust their actions and behaviors to the degree of discretion allowed in their industry. While the influence of personality and industry discretion is intuitively appealing, there is little rigorous empirical evidence to support it. Our findings present a theoretical and empirical contribution to this literature. We showed that CEOs behave in accordance to what their society expects of its leaders—that is, the country or CLTs. Our study of over 1,000 CEOs in 24 countries found that every society has a set of criteria to assess its leaders. Further, CEOs tend to behave in ways that are consistent with these expectations. In short, while the current strategic leadership literature tends to focus on industry level of analysis, our work offers the effect of variables at the societal level of analysis. It adds a cross-cultural perspective to the strategic leadership literature. It is, to our knowledge, the first research project comparing and contrasting CEOs across a large number of countries. This is an important direction since the current literature is almost all based on work with American and European executives.

In Chapter 7, we presented unique information about the leadership behaviors of CEOs in 24 countries. In Chapter 10, we presented information comparing superior and inferior CEOs in each of the 18 countries in our sample. Given the rapid pace of globalization in many industries, scholars need to develop a clear understanding of the role of CEOs and senior executives in many countries outside of the United States and Europe. As we have shown earlier, societies' expectations have an extremely important influence on CEO behavior.

Another major contribution of our work is our findings on the impact of CEO leadership behavior on TMTs. As explained in Chapter 2, the current strategic leadership literature has not sufficiently examined the relationship between CEOs and TMTs:

> Perhaps out of a zeal to move away from undue focus on the single top executive, researchers of top groups have been noticeably silent on the distinct role and impact of the group leader. As Jackson (1992) points out, there has been a tendency in top management team research to simply include the CEO as a member of the group, averaging in his or her characteristics in establishing overall group characteristics. Yet, everyday observation and a wealth of related literature indicates that the top group leader has a disproportionate, sometimes nearly dominating influence on the group's various characteristics and output. (Hambrick, 1994, p. 180)

Zaccaro (2001) also raised a similar concern: "Although there is a large and growing literature on TMTs, few studies have focused specifically on the relationship between the executive leader and his or her team, and specifically how executive leaders manage or lead their teams" (p. 193).

Our findings offer substantial information on the linkage between CEO leadership behavior and TMT outcomes. We have shown that four aspects of CEO leadership behavior clearly impact TMT Dedication: (1) Charismatic leadership, (2) Team-Oriented leadership, (3) Humane-Oriented leadership, and (4) Participative leadership. Furthermore, our comparison of the superior and inferior CEOs across countries showed that the CEOs with the highest levels of TMT Dedication are those who exceed their societies' expectations in terms of the previously listed four leadership dimensions. In conclusion, CEOs who are Charismatic, Team Oriented, Humane Oriented, and Participative *and* who exceed their societies' expectations on these dimensions, tend to lead highly dedicated TMTs. These findings are consistent with those of Ling, Simsek, Lubatkin, and Veiga (2008a), who showed that transformational leaders were associated with cohesive TMTs, but our findings go beyond by showing the impact of other aspects of CEO leadership behavior—namely, Team-Oriented, Humane-Oriented, and Participative leadership.

Finally, our findings shed light on the nature of the linkage between CEO leadership behavior and firm performance. As shown in Table 11.2 earlier in this chapter, two dimensions of CEO behavior clearly result in firm performance: (1) Charismatic leadership and (2) Team-Oriented leadership. All six primary dimensions of Charismatic leadership (visionary, inspirational, self-sacrificial, integrity, decisive, and performance oriented) and four of the five primary dimensions of Team-Oriented leadership (team integrator, diplomatic, collaborative team orientation, and administratively competent) are significantly correlated with firm performance. CEOs who excel in these two dimensions tend to lead competitively successful firms.

In support of these findings, the comparison of superior and inferior CEOs in our sample showed that inferior CEOs clearly fall short of their societies' expectations on both Charismatic and Team-Oriented leadership while superior CEOs tend to exceed expectations. The two groups also showed a similar pattern regarding Humane-Oriented leadership. These results contribute to the current literature on CEO-firm performance linkage. They support the work of Waldman and colleagues (2004); Ling and colleagues (2008a); and Wang and colleagues (2011), showing that charismatic CEOs do impact firm performance. But the current work goes beyond the work of other authors in important ways: It is the first large multicountry study of over 1,000 CEOs. It also examines other aspects of CEO leadership in addition to Charismatic leadership—in particular Team-Oriented leadership.

Managerial Implications of Our Findings

Our findings have important implications for senior executives and leaders across countries. Our work is helpful to executives who are leading corporations in any of the participating countries, as well as executives who have global responsibilities and need to lead groups of employees or work with managers and executives from other parts of the world in a strategic partnership or a joint venture. We highlight the key implications next.

Rigorous Findings and Lessons for Domestic Executives

Our work offers rigorous large-scale and scientific evidence in terms of what senior executives need to do to succeed in each of the participating countries. In several of such countries, our findings constitute the first information of its type and can thus be quite helpful. Based on the findings in GLOBE 2004, Figures 11.2 to 11.19 show societal expectations of leaders in the 18 participating countries. Each figure represents what a particular society like the United States, Taiwan, India, or China expects its leaders to do. For example, as shown in Figure 11.19, in the United States, leaders are expected to show impeccable levels of integrity and performance orientation. They are expected to develop and communicate an inspirational vision. They are also expected to effectively manage team dynamics and be administratively competent. They need to be decisive while demonstrating high levels of participation and diplomacy. They need to avoid self-centered and self-protective actions and work effectively with others.

In Taiwan, leaders are expected to show relatively high levels of integrity and performance orientation and communicate an inspirational vision (see Figure 11.17). But in contrast to the United States, they are expected to show higher levels of administrative competence and diplomacy while putting less emphasis on managing team synergy. They are also expected to

Figure 11.2   Austria Societal Leadership Expectations

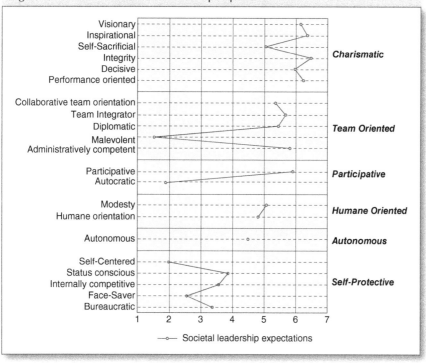

1 = This behavior or characteristic **greatly inhibits** a person from being an outstanding leader.

2 = This behavior or characteristic **somewhat inhibits** a person from being an outstanding leader.

3 = This behavior or characteristic **slightly inhibits** a person from being an outstanding leader.

4 = This behavior or characteristic **has no impact** on whether a person is an outstanding leader.

5 = This behavior or characteristic **contributes slightly** to a person being an outstanding leader.

6 = This behavior or characteristic **contributes somewhat** to a person being an outstanding leader.

7 = This behavior or characteristic **contributes greatly** to a person being an outstanding leader.

show much lower levels of participation while being much more internally competitive and much more status conscious.

Understanding societal expectations is the first step toward executive success. Following and matching the expectations is quite likely to enhance a local manager's ability to effectively lead a group or an organization and reap the rewards of success in their society. Our findings, explained in detail in the earlier chapters, have shown that executives who fall short of societal expectations are almost certain to fail as leaders. At the same time, as we have showed in Chapter 10, to be regarded a star and to perform exceptionally well, executives actually need to exceed societal expectations on many of these leadership attributes.

Figure 11.3 Brazil Societal Leadership Expectations

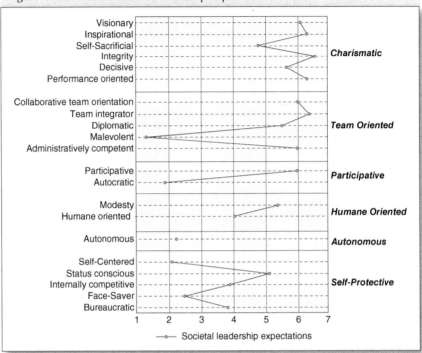

Figure 11.4 China Societal Leadership Expectations

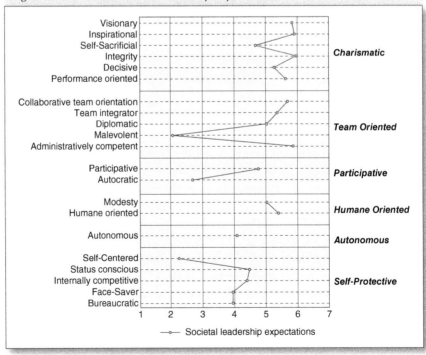

Figure 11.5   Estonia Societal Leadership Expectations

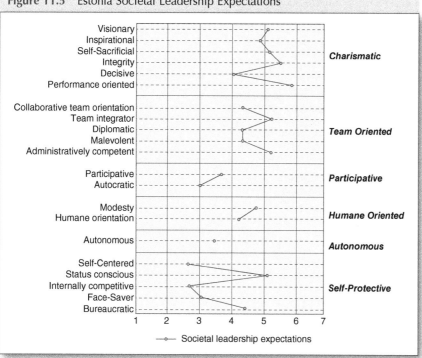

Figure 11.6   Germany Societal Leadership Expectations

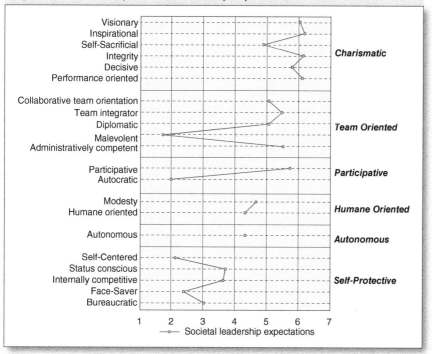

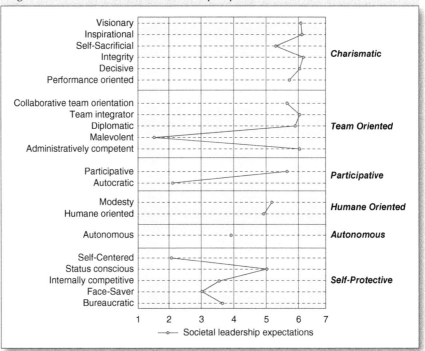

Figure 11.7   Greece Societal Leadership Expectations

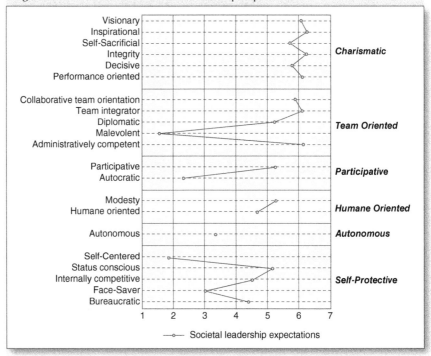

Figure 11.8   Guatemala Societal Leadership Expectations

Figure 11.9   India Societal Leadership Expectations

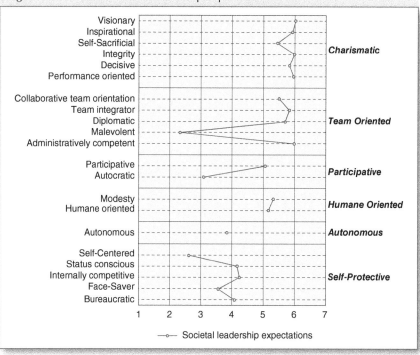

Figure 11.10   Mexico Societal Leadership Expectations

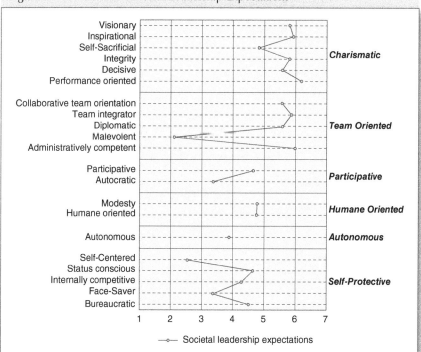

Figure 11.11 Netherlands Societal Leadership Expectations

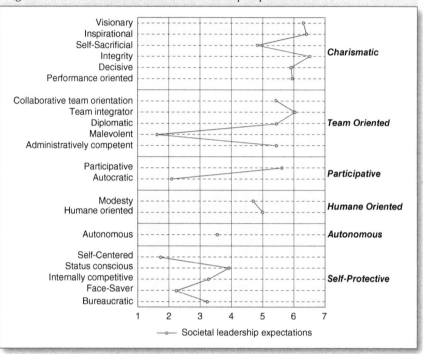

Figure 11.12 Nigeria Societal Leadership Expectations

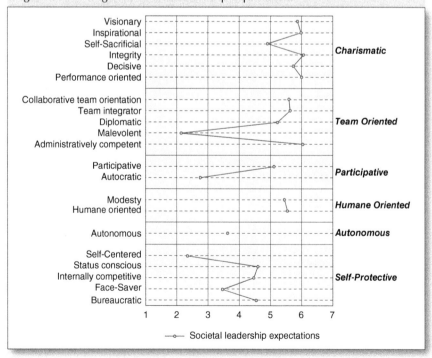

Figure 11.13   Romania Societal Leadership Expectations

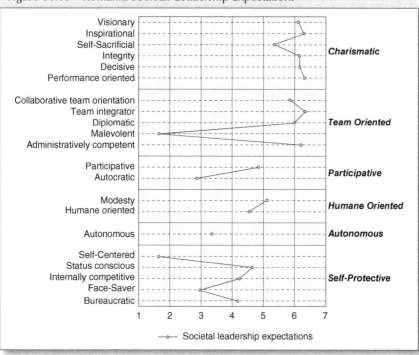

Figure 11.14   Russia Societal Leadership Expectations

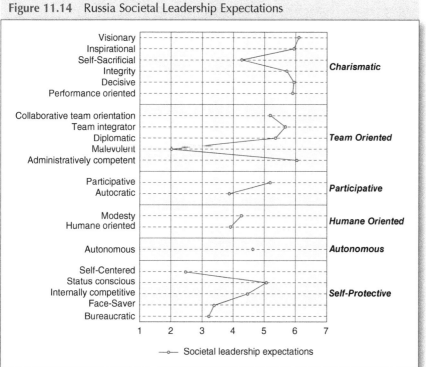

Figure 11.15 Slovenia Societal Leadership Expectations

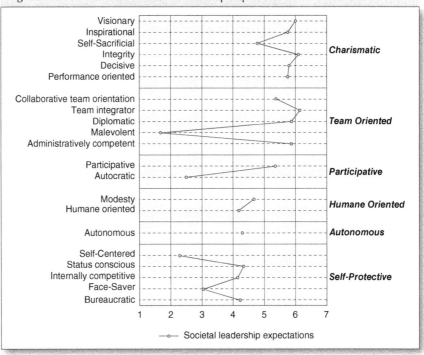

─○─ Societal leadership expectations

Figure 11.16 Spain Societal Leadership Expectations

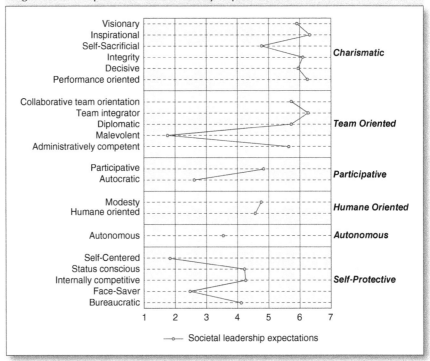

─○─ Societal leadership expectations

Figure 11.17   Taiwan Societal Leadership Expectations

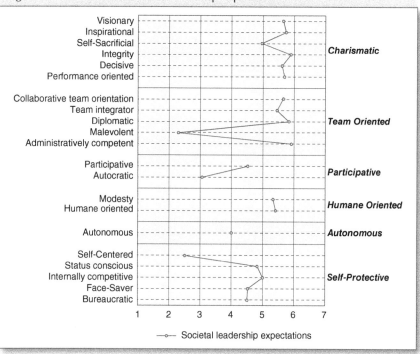

Figure 11.18   Turkey Societal Leadership Expectations

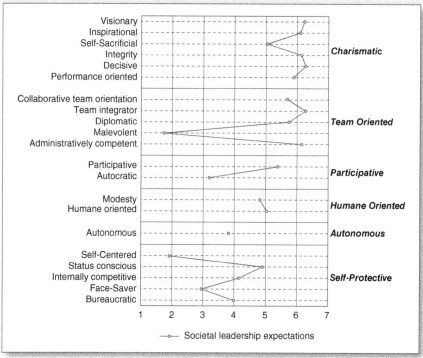

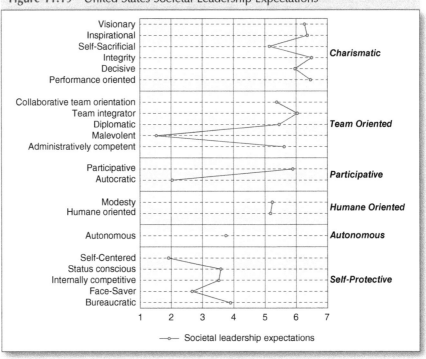

Figure 11.19 United States Societal Leadership Expectations

Rigorous Findings and Lessons for Global Executives

Our findings also have implications for executives who are in global roles and interact with executives and managers from other parts of the world, as employees, supervisors, colleagues, or otherwise. Our work is helpful in two important ways: (1) a general theory of strategic leadership and (2) an understanding of effective leadership across cultures. We explain each in detail next.

A General Theory of Strategic Leadership

The study of strategic leadership focuses on the characteristics, behaviors, styles, and outcomes of senior executives (Finkelstein et al., 2009). Our notion of a general theory of strategic leadership is a framework that identifies leadership behaviors that will lead to success for senior executives and the organizations they lead, across countries—in other words, those leadership behaviors that transcend national boundaries and lead to success in a variety of corporations in a variety of countries.

To offer a general theory of effective strategic leadership, we contrast the behavioral profile of the CEOs with superior results on both TMT Dedication and Firm Competitive Performance, with the behavioral profile of the CEOs with inferior results on both TMT Dedication and Firm Competitive

Performance. Figure 11.20 compares the two groups in terms of the 21 leadership behaviors. The dark blue bars show the average score of the CEOs who are leading highly dedicated TMTs and highly successful firms. The light blue bars show the profile of the CEOs who lead extremely low-performing firms and extremely low levels of Dedication among their TMTs. Both groups are from a variety of countries in our sample of over 1,000 firms in 24 countries.

The information in this figure offers several important insights about effective leadership in upper echelons of corporations. First, examining the

Figure 11.20   Comparison of Superior and Inferior CEOs (Combined Firm Competitve Performance and Top Management Team Dedication)

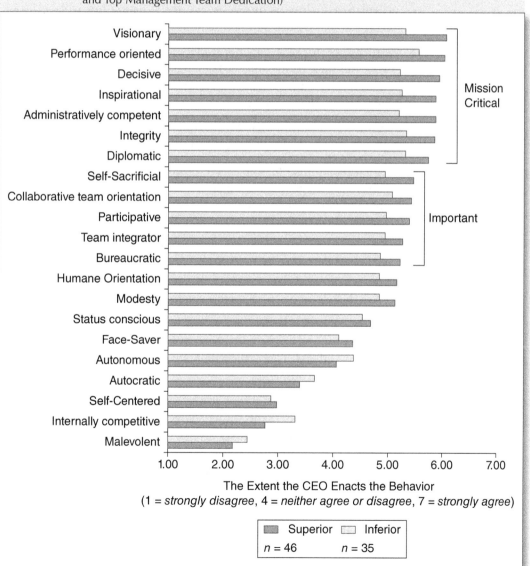

dark blue bars, we conclude that to succeed in senior ranks across countries, leaders need to perform two sets of activities: We call the first set *Mission Critical leadership competencies*. These are activities that are absolutely critical, and senior executives are required to perform these roles at very high levels to produce extraordinary results. The average scores for the star CEOs on these dimensions are very close to 6.0 on a 7-point scale. Furthermore, the average score of the top-performing CEOs is significantly and substantially higher than that of bottom-performing CEOs. The set of primary leadership competencies consists of seven critical requirements:

1. *Visionary:* Star leaders anticipate possible future events and prepare for them. They create and communicate a clear vision of the future, articulating a clear picture of where the organization will be in 5 years, and make plans and take actions to achieve it.

2. *Performance oriented:* Superior leaders strive for excellence for themselves and their teams and set high standards and goals. They communicate high performance expectations, work hard, and seek continuous performance improvement.

3. *Decisive:* Star leaders offer high levels of intuition and insight. They make decisions firmly and quickly based on logic and intuition.

4. *Inspirational:* Superior leaders are positive, energetic, enthused, and optimistic. They mobilize their teams by giving courage, confidence, hope, and praise. They emphasize the importance of being committed to values and beliefs.

5. *Administratively competent:* Star leaders are able to manage complex administrative systems and are highly organized and methodical. They clarify priorities and plan, organize, and coordinate the work of others. They explain the rules and procedures that employees are expected to follow.

6. *Integrity:* Superior leaders deserve to be trusted because they mean what they say and can be relied upon to keep their word. Their actions are always ethical. They articulate a strong sense of values and purpose and act accordingly.

7. *Diplomatic:* Star leaders have a strong world outlook. They have high levels of interpersonal skills through effective negotiation skills and by identifying solutions that satisfy diverse interests.

We call the second set of requirements *Important leadership competencies*. These are activities that are still important for leadership success, but they do not need to be performed at the high level of the first set of activities. Furthermore, the average score of top-performing CEOs is significantly higher than the bottom-performing CEOs but the difference is not as large as in the case of the Mission Critical competencies. Superior CEOs' average scores on these dimensions are between 5.0 and 5.5 on a 7-point scale. This set consists of five attributes.

1. *Self-sacrificial:* Star leaders are willing to forgo their own self-interest to serve the interests of the organization and their team members. As a result, they are viewed as persuasive by their teams.

2. *Collaborative:* Superior leaders have good relations with subordinates, are concerned about the welfare of the group, and are supportive in the face of difficulty or conflict.

3. *Participative:* Star leaders share critical information with subordinates and allow them a high degree of discretion in performing their work. They seek advice and recommendations from their team members and allow them to have influence on important decisions.

4. *Team integrator:* Superior leaders communicate frequently, openly, and effectively with their subordinates, clarifying what is expected of each team member. They work hard at getting team members to work together and integrating them into a cohesive team.

5. *Bureaucratic:*[1] Star leaders act according to established rules, guidelines, norms, and conventions. They use a common standard to evaluate all who report to them and administer rewards in a fair manner.

We did not include two other leadership behaviors, humane orientation and modesty, in this set even though the average score of top-performing CEOs was in the 5.0 to 5.5 range. The reason is that the difference between the average scores of top-performing and bottom-performing CEOs was not statistically significant.

The seven Mission Critical leadership competencies and the five Important leadership competencies constitute our general theory of strategic leadership. Senior executives who aspire to succeed in their roles need to

---

[1]The reader might be surprised to find the bureaucratic leadership dimension listed as moderately important for successful leadership. Not surprisingly, the term *bureaucratic* has a negative connotation in the literature. It often stands for the undesirable effects found in extremely bureaucratic organizations. As Bass (2008) noted, "Numerous case studies have suggested that when organizations become overly concerned with rules and formalities, they tend to lose touch with the external demands made on them and to become insensitive to the internal problems they generate" (p. 304). Burns (1978) identified the crux of the matter when noting that severe problems occur when consistency, predictability, and consistency are prized more than creativity. Our bureaucratic leadership dimension, however, should not be interpreted in this manner. Rather, this dimension simply refers to CEOs who act according to established rules, guidelines, norms, and conventions and who evaluate TMT members fairly when administering rewards in a fair manner. This view of bureaucratic behaviors is consistent with Bass's (2008) warning that completely unstructured environments also present major problems and lead to organizational chaos.

perform the former at very high levels and the latter at somewhat lower levels. Our findings show that these competencies lead to success across countries and are not unique to any specific country, although there will be cross-cultural differences in the degree of success. Senior executives in global roles are well advised to pay close attention to these dimensions to improve their own probability of success.

Figure 11.20 also offers information about CEOs who are inferior and are failing to develop dedicated TMTs and competitively successful firms. The light blue bars are the average scores of this group on leadership dimensions. It is important to note that as a group, inferior CEOs' average scores hover around 5.0 on a 7-point scale on Mission Critical and Important leadership roles, meaning that they are reported to behave at a modest level of these dimensions. In other words, what distinguishes superior and inferior CEOs is not that the former group behaves in ways that the latter group does not. Instead, it is the degree to which they enact the behaviors. For example, superior CEOs are much stronger visionaries and are much more performance oriented than inferior CEOs.

Effective Leadership Across Cultures

It is clear from the conclusion that was just given that as a general rule, senior leaders need to perform at high levels of the two sets of Mission Critical and Important leadership competencies. But a global executive still needs to know what a high level means in a particular country. For example, an Indian executive who leads an American team of managers needs to know how much of a vision, decisiveness, and participation she needs to demonstrate to effectively lead her American team. And how does this level compare to a situation where she leads a German team? In this book, we have offered two sets of empirical information to help answer these questions. First, in Figures 11.2 to 11.19, we showed how desirable each leadership dimension is in a particular country. For example, Figure 11.18 shows that Americans expect very high levels (average score of over 6.0 on a 7-point scale) of vision, inspiration, and decisiveness from their leaders. Second, in Chapter 10, we showed the profile of superior CEOs in each participating country. The profile of superior American CEOs, shown in Figure 10.19, points out that to produce superior results in the United States, leaders need to substantially exceed societal expectations.

In summary, to produce extraordinary results, global leaders need to understand and exceed the leadership expectations in the cultures they are interacting with. The information provided in this book should be useful for senior executives aspiring to, as well as leading organizations within and across cultural boundaries. Because talent acquisition and development are critical functions in modern organizations, HR directors should also be able to use these GLOBE findings in creating maximally effective selection systems and management development programs. However, grasping the importance of societal cultural expectations for leadership excellence is but a first step in what should be an ongoing company-wide and individual developmental undertaking.

_____ Future Research: What We Still Need to Know

The GLOBE project started with a research design that included four phases. We have completed the third phase, and it is time to step back and contemplate future GLOBE studies. The purpose of the proposed fourth GLOBE phase was to further validate hypotheses in the original GLOBE model by conducting laboratory and field studies (House et al., 2004, p. 18). Because we have answered a number of questions posed in the initial chapters of the current book, we can now pursue even more complicated questions. As discussed previously in this chapter, we need to examine how strategic organizational contingencies (e.g., size, organizational environment, and technological sophistication) affect organizational form, culture, and practices that in turn impact leadership behavior and effectiveness. Using the GLOBE model presented in this chapter as a guide for future research, the following additional studies would enhance the theoretical, methodological, and practical implications of the GLOBE project.

One obvious extension of the Phase 3 research would be to obtain a larger sample of female CEOs to further understand gender differences in leadership behavior and effectiveness. The female sample studied in this current project constituted less than 10% of the total sample. Although the field of gender studies has become much more sophisticated in recent years, to our knowledge, there are no large-scale empirical studies of female CEOs using a cross-cultural perspective. Do female CEOs lead in styles suggested in the new wave of gender-based research found in the popular press as well as in academic research (cf. Eagly & Carli, 2003)? That is, are female leaders more inclusive, team-oriented, and transformational than male leaders as some of this literature suggests? Further, is this phenomenon worldwide? Does it vary cross-culturally? Is it mostly found in low Power Distance and Individualistic countries? Are female CEOs gender-neutral with interactions of both male and female TMT members? These and a host of additional questions remain unanswered until a larger sample of female executives can be obtained and compared to male CEOs worldwide. Future GLOBE-based gender research is planned that will enable more sophisticated tests of the GLOBE hypotheses plus explicating gender differences between and within specific countries.

Because we now know which set of leadership behaviors seem to be universal or nearly universal in effectiveness, the fourth GLOBE research phase could include field studies of leadership development for global leaders and leaders who aspire to become CEOs in a global environment. Numerous developmental programs and techniques exist to enhance leadership skills such as mentoring, executive coaching, multisource feedback, and formal training programs to develop specific skills (e.g., implementing change in a crisis). While the findings from the set of GLOBE projects to date indicate that leaders need to fit into the cultural expectations of a leader in a society, our results also pointed out that truly successful leaders also go beyond cultural expectations for certain types of universal leadership dimensions. The field studies can disentangle whether the aforementioned developmental programs should emphasize the more universal skills identified by GLOBE or should they focus on developing the culture specific leadership profile, or perhaps a little of both? Clearly, field studies are needed to help us understand which of these techniques and programs are most effective in developing a truly successful cross-cultural leader.

As indicated previously in the section of theoretical implications, experimental, quasi-experimental, and field studies could also be used to explore a variety of GLOBE hypotheses not yet tested in the GLOBE model. Will the outcome suggested by our conceptual model be supported when a more rigorous research design is used? For example, while we statistically demonstrated the importance of cultural fit for leadership effectiveness, we could use a quasi-experimental design to more rigorously test the importance of fit. In such a design, one subdivision of an organization assigns expatriates to host countries as a function of fit between the expatriate's leadership style and host country's CLT and another division within that same organization assigns expatriates without consideration of the host country's CLT. Does the first division have a higher level of expatriate success than the second?

Also, the GLOBE model specifically includes hypotheses related to strategic organizational contingencies such as organizations' environment, size, and technology. They are predicted to directly affect organizational form, culture, and practices and indirectly affect leadership behaviors and effectiveness. Longitudinal quasi-experimentation approaches would seem to be an ideal methodology for exploring issues of organizational contingencies. To date, the GLOBE research program has not explicitly studied these variables. In addition, we should endeavor to help multinational organizations sort out practical problems related to cross-cultural interaction. For example, international mergers and acquisitions frequently encounter cultural problems that may limit the success of the merger/acquisition. The success of such mergers and acquisitions could be enhanced by simply training the new leaders to be aware of and enact society leadership expectations of the employees in the acquired organization.

Another avenue of future research would be to extend our knowledge regarding the CLT construct and how these leadership schemas are influenced by culture. The information processing model that drove our project was based on the classic symbolic information processing models that indicated that people held the content of different leadership categories in their memories. However, work in cognitive psychology has progressed beyond these symbolic models, and the utility of connectionist information processing models has been discussed for almost 30 years. Connectionist models differ from symbolic models in that connectionist models are more efficient, flexible, and provide a more nuanced approach to understanding the connection between schemas and behavior. Indeed, while symbolic models emphasize the content of the CLTs, connectionist models also emphasize the structure among the CLT content. Hanges, Lord, and Dickson (2000) used a connectionist model framework to explicate how culture and leadership schemas combine to influence leader and follower behavior. This model suggests that people with the same CLT content can still differ in the way they manifest leadership because of differences in how the CLT content is interconnected (i.e., differences in schema structure). For example, GLOBE 2004 demonstrated that administratively competent, trustworthy, and team integrator are universally held as three attributes of effective leaders. However, a person whose schema has a stronger association in trustworthy and team integrator, will enact different leadership behaviors than someone whose schema has a stronger association between trustworthy and administratively competent. The first person would be more likely to be participative and build teams whereas the second would focus on the management of task demands. The initial empirical work testing this perspective has been quite promising (Hanges et al., 2006).

We also to understand more about the incorporation of emotions into the cross-cultural leadership process. Traditional leadership research has typically taken a cognitive and rational approach to understanding leadership–follower relationships. However, during the past decade the importance of emotions in these relationships has been increasingly recognized (e.g., Dasborough & Ashkanasy, 2002). The ability to identify and regulate the emotions of oneself and others is a critical skill for forming, maintaining, and managing healthy interpersonal relationships. The recent scientific literature refers to this set of abilities as emotional intelligence (EI); however, the area of EI has proven to be controversial. Given that leadership quality is a function of the relationships between followers and the leader, it seems reasonable to hypothesize that EI is a critical competency for effective leadership. How leaders regulate their emotions and the emotions of their followers and the role that societal culture plays in this process is a critical question that is one of the avenues of future research in GLOBE.

One frequent suggestion by GLOBE members has been to validate the GLOBE questionnaire at the individual level. As is well known, GLOBE emphasizes the validity of the questionnaire attributes/dimensions at the national level for both the cultural dimensions and leadership constructs. However, most researchers are not capable of collecting data on many countries as done in the GLOBE study. Therefore, it would be a major contribution to validate the questionnaires at the individual level and/or to develop a parallel value questionnaire that can be applied at the individual level. As a corollary to validation of the GLOBE scales at the individual level, it would be worthwhile to create a research instrument whereby individuals could match their personal cultural values to the values found in various nations (e.g., level of desired Power Distance). This instrument could also measure and assess an individual's beliefs about critical leadership attributes in relation to those of each nation in the GLOBE project.

Methodological issues and a variety of research techniques that are ripe for cross-cultural investigation include exploring cultural response bias and discovering how to correct or minimize its influence. For example, does the statistical approach commonly used in the cross-cultural research to remove bias only remove response bias, or does it remove important variance due to the construct under investigation? To what extent would triangulation of constructs using different methodologies be a more effective way of minimizing cultural response bias than relying on a statistical correction procedure? Are different questionnaire response formats (e.g., forced choice) less susceptible to cultural response bias than the more traditional format used in questionnaires (i.e., Likert response scales)? Would item response theory (IRT) prove to be more effective at estimating cultural scores free from cultural response bias? Finally, current methods for establishing metric equivalence require that scales meaningfully vary within each country (i.e., the scales were designed to measure individual-level variability). New methods are needed to establish the metric equivalence of scales designed to measure culture level phenomena. Culture-level scales assume that individual level variation is noise and thus the current metric equivalence methods cannot be used.

In summary, cross-cultural leadership differences have become an ever-increasing and important field of study because of theoretical implications for the study of leadership and practical implications for leaders working in multicultural environments. GLOBE researchers believe that there are an almost unending number of topics and research questions worthy of study. They range from the more abstract questions such as, "Do certain cultural characteristics of a society make it more or less susceptible to leadership influence?" to more concrete questions such as "Does national culture matter equally with regard to mid-level versus executive leadership?" The previous paragraphs suggest a number of avenues to pursue and hopefully they will stimulate other promising research ideas.

Appendix A _____

Performance Orientation: This dimension is the degree to which a collective encourages and rewards (and should encourage and reward) group members for performance improvement and excellence.

Assertiveness: This dimension is the degree to which individuals are (and should be) assertive, confrontational, and aggressive in their relationship with others.

Future Orientation: This dimension is the extent to which individuals engage (and should engage) in future-oriented behaviors such as planning, investing in the future, and delaying gratification.

Humane Orientation: This dimension is the degree to which a collective encourages and rewards (and should encourage and reward) individuals for being fair, altruistic, generous, caring, and kind to others.

Institutional Collectivism: This dimension is the degree to which organizational and societal institutional practices encourage and reward (and should encourage and reward) collective distribution of resources and collective action.

In-Group Collectivism: This dimension is the degree to which individuals express (and should express) pride, loyalty, and cohesiveness in their organizations or families.

Gender Egalitarianism: This dimension is the degree to which a collective minimizes (and should minimize) gender inequality.

Power Distance: This dimension is the degree to which members of a collective expect (and should expect) power to be distributed equally.

Uncertainty Avoidance: This dimension is the extent to which a society, organization, or group relies (and should rely) on social norms, rules, and procedures to alleviate unpredictability of future events. The greater the desire to avoid uncertainty, the more people seek orderliness, consistency, structure, formal procedures, and laws to cover situations in their daily lives.

GLOBE Six Global Leadership Dimensions_____

Charismatic/Value-Based Leadership: Charismatic leaders inspire their followers with a desirable and realistic vision that is based on appropriate analysis and high performance expectations. They are viewed as sincere, decisive, and credible because of their integrity and willingness to sacrifice their own self-interest.

Team-Oriented Leadership: Team-oriented leaders are loyal to their teams and care for the welfare of their team members. They use their administrative and interpersonal skills to manage the team's internal dynamics and to create a cohesive working group.

Participative Leadership: Participative leaders believe that employees can contribute to decision making and should be engaged in the process of decision making and implementation. They also believe that debate, discussion, and disagreement are a natural part of good decision making and should not be suppressed.

Humane-Oriented Leadership: Humane-oriented leaders are unpretentious, show humility, and are reticent to boast. They are empathetic and likely to help and support team members in a humane manner by offering resources and other forms of assistance.

Autonomous Leadership: A newly defined leadership dimension. These leaders have extreme confidence in their own abilities and lack respect for others' abilities and ideas. They view themselves as unique and superior to others and as a result prefer to work independently and without collaboration with colleagues or direct reports.

Self-Protective Leadership: This newly defined leadership dimension refers to leaders who have a deep desire to succeed among a group of colleagues and direct reports who may act as competitors for the leaders' position and success. To protect themselves, these leaders defer to positions of power, hide information that might advantage potential competitors, follow rules and policies to avoid risk, and interact carefully with others to ensure they leave a positive impression.

GLOBE Twenty-One Primary Leadership Dimensions (Grouped by the Six Global Leadership Dimensions) _____

Charismatic/Value-Based Leadership

Visionary: This dimension describes leaders who clearly articulate his or her vision of the future and make plans and act based on future goals.

Inspirational: This dimension describes leaders who inspire others, increase morale of subordinates, and are energetic and confident.

Self-Sacrificial: This dimension indicates an ability to convince followers to invest their efforts in activities that do not have a high probability of success, to forgo their self-interest, and make personal sacrifices for the goal or vision.

Integrity: This dimension indicates a leader who is honest and trustworthy, keeps his or her word, and speaks and acts truthfully.

Decisive: This dimension indicates leaders who make decisions firmly, quickly, and logically and are insightful.

Performance oriented: This dimension describes leaders who set high goals, seek continuous improvement, and are excellence oriented for themselves and subordinates.

Team-Oriented Leadership

Collaborative team orientation: This dimension indicates a leader who is concerned with the welfare of the group and is collaborative and loyal.

Team integrator: This dimension indicates a leader who gets members to work together and integrates people into a cohesive working unit to achieve group goals.

Diplomatic: This dimension describes leaders who are diplomatic and skilled at interpersonal relations.

Malevolent: This dimension reflects leaders who are dishonest, vindictive, and deceitful and act negatively toward others.

Administratively competent: This dimension reflects leaders who are administratively skilled and well organized. They can effectively coordinate and control activities of the team members.

Participative Leadership

Participative: This dimension reflects leaders who share critical information with subordinates and give them a high degree of discretion to perform work.

Autocratic: This dimension indicates leaders who are dictatorial, do not tolerate disagreement, and expect unquestioning obedience of those who report to them (reverse scored in computations for the global Participative leadership dimension).

Humane-Oriented Leadership

Modesty: This dimension reflects leaders who do not boast, are modest, and present themselves in a humble and unassuming manner.

Humane orientation: This dimension emphasizes empathy for others by giving time, money, resources, and assistance when needed. It reflects concern for followers' personal and group welfare.

Autonomous Leadership

Autonomous: This dimension describes tendencies to act independently without relying on others, self-governing, and preferring to work and act separately from others.

Self-Protective Leadership

Self-Centered: This dimension reflects a leader who is self-absorbed, is a loner, is aloof, and stands off from others.

Status conscious: This dimension reflects a consciousness of one's own and others' social position, holding an elitist belief that some individuals deserve more privileges than others. A status-conscious leader adjusts his or her style of leadership and communication according to the status of the individual(s) he or she is dealing with.

Internally competitive (formerly labeled *conflict inducer*): This dimension reflects the tendency to view colleagues as competitors and to conceal information due to a lack of willingness to work jointly with others.

Face-Saver: This leadership dimension reflects the tendency to ensure followers are not embarrassed or shamed. A face-saving leader maintains good relationships by refraining from making negative comments and instead uses metaphors and analogies.

Bureaucratic (formerly labeled *procedural*): This dimension emphasizes leaders who habitually follow established norms, rules, policies, procedures, and routines.

GLOBE Culturally Contingent Leadership Dimensions (of the Twenty-One Primary Leadership Dimensions)_____

1. *Self-Sacrificial:* This dimension indicates an ability to convince followers to invest their efforts in activities that do not have a high probability of success, to forgo their self-interest, and make personal sacrifices for the goal or vision.

2. *Status conscious:* This dimension reflects a consciousness of one's own and others' social position, holding an elitist belief that some individuals deserve more privileges than others. A status-conscious leader adjusts his or her style of leadership and communication according to the status of the individual(s) he or she is dealing with.

3. *Internally competitive* (formerly labeled *conflict inducer*): This dimension reflects the tendency to view colleagues as competitors and to conceal information due to a lack of willingness to work jointly with others.

4. *Face-Saver:* This leadership dimension reflects the tendency to ensure followers are not embarrassed or shamed. A face-saving

leader maintains good relationships by refraining from making negative comments and instead uses metaphors and analogies.

5. *Bureaucratic* (formerly labeled *procedural*): This dimension emphasizes leaders who habitually follow established norms, rules, policies, procedures, and routines.

6. *Humane orientation*: This dimension emphasizes empathy for others by giving time, money, resources, and assistance when needed. It reflects concern for followers' personal and group welfare.

7. *Autonomous:* This dimension describes tendencies to act independently without relying on others, self-governing, and preferring to work and act separately from others.

CEO Dependent Variables

Internally Oriented Outcome of Top Management Team Dedication: This Outcome Measure Combines the Measures of Effort, Commitment, and Team Solidarity

Effort: This outcome variable reflects the level or amount of effort put forth by the TMT member. Respondents assess their agreement (or disagreement) with a set of questions, indicating that they put forth a very high level of effort, effort beyond expectations, and effort beyond the call of duty.

Commitment: This outcome variable indicates the level of commitment of the TMT member. Respondents assess their agreement (or disagreement) with a set of questions indicating commitment to the organization by indicating they expect to have a continuing employment relationship and are optimistic about their future and the organization's future.

Team solidarity: This outcome variable indicates the level of team solidarity of the TMT members' work unit. Respondents assess their agreement (or disagreement) with a set of questions, indicating that they work well together and TMT members work effectively as a team.

Externally Oriented Outcome of Firm Competitive Performance: This Outcome Measure Combines the Measures of Competitive Sales Performance and Competitive Industry Dominance

Competitive Sales Performance: This outcome variable indicates the perception of the CFO (or other knowledgeable top management team [TMT] member) of the financial sales performance of the firm in comparison to their major competitors.

Competitive Industry Dominance: This outcome variable indicates the perception of the CFO (or other knowledgeable TMT member) of the extent to which the firm dominates its industry.

Statistical Analysis Terms

Correlation: A correlation provides a standardized measure (theoretically, bounded between −1 and +1) of the relationship between two variables. A correlation coefficient close to +/−1 indicates a strong relationship, whereas a correlation coefficient close to 0 indicates a weak relationship.

HLM technique: Regression analyses have the underlying assumption that observations are independent, an assumption that is violated when observations are clustered within individuals, teams, organizations, and so forth. Random coefficient modeling (RCM) is a regression technique that accounts for dependence amongst observations. RCM is employed in the current study to account for dependence of observations within countries. RCM can be conducted by using several types of software, including HLM software, which has led this technique to be occasionally called hierarchical linear modeling (HLM).

HLM coefficients: RCM analyses yield unstandardized regression coefficients; when we call a coefficient an HLM coefficient, this indicates that the coefficient is an unstandardized regression coefficient derived through RCM analysis.

Fit: The GLOBE fit index assesses two aspects of the fit between CEO leader behavior and cultural expectations (CLTs). The first aspect of fit assesses the similarity in *patterns* or *profiles* between a CEO's leadership behavior profile and the country's expected leadership profile—that is, CLTs measured for each of the global leadership dimensions. This fit measure is described in Chapter 5 as a *profile pattern similarity* that is defined and measured as a within-person slope between their societal CLT and their corresponding 21 leadership behaviors. The second aspect of fit was an assessment of absolute level of agreement between CLTs and behavior. The second measure of fit calculates the *distance* between each of the CEO's behaviors and its corresponding CLT dimension. It reflects the overall similarity in *level* or magnitude between each CEO's observed behavior and the CLT dimensions. Fit measures were calculated for each global leadership dimension (e.g., Team Oriented) by using the two aspects of fit mentioned previously. In addition, an overall fit measure was calculated by using all 21 primary dimensions together. The latter is designated as the "Gestalt Fit" measure (see Chapter 9).

R^2: R^2 denotes the percentage of variance in the outcome (dependent variable) accounted for by the predictor (independent) variable(s).

Appendix B _____

Primary Leadership Dimension	Global Leadership Dimension	Leadership Survey Items
Visionary (Survey A)	Charismatic	Clearly articulates his/her vision of the future
		Anticipates possible future events
		Makes plans and takes actions based on future goals
		Inspires others to be motivated to work hard
		Smart, learns and understands easily
		Has a clear understanding of where we are going
Visionary (Survey B)	Charismatic	Anticipates and prepares in advance
		Has a vision and imagination of the future
		Has a clear sense of where he/she wants this organization to be in 5 years
Inspirational (Survey A)	Charismatic	Highly involved, energetic, enthused, motivated
		Gives courage, confidence, or hope through reassuring and advising
		Demonstrates and imparts strong positive emotions for work
		Increases morale of subordinates by offering encouragement, praise, and/or by being confident
Inspirational (Survey B)	Charismatic	Mobilizes and activates followers
		Emphasizes the importance of being committed to company values and beliefs
		Is generally optimistic and confident

(Continued)

(Continued)

Primary Leadership Dimension	Global Leadership Dimension	Leadership Survey Items
Self-Sacrificial (Survey A)	Charismatic	Foregoes self-interests and makes personal sacrifices in the interest of a goal or vision
		Can be trusted to serve the interests of his/her subordinates rather than him/herself
Self-Sacrificial (Survey B)	Charismatic	Views obstacles as challenges rather than threats
		Is usually able to persuade others of his/her viewpoint
Integrity (Survey A)	Charismatic	Talks to subordinates about his/her important values and beliefs
		Emphasizes the importance of having a strong sense of purpose
		Can be relied on to meet obligations
		Speaks and acts truthfully
		Acts according to what is right or fair
Integrity (Survey B)	Charismatic	Means what he/she says
		Deserves trust, can be believed and relied upon to keep his/her word
		Builds trust with subordinates
		Makes sure that his/her actions are always ethical
Decisive (Survey A)	Charismatic	Makes decisions firmly and quickly
		Has good intuition, insightful
		Applies logic when thinking
Performance oriented (Survey A)	Charismatic	Sets high goals; works hard
		Seeks continuous performance improvement
		Sets goals for my performance

Primary Leadership Dimension	Global Leadership Dimension	Leadership Survey Items
Performance oriented (Survey B)	Charismatic	Strives for excellence in performance of self and subordinates
		Sets high performance standards
		Communicates his/her performance expectations for group members
		Insists on only the best performance

Primary Leadership Dimension	Global Leadership Dimension	Leadership Survey Items
Collaborative team orientation (Survey A)	Team Oriented	Tends to be a good friend of subordinates
		Concerned with the welfare of the group
		Stays with and supports friends even when they have substantial problems or difficulties
		Intervenes to solve conflicts between individuals
Team integrator (Survey A)	Team Oriented	Easily understood
		Communicates with others frequently
		Integrates and manages work of subordinates
		Knowledgeable, is aware of information
		Integrates people or things into cohesive, working whole
Team integrator (Survey B)	Team Oriented	Works at getting members to work together
		Explains what is expected of each member of the group
		Is open in his/her communication with subordinates
Diplomatic (Survey A)	Team Oriented	Skilled at interpersonal relations
		Is able to negotiate effectively, able to make transactions with others on favorable terms
Diplomatic (Survey B)	Team Oriented	Able to identify solutions which satisfy individuals with diverse and conflicting interests
		Interested in temporal events, has a world outlook
		Is able to maintain good relationships with others

Primary Leadership Dimension	Global Leadership Dimension	Leadership Survey Items
Malevolent (Survey A)	Team Oriented	Tends to believe the worst about people and events
		Is sly, deceitful, full of guile
		Is not sincere, fraudulent
		Is actively unfriendly, acts negatively toward others
Malevolent (Survey B)	Team Oriented	Is punitive; has no pity or compassion
		Is vengeful; seeks revenge when wronged
		Pursues own best interests at the expense of others

(Continued)

(Continued)

Primary Leadership Dimension	Global Leadership Dimension	Leadership Survey Items
Administratively competent (Survey A)	Team Oriented	Is able to plan, organize, coordinate, and control work of
		large numbers (over 30) of individuals
		Explains the rules and procedures group members are expected to follow
		Has the ability to manage complex office work and administrative systems
Administratively competent (Survey B)	Team Oriented	Well-organized, methodical, orderly
		Is organized and methodological in work
		Clarifies priorities
Participative (Survey B)	Participative	Gives subordinates a high degree of discretion to perform their work
		Shares critical information with subordinates
		Allows subordinates to have influence on critical decisions
		Seeks advice concerning organizational strategy from subordinates
		Will reconsider decisions on the basis of recommendations by those who report to him/her

Primary Leadership Dimension	Global Leadership Dimension	Leadership Survey Items
Autocratic (Survey A)	Participative	Makes decisions in dictatorial way
		Is overbearing
		Forces his/her values and opinions on others
		Is inclined to dominate others
		Tells subordinates what to do in a commanding way
		Is an extremely close supervisor; one who insists on making all decisions

Primary Leadership Dimension	Global Leadership Dimension	Leadership Survey Items
Autocratic (Survey B)	Participative	Is in charge and does not tolerate disagreement or questioning; gives orders
		Acts like a tyrant or despot; imperious
		Does not allow others to participate in decision making
		Expects unquestioning obedience of those who report to him/her
Modesty (Survey A)	Humane Oriented	Not easily distressed
		Does not boast, presents self in a humble manner
		Given to being moody; easily agitated (Reverse Coded)
Modesty (Survey B)	Humane Oriented	Has and shows patience
		Is modest
Humane Orientation (Survey A)	Humane Oriented	Has empathy for others, inclined to be helpful or show mercy
		Willing to give time, money, resources, and help to others
Humane Orientation (Survey B)	Humane Oriented	Is aware of slight changes in others' moods
		Sees that the interests of subordinates are given due consideration
		Looks out for the personal welfare of others
Autonomous (Survey A)	Autonomous	Acts independently, does not rely on others
		Self-governing
Autonomous (Survey B)	Autonomous	Is individually oriented; places high value on preserving individual rather than group needs
Self-Centered (Survey A)	Self-Protective	Avoids people or groups, prefers own company
		Aloof, stands off from others, difficult to become friends with
		Self-absorbed, thoughts focus mostly on one's self

(Continued)

(Continued)

Primary Leadership Dimension	Global Leadership Dimension	Leadership Survey Items
		Is a loner, tends to work and act separately from others
Status conscious (Survey A)	Self-Protective	Is conscious of class and status boundaries and acts accordingly
		Believes that a small number of people with similar backgrounds are superior and should enjoy privileges
Status conscious (Survey B)	Self-Protective	Aware of others' socially accepted status
		Believes that all individuals are not equal and only some should have equal rights and privileges
		Does not show favoritism toward an individual or group of individuals
Internally competitive (Survey B)	Self-Protective	Holds people accountable for work over which they have no control
		Stimulates unrest
		Tends to conceal information from others
		Does not criticize subordinates without good reason (Reverse Coded)
		Is unwilling to work jointly with others
Face-Saver (Survey A)	Self-Protective	Refrains from making negative comments to maintain good relationships and save face
		Avoids disputes with members of his/her group
		Avoids saying no to impracticable requests
Face-Saver (Survey B)	Self-Protective	Ensures that subordinates are not embarrassed or shamed
Bureaucratic (Survey A)	Self-Protective	Administers rewards in a fair manner
		Uses a common standard to evaluate all who report to him/her
		Acts in accordance with rules, convention, and ceremonies
Bureaucratic (Survey B)	Self-Protective	Follows established rules and guidelines
		Tends to behave according to established norms, policies, and procedures

References _____

Adler, N. J. (1997). *International dimensions of organizational behavior.* Cincinnati, OH: South-Western College Publishing.

Agarwal, S., DeCarlo, T. E., & Vyas, S. B. (1999). Leadership behavior and organizational commitment: A comparative study of American and Indian salespersons. *Journal of International Business Studies, 30*(4), 727–743.

Agle, B. R., Nagaragan, N. J., Sonnenfeld, J. A., & Srinivasan, D. (2006). Does CEO charisma matter? An empirical analysis of the relationships among organizational performance, environmental uncertainty, and top management team perceptions of CEO charisma. *Academy of Management Journal, 49,* 161–174.

Aguinis, H., & Kraiger, K. (2009). Benefits of training and development for individuals and teams, organizations, and society. *Annual Review of Psychology, 60,* 451–474.

Aiken, J., Dorfman, P. W., Howell, J. P., & Hanges, P. J. (2012). *Gender and leadership: Effects of culture and institutions.* Manuscript in preparation.

Anderson, L. R. (1983). Management of the mixed-cultural work group. *Organizational Behavior and Human Performance, 31,* 303–330.

Ashford, S., Sully de Luque, M., Wollan, M., Wellman, N., & DeStobbelier, K. (2011). *Seeking from the top: CEO feedback seeking—a boon to firm performance?* Presented at the Annual Meeting of Society for Industrial Organizational Psychology (SIOP), Chicago.

Avolio, B. J., Walumbwa, F. O., & Weber, T. J. (2009). Leadership: Current theories, research, and future directions. *Annual Review of Psychology, 60,* 421–449.

Aycan, Z. (2006). Paternalism: Towards conceptual refinement and operationalization. In K. S. Yang, K. K. Hwang, & U. Kim (Eds.), *Scientific advances in indigenous psychologies: Empirical philosophical, and cultural contributions* (pp. 445–466). Cambridge, UK: Cambridge University Press.

Aycan, Z. (2008). Cross-cultural approaches to leadership. In M. F. Peterson, P. B. Smith, & D. C. Thomas (Eds.), *Handbook of cross-cultural management research.* Thousand Oaks, CA: Sage.

Ayman, R., & Chemers, M. M. (1983). Relationship of supervisory behavior ratings to work group effectiveness and subordinate satisfaction among Iranian managers. *Journal of Applied Psychology, 68*(2), 338–341.

Baer, M., & Frese, M. (2003). Innovation is not enough: Climates for initiative and psychological safety, process innovations, and firm performance. *Journal of Organizational Behavior, 23,* 45–68.

Barnard, C. I. (1938). *The functions of the executive.* Cambridge, MA: Harvard University Press.

Barnard, C. I. (Ed.). (1951). *Functions of status systems in formal organizations.* Englewood Cliffs, NJ: Prentice Hall.

Barrett, P. (2006). *Orthosim 2 v.01: Online help in manual form.* Retrieved from www.pbarrett.net/orthosim2.htm

Barrick, M., Stewart, G., Neubert, M., & Mount, M. (1998). Relating member ability and personality to work-team processes and team effectiveness. *Journal of Applied Psychology, 83*(3), 377–391.

Bass, B. M. (1985). *Leadership and performance beyond expectations.* New York: Free Press.

Bass, B. M. (1990). *Bass & Stogdill's handbook of leadership: Theory, research, and managerial applications* (3rd ed.). New York: Free Press.

Bass, B. M. (1997). Does the transactional-transformational leadership paradigm transcend organizational and national boundaries? *American Psychologist, 52*(2), 130–139.

Bass, B. M. (2008). Globalization and cross-national effects. In B. M. Bass & R. Bass (Eds.), *The Bass handbook of leadership: Theory, research, and managerial applications* (pp. 980–1048). New York: Free Press.

Bass, B. M., & Avolio, B. J. (1990). Developing transformational leadership: 1992 and beyond. *Journal of European Industrial Training, 14,* 21–27.

Bass, B. M., & Avolio, B. J. (1993). Transformational leadership: A response to critiques. In M. M. Chemers & R. Ayman (Eds.), *Leadership theory and research* (pp. 49–80). San Diego: Academic Press.

Bass, B. M., & Avolio, B. J. (1997). *Full range of leadership: Manual for the multifactor leadership questionnaire.* Palo Alto, CA: Mind Garden.

Bass, B. M., & Bass, R. (2008). *The Bass handbook of leadership: Theory, research, and managerial applications* (4th ed.). New York: Free Press.

Bass, B. M., Burger, P. C., Doktor, R., & Barrett, G. V. (1979). *Assessment of managers: An international comparison.* New York: Free Press.

Bass, B. M., & Steidlmeier, P. (1999). Ethics, character, and authentic transformational leadership. *Leadership Quarterly, 10,* 181–217.

Bass, B. M., & Yokochi, J. (1991, Winter/Spring). Charisma among senior executives and the special case of Japanese CEOs. *Consulting Psychology Bulletin, 1,* 31–38.

Beechler, S., & Javidan, M. (2007). Leading with a global mindset. *Advances in International Management, 19,* 131–169.

Bennett, M. (1977). Testing management theories cross-culturally. *Journal of Applied Psychology, 62*(5), 578–581.

Bennis, W. G., & Nanus, B. (1985). *Leaders: The strategies of taking charge.* New York: Harper & Row.

Bensman, J., & Rosenberg, B. (Eds.). (1960). *The meaning of work in bureaucratic society.* Glencoe, IL: Free Press.

Biffl, G. (2012). *Labour market integration of low skilled migrants in Europe: Economic impact.* Paper presented at the Conference on Managing Migration and Integration: Europe & the US, University of California-Berkeley.

Bliese, P. (Ed.). (2000). *Within-group agreement, nonindependence, and reliability: Implication for data aggregation and analysis.* San Francisco: Jossey-Bass.

Bliese, P. D., & Hanges, P. J. (2004). Being both too liberal and too conservative: The perils of treating grouped data as though they were independent. *Organizational Research Methods, 7*(4), 400–417.

Boal, K., & Hooijberg, R. (2001). Strategic leadership research: Moving on. *Leadership Quarterly, 11,* 515–549.

Bodinson, G., & Bunch, R. (2003, Spring). AQP's national team excellence award: Its purpose, value and process. *The Journal for Quality and Participation,* 37–42.

Boehnke, K., Bontis, N., DiStefano, J. J., & DiStefano, A. C. (2003). Transformational leadership: An examination of cross-national differences and similarities. *Leadership and Organization Development Journal, 24*(1), 5–15.

Bohnisch, W., Ragan, J. W., Reber, G., & Jago, A. (1988). Predicting Austrian leader behavior from a measure of behavioral intent: A cross-cultural replication. *Management under differing labour market and employment systems* (pp. 313–322). Berlin: Walter de Gruyter.

Bolchover, D. (2012). Competing across borders: How cultural and communication barriers affect business. *The Economist.*

Bolon, D. S., & Crain, C. R. (1985). *Decision sequence: A recurring theme in comparing American and Japanese management.* Paper presented at the Proceedings, Academy of Management, San Diego, CA.

Bottger, P. C., Hallein, I. H., & Yetton, P. W. (1985). A cross-national study of leadership: Participation as a function of problem structure and leader power. *Journal of Management Studies, 22,* 358–368.

Bowers, D. C., & Seashore, S. E. (1966). Predicting organizational effectiveness with a four factor theory of leadership. *Administrative Science Quarterly, 11,* 238–263.

Bradford, L. R., & Lippitt, R. (1945). Building a democratic work group. *Personnel, 22,* 142–148.

Brett, J. M., Tinsley, C. H., Janssens, M., Barsness, Z. I., & Lytle, A. L. (1997). New approaches to the study of culture in industrial/organizational psychology. In P. C. Early & M. Erez (Eds.), *New perspectives on industrial/organizational psychology* (pp. 75–127). San Francisco: New Lexington Press.

Brislin, R. W. (1980). Translation and content analysis of oral and written materials. In H. C. Triandis & J. W. Berry (Eds), *Handbook of cross-cultural psychology: Methodology* (pp. 389–444). Boston: Allyn & Bacon.

Brodbeck, F. C., Chhokar, J. S., & House, R. J. (2007). Culture and leadership in 25 societies: Integration, conclusions, and future directions. In J. S. Chhokar, F. C. Brodbeck, & R. J. House (Eds.), *Culture and leadership across the world: The GLOBE book of in-depth studies of 25 societies* (pp. 1025–1102). New York: Lawrence Erlbaum.

Brodbeck, F. C., & Eisenbeiss, S. A. (in press). Cross-cultural and global leadership. In D. V. Day (Ed.), *The Oxford handbook of leadership and organizations.*

Brodbeck, F. C., Frese, M., Akerblom, S., Audia, G., Bakacsi, G., Bendova, H., et al. (2000). Cultural variation of leadership prototypes across 22 European countries. *Journal of Occupational and Organizational Psychology, 73,* 1–29.

Brodbeck, F. C., Frese, M., & Javidan, M. (2002). Leadership made in Germany: Low on compassion, high on performance. *Academy of Management Executive, 16*(1), 16–30.

Bryk, A. S., & Raudenbush, S. W. (1992). *Hierarchical linear models: Applications and data analysis methods.* Thousand Oaks, CA: Sage.

Burke, C. S., Stagl, K. C., Klein, C., Goodwin, G. F., Salas, E., & Halpin, S. M. (2006). What type of leadership behaviors are functional in teams? A meta-analysis. *Leadership Quarterly, 17,* 288–307.

Burns, J. M. (1978). *Leadership*. New York: Harper & Row.

Cannella, A. A., Jr., & Monroe, M. J. (1997). Contrasting perspectives on strategic leaders: Toward a more realistic view of top managers. *Journal of Management, 23,* 213–238.

Carpenter, M. A., Geletkanycz, M. A., & Sanders, W. G. (2004). Upper echelons research revisited: Antecedents, elements, and consequences of top management team composition. *Journal of Management, 30,* 749–778.

Casimir, G., & Waldman, D. A. (2007). A cross cultural comparison of the importance of leadership traits for effective low-level and high-level leaders. *International Journal of Cross Cultural Management, 7*(1), 47–60.

Castel, P., Deneire, M., Kurc, A., Lacasagne, M. F., & Leeds, C. A. (2007). Universalism and exceptionalism: French business leadership. In J. S. Chhokar, F. C. Brodbeck, & R. J. House (Eds.), *Culture and leadership across the world: The GLOBE book of in-depth studies of 25 societies.* New York: Lawrence Erlbaum.

Catalyst. (2013). *Women CEOs of the Fortune 1000.* Retrieved January 5, 2013, from www.catalyst.org/knowledge/women-ceos-fortune-1000

Chakravarthy, B. S. (1986). Measuring strategic performance. *Strategic Management Journal, 7*(5), 437–458.

Chemers, M. M. (1983). Leadership theory and research: A systems-process integration. In P. B. Paulus (Ed.), *Basic group processes* (pp. 9–39). New York: Springer-Verlag.

Chemers, M. M. (1993). An integrative theory of leadership. In M. M. Chemers & R. Ayman (Eds.), *Leadership theory and research.* San Diego, CA: Academic Press.

Chemers, M. M. (1997). *An integrative theory of leadership.* London: Lawrence Erlbaum.

Chhokar, J. S., Brodbeck, F. C., & House, R. J. (Eds.). (2007). *Culture and leadership across the world: The GLOBE book of in-depth studies of 25 societies.* New York: Lawrence Erlbaum.

Child, J. (1972). Organizational structure, environment and performance: The role of strategic choice. *Sociology, 6,*(1), 1–22.

Child, J., & Tayeb, M. (1983, Winter). Theoretical perspectives in cross-national research. *International Studies of Management and Organization,* 32–70.

China Daily. (2012, April 27). Report.

Chong, L. M. A., & Thomas, D. C. (1997). Leadership perceptions in cross-cultural context: Pakeha and Pacific islanders in New Zealand. *Leadership Quarterly, 8*(3), 275–293.

Chow, I. H. (2007). Culture and Leadership in Hong Kong. In J. S. Chhokar, F. C. Brodbeck, & R. J. House (Eds.), *Culture and leadership across the world: The GLOBE book of in-depth studies of 25 societies.* New York: Lawrence Erlbaum.

CIA World Factbook. (n.d.). Retrieved May 1, 2013 from https://www.cia.gov/library/publications/the-world-factbook/rankorder/2119rank.html

Colbert, A. E., Kristof-Brown, A. L., Bradley, B. H., & Barrick, M. R. (2008). CEO transformational leadership: The role of goal importance congruence in top management teams. *Academy of Management Journal, 51,* 81–96.

Conger, J. A. (1990). The dark side of leadership. *Organizational Dynamics, 19*(2), 44–55.

Conger, J. A., & Kanungo, R. (1987). Toward a behavioral theory of charismatic leadership in organizational settings. *Academy of Management Review, 12,* 637–647.

Conger, J. A., & Kanungo, R. (1998). *Charismatic leadership in organizations.* Thousand Oaks, CA: Sage.

Croker, J., Fiske, S. T., & Taylor, S. E. (1984). Schematic bases of belief change. In J. R. Eisen (Ed.), *Attitudinal judgment* (pp. 197–226). New York: Springer-Verlag.

Cullen, J. B. (1998). *Multinational management: A strategic approach.* Cincinnati, OH: South-Western Publishing Company.

Cyert, R. M., & March, J. G. (1992). *A behavioral theory of the firm* (2nd ed.). Englewood Cliffs, NJ: Prentice Hall. (Original work published 1963)

Dasborough, M. T., & Ashkanasy, N. M. (2002). Emotion and attribution of intentionality in leader–member relationships. *The Leadership Quarterly, 13*(5), 615–634.

Davila, A., & Elvira, M. (2012). Performance management systems in Mexico. In B. Christensen (Ed.), *Cultural variations and business performance: Contemporary globalism.* Hershey, PA: IGI Global.

DeGroot, T., Kiker, D. S., & Cross, T. S. (2000). A meta-analysis to review organizational outcomes related to charismatic leadership. *Canadian Journal of Administrative Science, 17,* 356–371.

Delbecq, A., House, R., Sully de Luque, M., & Quigley, N. (2013). Implicit motives, leadership, and follower outcomes: An empirical test of CEOs. *Journal of Leadership and Organizational Studies, 20*(1), 3–20.

Den Hartog, D., House, R. J., Hanges, P. J., Ruiz-Quintanilla, S. A., Dorfman, P. W., et al. (1999). Culture specific and cross culturally generalizable implicit leadership theories: Are attributes of charismatic/transformational leadership universally endorsed? *Leadership Quarterly, 10*(2), 219–256.

Den Hartog, D. N., Van Muijen, J. J., & Koopman, P. L. (1994). *Transactional versus transformational leadership: An analysis of the MLQ in the Netherlands.* Paper presented at the 23rd International Congress of Applied Psychology, Madrid, Spain.

Deng, L., & Gibson, P. (2009). Mapping and modeling the capacities that underlie effective cross-cultural leadership: An interpretive study with practical outcomes. *International Journal, 16*(4), 347–366.

Deutschman, A. (2000). *The second coming of Steve Jobs.* New York: Broadway Books.

Dickson, M. W., Castaño, N., Magomaeva, A., & Den Hartog, D. N. (2012). Conceptualizing leadership across cultures. *Journal of World Business, 47*(4), 483–492.

Dickson, M., Den Hartog, D., & Mitchelson, J. K. (2003). Research on leadership in a cross-cultural context: Making progress, and raising new questions. *Leadership Quarterly, 14,* 729–768.

Doctors Without Borders. (2013). Retrieved from www.doctorswithoutborders.org/aboutus/?ref=nav-footer

Donaldson, L. (1993). *Anti-management theories of organization: A critique of paradigm proliferation.* Cambridge, UK: Cambridge University Press.

Dorfman, P. W. (1996). International and cross-cultural leadership research. In B. J. Punnett & O. Shenkar (Eds.), *Handbook for international management research* (pp. 267–349). Oxford, UK: Blackwell.

Dorfman, P. W. (2004). International and cross-cultural leadership research. In B. J. Punnett & O. Shenkar (Eds.), *Handbook for international management research* (2nd ed., pp. 265–355). Ann Arbor: University of Michigan.

Dorfman, P. W., Hanges, P. J., & Brodbeck, F. C. (2004). Leadership and cultural variation: The identification of culturally endorsed leadership profiles. In

R. J. House, P. J. Hanges, M. Javidan, P. W. Dorfman, & V. Gupta (Eds.), *Culture, leadership, and organizations: The GLOBE study of 62 societies* (pp. 667–718). Thousand Oaks, CA: Sage.

Dorfman, P. W., & House, R. J. (2004). Cultural influences on organizational leadership: Literature review, theoretical rationale, and GLOBE Project goals. In R. J. House, P. J. Hanges, M. Javidan, P. W., Dorfman & V. Gupta (Eds.), *Culture, leadership, and organizations: The GLOBE study of 62 societies* (pp. 49–71). Thousand Oaks, CA: Sage.

Dorfman, P. W., & Howell, J. P. (1988). Dimensions of national culture and effective leadership patterns. In R. N. Farmer & E. G. McGoun (Eds.), *Advances in international comparative management* (Vol. 3, pp. 127–150). London: JAI Press.

Dorfman, P. W., & Howell, J. P. (1997). Managerial leadership in the United States and Mexico: Distant neighbors or close cousins? In C. S. Granrose & S. Oskamp (Eds.), *Cross cultural work groups*. Thousand Oaks, CA: Sage.

Dorfman, P. W., Howell, J. P., Hibino, S., Lee, J. K., Tate, U., & Bautista, A. (1997). Leadership in Western and Asian countries: Commonalities and differences in effective leadership processes across cultures. *Leadership Quarterly, 8*(3), 233–274.

Dorfman, P. W., Javidan, M., Hanges, P., Dastmalchian, A., & House, R. (2012). GLOBE: A twenty year journey into the intriguing world of culture and leadership. *Journal of World Business, 47*(4), 504–518.

Dorfman, P. W., & Ronen, S. (1991). *Universal challenges to leadership theories.* Paper presented at the Annual Meeting of the Academy of Management, Miami.

Dyer, N. G., Hanges, P. J., & Hall, R. (2005). Applying multilevel confirmatory factor analysis techniques to the study of leadership. *The Leadership Quarterly, 16,* 149–167.

Eagly, A. H., & Carli, L.L. (2003). The female leadership advantage: An evaluation of the evidence. *Leadership Quarterly, 14,* 807–834.

Eagly, A. H., Johannesen-Schmidt, M. C., & van Engen, M. L. (2003). Transformational, transactional, and laissez-faire leadership styles: A meta analysis. *Psychological Bulletin, 129*(4) 569–591.

Earley, P. C. (1993). East meets West meets Mideast: Further explorations of collectivistic and individualistic work groups. *Academy of Management Journal, 36*(2), 319–348.

Earley, P. C. (1997). *Face, harmony, and social structure: An analysis of organizational behavior across cultures.* New York: Oxford University Press.

Echavarria, N. U., & Davis, D. D. (1994). *A test of Bass's model of transformational and transactional leadership in the Dominican Republic.* Paper presented at the 23rd International Congress of Applied Psychology, Madrid, Spain.

The Economist. (2013, January 21). Leaders without followers, World Economic Forum Report, Davos, Switzerland. Retrieved April 30, 2013, from www.economist.com/blogs/newsbook/2013/01/world-economic-forum-davos

Edwards, J. R. (1995). Alternatives to difference scores as dependent variables in the study of congruence in organizational research. *Organizational Behavior and Human Decision Processes, 64,* 307–324.

Edwards, J. R. (2002). Alternatives to difference scores: Polynomial regression analysis and response surface methodology. In F. Drasgow & N. W. Schmitt (Eds.), *Advances in measurement and data analysis* (pp. 350–400). San Francisco: Jossey-Bass.

Eisenhardt, K., & Bourgeois, L. J. (1988). Politics of strategic decision making in high-velocity environments: Toward a midrange theory. *Academy of Management Journal, 31,* 737–770.

Elenkov, D. S., & Manev, I. M. (2005). Top management leadership and influence on innovation: The role of sociocultural context. *Journal of Management, 31*(3), 381–402.

Elenkov, D. S., & Manev, I. M. (2009). Senior expatriate leadership's effects on innovation and the role of cultural intelligence. *Journal of World Business, 44,* 357–369.

Ensari, N., & Murphy, S. E. (2003). Cross-cultural variations in leadership perceptions and attribution of charisma to the leader. *Organizational Behavior and Human Decision Processes, 92*(1-2), 52–66.

Epitropaki, O., & Martin, R. (2005). From ideal to real: A longitudinal study of the role of implicit leadership theories on leader-member exchanges and employee outcomes. *Journal of Applied Psychology, 90*(4), 659–676.

Erez, M. (1997). A culture-based model of work motivation. In P. C. Earley & M. Erez (Eds.), *New perspectives on international industrial/organizational psychology* (pp. 193–242). San Francisco: The New Lexington Press.

Euwema, M. C., Wendt, H., & van Emmerik, H. (2007). Leadership styles and group organizational citizenship behavior across cultures. *Journal of Organizational Behavior, 28*(8), 1035–1057.

Farmer, R. N., & Richman, B. M. (1965). *Comparative management and economic progress.* Homewood, IL: Irwin.

Finkelstein, S. (1992). Power in top management teams: Dimensions, measurement, and validation. *Academy of Management Journal, 35,* 505–538.

Finkelstein, S., & Hambrick, D. C. (1996). *Strategic leadership: Top executives and their effects on organizations.* Minneapolis/St. Paul, MN: West.

Finkelstein, S., Hambrick, D. C., & Cannella, A. A. (2009). *Strategic leadership: Theory and research on executives, top management teams, and boards.* New York: Oxford University Press.

Fiske, S. T., & Taylor, S. E. (1991). *Social cognition* (2nd ed.). New York: McGraw-Hill.

Fleishman, E. A. (1953). The description of supervisory behavior. *Personnel Psychology, 37,* 1–6.

Fleishman, E. A., Harris, E. F., & Burtt, H. E. (1955). *Leadership and supervision in industry.* Columbus: Bureau of Educational Research, The Ohio State University.

Flood, P. C., Hannan, E., Smith, K. G., Turner, T., West, M. A., & Dawson, J. (2000). Chief executive leadership style, consensus decision making, and top management team effectiveness. *European Journal of Work and Organizational Psychology, 9*(3), 401–420.

Foster, M. (2008). *Multi-polar world 2: The rise of the emerging-market multinational.* Accenture. Retrieved from www.accenture.com/SiteCollectionDocuments/PDF/MPW2.pdf.

Fu, P. P., Tsui, A. S., Liu, J., & Li, L. (2010). Pursuit of whose happiness? Executive leaders' transformational behaviors and personal values. *Administrative Science Quarterly, 55*(2), 222–254.

Fu, P. P., & Yukl, G. (2000). Perceived effectiveness of influence tactics in the United States and China. *Leadership Quarterly, 11,* 252–266.

Gelfand, M. J., Erez, M., & Aycan, Z. (2007). Cross-cultural organizational behavior. *Annual Review of Psychology, 58,* 1–35.

Gelfand, M. J., Raver, J. L., Nishii, L., Leslie, L. M., Lun, J., Lim, B. C., et al. (2011). Differences between tight and loose cultures: A 33-nation study. *Science, 332*(6033), 1100–1104.

Gerstner, C. R., & Day, D. V. (1994). Cross-cultural comparison of leadership proto-types. *Leadership Quarterly, 5*(2), 121–134.

Gerstner, C. R., & Day, D. V. (1997). Meta-analytic review of leader-member exchange theory: Correlates and construct issues. *Journal of Applied Psychology, 82,* 827–844.

Goldstein, H. (1995). *Multilevel statistical models* (2nd ed.). London: John Wiley.

Goodsell, C. T. (1983). *The case for bureaucracy: A public administration polemic.* Chatham, NJ: Chatham House.

Grachev, M. V., Rogovsky, N. G., & Rakitski, B. V. (2007). Leadership and culture in Russia: The case of transitional economy. In J. S. Chhokar, F. C. Brodbeck, & R. J. House (Eds.), *Culture and leadership across the world: The GLOBE book of in-depth studies of 25 societies.* New York: Lawrence Erlbaum.

Graen, G. B. (2006). In the eye of the beholder: Cross-cultural lessons in leadership from project GLOBE: A response viewed from the third culture bonding (TCB) model of cross-cultural leadership. *Academy of Management Perspectives, 20*(4), 95–101.

Graumann, C. F., & Moscovici, S. (1986). *Changing conceptions of leadership.* New York: Springer-Verlag.

Green, W. (2009). *Letter to shareholders.* Accenture. Retrieved from www.accenture.com/SiteCollectionDocuments/PDF/Accenture_2009_Letter_from_Our_Chairman_and_CEO.pdf

Grothe, M. (2004). *Oxymoronica: Paradoxical wit and wisdom from history's great-est wordsmiths.* New York: HarperCollins.

Gupta, V., & Hanges, P. J. (2004). Regional and climate clustering of societal cultures. In R. J. House, P. J. Hanges, M. Javidan, P. W. Dorfman, & V. Gupta (Eds.), *Culture, leadership, and organizations: The GLOBE study of 62 societies.* Thousand Oaks, CA: Sage.

Hackman, J. R. (2002). *Leading teams: Setting the stage for great performance.* Boston: Harvard Business School Press.

Haire, M., Ghiselli, E. E., & Porter, L. (1966). *Managerial thinking: An international study.* New York: Wiley.

Hambrick, D. C. (1994). Top management groups: A conceptual integration and reconsideration of the "team" label. *Research in Organizational Behavior, 16,* 171–213.

Hambrick, D. C. (2007). Upper echelons theory: An update. *Academy of Management Review, 32*(2), 334–343.

Hambrick, D. C., & Finkelstein, S. (1987). Managerial discretion: A bridge between polar views of organizational outcomes. In L. L. Cummings & B. M. Staw (Eds.), *Research in organizational behavior* (Vol. 9, pp. 369–406). Greenwich, CT: JAI Press.

Hambrick, D. C., & Mason, P. A. (1984). Upper echelons: The organization as a reflection of its top managers. *Academy of Management Review, 9*(2), 193–206.

Hanges, P. J. (2004). Response bias correction procedure used in GLOBE. In R. J. House, P. J. Hanges, M. Javidan, P. W. Dorfman, & V. Gupta (Eds.), *Culture, leadership, and organizations: The GLOBE study of 62 societies* (pp. 737–752). Thousand Oaks, CA: Sage.

Hanges, P. J., & Dickson, M. W. (2004). The development and validation of the GLOBE culture and leadership scales. In R. House, P. J. Hanges, M. Javidan, P. W. Dorfman, & V. Gupta (Eds.), *Culture, leadership, and organizations: The GLOBE study of 62 societies* (pp. 122–151). Thousand Oaks, CA: Sage.

Hanges, P. J., Dorfman, P. W., Shteynberg, G., & Bates, A. (2006). Culture and leadership: A connectionist information processing model. In W. H. Mobley & E. Weldon (Eds.), *Advances in global leadership* (Vol. 4, pp. 7–37). New York: JAI Press.

Hanges, P. J., Lord, R. G., & Dickson, M. W. (2000). An information processing perspective on leadership and culture: A case for connectionist architecture. *Applied Psychology: An International Review, 49,* 133–161.

Hanges, P. J., & Wang, M. (2012). Seeking the Holy Grail in organizational science: Uncovering causality through research design. In S. W. J. Kozlowski (Ed.), *The Oxford handbook of organizational psychology* (pp. 79–116). New York: Oxford University Press.

Hannan, M. T., & Freeman, J. H. (1977). The population ecology of organizations. *American Journal of Sociology, 82,* 929–964.

Heller, F. A., Drenth, P., Koopman, P. L., & Rus, V. (1988). *Decisions in organizations.* Newbury Park, CA: Sage.

Heller, F. A., & Wilpert, B. (1981). *Competence and power in managerial decision-making: A study of senior-levels of organization in eight countries.* London: Wiley.

Hemphill, J. K., & Coons, A. E. (Eds.). (1957). *Development of the leader behavior description questionnaire.* Columbus: Bureau of Business Research, The Ohio State University.

Hickson, D. J., Hinings, C. R., McMillan, J., & Schwitter. (1974). The culture-free context of organization structure: A tri-national comparison. *Sociology, 8,* 59–80.

Hitt, M. A., & Tyler, B. B. (1991). Strategic decision models: Integrating different perspectives. *Strategic Management Journal, 12,* 327–351.

Hofmann, D. A. (1997). An overview of the logic and rationale of hierarchical linear models. *Journal of Management, 23*(6), 723–744.

Hofmann, D. A., Griffin, M. A., & Gavin, M. B. (2000). The application of hierarchical linear modeling to organizational research. In K. J. Klein & S. W. Koslowski (Eds.), *Multilevel theory, research, and methods in organizations* (pp. 467–511). San Francisco: Jossey-Bass.

Hofstede, G. (1976). Nationality and espoused values of managers. *Journal of Applied Psychology, 61,* 148–155.

Hofstede, G. (1980). *Culture's consequences: International differences in work-related values.* Beverly Hills, CA: Sage.

Hofstede, G. (1993). Cultural constraints in management theories. *Academy of Management Executive, 7*(1), 81–94.

Hofstede, G. (2001). *Culture's consequences: Comparing values, behaviors, institutions, and organizations across nations.* Thousand Oaks, CA: Sage.

Hofstede, G. (2006). What did GLOBE really measure? Researchers' minds versus respondents' minds. *Journal of International Business Studies, 37,* 882–896.

Hollenbeck, G. P., & McCall, M. W. (2003). Competence, not competencies: Making global executive development work. In W. Mobley & P. W. Dorfman (Eds.), *Advances in global leadership* (Vol. 3). Oxford: JAI Press.

Holmberg, I., & Akerblom, S. (2006). Modelling leadership: Implicit leadership theories in Sweden. *Scandinavian Journal of Management, 22*, 307–329.

Hoppe, M. H. (2004). Cross-cultural issues in the development of leaders. In C. D. McCauley & E. Van Velsor (Eds.), *The Center for Creative Leadership handbook of leadership development* (2nd ed., pp. 331–360). San Francisco: Jossey-Bass.

Hoppe, M. H., & Bhagat, R. S. (2007). Leadership in the United States of America: The leader as cultural hero. In J. S. Chhokar, F. C. Brodbeck, & R. J. House (Eds.), *Culture and leadership across the world: The GLOBE book of in-depth studies of 25 societies*. New York: Lawrence Erlbaum.

House, R. J. (1977). A 1976 theory of charismatic leaders. In J. G. Hunt & L. L. Larson (Eds.), *Leadership: The cutting edge* (pp. 189–207). Carbondale: Southern Illinois University Press.

House, R. J., Dorfman, P., Sully de Luque, M. F., Hanges, P., & Javidan, M. (2010, August). *Strategic leadership across cultures: The new GLOBE multinational study: The new GLOBE study, all-academy showcase symposia.* Presented at the Annual Meeting of Academy of Management, Montreal, Canada.

House, R. J., Hanges, P. J., Javidan, M., Dorfman, P. W., & Gupta, V. (2004). *Culture, leadership, and organizations: The GLOBE study of 62 societies.* Thousand Oaks, CA: Sage.

House, R. J., Hanges, P. J., Ruiz-Quintanilla, S. A., Dorfman, P. W., Javidan, M., Dickson, M., et al. (1999). Cultural influences on leadership and organizations: Project GLOBE. In W. F. Mobley, M. J. Gessner, & V. Arnold (Eds.), *Advances in global leadership* (Vol. 1, pp. 171–233). Stamford, CT: JAI Press.

House, R. J., & Javidan, M. (2004). Overview of GLOBE. In R. J. House, P. J. Hanges, M. Javidan, P. W. Dorfman, & V. Gupta (Eds.), *Culture, leadership, and organizations: The GLOBE Study of 62 societies* (pp. 9–48). Thousand Oaks, CA: Sage.

House, R. J., Rousseau, D. M., & Thomas, D. (1995). The MESO paradigm: A framework for the integration of micro and macro organizational behavior. In L. L. Cummings & B. M. Staw (Eds.), *Research in organizational behavior* (pp. 71–114). Greenwich, CT: JAI Press.

House, R. J., & Shamir, B. (1993). Toward the integration of transformational, charismatic and visionary theories. In M. M. Chemers & R. Ayman (Eds.), *Leadership theory and research: Perspectives and directions* (pp. 81–107). San Diego: Academic Press, Inc.

House, R. J., Wright, N. S., & Aditya, R. N. (1997). Cross-cultural research on organizational leadership: A critical analysis and a proposed theory. In P. C. Earley & M. Erez (Eds.), *New perspectives in international industrial/organizational psychology* (pp. 535–625). San Francisco: The New Lexington Press.

Howard, A., & Wellins, R. S. (2008). *Global leadership forecast 2008–2009: Overcoming the shortfalls in developing leaders.* Pittsburgh, PA: Development Dimensions International.

Howell, J. M., & Avolio, B. J. (1993). Transformational leadership, transactional leadership, locus of control and support for innovation. *Journal of Applied Psychology, 78*, 891–902.

Howell, J. M., & Frost, P. J. (1989). A laboratory study of charismatic leadership. *Organizational Behavior and Human Decision Processes, 43*(2), 243–269.

Howell, J. P. (2013). *Snapshots of great leadership.* New York: Routledge.

Inglehart, R., Basanez, M., & Moreno, A. (1998). *Human values and beliefs: A cross-cultural sourcebook*. Ann Arbor: University of Michigan Press.

International Security Assistance Force. (2013, May 7). *Troop numbers and contributions*. Retrieved from http://www.isaf.nato.int/troop-numbers-and-contributions/index.php

Isaacson, W. (2011). *Steve Jobs*. New York: Simon & Schuster.

Ivancevich, J. M., Schweiger, D. M., & Ragan, J. W. (1986). *Employee stress, health, and attitudes: A comparison of American, Indian and Japanese managers*. Paper presented at the Academy of Management, Chicago.

Jackson, C. L., Colquitt, J. A., Wesson, M. J., & Zapata-Phelan, C. P. (2006). Psychological collectivism: A measurement validation and linkage to group member performance. *Journal of Applied Psychology, 91*(4), 884–899.

Jacobsen, C., & House, R. J. (2011). Dynamics of charismatic leadership: A process theory, simulation model, and tests. *Leadership Quarterly, 12*, 75–112.

James, L. R. (1982). Aggregation bias in estimates of perceptual agreement. *Journal of Applied Psychology, 76*, 219–229.

James, L. R., Demaree, R. G., & Wolf, G. (1984). Estimating within-group interrater reliability with and without response bias. *Journal of Applied Psychology, 69*(1), 85–98.

Javidan, M. (2004). Performance Orientation. In R. J. House, P. J. Hanges, M. Javidan, P. W. Dorfman, & V. Gupta (Eds.), *Culture, leadership, and organizations: The GLOBE study of 62 societies* (pp. 239–281). Thousand Oaks, CA: Sage.

Javidan, M., & Carl, D. E. (2005). Leadership across cultures: A study of Canadian and Taiwanese Executives. *Management International Review, 45*(1), 23–44.

Javidan, M., & Dastmalchian, A. (2009). Managerial implications of the GLOBE project: A study of 62 societies. *Asia Pacific Journal of Human Resources, 47*, 41–58.

Javidan, M., Dorfman, P. W., Howell, J. P., & Hanges, P. J. (2010). Leadership and cultural context: A theoretical and empirical examination based on Project GLOBE. In N. Nohria & R. Khurana (Eds.), *Handbook of leadership theory and practice*. Boston: Harvard Business Press.

Javidan, M., Dorfman, P. W., Sully de Luque, M., & House, R. J. (2006). In the eye of the beholder: Cross cultural lessons in leadership from Project GLOBE. *Academy of Management Perspectives, 20*(1), 67–90.

Javidan, M., & House, R. (2001). Cultural acumen for the global manager: Lessons from GLOBE [30th anniversary special issue]. *Organizational Dynamics, 29*(4), 289–305.

Javidan, M., House, R., Dorfman, P. W., Hanges, P. J., & Sully de Luque, M. (2006). Conceptualizing and measuring cultures and their consequences: A comparative review of GLOBE's and Hofstede's approaches. *Journal of International Business Studies, 37*, 897–914.

Jilani, Z. (2011). *Taking a moral stand, American Airlines CEO retires with no severance package as company goes bankrupt*. ThinkProgress. Retrieved from http://thinkprogress.org/economy/2011/12/02/380768/american-airlines-ceo-retires

Judge, T. A., & Piccolo, R. F. (2004). Transformational and transactional leadership: A metaanalytic test of their relative validity. *Journal of Applied Psychology, 89*, 755–768.

Jung, D., & Avolio, B. J. (1999). Effects of leadership style and followers' cultural orientation on performance in groups and individual task conditions. *Academy of Management Journal, 42*, 208–218.

Jung, D., Butler, M. C., & Baik, K. B. (1998). *Effects of transformational leadership on group members collective efficacy and perceived performance.* Paper presented at the Society for Industrial and Organizational Psychology, New Orleans, LA.

Jung, D., Wu, A., & Chow, C. (2008). Towards understanding the direct and indirect effects of CEO's transformational leadership on firm innovation. *Leadership Quarterly, 19,* 582–594.

Jung, D., Yammarino, F. J., & Lee, J. K. (2009). Moderating role of subordinates' attitudes on transformational leadership and effectiveness: A multi-cultural and multi-level perspective. *Leadership Quarterly, 20,* 586–603.

Kanter, R. M. (1968). Commitment and social organization: A study of commitment mechanisms in utopian communities. *American Sociological Review, 33,* 499–517.

Katz, D., & Kahn, R. L. (1978). *The social psychology of organizations* (2nd ed.). New York: John Wiley.

Katzenbach, J. R., & Smith, D. K. (1993). *The wisdom of teams.* Cambridge, MA: Harvard University Press.

Keller, T. (2003). Parental images as a guide to leadership sensemaking: An attachment perspective on implicit leadership theories. *Leadership Quarterly, 14,* 141–160.

Kennedy, J. C. (2007). Leadership and culture in New Zealand. In J. S. Chhokar, F. C. Brodbeck, & R. J. House (Eds.), *Culture and leadership across the world: The GLOBE book of in-depth studies of 25 societies.* New York: Lawrence Erlbaum.

Kennis, I. (1977). A cross-cultural study of personality and leadership. *Group and Organizational Studies, 2*(1), 49–60.

Kirkman, B. L., Chen, G., Farh, J. L., Chen, Z. X., & Lowe, K. B. (2009). Individual power distance orientation and follower reactions to transformational leaders: A cross-level, cross-cultural examination. *Academy of Management Journal, 52*(4), 744–764.

Klein, H., Becker, T., & Meyer, J. (2009). *Commitment in organizations: Accumulated wisdom and new directions.* New York: Routledge.

Klein, K. J., Dansereau, F., & Hall, R. J. (1994). Levels issues in theory development, data collection, and analysis. *Academy of Management Review, 19*(2), 195–229.

Koene, H., Pennings, H., & Schreuder, M. (1991). Leadership, culture, and organizational effectiveness. In K. E. Clark, M. E. Clark, & D. P. Campbell (Eds.), *The impact of leadership.* Greensboro, NC: Center for Creative Leadership.

Koh, W. L. (1990). An empirical validation of the theory of transformational leadership in secondary schools in Singapore. Doctoral dissertation, University of Oregon. *Dissertation Abstracts International, 52* (2), 602A.

Koh, W. L., Terborg, J. R., & Steers, R. M. (1991). The impact of transformational leaders on organizational commitment, organizational citizenship behavior, teacher satisfaction and student performance in Singapore. Paper presented at the Academy of Management, Miami, FL.

Kohn, M. L. (1971). Bureaucratic man: A portrait and an interpretation. *American Sociological Review, 36,* 461–474.

Kouzes, J. M., & Posner, B. Z. (1987). *The leadership challenge: How to get extraordinary things done in organizations.* San Francisco: Jossey-Bass.

Kozlowski, S., & Bell, B. S. (2003). Work groups and teams in organizations. In W. C. Borman, D. R. Ilgen, & R. J. Klimoski (Eds.), *Handbook of psychology (Vol. 12): Industrial and organizational psychology* (pp. 333–375). New York: Wiley.

Kozlowski S., & Ilgen, D. (2006). Enhancing the effectiveness of work groups and teams. *Psychological Science and the Public Interest, 7*(3), 77–125.

Kozlowski, S., & Klein, K. J. (2000). A multilevel approach to theory and research in organizations: Contextual, temporal, and emergent processes. In K. J. Klein & S. W. J. Kozlowski (Eds.), *Multilevel theory, research, and methods in organizations* (pp. 3–90). San Francisco: Jossey-Bass.

Kreft, I., & Leeuw, J. D. (1998). *Introducing multilevel modeling.* Thousand Oaks, CA: Sage.

Landy, F. J., & Conte, J. M. (2010). *Work in the 21st century: An introduction to industrial and organizational psychology* (3rd ed.). New York: John Wiley.

Lawrence, P. R., & Lorsch, J. W. (1967). *Organization and environment.* Cambridge, MA: Harvard University Press.

Leana, C. R., Locke, E. A., & Schweiger, D. M. (1990). Fact and fiction in analyzing research on participative decision making: A critique of Cotton, Wollrath, Froggatt, Lengnick-Hall, and Jennings. *Academy of Management Review, 15,* 137–146.

Leong, L. Y. C., & Fischer, R. (2011). Is transformational leadership universal? A meta-analytical investigation of multifactor leadership questionnaire means across cultures. *Journal of Leadership & Organizational Studies, 18*(2), 164–174.

Leung, K., Bhagat, R. S., Buchan, N. R., Erez, M., & Gibson, C. B. (2005). Culture and international business: Recent advances and their implications for future research. *Journal of International Business Studies, 36,* 357–378.

Lewin, K., Lippitt, R., & White, R. K. (1939). Patterns of aggressive behavior in experimentally created social climates. *Journal of Social Psychology, 10,* 271–301.

Likert, R. (1961). *New patterns of management.* New York: McGraw-Hill.

Likert, R. (1967). *The human organization.* New York: McGraw-Hill.

Lindsay, C. P., & Dempsey, B. L. (1985). Experiences in training Chinese business people to use U.S. management techniques. *Journal of Applied Behavioral Science, 21,* 65–78.

Ling, Y., Simsek, Z., Lubatkin M. H., & Veiga, J. F. (2008a). The impact of transformational CEOs on the performance of small- to medium-sized firms. Does tenure or founder status matter? *Journal of Applied Psychology, 4,* 923–934.

Ling, Y., Simsek, Z., Lubatkin, M. H., & Veiga, J. F. (2008b). Transformational leadership's role in promoting corporate entrepreneurship: Examining the CEO-TMT Interface? *Academy of Management Journal, 51,* 557–576.

Lok, P., & Crawford, J. (2004). The effect of organisational culture and leadership style on job satisfaction and organisational commitment: A cross-national comparison. *Journal of Management Development, 23*(4), 321–338.

Lonner, W. J. (1980). The search for psychological universals. In H. C. Triandis & W. W. Lambert (Eds.), *Handbook of cross-cultural psychology* (Vol. 1, pp. 143–204). Boston: Allyn & Bacon.

Lord, R. G., & Brown, D. J. (2004). *Leadership processes and follower self-identity.* Hillsdale, NJ: Lawrence Erlbaum.

Lord, R. G., Foti, R. J., & De Vader, C. L. (1984). A test of leadership categorization theory: Internal structure, information processing, and leadership perceptions. *Organizational Behavior and Human Performance, 34*(3), 343–378.

Lord, R. G., Hanges, P. J., & Godfrey, E. G. (2003). Integrating neural networks into decision-making and motivational theory: Rethinking VIE theory. *Canadian Psychology/Psychologie Canadienne, 44*(1), 21.

Lord, R. G., & Maher, K. J. (1990). Leadership perceptions and leadership performance: Two distinct but interdependent processes. In J. S. Carroll (Ed.), *Applied social psychology and organizational settings* (pp. 129–154). Hillsdale, NJ: Lawrence Erlbaum.

Lord, R. G., & Maher, K. J. (1991). *Leadership and information processing: Linking perceptions and performance* (Vol. 1). Cambridge, MA: Unwin Hyman.

Machiavelli, N. (1961). *The prince* (G. Bull, Trans.). London: Penguin. (Original work published 1532).

Magnusson, P., & Boggs, D. J. (2006). International experience and CEO selection: An empirical study. *Journal of International Management, 12*(1), 107–125.

Makri, M., & Scandura, T. A. (2010). Exploring the effects of adaptive and expansive CEO leadership on innovation in high-technology firms. *The Leadership Quarterly, 21,* 75–88.

Marion, R., & Uhl-bien, M. (2001). Leadership in complex organizations. *The Leadership Quarterly, 12,* 389–418.

McCall, M., & Hollenbeck, G. (2002). *Developing global executives: The lessons of international experience.* Boston: Harvard Business School Publishing.

McClelland, D. C. (1961). *The achieving society.* Princeton, NJ: Van Nostrand.

McClelland, D. C. (1985). *Human motivation.* Glenview, IL: Scott-Foresman.

McKeown, B. (1988). *Q methodology.* Newbury Park, CA: Sage.

Mehra, P., & Krishnan, V. R. (2005). Impact of Svadharma-orientation on transformational leadership and followers' trust in leader. *Journal of Indian Psychology, 23*(1), 1–11.

Meindl, J. R., Ehrlich, S. B., & Dukerich, J. M. (1985). The romance of leadership. *Administrative Science Quarterly, 30,* 78–102.

Meindl, J. R., Ehrlich, S. B., & Dukerich, J. M. (1985). The romance of leadership. *Administrative Science Quarterly, 30,* 78–102.

Menon, T., Sim, J., Ho-Ying Fu, J., Chiu, C.-y., & Hong, Y.-y. (2010). Blazing the trail versus trailing the group: Culture and perceptions of the leader's position. *Organizational Behavior and Human Decision Processes, 113,* 51–61.

Meyer, J. P., & Allen, N. J. (1991). A three-component conceptualization of organizational commitment. *Human Resource Management Review, 1,* 61–89.

Meyer, J. P., & Allen, N. J. (1997). *Commitment in the workplace: Theory, research, and application.* Thousand Oaks, CA: Sage.

Mintzberg, H. (1973). *The nature of managerial work.* New York: Harper & Row.

Mintzberg, H. (2004). Enough leadership. *Harvard Business Review, 82*(11), 22.

Mintzberg, H. (2006). The leadership debate with Henry Mintzberg: Communityship is the answer. *Financial Times.* Retrieved from www.ft.com/intl/cms/s/2/c917c904-6041-11db-a716-0000779e2340.html#axzz28dMdmrmU

Mintzberg, H. (2009). *Managing.* San Francisco: Berrett-Koehler.

Morrow, P. C. (1993). *The theory and measurement of work commitment.* Greenwich, CT: JAI Press.

Mowday, R. T., Porter, L. W., & Steers, R. M. (1982). *Organizational linkages: The psychology of commitment, absenteeism, and turnover.* San Diego, CA: Academic Press.

Naisbitt, J. (1982). *Megatrends: Ten new directions transforming our lives.* New York: Warner Books.

Newman, K. L., & Nollen, S. D. (1996). Culture and congruence: The fit between management practices and national culture. *Journal of International Business Studies, 27,* 753–779.

Nisbett, R. E. (2003). *The geography of thought: How Asians and Westerners think differently…and why.* New York: Free Press.

O'Connell, M. S., Lord, R. G., & O'Connell, M. K. (1990, August). *Differences in Japanese and American leadership prototypes: Implications for cross-cultural training.* Paper presented at the Academy of Management Annual Meeting, San Francisco.

Offermann, L. R., Kennedy, J. K., & Wirtz, P. W. (1994). Implicit leadership theories: Content, structure, and generalizability. *The Leadership Quarterly, 5*(1), 43–58.

O'Reilly, C. A., III, Chatman, J., & Caldwell, D. F. (1991). People and organizational culture: A profile comparison approach to assessing person-organization fit. *Academy of Management Journal, 34,* 487–516.

Oxfam International. (2013). Retrieved from www.oxfam.org/en/about

Palrecha, R., Spangler, W. D., & Yammarino, F. J. (2012). A comparative study of three leadership approaches in India. *The Leadership Quarterly, 23,* 146–162.

Parboteeah, K. P., Hoegl, M., & Cullen, J. B. (2008). Managers' gender role attitudes: A country institutional profile approach. *Journal of International Business Studies, 39,* 795–813.

Paris, L. D., Howell, J. P., Dorfman, P. W., & Hanges, P. J. (2009). Preferred leadership prototypes of male and female leaders in 27 countries. *Journal of International Business Studies, 40,* 1396–1405.

Peng, M. M., & Luo, Y. (2000). Managerial ties and firm performance in a transition economy: The nature of a micro-macro link. *Academy of Management Journal, 43,* 486–501.

Peng, T. K., Peterson, M. F., & Shyi, Y. (1991). Quantitative methods in cross-national management research: Trends and equivalence issues. *Journal of Organizational Behavior, 12,* 87–107.

Pereira, D. (1987). *Factors associated with transformational leadership in an Indian engineering firm.* Paper presented at the Administrative Science Association of Canada, Vancouver.

Peterson, M. F. (2004). [Review of the book *Culture, leadership, and organizations: The GLOBE study of 62 societies*]. *Administrative Science Quarterly, 49,* 641–647.

Peterson, M. F., & Hunt, J. G. (1997a). International perspectives on international leadership. *Leadership Quarterly, 8*(3), 203–231.

Peterson, M. F., & Hunt, J. G. (1997b). Overview: International and cross-cultural leadership research (Part II). *Leadership Quarterly, 8*(4), 339–342.

Peterson, R. S., Smith, D. B., Martorana, P. V., & Owens, P. D. (2003). The impact of chief executive officer personality on top management team dynamics: One mechanism by which leadership affects organizational performance. *Journal of Applied Psychology, 88,* 795–808.

Peterson, S. J., Walumbwa, F. O., Byron, K. L., & Myrowitz, J. (2009). CEO positive psychological traits, transformational leadership, and firm performance in high-technology start-up and established firms. *Journal of Management, 35,* 348–368.

Pfeffer, J. (1977). The ambiguity of leadership. *Administrative Science Review, 2,* 104–112.

Pillai, R., Scandura, T. A., & Williams, E. A. (1999). Leadership and organizational justice: Similarities and differences across cultures. *Journal of International Business Studies, 30*(4), 763–779.

Podsakoff, P. M., MacKenzie, S. B., Jeong-Yeon, L., & Podsakoff, N. P. (2003). Common method biases in behavioral research: A critical review of the literature and recommended remedies. *Journal of Applied Psychology, 88*(5), 879.

Podsakoff, P. M., MacKenzie, S. B., Moorman, R. H., & Fetter, R. (1990). Transformational leader behaviors and their effects on followers' trust in leader, satisfaction, and organizational citizenship behaviors. *Leadership Quarterly, 1,* 107–142.

Poortinga, Y. H., & Malpass, R. S. (1986). Making inferences from cross-cultural data. In W. J. Lonner & J. W. Berry (Eds.), *Field methods in cross-cultural research* (pp. 12–46). Beverly Hills, CA: Sage.

Priem, R. L., Lyon, D. W., & Dess, G. G. (1999). Limitations of demographic proxies in top management team heterogeneity research. *Journal of Management, 6,* 935–953.

Rauch, C. F., & Behling, O. (1984). Functionalism: Basis for an alternate approach to the study of leadership. In J. G. Hunt, D. M. Hosking, C. A. Schriesheim, & R. Stewart (Eds.), *Current studies in social psychology* (pp. 45–62). New York: Holt, Rinehart & Winston.

Reber, G., Jago, A., & Bohnisch, W. (1993). Interkulturelle unterschlede im fuhrungs-suerhalten *Globalisierung der Wirtschaft-Einvirkungen auf die Betribswirtschaftslehre* (pp. 217–240). Stuttgart: Verlag Paul Haupt Bern.

Recht R., & Wilderom C. (1998). Kaizen and culture on the transferability of Japanese suggestion systems. *International Business Review, 7*(1), 7–22.

Reicher, S. D., Haslam, S. A., & Hopkins, N. (2005). Social identity and the dynamics of leadership: Leaders and followers as collaborative agents in the transformation of social reality. *Leadership Quarterly, 16,* 547–568.

Richards, D., & Engle, S. (1986). After the vision: Suggestions to corporate visionaries and vision champions. In J. D. Adams (Ed.), *Transforming leadership* (pp. 199–214). Alexandria, VA: Miles River Press.

Robbins, S. P., & Judge, T. A. (2011). *Organizational behavior* (14th ed.). Upper Saddle River, NJ: Prentice Hall.

Romero, E. J. (2004). Latin American leadership: El Patrón and El Líder moderno. *Cross Cultural Management: An International Journal, 11,* 25–37.

Ronen, S. (1986). *Comparative and multinational management.* New York: Wiley.

Ronen, S., & Kraut, A. I. (1977). Similarities among countries based on employee work values and attitudes. *Columbia Journal of World Business, 12*(2), 89–96.

Ronen, S., & Shenkar, O. (1985). Clustering countries on attitudinal dimensions: A review and synthesis. *Academy of Management Review, 10,* 435–454.

Ronen, S., & Shenkar, O. (2010). *Country clusters: A cultural guiding map to global business.* Invited keynote address at International Society for the Study of Work and Organizational Values, Portugal.

Rosch, E. (1975). Cognitive representations of semantic categories. *Journal of Experimental Psychology: General, 104*(3), 192.

Rousseau, D. M. (1985). Issues of level in organizational research: Multilevel and cross-level perspectives. In L. L. Cummings & B. Staw (Eds.), *Research in organizational behavior* (pp. 1–37). Greenwich, CT: JAI Press.

Sachs, J. (2000). Using a small Sample Q sort to identify item groups. *Psychological Reports, 86,* 287–294.

Sagie, A., & Aycan, Z. (2003). A cross-cultural analysis of participative decision-making in organizations. *Human Relations, 56,* 453–473.

Sagie, A., & Koslowsky, M. (2000). *Participation and empowerment in organizations.* Thousand Oaks, CA: Sage.

Salancik, G. R., & Meindl, J. R. (1984). Corporate attributions as strategic illusions of management control. *Administrative Science Quarterly, 29,* 238–254.

Sapienza, H. J., Smith, K. G., & Gannon, M. J. (1988, Winter). Using subjective evaluations of organizational performance in small business research. *American Journal of Small Business,* 45–53.

Scandura, T. A., Von Glinow, M. A., & Lowe, K. B. (1999). When East meets West: Leadership "best practices" in the United States and the Middle East. In W. Mobley, M. J. Gessner, & V. Arnold (Eds.), *Advances in global leadership* (Vol. 1, pp. 235–248). Greenwich, CT: JAI Press.

Schein, E. H. (1985). *Organizational culture and leadership.* San Francisco: Jossey-Bass.

Schmidt, A. (2013). *Antecedents and outcomes of toxic leadership.* Unpublished doctoral dissertation, University of Maryland, College Park.

Schyns, B., Kiefer, T., Kerschreiter, R., & Tymon, A. (2011). Teaching implicit leadership theories to develop leaders and leadership: How and why it can make a difference. *Academy of Management Learning & Education, 10*(3), 397–408.

Shahin, A. I., & Wright, P. L. (2004). Leadership in the context of culture: An Egyptian perspective. *Leadership and Organization Development Journal, 25*(6), 499–511.

Shamir, B., House, R. J., & Arthur, M. B. (1993). The motivational effects of charismatic leadership: A self-concept theory. *Organization Science, 4,* 1–17.

Shaw, J. B. (1990). A cognitive categorization model for the study of intercultural management. *Academy of Management Review, 15*(4), 626–645.

Shondrick, S. J., Dinh, J. E., & Lord, R. G. (2010). Developments in implicit leadership theory and cognitive science: Applications to improving measurement and understanding alternatives to hierarchical leadership. *Leadership Quarterly, 21,* 959–978.

Shrout, P. E., & Fleiss, J. L. (1979). Intraclass correlations: Uses in assessing rater reliability. *Psychological Bulletin, 86,* 420–428.

Sinha, J. B. P. (1980). *The nurturant task leader.* New Delhi, India: Concept.

Sinha, J. B. P. (1995). *The cultural context of leadership and power.* Thousand Oaks, CA: Sage.

Sirota, D., & Greenwood, J. M. (1971). Understand your overseas work force. *Harvard Business Review, 49*(1), 53–60.

Smith, K. G., & Hitt, M. A. (2005). *Great minds in management: The process of theory development.* Oxford, UK: Oxford University Press.

Smith, P. B., Dugan, S., & Trompenaars, F. (1996). National culture and the values of organizational employees: A dimensional analysis across 43 nations. *Journal of Cross-Cultural Psychology, 27*(2), 231–264.

Smith, P. B., & Peterson, M. F. (1988). *Leadership, organizations and culture: An event management model.* Newbury Park, CA: Sage.

Smith, P. B., & Peterson, M. F. (1995). *Beyond value comparisons: Sources used to give meaning to management events in 30 countries.* Paper presented at the Academy of Management Annual Meeting, Vancouver, Canada.

Smith, P. B., Peterson, M. F., & Schwartz, S. H. (2002). Cultural values, sources of guidance, and their relevance to managerial behavior: A 47-nation study. *Journal of Cross-Cultural Psychology, 33*(2), 188–208.

Smith, P. B., Peterson, M. F., & Thomas, D. C. (2008). *The handbook of cross-cultural management research*. Thousand Oaks, CA: Sage.

Smith, P. B., Peterson, M. F., & Wang, Z. M. (1996). The manager as mediator of alternative meanings: A pilot study from China, the U.S.A. and U.K. *Journal of International Business Studies, 27*(1), 115–138.

Smith, P. B., Wang, Z. M., & Leung, K. (1997). Leadership, decision-making and cultural context: Event management within Chinese joint ventures. *Leadership Quarterly, 8*(4), 413–431.

Spector, P. E. (2006). Method variance in organizational research: Truth or urban legend? *Organizational Research Methods, 9,* 221.

Spreitzer, G. M., Perttula, K. H., & Xin, K. R. (2005). Traditionality matters: An examination of the effectiveness of transformational leadership in the United States and Taiwan. *Journal of Organizational Behavior, 26*(3), 205–227.

Stahl, G. K., & Javidan, M. (2009). Cross-cultural perspectives on international mergers and acquisitions. In R. S. Bhagat & R. Steers (Eds.), *Culture, organizations and work* (pp. 118–147). Cambridge, UK: Cambridge University Press.

Steenkamp, J. E. M., & Baumgartner, H. (1998). Assessing measurement invariance in cross-national consumer research. *Journal of Consumer Research, 25,* 78–107.

Stewart, R., Barsoux, J. L., Kieser, A., Ganter, H. D., & Walgenbach, P. (1994). *Managing in Britain and Germany*. London: St. Martin's Press/MacMillan.

Stogdill, R. M. (1974). *Handbook of leadership: A survey of the literature*. New York: Free Press.

Swidler, A. (1986). Culture in action: Symbols and strategies. *American Sociological Review, 51,* 273–286.

Tabuchi, H. (2011, May 20). Head of Japanese utility steps down after nuclear crisis. *New York Times* (online). Retrieved from www.nytimes.com/2011/05/21/business/global/21iht-tepco21.html?pagewanted=all&_r=0

Tan, J. J., & Litschert, R. J. (1994). Environment-strategy relationship and its performance implications: An empirical study of the Chinese electronics industry. *Strategic Management Journal, 15,* 1–20.

Tosi, H. L., Misangyi, V. F., Fanelli, A., Waldman, D. A., & Yammarino, F. J. (2004). CEO charisma, compensation, and firm performance. *Leadership Quarterly, 15,* 405–421.

Triandis, H. C. (1993). The contingency model in cross-cultural perspective. In M. M. Chemers & R. E. Ayman, *Leadership theory and research: Perspectives and directions* (pp. 167–188). San Diego: Academic Press.

Triandis, H.C. (1994). Cross-cultural industrial and organizational psychology. In H. C. Triandis, M. D. Dunnette, & L. M. Hough (Eds.), *Handbook of industrial and organizational psychology* (2nd ed., Vol. 4, pp. 103–172). Palo Alto, CA: Consulting Psychologists Press.

Triandis, H. C. (1995). *Individualism and collectivism*. Boulder, CO: Westview Press.

Triandis, H. C. (2004). Foreword. In R. House, P. J. Hanges, M. Javidan, P. W. Dorfman, & V. Gupta (Eds.), *Culture, leadership, and organizations: The GLOBE study of 62 societies* (pp. xv–xix). Thousand Oaks, CA: Sage.

Tsui, A. S., Nifadkar, S. S., & Ou, A. Y. (2007). Cross-national, cross-cultural organizational behavior research: Advances, gaps, and recommendations. *Journal of Management, 33*(3), 426–478.

Tung, R. L. (2004). Female expatriates: The model global manager? *Organizational Dynamics, 33*(3), 243–253.

Turley, J. (2010). *Redrawing the map: Globalization and the changing world of business, featuring excerpts from The Globalization Index compiled by the Economist Intelligence Unit.* Ernst & Young Report.

Union of International Associations (Ed.). (2012). Number of international organizations by type. *The yearbook of international organizations* (49th ed., Vol. 3, App. 3, Table 1). Boston: Brill.

U.S. Department of Defense. (2010, December 31). Active duty military personnel strengths by regional area and by country (309A). Retrieved from http://siadapp.dmdc.osd.mil/personnel/MILITARY/history/hst1012.pdf 1

Van de Vijver, F., & Leung, K. (1997). *Methods and data analysis for cross-cultural research.* Thousand Oaks, CA: Sage.

Van der Vegt, G. S., & Bunderson, J. S. (2005). Learning and performance in multifunctional teams: The importance of collective team identification. *Academy of Management Journal, 48,* 532–547.

van Dyck, C., Frese, M., Baer, M., & Sonnentag, S. (2005). Organizational error management culture and its impact on performance: A two-study replication. *Journal of Applied Psychology, 90,* 1228–1240.

van Quaquebeke, N., van Knippenberg, D., & Brodbeck, F. C. (2011). More than meets the eye: The role of subordinates' self-perceptions in leader categorization processes. *Leadership Quarterly, 22*(2), 367–382.

Vroom, V. H., & Jago, A. G. (1988). *The new leadership: Managing participation in organizations.* Englewood Cliffs, NJ: Prentice-Hall.

Vroom, V. H., & Yetton, P. W. (1973). *Leadership and decision-making.* Pittsburgh, PA: University of Pittsburgh Press.

Waldman, D. A., de Luque, M. S., Washburn, N., House, R. J., Adetoun, B., Barrasa, A., et al. (2006). Cultural and leadership predictors of corporate social responsibility values of top management: A GLOBE study of 15 countries. *Journal of International Business Studies, 37,* 823–837.

Waldman, D. A., Javidan, M., & Varella, P. (2004). Charismatic leadership at the strategic level: A new application of upper echelons theory. *Leadership Quarterly, 15,* 355–381.

Waldman, D. A., Ramirez, G. A., House, R. J., & Puranam, P. (2001). Does leadership matter? CEO leadership attributes and profitability under conditions of perceived environmental uncertainty. *Academy of Management Journal, 44,* 134–143.

Waldman, D. A., & Yammarino, F. J. (1999). CEO charismatic leadership: Levels-of-management and levels-of-analysis effects. *Academy of Management Review, 24,* 266–285.

Waller, D. (2001). *Wheels on fire: The amazing inside story of the Daimler Chrysler merger.* London: Hodder & Stoughton.

Walsh, J. P., & Seward, J. K. (1990). On the efficiency of internal and external corporate control mechanisms. *Academy of Management Review, 15,* 421–458.

Walumbwa, F. O., & Lawler, J. J. (2003). Building effective organizations: Transformational leadership, collectivist orientation, work-related attitudes and withdrawal behaviours in three emerging economies. *International Journal of Human Resource Management, 14*(7), 1083–1101.

Wang, H., Tsui, A. S., & Xin, K. R. (2011). CEO leadership behaviors, organizational performance, and employees' attitudes. *Leadership Quarterly, 22,* 92–105.

Wang, H., Waldman, D. A., & Zhang, H. (2012). Strategic leadership across cultures: Current findings and future research directions. *Journal of World Business, 47*(4), 479–706.

Weber, M. (1947). *The theory of social and economic organizations* (T. Parsons, Trans.). New York: Free Press.

Weiss, J. W., & Bloom, S. (1990). Managing in China: Expatriate experiences and training. *Business Horizons, 33,* 23–29.

Wendt, H., Euwema, M. C., & Van Emmerik, H. (2009). Leadership and team cohesiveness across cultures. *Leadership Quarterly, 20*(3), 358–370.

Werther, W. B. J. (1996). Toward global convergence. *Business Horizons, 39*(1), 3–9.

Westphal, J. D., & Zajac, E. J. (1995). Who shall govern? CEO/board power, demographic similarity, and new director selection. *Administrative Science Quarterly, 40*(1), 60–83.

Wolgemuth, L. (2010). What the resumes of top CEOs have in common. *US News Report.*

World Trade Organization's Regional Trade Agreement Database. (2012). Retrieved from http://rtais.wto.org/ui/PublicMaintainRTAHome.aspx

Yavas, B. F. (1995). Quality management practices worldwide: Convergence or divergence? *Quality Progress, 28*(10), 57–61.

Young, J. S. & Simon, W. L. (2005). *iCon Steve Jobs: The greatest second act in the history of business.* Hoboken, NJ: Wiley.

Yukl, G. (2001). *Leadership in organizations* (5th ed.). Upper Saddle River, NJ: Prentice Hall.

Yukl, G. (2006). *Leadership in organizations* (6th ed.). Upper Saddle River, NJ: Prentice Hall.

Yukl, G. (2008). How leaders influence organizational effectiveness. *Leadership Quarterly, 19,* 708–722.

Yukl, G. (2010). *Leadership in organizations* (7th ed.). Upper Saddle River, NJ: Pearson Education.

Yukl, G. (2012). Effective leadership behavior: What we know and what questions need more attention. *Leadership Quarterly, 23,* 66–85.

Yukl, G. (2013). *Leadership in organizations* (8th ed.). Upper Saddle River, NJ: Prentice Hall.

Zaccaro, S. J. (2001). *The nature of executive leadership: A conceptual and empirical analysis of success.* Washington, DC: American Psychological Association.

Zaccaro, S. J., & Klimoski, R. J. (2001). *The nature of organizational leadership: Understanding the performance imperatives confronting today's leaders.* San Francisco: Jossey-Bass.

Zaccaro, S. J., Rittman, A. L., & Marks, M. A. (2001). Team leadership. *Leadership Quarterly, 12,* 451–484.

Name Index _____

Subject Index _____

Note: In page references, f indicates figures and t indicates tables.

$SAGE researchmethods

The essential online tool for researchers from the world's leading methods publisher

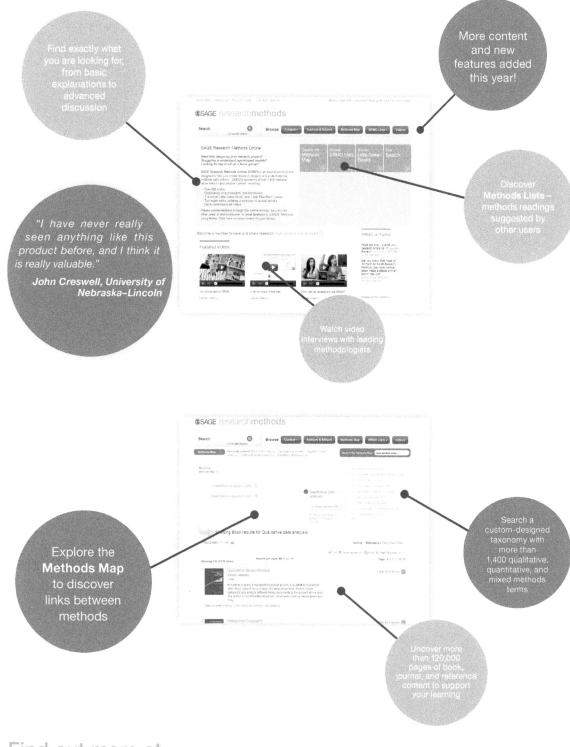

Find exactly what you are looking for, from basic explanations to advanced discussion

More content and new features added this year!

"I have never really seen anything like this product before, and I think it is really valuable."
John Creswell, University of Nebraska–Lincoln

Discover **Methods Lists** – methods readings suggested by other users

Watch video interviews with leading methodologists

Explore the **Methods Map** to discover links between methods

Search a custom-designed taxonomy with more than 1,400 qualitative, quantitative, and mixed methods terms

Uncover more than 120,000 pages of book, journal, and reference content to support your learning

Find out more at
www.sageresearchmethods.com

CPSIA information can be obtained
at www.ICGtesting.com
Printed in the USA
LVHW102240061218
599562LV00010B/187/P

9 781412 995948